MARXISM
an historical and critical study

GEORGE LICHTHEIM

Columbia University Press
New York

FOR

I. A.

Library of Congress Cataloging in Publication Data

Lichtheim, George, 1912–1973
    Marxism, an historical and critical study.

    Reprint. Originally published: 2nd ed.,
rev. New York: Praeger, 1969 printing, c1964.
    Includes bibliographical references and
index.
    1. Socialism—History.   2. Communism—History.
I. Title.
HX36.L48   1982   335.4′09   81-17066
ISBN 0-231-05424-6   AACR2
ISBN 0-231-05425-4 (pbk.)

Library of Congress Catalog Card Number: 61-8694
Printed in the United States of America

Columbia University Press
New York
Columbia University Press Morningside Edition 1982

Clothbound editions of Columbia University Press books are Smyth-sewn and printed
on permanent and durable acid-free paper.

CONTENTS

CONTENTS

Part Four

THE THEORY OF BOURGEOIS SOCIETY
1850–1895

Part Five

MARXIAN SOCIALISM, 1871–1918

Part Six

THE DISSOLUTION OF THE MARXIAN
SYSTEM, 1918–1948

PREFACE

A STUDY which sets out to present an integrated account of Marxian theory since its first formulation, and of the Marxist movement from its inception in 1848 to its petrifaction a century later, cannot hope to satisfy those who look for a neat dissection of topical problems. Nor is it intended to rival the work of scholars who have examined in detail one particular corner of the field. The task of assembling so many different elements of social and intellectual history under one general heading imposes limitations of which the author is only too conscious. Some of the resulting difficulties are considered in the Introduction. It may be pertinent, however, to state at the outset that it is not proposed here to do more than indicate the general sense of the movement and the period under review. This cannot be done without trespassing upon ground normally reserved for specialists, to whom every writer must be grateful, and who in their turn may acknowledge the usefulness of an attempt to bring together what is commonly treated separately. For his part the author only claims that extent of familiarity with the subject which is required to distinguish what is relevant from the boundless accretion of other data. The principle of selection, and the exigencies of space, may perhaps be thought to have resulted in a degree of compression unusual in a work intended for the general reader. If so, the defence must be that an analysis of so complex a subject is not achieved without rigid concentration upon essentials and ruthless disregard of mere detail. As for the standpoint here chosen, it will be enough to say that it represents no commitment to anything save the critical method inherent in the exercise of rational thinking.

While the actual writing of this book has not occupied me for very long, the subject is one which for many years has furnished the theme of constant discussion with friends and acquaintances sharing the same interest. In mentioning a few names, I am conscious of the manifold intellectual debts incurred in the process. The late Franz Borkenau probably had the greatest influence upon the general approach adopted in this work, although he would have been unlikely to agree with all its conclusions. I take this opportunity of paying tribute to the memory of one of the most original and penetrating intellects of our time—an Argonaut of the spirit, daring and even reckless in the discovery of new territory. My other debts are more easily discharged. Several chapters have been read in manuscript by friends among whom I particularly want to mention Dr. Francis Carsten, of London University; Mr. Leo Labedz; and Mr. Morris Watnick, of the Russian Research Centre at Harvard. I am obliged to Mr. Richard Lowenthal for the loan of material and for some stimulating monologues; to Professor S. F. Bloom, of Brooklyn College, New York, and to Professor J. L. Talmon, of the Hebrew University, Jerusalem, for the benefit derived from lengthy conversations with them; to the Congress for Cultural Freedom, for a research grant which greatly facilitated my work; to the Internationaal Instituut voor Sociale Geschiedenis, Amsterdam, and to the Istituto Giangiacomo Feltrinelli, Milan, for literature supplied to me; to Miss Marion Bieber for her kind assistance in procuring research material; to Linda Hamilton and Ruth Sharon for secretarial assistance; and last but not least to Mrs. Esther Howell, who patiently bore the burden of typing and retyping the manuscript.

NOTE ON SOURCES

NO FORMAL BIBLIOGRAPHY is appended to this work. To have done
so would have meant stretching to intolerable length the list of works
either referred to in the text or taken for granted in the presentation
of the argument. What a really comprehensive survey would entail
may be gathered from the fact that M. Maximilien Rubel's invaluable
Bibliographie des Oeuvres de Karl Marx (Paris, 1956) runs to 258
pages and lists 885 titles for Marx alone, not counting a mere selection of 151 for Engels. A full-scale bibliography of Marxist literature
—not to mention socialism in general—would certainly exceed the
dimensions of the present work. For the socialist movement as a
whole, the fullest select bibliography known to the author is that
appended to the five volumes of Professor G. D. H. Cole's *History of
Socialist Thought* (London, 1955–60). Though selective, it includes
nearly all the general studies dealing with the subject, at any rate in
English and French, less so in German. In the latter language, one of
the best select reading lists is that contained in the notes to the two-
volume biography of Engels by Gustav Mayer (The Hague, 1934);
it is, however, inevitably centred on the history of German socialism.
As regards the Russian Revolution and the history of Russian
Marxism, the reader must be referred to the bibliographies given by
the authors cited in the course of this study. Listing these and other
sources here would entail an altogether useless duplication. On the
other hand, no good purpose would be served by compiling a list
based solely on works cited in the text. A selection of this kind would
in fact be seriously misleading, in that it would leave out of account
a number of general and specialised studies not specifically mentioned
in the text, but which form the indispensable background of any
serious work on the subject.

For practical purposes, then, the bibliography is contained in
the Notes. The latter refer in general to writings in their original

language, though in the case of Marx and Engels preference has been given where possible to English translations. Some of the latter being incomplete or inadequate, the German and the English text are occasionally listed side by side. Thus a reference to MEGA (*Karl Marx-Friedrich Engels: Historisch-Kritische Gesamtausgabe*, Marx-Engels Verlag, Frankfurt-Berlin, 1927–32: the incomplete but indispensable German-language edition containing the works down to 1848 and the entire Marx-Engels correspondence) is frequently followed by a parallel reference to the two-volume English-language selection cited as MESW (*Marx-Engels Selected Works*), or to the one-volume *Selected Correspondence* (MESC). These are Soviet editions, and the same applies to such titles as the English edition of Engels's *Anti-Dühring* (*Herr Eugen Dühring's Revolution in Science*), or the more recently published translation of Marx's so-called *Paris Manuscripts* of 1844. Where the editing appeared to be inadequate or tendentious, this has been remarked upon, but in general it has not been found necessary to contrast the original text with the translation.

References to *Capital*, vol. I, are in general to the London, 1938, edition of the original Moore-Aveling translation first published in 1887 under Engels's editorship. Volumes II and III are quoted in the Kerr (Chicago) edition, unless otherwise stated. All three volumes are now available in an official Soviet translation into English, of which occasional use has been made. In one or two places the text refers to the recent German edition, *Das Kapital*, (Berlin, 1949.) The posthumously published *Grundrisse der Kritik der politischen Oekonomie* are quoted in the only available German edition (Berlin, 1953). The *Theories of Surplus Value* are cited from the one-volume selection published in London in 1951, the original three-volume edition (*Theorien ueber den Mehrwert*, ed. Kautsky, 1905–10) not being available in full translation. Most of Marx's minor works have now been translated, not always adequately. References to Lenin's writings are either to the two-volume English *Selected Works* (London, 1947) or to individual works available in official English versions, e.g., *Materialism and Empirio-Criticism*. With Trotsky and some others there is the problem that the only collected editions of their works are the incomplete versions published in Russian in the 1920's. In general, reference has been made to German or English translations, but in the case of some of Trotsky's more important writings, the Russian original is cited. No corresponding difficulty arises for Stalin, whose writings are available in all known languages.

The secondary works cited in the text are mostly in English, French, or German. Apart from the German sources already referred to, which relate chiefly to the nineteenth century, the student can obtain a very comprehensive reading list from the bibliographical essay appended to Carl E. Schorske's *German Social-Democracy 1905–1917* (Harvard, 1955). This is not merely the best historical account of the dissensions within the German socialist movement, but also a considerable aid to further reading. Central European socialism before and after 1914 is a world in itself, and its understanding requires at least some familiarity with its voluminous literature, including its more important periodicals. In view of the relative paucity of citations in the text, it may be worth remarking that only a fraction of the sources consulted for this topic are expressly referred to in the footnotes. The same applies *a fortiori* to general literature, and in particular to historical writings on the 1871–1914 period, which is the subject of a special chapter. Thus it would have been impracticable to back the few and brief references to British economics and Fabian socialism with extensive bibliographical references. This rule also holds good for the history of the Second and Third Internationals, where it is perforce assumed that the reader will be familiar with the basic facts. Any other procedure would have burst the bounds of what is after all primarily meant to be a critical history of Marxist theory. For the vast field of Soviet Marxism—considered as an ideological phenomenon—there now exists the very comprehensive bibliography of Russian sources given in G. A. Wetter's *Dialectical Materialism* (London, 1958). Like other students of the subject I owe a debt to the recent work of Professor Marcuse, and I have also gained some insights from an unpublished MS. by Dr. Eugene Kamenka. The post-war discussion on Marxism in Western Europe is referred to only incidentally. What a reading list would involve for France alone may be gauged from the bibliography of Jean-Yves Calvez' massive work, *La Pensée de Karl Marx* (Paris, 1956); here a number of important writings are listed which during the past few years have proved to be merely the precursors of a whole new department of French academic scholarship. In general, the reader does well to bear in mind that in what follows he is presented with no more than a bare outline of a subject whose proper study would exhaust the combined resources of a major research institute.

INTRODUCTION

A NOTE ON METHODOLOGY

MARXISM IS A TERM which has come to stand for so many different things that it is relevant at the outset to clarify its intended use here. An attempt will be made in the following pages to trace the development of Marxian theory and to give an account of the manner in which the tradition thus established interacted with other currents to bring about those theoretical and practical results which have become so large a part of our present preoccupations. Viewed under this aspect Marxism can be regarded as one intellectual construction among others; alternatively, it can be assigned a definite place among the socialist movements of the nineteenth century which arose from the impact of the industrial revolution on European society. Either approach is legitimate, though one leads to a critical study of the system, the other to an historical account of the movement, both of which go under the name of Marxism.

Thus defined, the Marxian synthesis appears as the historical counterpoint to the liberal integration, and indeed there is a sense in which liberalism and socialism can be described as alternative reactions to the challenge posed by the industrial revolution. But unless Marxism and socialism are equated, it will not do to speak of a Marxian system as opposed to a liberal one. There have been socialist movements other than Marxism, while conversely there are elements common to liberal and Marxian thought that are missing from some distinctively socialist systems—that of Proudhon for example. Again, there is little purpose in contrasting Marx with some representative figure of nineteenth-century liberalism, J. S. Mill being the obvious example. For even if it were possible to take Mill more seriously as a theorist of society (his philosophical standing is another matter) he cannot be said to have furnished modern liberalism with a working model for everyday political use, whereas the 'union of theory and practice' is the distinguishing trait of Marxism; hence Marx cannot be discussed merely as a theorist, but must be understood in terms of those historic changes which he both predicted and helped to bring about.

It follows that a study of Marxism which attempts to be at once critical and historical—i.e., addressed to the theoretical structure as well as to the historical movement comprised under the same term—must display some such unity within its own methodical frame. The nineteenth century was indeed a great age of system-building; it was also an epoch rich in revolutionary social currents. But the two came together only in the person of Marx—they signally failed to do so in the case of Comte, Mill or Spencer, to mention three of the leading claimants to celebrity in the field of social philosophy. The unmistakable aura of absurdity which clings to figures like Comte or Spencer (to say nothing of such latter-day saviours of society as Henry George), and the diminishing relevance even of Mill, suggests a failure rendered all the more conspicuous by Marx's achievement. The fact is noteworthy quite apart from its historical consequences, but it is of course the latter that are intended when one speaks of Marxism as a whole. There is indeed no plausible way of divorcing one from the other, and it is just this which renders the subject at once so important and so difficult to analyse.

In principle this procedure is consistent with the Marxian approach, the ability to view itself historically being one of its peculiar intellectual charms. Yet if the term 'Marxism' is allowed to comprise all the theoretical and practical modifications introduced in the course of time, under circumstances unforeseen by the founding fathers, the historical approach becomes self-validating only at the cost of being emptied of meaning. We are thus back at the beginning—Marxism must be defined historically, but to define it so is to neglect its *theoretical* significance.

A possible way out of the difficulty lies in grasping the historical nettle rather more firmly. Marx himself was not averse to treating theoretical constructions functionally, in terms of what they accomplished in the particular age for which they were relevant. Why not follow his example? It is hardly necessary to stress that such an approach does not exempt one from the duty of attending to the scientific standing of those parts of the whole which clearly call for critical (as distinct from historical) treatment. The notion, e.g., that

Marxism represents a link—possibly the most important link—between the French and the Russian Revolution has a definite theoretical content, in addition to suggesting a particular understanding of European history between 1789 and 1917. What took place during this period is more clearly understood in the light of Marxism than in the illumination shed by rival doctrines. Yet this consideration also serves to 'place' Marxism as the theory of one particular kind of revolutionary movement—that which arose from the impact of early industrialism upon the highly stratified society of nineteenth-century Europe.

There is, however, a methodical difficulty which must be faced at the outset. Although it is quite in accordance with Marx's own manner to take an historical view of his work, such an approach presupposes a vantage-point made available by developments beyond the stage reflected in the Marxian system—in other words, it assumes that the Marxian categories are no longer quite applicable to current history. For obvious reasons this is an admission which orthodox Marxists find it hard to make, while others may wonder why this particular scruple should arise in the first place. Its emergence is due to the fact that Hegel and, following him, Marx took a view of history which is not the familiar positivist one. They saw history as a process whose meaning reveals itself by stages, the succession of the latter reflecting man's growing awareness of his role in creating the historical world. To comprehend its past mankind must raise itself to a higher level; hence our ability to understand our predecessors suggests that we have reached a new altitude. This consideration originally presented itself to Hegel as a consequence of his discovery that philosophical systems had a tendency to age: they appeared to be historical, not merely in the sense of being conditioned by circumstances (no one had ever doubted this), but in the more alarming sense of tending to evaporate with the circumstances that attended their birth. Hegel tried to meet the difficulty by establishing an intrinsic relationship between the philosophy of history (his own) and the history of philosophy: *his* system, if not guaranteed to withstand the flux of time, was at any rate promoted to a special dignity by its ability to give an account of the process which had swallowed up all its predecessors. A philosophy which traced the unfolding of the *logos* through all its stages, from inanimate nature, via human history, to the realm of spirit, could assign their proper place to the various philosophical systems, including that in which the process had eventually culminated: Hegel's own. The categories of logic were also those of history, or the historical process exemplified the march of reason: no matter how it was put, the philosopher retained his hold on the totality of the system, which was identical with the world. In Hegel's philosophy—unquestionably the greatest speculative construction of all time—the history of logic and the logic of history have the same goal: the gradual unfolding of the Absolute Idea comes to a climax at the point where the human mind discovers the identity of mind-matter. The universe yields its secret to Reason because it is itself the creation of Reason.[1]

It is today widely taken for granted that the gradual disappearance of these metaphysical certainties has introduced a relativist element into the philosophy of history—on this account frequently described as 'historicism' by an influential academic school.[2] If it is not always apparent whether the target aimed at by these writers is the Hegelian absolutism or the post-Hegelian adoption of a purely human standpoint, it is at any rate evident that they are not happy with an approach which seeks to comprehend both the history and the logic of intellectual phenomena. Since this criticism is directed against thinkers so widely different in their political outlook as Hegel, Marx and Croce, it clearly reflects a genuine philosophical difficulty. Those who take a different view of what is entailed by the philosophy of history are thus under an obligation to define their own standpoint. This, however, is best done by letting the results speak for themselves. At any rate it is the thesis of this study that Marxism is to be understood as an historical phenomenon, as against the now standard analysis of Marxian theory in terms of its compatibility with modern thought. Not that such investigations are without value—few scholarly endeavours are wholly useless, and a sustained indictment of 'historicism', however unconvincing to non-empiricists, may at any rate help to clarify the issue. But whatever the benefit to be obtained from such studies, their aim is different from that of the present enquiry, which sets out to derive the significance of a corpus of thought from its historic function; to trace the link connecting the French Revolution—via German philosophy and German history— with the East European cataclysm of our own age; and to do so in

---

[1] For an analysis of this aspect of Hegel's thought, cf. Herbert Marcuse, *Reason and Revolution*, New York and London, 1941 (2nd edn., 1955), pp. 224–48.

[2] Cf. K. R. Popper, *The Poverty of Historicism*, London, 1957, passim.

terms of an analysis relevant both to the movement of thought and the actions of men, no distinction being drawn between what people thought and what they did. For if it is true that we are dealing with a social transformation of which Marxism was both the theoretical reflection and the political agent, there is no point in confining the discussion to either the historical or the theoretical side. What is required rather is an effort to comprehend the manner in which both came together to bring about the situation now confronting us.

An attempt must nonetheless be made to relate Marxism to contemporary thought in general—in other words, to criticise it. For in dealing with a theoretical structure the genetic approach by itself is of course inadequate. It is not, however, irrelevant. The naive view that doctrines are either true or false, no other judgment being allowed, takes no account of the practical significance of theory: its relevance to the circumstances it sets out to explain. This is not just a matter of sound conclusions being accidentally derived from faulty premises; rather the problem consists in trying to identify those theoretical elements which at a particular point in time are genuinely productive of insight. This topic is commonly subsumed under the general heading of intellectual progress, as though it were simply a matter of each generation marching further along the same road and in the process correcting the errors of its predecessors. In reality the interaction of analysis and actual experience is a good deal more complicated. Thus, to take a well-known example, the labour market and the labour theory of value came into existence roughly at the same time, in the late eighteenth and early nineteenth century; and although it is a commonplace of present-day discussion that the labour theory has been superseded as an instrument of economic analysis, it may still be granted that, for the purpose for which it was originally intended, it was, broadly speaking, adequate. Yet it would clearly be absurd to say that the theory was 'true' when Smith and Ricardo suggested it, less true when Marx elaborated it, and altogether untrue half a century later. In a sense the determination of value by embodied labour always rested on a tautology; yet as an intellectual tool designed to accomplish a particular task it was at one time important, in that it made possible a broadly accurate analysis of the manner in which the social product was distributed among various classes. That it did so with the help of equivocations which proved troublesome later on, is another matter. Intellectual progress

xvii

consists largely in the substitution of one imperfect set of tools for another.

Methodically, the line of advance suggested by this example implies a departure from the customary distinction between factual and value judgments. The usual question with regard to the author of a systematic body of thought is: (1) What did he teach? (2) Is what he taught true? It is questionable whether this approach can ever be very helpful, and it is quite certainly useless in dealing with Marx, the more so as his theories emerged in response to developments which he was the first to identify. We cannot discover what he said without considering the problems he set out to solve, and we cannot analyse the problems without judging the validity of his attempted solutions. And since a problem for Marx was never simply a theoretical question, we cannot consider his solutions without taking a stand on the issues involved. That is why all attempts to discuss Marxism in a morally neutral atmosphere are from the start condemned to failure.

It remains to indicate briefly the general line of approach which has been followed. Our starting-point is not 'dialectical materialism', or some such abstraction, but the French Revolution and its impact on Germany at the beginning of the nineteenth century; along with the industrial revolution and its repercussions in the theoretical sphere, i.e., among the late eighteenth-century and early nineteenth-century British and French writers who were then engaged in working out the analytical tools appropriate to the study of the new society. From this point the discussion moves forward in time, and eastward in space, its preliminary locus being Central Europe, and its temporary halting-point the abortive upheaval of 1848–9 which prefigured the greater cataclysm of 1917–19. There follows a period characterised by the gradual formation of the Marxist system and its political counterpart, Central European Social-Democracy, the system and the movement both relating back to the failure of the 1848 revolution. The full development of this orthodoxy, from about 1890 to 1914, is shown to depend upon an unstable balance of political factors in Central Europe whose disappearance, during and after the first world war, released explosive forces hitherto concealed beneath the surface of seemingly innocuous theoretical wrangles among 'revisionist' and 'radical' interpreters of the orthodox synthesis elaborated by the theorists of the pre-revolutionary era: Engels, Kautsky and Plekhanov. In consequence of this two-fold development—for the political splits and upheavals were both occasioned by, and reflected in, theoretical divergencies—the subsequent process is shown to involve a further eastward shift, away from the industrially and politically developed societies of Western and Central Europe, hitherto principally concerned in the growth of the socialist movement. The dissolution of Marxian socialism as formulated before 1914, and the emergence of Soviet Marxism (or 'Marxism-Leninism') is thus seen to parallel the decline of German (and Austrian) influence in Central and Eastern Europe.

As against this eastward shift it finally becomes necessary to consider those elements in the original Marxian synthesis which appear to have retained their relevance for modern society: notably the critique of liberal economics and the first approximation towards a unified theory of the state. Here an attempt is made to trace the line of development from the classics of political economy via Marx to present-day economics, and the parallel line from the political theorists of the eighteenth century to the sociology of our own day. If this seems a needless undertaking, one has only to consider what a history of liberalism would be like without mention of Locke, Turgot, Smith, and the authors of the American Constitution on the one hand, and the further development of their thought down to Russell, Dewey, Keynes, and the theorists of the welfare state, on the other. There is in fact no clear dividing line between the history of social theory and the history of society in general, though there may be different views about their interaction.[1]

Clearly it is impossible to discuss so complex a subject without making a great many affirmations about matters of fact, some of which will necessarily be controversial. The author can only plead that this need has been imposed upon him by his method, which for the rest must justify itself by the results it yields. Since the standpoint here chosen is historical, in the sense common to Hegel, Marx and Croce—not to mention a list of contemporary philosophers, sociologists, and historians, which could easily be stretched to accommodate both conservatives and radicals—it will not be possible to please critics to whom 'historicism' is abhorrent. Neither is agreement to be expected from those who maintain a vested interest in traditional interpretations of the subject. In general it is here assumed that

[1] For the purpose of this argument, the distinction between Marxism and socialism in general can be ignored. Marxism is after all the predominant element in the socialist movement, at any rate during the period under discussion; and conversely there are non-classical variants of liberalism, e.g., the physiocrats; not to mention Rousseau and his Jacobin progeny.

modern society has moved beyond the stage with whose analysis Marx was primarily concerned. In this sense the Marxian breakthrough may now be said to have been absorbed, not least through the instrumentality of the socialist movement itself. Such paradoxical accomplishments furnish the stuff of history. Indeed, they alone make it possible to interpret the past to the present, with which it is connected through the medium of those half-conscious convulsions which we call revolutions and which never fail to carry their own misinterpretations along with them. If this conclusion has the ring of scepticism, it also suggests (to the author at any rate) the truth of Hegel's dictum that genuine comprehension occurs after the event: Minerva's owl flies out at dusk. We are able to understand Marx because we have reached a point where neither his own modes of thought, nor those of his nineteenth-century opponents, are altogether adequate to the realities.

PART ONE

THE HERITAGE
1789–1840

1

GERMAN IDEALISM

CLASSICAL GERMAN philosophy has been described as a secularised form of Protestantism; it has also been called the theory of the French Revolution. There is no need to argue the respective merits of these interpretations. They are compatible, for the effect of the French Revolution upon the German Enlightenment was to accentuate certain traits which had their roots in the Reformation: principally the radical dissociation of the individual soul, and therewith the realm of freedom, from the wretchedness of earthly existence. German idealist philosophy, like German Protestant theology before it, transforms the aims of men into spiritual values; it thus renounces as hopeless the task of anchoring them in material reality.

In its origins the German Enlightenment of the eighteenth century proceeded from motives held in common with sceptical and deist movements elsewhere in Europe, until in the person of Kant it brought forth a thinker who combined these intellectual strands with the heritage of the Reformation and the first stirrings of the Romantic movement—the latter by way of Rousseau whose growing influence among the educated elite of Germany prepared the way for a sympathetic reception of the French Revolution in its earlier, pre-terrorist, phase. In this manner the Enlightenment came to rest upon an intellectual assent to changes occurring beyond the frontiers and involving no more than a theoretical acceptance of events which had no counterpart in Germany. This attitude (which as time went on was modified by disapproval first of the Jacobin dictatorship and later of the Napoleonic empire) entailed no corresponding change in the contemplative outlook of the elite which had made itself responsible for the guardianship of intellectual values. As before, the life of the spirit was conceived as an autonomous realm unconnected with the sordid circumstances of material existence. Indifferent to the public sphere, because impotent to shape it in accordance with their ideals, the educated strata who around 1800 sustained the flowering of the German Renaissance in the classical Weimar culture, entrenched themselves in the unconquerable regions of philosophy, literature, and art. In so doing they evolved an awareness of personal freedom and a way of life that stood in stark contrast to the realities surrounding them. At the same time they made it more difficult for themselves to break out of their isolation and find the way back to ordinary human community, society, the state.[1]

In this process may be traced the final consummation of tendencies latent in German society since the Reformation—tendencies which signalised the subsequent failure to bring the public realm into correspondence with the aims of the liberal intellectuals, when under the impulsion of social and economic change they finally descended into the political arena. In preparing the way for their discomfiture in the abortive 1848 revolution, the liberals simultaneously laid the groundwork for the theoretical justification of their repeated failures : henceforth every new defeat would serve as additional proof that mankind was neither worth saving nor capable of being saved. Only a few chosen spirits had access to the realm of freedom, truth, and beauty, and for them alone did these supreme values possess concrete existence. For the mass of the people there remained the consolations of religion, concerning whose illusory character Goethe and Hegel entertained as little doubt as did Feuerbach, Schopenhauer or Nietzsche. Thus the German Renaissance, originally the offspring of Northern Germany's traditional Protestant culture, issued in an idealist philosophy which from a secret doctrine of the elect evolved by stages into an openly proclaimed cult of the elite.[2]

[1] Marcuse, op. cit., passim; Ernst Troeltsch, 'Der deutsche Idealismus', in *Aufsaetze zur Geistesgeschichte und Religionssoziologie*, Tuebingen, 1925, pp. 532 ff.

[2] Karl Barth, *Die protestantische Theologie im 19. Jahrhundert*, Zurich, 1947, passim; also by the same author, 'Mensch und Mitmensch', in *Die kirchliche*

Hegel's philosophy represents a crucial stage in this process, for it marks both the climax of the idealist movement and the point where its inner tensions threaten to disrupt the philosophic integument. Hegel himself stood midway between the rationalist doctrine formulated by Kant and Fichte, and the reaction which arose from the failure of the French Revolution to translate the aims of the Enlightenment into reality. Opposed alike to the doctrinaire intransigence of the Jacobins, and to the conservative reaction dominant during the Restoration period after 1815, he consistently maintained an intermediate position which in the end led him back to a qualified acceptance of his native Lutheranism and its political sanction: the absolutist state. Yet the growing conservatism of the ageing Hegel was superimposed upon a rationalist system incompatible with religious orthodoxy and the ideology of the Prussian monarchy. The tension, never resolved in his life-time, exploded after his death. It then became apparent that the contradictions which ultimately tore the system apart had been held together by an act of will on Hegel's part. When in 1831 he left the scene, his followers drifted into incompatible positions which finally coincided with the emerging political line-up on the eve of the 1848 crisis. In conformity with the underlying gravitational pull of German history throughout the nineteenth century, the majority chose the conservative side.[1]

The disintegration of Hegelianism thus went parallel with the gradual formation of a movement hostile to absolutism and religious orthodoxy. This coincidence of philosophical and political stirrings is an index to the backwardness of mid-nineteenth-century Germany. In Western Europe it was no longer possible to assemble a radical party under the banner of slogans directed primarily against the 'union of throne and altar', whereas Germany in the 1840's was still struggling with the heritage of absolutism, not to mention the Middle Ages. In Prussia as in Austria, the church—Lutheran in the one case, Catholic in the other—provided both the principal safeguard of authority and its ideological justification. In this respect as in others, the two leading German states were closer to Russia than to Western Europe. This contrast was already noticeable during the Napoleonic era and it became more marked after the disintegration of the

Dogmatik, vol. III, 2; published separately, Zurich, 1954; cf. Karl Loewith, *Von Hegel zu Nietzsche*, Stuttgart, 1950, pp. 33 ff.

[1] For Hegel's conservatism, cf. Loewith, op. cit., pp. 39–42; Marcuse, op. cit., pp. 169 ff. For the incompatibility of Hegel's philosophy of religion with Protestant orthodoxy, cf. Barth, *Die protestantische Theologie etc.*, pp. 343–78.

Bourbon monarchy in France during the 1830 revolution: an event that coincided with the close of the classical age in German literature and philosophy.[1]

Hegel's philosophy must be viewed against this background of slowly mounting dissatisfaction with the continued existence of the Old Regime, after the latter had been eliminated in France and other parts of Western Europe. The tendency of his thought is to comprehend all possible antagonisms within the unity of a system which allows for conflict only as the motor of gradual progress towards a predetermined goal. The real and the rational are identical. Ultimately this is a theological conception, and the final tendency of Hegel's philosophy is to substitute itself for religion. On the political plane it reflects that reconciliation of (critical) thought with (unchanging) reality which is the common trait of all forms of German Idealism. Like the classical Weimar culture, of which it is the philosophical counterpart, the Hegelian system provides a transcendental resting-place for ideals not realised in actuality. It holds out to men the promise not of freedom, but of the idea of freedom; it envisages not the actual domination of reason in human affairs, but the recognition of the march of reason through history. It thus embodies both the ultimate aims of mankind—liberty and rationality—and their renunciation.

Hegel stands midway between the rationalism of the Enlightenment, which looked forward to a golden age of ordered freedom, and the radicalism of the post-1830 generation, determined to resume the advance where the French Revolution had been brought to a halt. His death in 1831 terminates the half-century of Germany's classical period which had opened with Kant's publication of the *Critique of Pure Reason* in 1781. The equivocal character of Hegel's pronouncements served for a while to conceal the fact that his system embodied, albeit in an obscure and mystifying fashion, some of the aims for which the French Revolution had been fought. Yet the radicals who broke away from him after his death were on solid ground when they denounced the conservative and contemplative bent of his philosophy. The 'reconciliation of idea and reality' is the central motive of Hegel's thought, as the transformation of reality is that of Marx.

---

[1] Goethe's death in 1832 marks the end of an epoch as much as Hegel's departure the year before. For a conservative interpretation of this turning-point, cf. Loewith, op. cit., pp. 28 ff; for the conventional Marxist-Leninist view cf. G. Lukács, *Der junge Hegel*, Zurich, 1948, pp. 27–45.

Hence the Hegelian dialectic in its orthodox form could not serve as an instrument of change, though a time was to come when it would be hailed as the 'algebra of revolution' by Herzen, invoked in support of radical revolt by Bakunin, and acclaimed as the esoteric doctrine of revolution by Engels.[1]

Contrary to a widespread notion, the triad thesis-antithesis-synthesis is not essential to Hegel's system, whose motor is rather to be found in the dialectic of the whole and its parts. There is no foundation for the legend that he attempted to deduce the empirical sequence of actual events from the triadic march of logical categories, though this criticism can reasonably be urged against the pseudo-Hegelianism of Lassalle or Lorenz von Stein—neither of whom understood Hegel, or indeed knew how to handle logical concepts.[2]

The dialectical method is meant to conform to the actual structure of reality, conceived as a process in which the logical subject unfolds itself into its own predicates. Hegel's marvellously compressed discussion of this theme in the Preface to the *Phenomenology of Mind* is still sufficiently lengthy and involved to defy summary exposition. For our purpose it is enough to say that he breaks away from formal logic, with its apparatus of fixed categories adapted to the empty

[1] Cf. F. Engels, *Ludwig Feuerbach and the End of Classical German Philosophy*, in Marx-Engels, *Selected Works*, Moscow, 1951, II, pp. 324 ff; cited hereafter as MESW. For Bakunin's views, cf. M. Bakunin: 'Reaktion in Deutschland', in *Deutsche Jahrbuecher*, vol. 17, 21st Oct. 1842, especially p. 1009: 'Let us put our trust therefore in the eternal spirit who shatters and destroys only because he is the unfathomable and eternally creative source of life. The desire to destroy is itself a creative desire.' (Quoted in D. Chizhevski, *Hegel bei den Slawen*, Reichenberg, 1934, p. 203.) For a more considered statement by a Polish pupil of Hegel, cf. August von Cieszkovski, *Prolegomena zu einer Historiosophie*, Berlin, 1838. There is evidence that Marx was influenced by him; cf. Auguste Cornu, *Karl Marx et Friedrich Engels*, Paris, 1955, vol. I, pp. 142 ff.

[2] For a brief account of the traditional confusion over Hegel's alleged dependence on the 'triad', cf. Gustav E. Mueller, 'The Hegel Legend of "Thesis-Antithesis-Synthesis" ', in *Journal of the History of Ideas*, New York, June 1958, vol. XIX, nr. 3, pp. 411–14. The author exaggerates Marx's part in furthering the misconception and makes no mention of Schopenhauer's frenzied polemics which are still quoted as valid criticism of Hegel: cf. K. R. Popper, *The Open Society and its Enemies*, vol. II, pp. 30 ff. The terms 'thesis, antithesis, synthesis' are employed by Fichte; they occur nowhere in Hegel's writings. This is not to say that the misunderstanding did not have some effect on later writers who believed themselves to be in the Hegelian tradition. It was Marx's criticism of such writers which unwittingly contributed to the further spread of the legend. Cf. his remarks on Stein, in a letter to Engels of January 8, 1868, in *Marx-Engels Gesamtausgabe* (hereafter cited as MEGA), Section III, vol. 4, p. 5.

certainties of mathematics, into a realm where the content and the method of philosophical enquiry are seen to coincide. The result of his enquiry is to demonstrate that reality is not as it appears to empirical perception, but as it is revealed by philosophical reflection. This certainty constitutes the inmost essence of German Idealism, and the source of its unbridgeable opposition to every form of empiricism. Insofar as Marxism embodies a similar conviction, with particular respect to history, it is still within the tradition of classical German philosophy.

Since for Hegel the truth of a philosophical proposition is demonstrated by what actually happens to the subject of the proposition— e.g., the truth that freedom is essential to men by the course of human history—there is for him no cleavage between the subject-matter of thought and the realm of actuality. Philosophical reflection discloses reason to be the ultimate essence of the world with which philosophy is concerned, and reason is likewise the instrument whereby in the course of time this truth is brought to the level of human awareness. This is the core of what has been called Hegel's pan-logism, or his rediscovery of Aristotle's ontology. It is also the starting-point of all the subsequent assaults on his system—by Feuerbach, by Marx and the other Young Hegelians, and lastly by Kierkegaard.[1]

The Hegelian scheme is operative because for Hegel there is in the last analysis no distinction between mind and its object. Both have a common denominator, which Hegel calls Reason and which appears under the guise of Spirit in the historical world. Spirit is both subjective and objective, and its 'internal contradictions' are resolved in the dialectical process, whereby the potentialities of all things unfold in a pattern of self-transcendence to a higher unity. Dialectical progress, though mirrored in thought, is the objective history of the real world, which arrives at self-consciousness in philosophy. The traditional criticism of this form of idealism is that it subordinates existence to logic. This misses the point, for in Hegel's system philosophical cognition has itself an existential quality: it enables the individual to recover his essence, which is reason. Yet this identification of thought and reality was precisely the target against which Feuerbach and Marx—and from a different standpoint Kierkegaard —directed their shafts. These attacks proceeded independently of

[1] For the parallelism between the Marxian and the Kierkegaardian revolt against Hegel, cf. Loewith, op. cit., pp. 125 ff; Marcuse, op. cit., pp. 262 ff.

each other. Marx knew nothing of Kierkegaard, and would not have considered his critique of Hegel important, save insofar as it emphasised the other-worldly nature of Christianity.

All the thinkers in question, including Marx, operated within the context of a secularised Protestant culture. The significance of this fact is not limited to the accidental circumstance that Hegel's philosophy became for a while the ideological sanction of the Prussian State. It extends to the core of the Hegelian system, and the subsequent revolt against it. Hegel had conceived the identity of the rational and the real in terms which ultimately went back to Christian theology. Behind the unfolding of Spirit in the universe lies the notion of creation. Spirit creates the world by externalising itself, and eventually returns to itself after arriving at self-consciousness. This process is mediated by toil and suffering, symbolised for Hegel by the image of the Cross. Reconciliation—the union of idea and reality —takes place only after the idea has undergone the lengthy travail of passing through successive incarnations in a medium—reality— which is alien to it, but gradually becomes one with the spirit that permeates it. The concrete identity of the real and the rational is the concept (notion) which embodies the essence of things—not as they appear in actuality, but as they are in reality. The concept is the logical form of the universal, i.e., that which determines the existence of particulars—as, e.g., Man is logically prior to particular men, who exist as such only by virtue of what is common to all. Thus the concept mediates between (spiritual) reality and (material) appearance, as Christ mediates between God and the world. Hence the *logos*-concept is Christ, and philosophy, which conceives the identity of reality and the absolute idea (God), becomes theology. But since the idea (*logos*) unfolds through all the successive stages of nature and history, philosophy must concern itself with reality and become science. Yet not empirical science, which never rises above the mere data of existence, but rather knowledge of the essential reality that manifests itself through the march of events in the world.

Since we are here concerned not with Hegel's philosophy—the briefest outline of which would fill an entire volume—but with its role in Germany on the eve of the 1848 revolution, it will be sufficient to indicate its relevance to the events which were shortly to dethrone it as the quasi-official ideology of the Prussian State, while incorporating some of its elements into a theory of total revolution.

It has been noted that, owing to the peculiar character of the

Hegelian dialectic of subject-object, Hegel's system mirrors its own theme. Another way of putting this is to say that while philosophy provides the general categories for the understanding of history, it also turns out to be the secret of history, inasmuch as the latter is revealed as embodied reason, now brought to self-consciousness. In principle it would have been sufficient for Hegel to state this as an axiom of thought; in fact he postulated it as an achievement that had already taken place: history had reached its appointed goal (in the *status quo*), and the reconciliation of idea and reality—Hegel's fundamental aim ever since the spiritual crisis which terminated his youthful revolutionary phase—was presumed to have taken place. This notion was not merely unacceptable to Feuerbach and the Young Hegelians of the next generation for political reasons: it represented a claim which was plainly unbelievable, namely that the identity of subject and object, thought and reality, had been attained in the true 'system of science', i.e., Hegel's own. This conclusion did not follow from the conception of history as the march of mankind to domination over nature and possession of the world through reason: but it followed necessarily from Hegel's belief that his system mirrored the totality of the world. Once this was granted, philosophy was reduced to contemplation of the idea's progress through history, now brought to a close in the comprehension of that necessity which had given birth, among others, to Hegel's own system of thought. Alternatively, if it was accepted that philosophy could not go beyond the comprehension of the actual state of affairs as necessary and therefore rational, those who wished to alter the existing condition of things were impelled to advance beyond the contemplative stage.[1]

The conventional account of this chapter in the history of German philosophy is content to register the dissolution of the Hegelian school into conflicting groups, among whom the left-wingers—principally D. F. Strauss, Bruno Bauer, and Feuerbach—eventually

---

[1] For Hegel's spiritual crisis during his Frankfurt period (1797–1800), i.e., before the first tentative elaboration of his thought, in conjunction with Schelling in Jena (1801–2), cf. Lukács, op. cit., pp. 131 ff. Although the interpretation supplied by L. is both banal and misleading, the relevant facts are stated. For Hegel's conceptual scheme cf. Marcuse, op. cit., pp. 121 ff. Among recent literature on the subject, Georges M.-M. Cottier, *L'Athéisme du jeune Marx: ses origines hégéliennes*, Paris, 1959, presents a critical view of both Hegel and Marx from the Thomist standpoint. For an interpretation of Hegel which combines Marxist and existentialist viewpoints, cf. Alexandre Kojève, *Introduction à la lecture de Hegel*, Paris, 1947. Cf. also Jean Hyppolite, *Etudes sur Marx et Hegel*, Paris, 1955.

prepared the way for Marx. This hardly takes account of the complexities of a situation in which a radical critic of traditional theology like Strauss could figure as the leader of the left wing around 1836-8, only to become a highly conservative figure in the political field a decade later. What was originally at issue among Hegel's followers after his death (1831) was the philosophy of religion, and specifically the literal truth of Scripture. The 'right wing' and the 'centre' were defined by their respective attitudes towards the theological iconoclasm of Strauss, for whom Lutheran orthodoxy rather than the Prussian State was the enemy; while some typical 'Old Hegelians' maintained their allegiance to the system during the second half of the century, long after the 'Young Hegelians' had abandoned the philosophical arena. To be an orthodox member of the school it was sufficient to be neutral on the religious issue, following Hegel's own example. In a country where the government was then busy promoting a somewhat artificial union of the Lutheran and Reformed churches, with a view to giving the State a solid Evangelical foundation, such neutrality did indeed amount to passive support of the *status quo*; but not every member of the school in the 1830's was necessarily aware of this fact. Strauss was the exception, which was precisely why he initiated the practice of referring publicly to a 'right' and 'left' wing among Hegelians—following the terminology (then novel and alarming) of French politics.

Strictly speaking no 'Young Hegelian' group existed before the 1840's. By then the excitement over Strauss's critique of theology had yielded to the far greater stir produced by Feuerbach's assault on religion as such, while at the same time Arnold Ruge, Moses Hess, and the Bauers (Bruno and Edgar), made their first tentative excursions into the critical field. Even then the debate was still partly conducted in metaphysical terms. It could not well be otherwise, since Hegel's doctrine of Right (the term under which he introduced the political realm) was grounded in his philosophy of history, which in turn sought to demonstrate the essential harmony of reason and the actual world. Its categories terminated in the existing condition of things, which in Prussia was characterised by the alliance of the State and the Lutheran Church against liberalism, i.e., against the contemporary form of the Enlightenment. But the Enlightenment was likewise the source of that strand in Hegel's thinking which affirmed the universality of reason and the consequent rationality of the universe. These contradictions would have exploded the system even if in 1840 the accident of a dynastic change in Prussia had not pre-cipitated the long-delayed conflict between the government—fully supported by the State Church—and the nascent radical movement. It was as representatives of the latter that the 'Young Hegelians' found themselves harried by the 'Christian-German' orthodoxy which had recently found a programme in Romantic medievalism, and a leader in the new king, Frederick William IV. If the 1840's are the most exciting period in nineteenth-century German intellec-tual history, the reason is that they witnessed the first principled con-frontation of the *Ancien Régime* with the heirs of the French Revolu-tion on German soil. For a century to come, the ideas that emerged from this crucible were to place their stamp on every movement originating from similar circumstances. And here it is worth stressing that the assault on absolutism and conservatism began at a time when the middle-class was still politically passive, and the industrial proletariat had hardly emerged. The radical intellectuals who incor-porated the new outlook were not merely the heralds of a coming storm; their dissatisfaction with the existing order crystallised a mood which had been growing in Western Europe for some decades. Past and future mingled oddly in the ideology of a new social stratum which had not yet found its bearings, and whose confused gropings could be formulated alternatively in traditional liberal, or new-fangled socialist, terms. On the eve of the German pseudo-revolution, which was to satisfy national longings while leaving democratic aspirations unfulfilled, we encounter a new and potentially important group: the intelligentsia.

2

PHILOSOPHIC RADICALISM

IF THE EUROPEAN nineteenth century is defined as the era between the French and the Russian Revolution, the role played by German philosophy during this period appears in a paradoxical light. Germany resisted the impact of both upheavals, yet produced the essential link between them—Marxism. Moreover, this connection was established with the help of the Hegelian synthesis: a philosophy of contemplation and reconciliation, explicitly addressed to the task of mediating between the liberalism of the Enlightenment and the conservatism of the Restoration. The problem is not rendered easier by the corresponding circumstance that Hegelianism was having an unsettling effect upon East European intellectuals of aristocratic and conservative background long before Marx appeared on the scene.[1]

The general character of German political evolution throughout this period is one of negative reaction to the upheavals produced, first in France and then in Russia, by the application to society of the doctrines of philosophic radicalism. The helpless passivity of the thin stratum of German sympathisers with the early phase of the French

[1] Cf. Gustav A. Wetter, *Dialectical Materialism*, London, 1958, p. 8. In addition to the Russian and Polish aristocrats among the Berlin Hegelians, mention must be made of those with whom Marx subsequently came into personal contact; cf. his correspondence with P. V. Annenkov in *Marx-Engels Selected Correspondence*, Moscow, 1954 (cited hereafter as MESC), pp. 39–51.

Revolution has already been noted. It corresponded not merely to the material weakness of the German middle class, but to its state of mind, which remained timidly conservative at least down to the middle of the nineteenth century. Thereafter the brief revolutionary effervescence of 1848–9 turned out to be a false dawn. German liberalism became progressively less combative as the century drew on, and after 1871 it was increasingly absorbed into the quasi-official ideology of National Liberalism. It thus continued the traditional role of the German middle class: that of a socially influential, but politically passive, adjunct to the autocracy.

Although on the eve of 1848 this peculiar constellation was not yet fully observable, it was already foreshadowed by the weakness of the radical intelligentsia and its isolation from the bulk of the educated middle-class public. In part the intellectuals compensated for this lack of influence by the intransigence of their theoretical formulations, as did their opposite numbers in France during and after the Bourbon restoration. But whereas the French ideologists of the 'Left' formed a coherent stratum which resisted official pressures and in the end imposed its outlook upon society, in Germany philosophic radicalism—the system of ideas and values held by the opponents of autocratic rule—disintegrated steadily throughout the second half of the century, leaving a vacuum which was not adequately filled by scientific materialism and positivism. As time went on, the entire complex of ideas associated with the French Revolution—ideas which in the 1840's had become the credo of the Young Hegelians and through them of the liberal opposition, though in a diluted form—disappeared from the consciousness of the educated classes. It became common form to assert the existence of an unbridgeable barrier between 'Western' rationalism (as though Kant had never existed) and the truly 'German' philosophy of Romanticism. This outcome casts a revealing light upon the intellectual situation on the eve of 1848, and in particular upon the significance of Feuerbach as the philosopher of Germany's aborted democratic revolution.

For reasons unconnected with his status in the history of philosophy, Feuerbach has come to be known chiefly as a precursor of Marx, or—more quaintly still—of 'dialectical materialism'. This is to ignore his significance as a critic of religion, and of the Hegelian system insofar as it embodied certain remnants of the theological world-view. From a formal viewpoint, Feuerbach's doctrine can be described as inverted Hegelianism. It can even be claimed that his inversion of Hegel's idealism (e.g., his treatment of spirit as the 'negation' of matter) anticipates some of the tenets of 'dialectical materialism'. But here we are concerned with his role in preparing the way for the emergence of a non-religious world view, i.e., for the completion of the Enlightenment on German soil. The understanding of this subject is not helped by emphasis upon the formal peculiarities of Feuerbach's philosophy. What matters is the effect of his teaching, which was to emancipate the radical intellectuals from the hold of institutional religion and its last remaining theological bulwark, Hegelian metaphysics.[1]

Feuerbach begins and ends as a critic of religion, and of philosophical idealism—in his eyes a diluted form of theological idealism. The religious 'alienation' (the term, but not its application, goes back to Hegel) is viewed as the source of the philosophical alienation, of which Hegel's system is the last and greatest expression.[2] Apart from the critique of religious and speculative idealism, Feuerbach strictly speaking has no major aim in view. His attack on the Hegelian system, starting a little hesitantly and gradually rising to a climax in which the former disciple repudiates the master's teachings, turns wholly upon the destruction of speculative 'other-worldliness'. He himself was quite conscious of the fact that his substitution of anthropology for theology was the core of his thinking.[3]

This thinking has a passionate, almost lyrical, quality absent in

[1] Cf. Engels, *Ludwig Feuerbach, etc.*, MESW II, pp. 331 ff. The extent of Engels's commitment to the optimistic naturalism of the Enlightenment, which Feuerbach introduced into the post-Hegel discussion, is obscured by his strictures upon the inadequacy of Feuerbach's thought. Both men believed in the unification of philosophy and (natural) science, though at a level higher than that of the 'vulgar materialists' whom Feuerbach, like Engels, had repudiated. 'Dialectical materialism' (first so described by Plekhanov) was to be the concrete realisation of this positivist programme. Cf. Engels, op. cit., pp. 337 ff.

[2] Cf. *Vorlaeufige Thesen zur Reform der Philosophie*, in Ludwig Feuerbach, *Saemtliche Werke*, Stuttgart, 1904, vol. II, p. 249: 'The Hegelian philosophy has alienated man from himself, its entire system resting upon . . . abstractions.' 'The "absolute spirit" is the "departed spirit" of theology which leads a ghostly existence in Hegel's philosophy.' (Ibid.) 'Theology is belief in ghosts. Ordinary theology has its ghosts in sensual imagination, speculative theology in unsensual abstraction.' (Ibid.)

[3] 'The secret of theology is anthropology.' (Ibid.) 'God was my first thought, reason my second, and man my third and last.' (*Philosophical Fragments*, in *Saemtliche Werke*, vol. II, p. 388.) '. . . my writings all . . . have one and the same object . . . one and the same theme. That theme is religion and philosophy, and everything connected with it.' (*Vorlesungen ueber das Wesen der Religion*, p. 6; in *Saemtliche Werke*, vol. VIII.)

Hegel, but common enough in the Romantic movement. It was the peculiar achievement of Feuerbach to enlist the Romantic strain in the service of humanism. His affirmation of nature, man, the life of the senses, recalls Rousseau, with whom he also shares a certain sentimentality; while his radical rejection of Christianity foreshadows Nietzsche. At the same time he is totally free from Nietzsche's hysteria, which heralds the subsequent collapse of atheist humanism into nihilism. In the emancipation of the German mind from theology he represents the forward-looking stage, when rationalism still sounded an optimistic note. If religion is disclosed to be an illusion, it is also seen to constitute a human creation which flatters its originator, since the attributes of God are in fact those of Man. 'The divine being is nothing else than the human being, or rather, the human nature purified, freed from the limits of the individual man, made objective —i.e., contemplated and revered as another, a distinct being.'[1]

Feuerbach—like Hegel and almost every other representative of classical German philosophy a Protestant in his ethic, though not in his theological beliefs—attempts to rescue the religious kernel from the metaphysical husk. The outcome is a system of 'religious atheism' which has man for its unique centre of reference.

Who then is our Saviour and Redeemer? God or Love? Love; for God as God has not saved us, but Love, which transcends the difference between the divine and human personality. As God has renounced himself out of love, so we, out of love, should renounce God; for if we do not sacrifice God to love, we sacrifice love to God, and, in spite of the predicate of love, we have the God—the evil being—of religious fanaticism.[2]

The time has come to transform theology into anthropology. 'In the Incarnation religion only confesses what in reflection on itself, as theology, it will not admit; namely, that God is an altogether human being.' The statement 'God loves man' is an 'Orientalism' for 'love of man is the highest'. Feuerbach has no use for a God who plainly is nothing but the Oriental paterfamilias writ large, but his critique proceeds from this somewhat sentimental objection to the demonstration that 'God' is an imaginary substitute for the real world. Religion has sacrificed man to God. Now '. . . we need only . . . invert the religious relation—regard that as an end which religion supposes to be a means—exalt that into the primary which

[1] L. Feuerbach, *Das Wesen des Christentums*, in *Saemtliche Werke*, vol. VI, p. 17; translated as *The Essence of Christianity*, by Marian Evans (George Eliot), London, 1854, (2nd edn., 1881) p. 14.
[2] *Essence of Christianity*, p. 53.

in religion is subordinate . . . at once we have destroyed the illusion, and the unclouded light of truth streams in upon us.'[1]

The loss of the religious illusion leads straight to the recognition that philosophy, to fulfil its task, must promote the emancipation of mankind from all obstacles which hamper the free development of human faculties. The positive content of philosophy is furnished by study of the real existence of man—not man in the abstract, but the empirical human beings whose liberty and happiness are at stake:

He who says no more of me than that I am an atheist, says and knows nothing of me. The question as to the existence or non-existence of God, the opposition between theism and atheism, belongs to the sixteenth and seventeenth centuries, but not to the nineteenth. I deny God. But that means for me that I deny the negation of man. In place of the illusory, fantastic, heavenly position of man, which in actual life necessarily leads to the degradation of man, I substitute the tangible, actual, and consequently also the political and social position of mankind. The question concerning the existence or non-existence of God is for me nothing but the question concerning the existence or non-existence of man.[2]

In religion, man 'alienates' himself from himself, worships a self-generated image of perfection, and renders himself uselessly miserable. True philosophy breaks this enchantment and brings man back to himself. It does so by illuminating the sources of the religious illusion. 'The historical progress of religion consists in this: that what by an earlier religion was regarded as objective, is now recognised as subjective; that is, what was formerly contemplated and worshipped as God, is now perceived to be something human.'[3]

Feuerbach conceived his philosophy to be the realisation of all preceding systems—in this respect following in Hegel's footsteps. But he repudiated Hegel's procedure, including his identification of the real and the rational. Philosophy must take its start not from Hegel's abstract 'idea', but from concrete nature and historical reality. It must trace the natural conditions of human freedom, and understand man as a being whose relationship to nature is mediated by the senses. It must realise that 'thought is preceded by suffering', and that cognition enters the picture only after man has been formed by nature. Above all, it must cease to judge men by the illusory idols they set up, notably the religious idol which estranges them from their own nature. Here Feuerbach spells out the implications of Goethe's

[1] Ibid., p. 271.   [2] Preface to vol. I of *Saemtliche Werke*.
[3] *Essence of Christianity*, p. 12.

pantheist world-view which by the 1840's had become the esoteric doctrine of the intellectual elite. For all its political conservatism and the calculated ambiguity of its public utterances, the 'spirit of Weimar' had always been profoundly subversive of religious orthodoxy.

There is an obvious retort to all this: *Why* does man experience the need to project the 'spiritual' part of his nature in this curious fashion? One need not be a theologian or an idealist philosopher to see that Feuerbach has to some extent begged the question. But the philosophical inadequacy of a doctrine has never yet prevented it from becoming socially important. The problem for the historian is why Feuerbach's influence on the subsequent development of German thought was so much less than that of a thinker like Nietzsche who shared his atheism, but not his humanism. To put it differently, why did those elements in German national life who continued to adhere to Feuerbach's outlook have to become socialists? This question leads back to politics, and specifically to the failure of German democracy in what for a moment promised to be its *annus mirabilis*: 1848.

Feuerbach's position, by and large, corresponds to that of the French materialists and rationalists on the eve of 1789, when the radical intellectuals entered the political arena. In the German setting these tendencies were necessarily reflected in a caricatured form. The place of the Girondins (not to mention the Jacobins, who had no German counterparts save Marx and his friends) was occupied by those democrats who formed the left wing of the National Assembly in 1848–9, and who subsequently maintained an increasingly hopeless resistance to the alliance between the Prussian state and the North German National-Liberals. This opposition in turn contained an even smaller and weaker republican element, largely concentrated in the South and actuated by particularist dislike of Prussia. Feuerbach is the philosopher of this republican-democratic opposition. Its failure is also his failure. With its growing elimination from public life, his own influence declined, until by the time of his death (1872) he was isolated and almost forgotten. Yet his legacy was incorporated within the body of Marxist, or quasi-Marxist, doctrine which at about that time began to permeate the nascent labour movement. This renaissance of his influence proceeded *pari passu* with the spread of a vulgarised scientific materialism among the middle-class public— now politically quiescent, but still anti-clerical and vaguely liberal. Since he had been among the first to demand the unification of philosophy and science, he could in retrospect be viewed as a fore-runner of positivism as well as Marxism. In practice it depended largely upon shifting political affiliations which aspect received the greatest prominence. In the ideology of Social-Democracy, as formu-lated by Engels around 1880, both elements managed to coexist quite happily, albeit at the expense of the Hegelian heritage which Feuer-bach had never quite repudiated. It was now taken for granted that Feuerbach's 'materialism', i.e., his naturalist humanism, offered the necessary corrective to Hegel's metaphysics. At the same time the development of (natural) science was welcomed as a solvent of specu-lative idealism and the most reliable reinforcement of the new positivist world-view.

All this was a far cry from the situation on the eve of 1848, when radical humanism was the fighting creed of a small but determined body of intellectuals who hoped to take the leadership in the impend-ing revolution. The latter was envisaged in terms derived from French experience, and the radical intellectuals drifted towards Feuerbach's materialism, and away from their traditional idealist moorings, be-cause the struggle against Church and State had begun to reproduce some of the features of the earlier revolt against the *ancien régime* in France. The extraordinary certainty of victory displayed by all the radicals, including Marx and Engels, in 1848–9 was due to their con-viction that history was about to repeat itself.[1]

In passing one may note the remarkable parallelism between the thought of Feuerbach and that of the Saint-Simonist school in France. Whether by coincidence or not, both stress the transformation of theology into anthropology: the kingdom of heaven is to be brought down to earth. When Feuerbach proclaims as his aim 'the realisation of the Hegelian and generally of the preceding philosophy',[2] he

[1] Engels, op. cit., p. 332: 'The main body of the most determined Young Hegelians was, by the practical necessity of the fight against organised religion, driven back to Anglo-French materialism. This brought them into conflict with their school system.' Cf. also Lukács, *Der junge Hegel*, p. 342: 'Die Grundlinie der klassischen deutschen Philosophie ist ein Kampf gegen den philosophischen Materialismus.' (The basic line of classical German philosophy is a struggle against philosophical materialism.) For L. this is an awkward admission to have to make, since his general tendency is to represent classical German thought as the ideological reflex of the French Revolution—ignoring its derivation from Lutheran Protestantism which from the start gave it a conservative bent and subsequently led its more influential adherents to look to England rather than France as the political model.

[2] *Grundsaetze der Philosophie der Zukunft*, in *Saemtliche Werke*, vol. II, para. 20.

not merely anticipates Marx, but echoes a theme which had already been sounded by the French 'utopian socialists'.[1] The secularisation of religion, i.e., the transforming of religious into humanist motivations, was an aim common to radical movements on both sides of the Rhine, with the French generally setting the pace, while the more pedestrian Germans brought up the rear, but in the process deepened the French concepts into a systematic critique of theology and metaphysics. To gain a clear picture of Marx's background one has to bear in mind that his birthplace, the Rhineland, lay at the crossroads of all these movements. It seems probable that he had already made the acquaintance of Saint-Simonism before he took up his studies. He was still a high-school pupil in Trier when a resident Saint-Simonian propagandist in 1835 attracted the unfavourable attention of the authorities with a pamphlet on 'The Privileged Classes and the Working Classes': perhaps the first time that this now familiar battle-cry had been sounded on German soil.[2]

[1] For a thorough analysis of this subject, cf. H. J. Hunt, *Le socialisme et le romantisme en France*, Oxford, 1955. For Saint-Simonian influence on German thinkers of the period, cf. E. M. Butler, *The Saint-Simonian Religion in Germany*, London, 1926, passim.

[2] The author in question, Ludwig Gall, seems to have been connected with an 'advanced' liberal circle of which Marx's father, and the headmaster of his school, were members: cf. B. Nicolaevsky and O. Maenchen-Helfen, *Karl Marx: Man and Fighter*, London, 1936, pp. 9 ff. There is reason to believe that Marx's future father-in-law, Ludwig von Westphalen, was likewise attracted to Saint-Simonism; cf. *Karl Marx: Selected Writings in Sociology and Social Philosophy*, ed. T. B. Bottomore and M. Rubel, London, 1956, p. 9.

3

EARLY SOCIALISM

THE FRENCH REVOLUTION, whose impact on the European consciousness has so far been discussed only in terms appropriate to the history
of philosophy, is today generally acknowledged to have been the
source of the modern socialist movement.[1] Though unchallenged, this
reading of the facts lacks some of the overwhelming certainty which
it necessarily possessed for contemporaries. At our present distance
from the scene, the suggestion that socialism might equally well have
come to birth under different circumstances has at least the plausibility of an academic hypothesis. To any European living between
1830 and 1870, such a notion would have appeared grotesque, just as
it would have seemed palpably absurd to associate democratic
radicalism with any country but France, and with any tradition save
that of the Jacobins. (Switzerland was republican, but far from
radical.) In 1848, and for some decades before and after this crucial
watershed, the derivation of socialism from France was as plain as
the Russian origin of modern communism is to us. To pursue socialist
aims was to think along lines suggested by the evolution of France

---

[1] Cf. J. L. Talmon, *The Origins of Totalitarian Democracy*, London, 1952,
part III, pp. 167 ff; Elie Halévy, *Histoire du socialisme européen*, Paris, 1948,
passim; G. D. H. Cole, *Socialist Thought:* vol. I, *The Forerunners 1789–1950*,
London, 1955, pp. 11 ff.

since 1789. This statement holds good for all the early socialist groups, including the Owenite socialists in England whose thinking was wholly determined by the manner in which the French Revolution had posed the social problem: namely as a problem calling for the rational reorganisation of society. There was nothing in the intellectual tradition of either Germany or England before 1789 to suggest such an approach—not to mention other European countries. Nor was there any conscious formulation of a general socialist programme prior to 1830, when 'utopian' socialism crystallised in Paris. After 1830 the situation had altered inasmuch as France now exported socialist ideas and tendencies instead of keeping them at home; but as late as 1848 there was no major socialist *movement* outside France, and even in 1870–1 the fate of the First International was determined by the catastrophe of the Paris Commune.[1]

For our purpose—since we are not concerned with the history of early socialism, but with the socialist component in the Marxian synthesis—the crucial period is that of 1830–48. Those were the years when socialism transformed itself from a doctrine into a movement. That it did so in France, and not in England where industrial society was much further advanced, should alone have been enough to put the quietus on all attempts to establish a mechanical cause-and-effect relationship between economics and politics. Eventually something like a socialist labour movement spread to other areas, e.g., Belgium, where similar circumstances had not previously given rise to parallel forms of thinking or organisation. But the original breakthrough occurred in France, and in France alone. Unless the full implications of this fact are grasped, the subsequent history of the socialist movement remains mysterious. In particular it becomes incomprehensible that the Russian Revolution should have reached back, across Marxism and Germany, to France for its inspiration.

[1] Cf. Halévy, op. cit., passim. Attempts have been made, with little success, to read socialist implications into the programme of the extreme left wing in the English Revolution of 1640–60; but even if the democratic radicalism of the period is to be designated by this term, it can hardly be held to foreshadow the upheaval of the industrial revolution. There was no anticipation of Chartism, for all its primitive agrarian overtones. The case of Germany is even clearer. Fichte's *Geschlossener Handelsstaat* (1800) is reactionary rather than utopian, but those who stress his originality have to face the awkwardness of explaining why he should have elaborated his scheme at the height of his concern with the French Revolution. For the rest, Weitling remains the first German working-class socialist, and in his case it is beyond doubt that he underwent his political schooling in the Paris of the 1830's. Cf. Thilo Ramm, *Die grossen Sozialisten*, Stuttgart, 1955, vol. I, pp. 475–514.

Yet the fact is undeniable; to this day, Russia and France remain linked by the common experience of a dramatic break with the Old Regime: a chapter missing in the history of Germany. They call to each other across that unconquered fortress of a different tradition; and this although the impulse of the French Revolution reached Russia by way of Germany, and although German philosophy has been the proximate source of all Russian theorising since at least 1917, if not earlier.

The mystery of course ceases to be one if the French Revolution is recognised as the starting-point of modern political thinking, at any rate on the European Continent, if not in the Anglo-American world with its somewhat different traditions. By 1830 this recognition had become sufficiently general to inspire all existing governments with an altogether exaggerated fear of further volcanic eruptions, while the revolutionaries naturally went to the same source for instruction. The dates 1830 and 1848 are crucial, for during this period the nascent socialist movement—then running in harness with democratic repub-licanism, i.e., neo-Jacobinism—became fully impregnated with the revolutionary tradition as it was then understood in France. This interaction was to prove more lasting in its effects than the simul-taneous infusion of Jacobin tendencies into the European liberal movement. The latter always had an alternative model in the England of the Whigs and parliamentary rule, while the socialists could look only to France—or rather to the revolution that had partly trans-formed France. It is for this reason that the literature of pre-1848 socialism, irrespective of authorship, so often suggests a conscious harking back to the Convention and the Commune of 1793-4.[1]

But although the decisive formulation of the new doctrine occurred in France, the social matrix out of which the movement arose was already common to the whole of Western Europe. There is no parti-cular point in listing once again the consequences produced by the impact of nascent industrial capitalism upon the European Continent on the morrow of the Napoleonic wars. The conjunction of these two upheavals was crucial for the turn then given to the European mind —in more precise terms, to the thinking of the intellectuals. Unless one bears in mind that the industrial and the political revolutions went hand in hand, interacting on one another and helping to

[1] Halévy, op. cit., pp. 48 ff; Edouard Dolléans, *Histoire du mouvement ouvrier*, Paris, 1946/7, vol. I, pp. 51 ff; Th. Ramm (ed.), *Der Fruehsozialismus*, Stuttgart, 1956, passim.

accelerate each other, one obtains no adequate picture of the period —or for that matter of the 'materialist conception of history' which, not surprisingly, arose at that particular moment in time and at the intersection of all these new currents. Marxism, in one of its aspects, is also a theory of the industrial revolution—at any rate in its European setting.[1]

Perhaps the simplest way of formulating the doctrinal issue—since we are here concerned with what the theorists thought of the new situation—is to say that the liberal vision was challenged at the precise moment when it had ceased to be altogether utopian, i.e., when it was about to descend from the heaven of philosophy to the solid earth of economic relations. In real terms, liberalism—then and later on—meant bourgeois society, or at least it rested upon that society as its foundation. Bourgeois society having given birth to industrial capitalism (thereby transcending its own safely non-industrial origins) it became urgently necessary to decide whether the promised advance in freedom and welfare was really worth the altogether monstrous birth-pangs of the new social order; or indeed whether the promise itself might not be fraudulent. As everyone knows, it was at this point that a split became manifest in the hitherto united army marching forward from the positions occupied by the French Revolution: socialist progressives parted company with liberal progressives, sometimes to the accompaniment of battle-cries which sounded not altogether unlike the despairing complaints of agrarian conservatives and religious traditionalists. The familiar tripartite political spectrum of the European nineteenth century—conservatives, liberals, socialists—was about to emerge. All this took place amid a welter of confusing claims and assertions, but in its essentials the socialist protest was already plain enough. It concerned the centre-piece of the liberal system: private property and the market; and the heart of the liberal programme: unbridled individualism. Both were rejected as potentially destructive of social solidarity and human welfare.[2]

Put thus baldly, the matter appears simpler than it really was. What confronted the contemporaries was a revolution which altered not merely the political structure, but the total culture of society. In

[1] Cf. Karl Polanyi, *The Great Transformation*, London, 1944, for some of the social consequences; see also E. Halévy, *A History of the English People*, London, 1961, vol. III, pp. 119 ff.

[2] Polanyi, op. cit., ch. 11; Dolléans, op. cit., vol. I, pp. 113 ff.

particular, social life was rapidly becoming unresponsive to the values of communal existence. Today, with the crisis behind us, we are able to view this disintegration as a stage on the road towards new forms of collectivity, but in the early nineteenth century the situation looked alarming enough, both to conservatives and to those radicals who were trying to extricate themselves from what seemed to them the blind optimism of the liberals. There was a very real sense of cultural dissolution coming on top of the appalling social conditions created by early capitalism—circumstances which the fashionable liberal ideology either denied or dismissed as the inevitable price of progress. On both counts the socialist opponents of the new order at first sounded the kind of alarm that had already been expressed by conservative critics of liberal individualism.[1] At this stage it is often difficult to differentiate conservative from socialist protests. The Saint-Simonians, though in the tradition of the French Revolution, were critical of its individualism and eventually proposed not merely a new social integration, but a renovated religious faith as well. Across the Rhine, the 'true socialism' mocked by Marx and Engels in the *Manifesto* drew from the Romantics (and from Feuerbach) its somewhat sentimental appeal for a restoration of social solidarity. A 'primitive communist' like Weitling argued on much the same lines as the sophisticated pupils of Saint-Simon in France, or the 'Christian socialists' in England: modern civilisation was setting people against each other, atomising society, and introducing an individualism hostile to the precepts of traditional morality. At a more elevated level the same theme is encountered in Comte.[2]

Behind the social protest there is to be sensed a growing alarm at the threatened isolation of the individual in an atomised society in which communal religion has ceased to function and nothing is taking its place. This has become a familiar theme and one that tends to be shrugged off. In the early nineteenth century it represented a novel situation, and one which most intellectuals were not well

[1] Cf. Max Beer, *A History of British Socialism*, London, 1919 (revised edns., 1929, 1940, 1953).
[2] Cf. Cole, op. cit., pp. 37 ff. The Saint-Simonian literature is too voluminous to cite. Its main documents are contained in *Saint-Simon: Oeuvres choisies*, 3 vols., Brussels, 1859. Cf. also S. Charléty, *Histoire du Saint-Simonisme*, Paris, 1931. For the early French socialists generally, cf. Hunt, op. cit., passim. Weitling's *Evangelium eines armen Suenders* (1843—new edn. in *Der Fruehsozialismus*, Stuttgart, 1956) is significant for its naive attempt to give a socialist twist to the Christian tradition—neither the first nor the last effort in this direction.

equipped to handle, since it cut across their newly discovered sense of freedom from traditional (religious and social) sanctions. The socialist protest could easily be confused with the Romantic lament, and both with utopian schemes for reviving medieval ways of life. Before socialism could constitute itself in opposition to the now dominant liberal school and to the still strongly entrenched conservatism of the old order, it had to formulate its critique in such a way as to preserve the inheritance of rationalism and the French Revolution. By 1840 this task had been more or less completed, and the political movement could get under way.[1]

It could not, however, progress very far without an economic doctrine, and something like a coherent view of society. The first was gradually elaborated with the help of the labour theory of value in its simplified form, i.e., the doctrine that labour is the sole creator of society's wealth; the second required a more philosophical approach. If individualism was to be overcome, its picture of society had to be shown up as defective. Above all, the role of the individual needed to be clarified. At the outset this task devolved upon writers who were anything but politically neutral—the Comteists in France and the Owenites in England—though in the end their criticism of the liberal ethic was incorporated in the generally accepted body of academic philosophy. In England this important movement of thought away from 'rugged individualism' and towards a modified collectivism started the slow erosion of Benthamite orthodoxy. The crucial figure in this process is John Stuart Mill—Marx's contemporary and in a sense his only serious rival, insofar as he is one of the ancestors of Fabianism and welfare socialism generally. Here we are merely concerned to note Mill's place in the nineteenth-century debate on the role of the individual, a controversy in which the new socialist view of man as a creation of society for the first time confronted the liberal thesis that society exists for the benefit of the individuals whose sum total it is.[2]

In these early socialist writers the relation of the individual to society is analysed from a critical viewpoint which does not question

[1] J. L. Talmon, *Political Messianism*, London—New York, 1960, passim; Emile Durkheim, *Socialism and Saint-Simon*, London, 1959 (cf. Durkheim, *Le Socialisme*, Paris, 1928).

[2] So far as Britain is concerned the effective formulation of the post-liberal standpoint belongs to the 1890's, but it is already foreshadowed in the later writings of Mill, with their growing stress on the involvement of the individual in society.

the presuppositions of liberalism, but seeks to go beyond them. It is accepted that, once personal freedom has become historically possible, society exists for the sake of furthering and protecting its growth. As against the traditional religious world-view it is likewise taken for granted that freedom is not to be understood as the illusory possession of an 'inner' spiritual realm compatible with actual enslavement, but as concrete individual liberty, i.e., the right to self-determination. The clash occurs over the socialist insistence upon the responsibility of society to ensure the welfare of all its members. The individual is a social creation. As it cannot develop outside society, so its individual characteristics are, in part at least, chargeable to the community. The latter is thus morally responsible for the fate of its members. Although these conclusions are put forward in the interest of reforming currents—specifically Owenite socialism in England and its various counterparts in France—they embody an embryonic sociology destined to flower into a new academic discipline: not accidentally the achievement of a writer who had made his start in the early socialist movement.[1]

A rudimentary sociology is likewise implicit in the work of those economists who after 1815 set out to give a critical estimate of the new market economy. Here it is customary to mention Sismondi, of whom no more need be said than that he deserved better treatment than was meted out to him by Marx in the *Communist Manifesto*.[2] Although it has been questioned whether he should be described as a socialist[3] he was sufficiently critical of *laissez-faire* to warrant inclusion among the opponents of the new orthodoxy. The same clearly cannot be said of those former Saint-Simonists whose technological

[1] H. B. Acton, 'Comte's Positivism and the Science of Society', *Philosophy*, London, October 1951, vol. XXVI, No. 99, pp. 291–310. The sociology of Comte clearly cannot be considered apart from the Saint-Simonian movement, but since Comte (unlike Saint-Simon) had no influence on Marx, this circumstance is simply noted. Marx appears to have read him for the first time in 1866, and his comments on Comte's 'trashy positivism' (cf. MESC, p. 218) are far from flattering. This of course does not exclude the possibility that Comte may have anticipated some sociological notions which later occur in Marx—though in point of fact he does not seem to have done so.

[2] Cf. J. A. Schumpeter, *History of Economic Analysis*, New York, 1954, pp. 493 ff. In a history of socialism, Sismondi's *Nouveaux principes d'économie politique* (1819–27) unquestionably deserves a place; but although his views on pauperism, under-consumption, etc., are dimly echoed in all the socialist literature of the period, down to the *Communist Manifesto*, he cannot be said to have had any real influence on Marx, and we are therefore obliged to pass on.

[3] Cole, op. cit., p. 84.

enthusiasm gradually turned them into pioneers of liberalism.[1] In general the difficulty about this period is that the socialist writers were weak in economics, while the economists dwelt in happy ignorance of sociology. This at any rate is true of France, despite the proliferation of socialist literature after 1830. It is less true of England, where the conjunction of Owenite socialism and Ricardian economics for a while gave promise of a genuine theoretical synthesis. That this was not brought about either by the Owenites or by the Ricardians, nor yet by writers like Mill who stood midway between the two, but had to await the coming from Marx, is one of those baffling circumstances of which history is full. The next step then is to set out the theoretical position established by the 'Ricardian socialists', leaving for a later chapter a more detailed consideration of Ricardian economics and their influence upon Marx.

All the writers in question were adherents of the labour theory of value; this is virtually their only link with Ricardo, and the only good reason for treating them as forerunners of Marx.[2] It is of course an extremely important link, since the labour theory—when combined with the notion that labour is itself a commodity—leads straight to a doctrine of exploitation which is at least implicitly socialist.[3] Yet Owen managed without an exploitation theory, while some of the Ricardian socialists did not share the Owenite dislike of competition and advocacy of co-operation.[4] The workers' claim to the 'whole product' of labour could in principle be put forward without going into the further question how industry should be organised. The Owenites did, however, have an answer to this question, while those radicals who developed Ricardo's views on labour as the source of wealth were imperceptibly moving away from him, and towards Owen's view of society. All they had to do was to spell out the implications of the labour theory; from there it was a short step to criticism

[1] Cf. Schumpeter, op. cit., pp. 496-7, for an estimate of Michel Chevalier.

[2] Cf. Mark Blaug, *Ricardian Economics. A Historical Study*, Yale University Press, 1958, pp. 140-50.

[3] Cf. Schumpeter, op. cit., p. 479.

[4] Blaug, op. cit., pp. 142-3. Ricardo seems not to have noticed that Ravenstone, generally regarded as the earliest 'Ricardian socialist', was a follower of Owen. Conversely, the Owenites at first tried rather naïvely to secure Ricardo's support, without troubling to establish a connection between his doctrine and theirs. In 1820 Owenism signified either philanthropy or hostility to competition and the cash nexus. A 'Ricardian socialist' like Hodgskin, who was indifferent to this issue while laying stress on the exploitation of labour, seemed to the Owenites not to have grasped the overriding importance of replacing the market economy by a co-operative order.

of a social order which guaranteed to the capitalist the lion's share of the total product. Hodgskin, who angered the Owenites by his indifference to their co-operative shibboleth, was quite clear that private ownership of the means of production was the real issue: 'It is the overwhelming nature of the demands of capital, sanctioned by the laws of society, sanctioned by the customs of men, enforced by the legislature, and warmly defended by political economists, which keep, which ever have kept, and which ever will keep, as long as they are allowed and acquiesced in, the labourer in poverty and misery.'[1]

These conclusions were derived from the labour theory of value, in the form given to it by Ricardo. A good many writers of the time seem not to have been aware that Ricardo had been anticipated on this point by A. Smith, and even by Locke. In any event the assertion that labour was exploited came to be associated with Ricardianism, and had its share in causing Ricardo's system to lose favour among professional economists within a few years of his death in 1823. But there was more than this: Ricardo's *Principles of Political Economy* appeared in 1817, at a time when the conflict between landowners and manufacturers was sharp enough to encourage a discussion of economic relations in terms of divergent class interests.[2] In its classical form, Ricardo's doctrine assumes an identity of interest among manufacturers and workers, but it holds out no very hopeful prospect of improvement for the latter. This pessimism, however, arises from an acceptance of conditions which the socialists soon came to regard as historical and transitory. The obverse of this picture is Ricardo's realistic treatment of the antagonism between the owners of the soil and the industrial producers—the latter term comprehending both manufacturers and labourers, just as it does in Saint-Simon. Such an outlook seemed disturbing to his contemporaries, and with the growth of socialist influence after 1830 it became altogether intolerable to writers whose political inclinations were

[1] Thomas Hodgskin, *Labour Defended Against the Claims of Capital*, London, 1825; reprinted London, 1932, p. 80; cf. also J. F. Bray, *Labour's Wrongs and Labour's Remedy*, London, 1839 (reprinted London, 1931).

[2] Blaug, op. cit., p. 148. 'It is no accident that the writers who did criticize the Ricardian socialists—Read, Scrope and Longfield—were not only opponents of Ricardo's theories but were also among the first to develop the abstinence theory of profit.' The more usual method of dealing with the economic radicals was to ignore them, a practice followed even by J. S. Mill, at least in regard to the Owenites. Mill seems to have thought that the only socialists worth controverting were the French; cf. his *Autobiography*.

conservative. Conversely, Ricardo's unflinching acceptance of an antagonism of interest between the major classes of society acquired enormous importance for those radicals who were already groping towards a new political doctrine. There was, after all, no need to share his gloom, which arose in part from his quasi-acceptance of the Malthusian population doctrine. If his theory could be given a more hopeful aspect without doing injury to its scientific character, it might be integrated into the emerging socialist world-view.[1]

In retrospect it would appear that what prevented the early socialists in Britain—who by 1840 had merged with the general stream of Owenism—from taking this step was not so much theoretical incompetence as lack of historical imagination and failure to raise their generalisations to the philosophical level; while the French socialists, from Louis Blanc to Proudhon, were hampered by ignorance of economics. In any event it is an historical fact that the writer destined to place Ricardian socialism in the service of a new vision of society was neither a British economist nor a French historian, but a German philosopher.

[1] Cole, op. cit., pp. 106–7; Blaug, op. cit., p. 149. There are differences of opinion over the importance of this factor in promoting the growing reaction against the Ricardian school; but the more vocal anti-Ricardians at least had no doubt that the implications of Ricardo's doctrine were politically dangerous, even when they were not interpreted in a socialist sense. For a detailed exposition of the views held, and the writings published, by the earliest British socialists, cf. Beer, op. cit., vol. I, pp. 182 ff (1953 edn.); for the conservative and Christian-Socialist critics of the new social order, cf. vol. II, pp. 175 ff.

PART TWO

THE MARXIAN SYNTHESIS
1840–1848

1

THE LOGIC OF HISTORY

THE TRANSITION from Hegel to Marx represents in every respect a radical break in the continuity of nineteenth-century history. Although the long-term consequences of this rupture have become fully manifest only in recent years, those who witnessed the dissolution of the Hegelian system already had an inkling of what this event portended. There is no lack of evidence that the more thoughtful contemporaries realised the dimensions of the failure of this last grandiose attempt to reconcile theology with philosophy, and both with the modern consciousness. After 1830, and *a fortiori* after 1848—when European society was violently disrupted by conflicts which had hitherto been fought out only in the pages of learned journals—belief in the possibility of stating valid principles binding upon all was gradually abandoned. Politics, science, philosophy, and religion went their separate ways, in the name of freedom, but under the guardianship of authoritarian regimes whose powers were frequently invoked to prevent liberty from degenerating into what the propertied classes regarded as the threat of democracy, if not anarchy: the two tending to become increasingly linked in the conservative ideology which spread among the German middle class after the failure of the 1848/9 revolution.[1]

[1] Franz Schnabel, *Deutsche Geschichte im neunzehnten Jahrhundert*, Freiburg,

33

The universalism of Hegel's system corresponded to a state of affairs which Comte had in mind when he urged his contemporaries to abandon metaphysics for science. The conservative character of Comte's sociology and the triviality of his conceptual apparatus need not hinder the recognition that his positivism is in the general line of advance first sketched by the French Enlightenment: even his lack of originality reflects the circumstance that he is in the tradition of Turgot and d'Alembert, who almost a century earlier had anticipated his quest for 'invariable laws' of nature and society. The French development—contrary to what students of 'national psychology' might have expected—had been more gradual than the German. The process of rationalisation had begun so early that by the mid-nineteenth century French liberalism was in possession of a fully developed world-view, including a scheme of constitutional government and a doctrine of liberal economics; whereas Germany was still struggling to emerge from the Middle Ages, and not succeeding too well. Conversely, the fact that Germany had to emancipate itself all at once from political and ideological traditions which in the West had gradually disappeared, made for greater radicalism in the theoretical sphere. The frantic production of philosophical 'systems' by the Young Hegelians between 1840 and 1847 loses its comic aspect when it is seen to herald the approaching storm. For the bewildering speed with which these intellectual productions succeeded one another— each claiming to represent the consummation of all the others— corresponded to the hurried telescoping of historical phases on the eve of the 1848 outbreak, when Germany all at once tried to make the transition from particularism to unification in national life; from authoritarian rule to liberalism in politics; and from medievalism to modernism in morals. That the attempt was a failure, which already foreshadowed the greater debacles of 1918 and 1933, does not detract from its importance.[1]

1951, vol. IV, pp. 529–77; K. Barth, *Die protestantische Theologie, etc.*, pp. 343 ff; Loewith, op. cit., pp. 78 ff.; Marcuse, op. cit., pp. 258 ff; Ludwig Landgrebe, 'Hegel und Marx', in *Marxismusstudien*, Tuebingen, 1954, vol. I, pp. 39–53.

[1] Marx, Introduction to 'Feuerbach', in *Die deutsche Ideologie*, ed. Adoratskij, Moscow, 1932, pp. 7 ff. (Cf. *The German Ideology*, Moscow, 1959.) The gusto with which Marx in this polemical tract dwells upon the frenzied intellectual activity displayed by Bauer, Hess, Stirner *et al.*, their reluctance to abandon their metaphysical cloud-cuckooland for solid ground etc., tends to obscure the fact that he was at that time (1845/6) still in the process of disengaging himself from his erstwhile associates.

The 'total' character of the crisis of German society in 1848 needs to be borne in mind when considering what preceded and followed the revolutionary upheaval. The events themselves will be discussed elsewhere. What concerns us here is the interrelation of philosophy and politics which gave birth to Marxism as a theory—and the practice of that theory. It is true that down to 1848 the only *praxis* on which Marx could reflect was that of the Jacobins and their heirs among the radical sects in Paris: while his (and Engels's) economics were already those of the Ricardian and Owenite socialists in Britain. But the arsenal of conceptual tools which he brought to bear on the facts included an element that neither French rationalism nor British empiricism could supply: Hegel's philosophy of history and—standing behind it—the conviction that the totality of the world is an ordered whole which the intellect can comprehend and master. Feuerbach's assault on Hegel had not shaken this faith; it had merely compelled the Young Hegelians to cast the theological remnants of the system overboard and place Man in the centre of the universe, from which he was henceforth not to be dislodged by spiritualist metaphysics. It now remained for Marx to draw the appropriate conclusion. This conclusion owed a great deal to Feuerbach's rebellious materialism: his defence of the senses and natural existence against the abstractions of idealist metaphysics; it owed little to his positive sentiments, for by the time Marx began to formulate his views he had gone from Feuerbach to the ultimate source of the latter's naturalist and atheist doctrine: the radical phase of the French Revolution and the writers who prepared it.

Here was a cause of potential discord not merely with Feuerbach, but with the 'Young Hegelians' in whose company the youthful Marx had originally learned to turn the Hegelian dialectic into an instrument of radical criticism; above all Bruno Bauer, their acknowledged leader and Marx's first teacher. Unlike these former allies, Marx had no use for Feuerbach's 'religious atheism' which even in its heterodox guise still trailed transcendental clouds of glory; or for his religion of humanity, addressed impartially to all and sundry, and consequently lacking the revolutionary impulse which in Marx sprang from the conviction that men could free themselves only by overturning the established order.

In going back to the French Revolution, Marx was also, without knowing it, reaching back across Feuerbach to the youthful Hegel, whose early writings—unpublished in his lifetime and for a century

35

thereafter—had sketched a scheme of liberation as far-reaching as anything envisaged in the *Communist Manifesto* or the *Critique of the Gotha Programme*. In 1795–6, with Paris still the seat of a victorious revolution, Hegel had expressed himself in a fashion not to be mistaken: '. . . the halo which has surrounded the leading oppressors and gods of the earth has disappeared. Philosophers demonstrate the dignity of man: the people will learn to feel it and will not merely demand their rights, which have been trampled in the dust, but will themselves take them—make them their own. Religion and politics have played the same game. The former has taught what despotism wanted to teach: contempt for humanity and the incapacity of man to realise the good and achieve something through his own efforts.'[1] And yet more strikingly:

> I shall demonstrate that, just as there is no idea of a machine, there is no idea of the State; for the State is something mechanical. Only that which is an object of freedom may be called an idea. We must, therefore, transcend the State. For every State is bound to treat free men as cogs in a machine. And this is just what it ought not to do; hence the State must perish.[2]

This was an aspect of Hegel which remained unknown to Marx. It is the more remarkable that his own youthful writings reflect the spirit of revolt which the ageing Hegel had abandoned, but to which the early Marx paid tribute in the preface to his doctoral dissertation (1841) when he wrote: 'Prometheus is the foremost saint and martyr in the philosophical calendar.' Prometheus is the hero of all youthful rebels, but it takes more than natural rebelliousness—or even the combined effect of a Jewish heritage and a classical education—to keep this spirit alive. Marx preserved his vision at the cost of failing to integrate it into the body of his scientific work. The sociologist in him could have discovered ample ground for discarding the idea of total freedom from external constraint as an impossible dream; but to have done so would have meant abandoning the central energising concept which in the 1840's turned the youthful Marx into a revolutionary: long before he had come across socialism or envisaged the

[1] Letter to Schelling, April 1795, in *Briefe von und an Hegel*, ed. Karl Hegel, Leipzig, 1887.
[2] Hegel, *Erstes Systemprogramm des deutschen Idealismus*, in *Dokumente zu Hegels Entwicklung*, ed. J. Hoffmeister, Stuttgart, 1936, pp. 219 ff. For the radical difference between Hegel's and Marx's thinking which underlies the similarity of their early views, cf. Ludwig Landgrebe, 'Das Problem der Dialektik', in *Marxismusstudien*, Tuebingen, 1960, vol. III, pp. 1–65.

possibility of a proletarian upheaval which would make all things new.

Marx in fact joins Hegel—notably the early Hegel—in treating as irrelevant and 'merely empirical' every mode of reality which presents an obstacle to the unfolding of man's inner essence. This theme is already present in his doctoral dissertation, which is Hegelian to the last degree, and it is expounded with gradually mounting emphasis in the semi-philosophical writings (1842–4) which herald his eventual rupture with Hegel. This rupture has for its cause the discovery that Hegel's system of total comprehension leads to the reconciliation of mind with the world as it is, instead of turning thought into an instrument for transforming the world in accordance with the principles of philosophy. 'The owl of Minerva spreads its wings when the shades of dusk are falling', Hegel had written in the preface to the *Philosophy of Right*: a warning to his pupils to remain true to the conception of philosophy as an activity of the spirit which can make its appearance only after consciousness has comprehended the necessity of what has gone before. Marx rejected this interpretation; yet he remained sufficiently faithful to the teachings of his master to repudiate with equal intransigence the traditional dualism of reality and the ideal. The world was to be transformed not by an appeal to 'eternal' principles, but by the progressive unfolding of its own essence, which was freedom. It is only because the youthful Marx, following Hegel—but also Kant, Rousseau and the Enlightenment generally—believes freedom to be inherent in the very nature of man, that he is confident of being able to dissolve all existing structures, and challenge every traditional authority, by raising the demand that man should be allowed to rule himself.[1]

Marx takes issue with Hegel on the grounds that his system contradicts his own insight into the condition of human existence. Freedom demands self-determination, but Hegel had come to justify the existing state of affairs which rested on the imposition of external authority upon unfree individuals. Marx develops this theme in his early writings (1842–3) which, for all their longwindedness and their devotion to philosophical jargon, succeed well enough in making the

---

[1] 'Freedom is so much the essence of man that its very enemies realise it in struggling against its reality. . . . No man fights against freedom; at most he fights against the freedom of others. Hence every form of freedom has existed since time immemorial, whether as a special privilege, or as a general right.' Marx, 'Debate on the Liberty of the Press', *Rheinische Zeitung*, May 12, 1842, MEGA I/1, p. 202.

point—already suggested by Feuerbach—that in Hegel's philosophy of civil society the state is the only real subject, while individual men, social classes, and society itself, appear as its predicates. Marx is here still guided by Feuerbach, from whom he was soon to emancipate himself; his standpoint is that of a typical radical democrat of the period: not a socialist, let alone a communist. The socialist critique of bourgeois society entered his horizon only after he had removed to Paris in 1843.

At this point, philosophy and politics once more coincide. The revolt against the Hegelian system, as the theoretical defence of the *status quo*, from the start transcended the limits of philosophic discourse. It was the work of men who conceived their aim to be a radical critique of all existing institutions, with a view to their eventual destruction. On this point all the Left Hegelians were in agreement, however much they might differ over ends and means. Feuerbach, Ruge, Hess, Bauer, Stirner, Bakunin, Marx, and Engels (not to mention the numerous minor figures) formed a party in the true sense, though they spent much of their time squaring accounts and disputing one another's title to the leadership of the coming upheaval: the revolution that would destroy the old regime, dissolve religion, renovate society, unify Germany, liberate Europe, and emancipate the proletariat.[1]

So far from being more utopian than the others in the group, Marx was distinguished by his greater realism. For if it was fanciful to expect all these results to follow from the next turn of the revolutionary wheel in Paris, it was clearly absurd to suppose that the walls of autocracy would collapse at the mere sound of critical trumpets. Yet the Young Hegelians still retained their faith in the efficacy of theoretical criticism—for the most part criticism of revealed religion —at a time when Marx had already discovered economics and the proletariat. They were, it is true, domiciled in Berlin—already a growing city, but no metropolis—or in small university towns, where their energies were absorbed by the struggle between the philosophical and the theological faculties. Germany, then as in later days, was far from being an ideal training ground for revolutionaries. The theory

[1] The *locus classicus* is undoubtedly Marx's 'Introduction to a Critique of Hegel's Philosophy of Right', in *Deutsch-Franzoesische Jahrbuecher*, February 1844 (MEGA I/1, pp. 607 ff). The significance of this essay derives from the fact that it was written before Marx had broken with Ruge and the other liberals, and turned to communism; he was then still as it were a German Jacobin for whom the proletariat existed primarily as the instrument of revolution.

as well as the practice of the coming upheaval had to be worked out in Paris. To say this, however, is merely to underline the central paradox of Marxism: what was it that enabled Marx to conceive the alliance between German philosophy and the French proletariat in the form of a revolutionary doctrine which for a time actually drew together some of the most explosive elements in the situation? Why did he succeed where others failed? And what is to be made of the fateful synthesis he established, in the light of his—and Engels's—subsequent attempt to restate the original concept in a more scientific (and correspondingly less revolutionary) form?

It is customary to answer this question by pointing to Marx's radical inversion of Hegel's philosophy with the aid of the French materialist doctrines, whose current representatives were the socialist revolutionaries he encountered in Paris during his stay there (1843–5). Men like Blanqui and his followers, or writers like Cabet, had indeed already arrived at a standpoint which was to be that of Marx only from 1845 onwards. They evidently did not need to be told that materialist humanism led straight to socialism.[1] That was their own discovery, as it was their disillusionment with the social achievements of the French Revolution which had impelled them to go beyond the Jacobin demand for political equality. Though his encounter with these men turned Marx from a radical democrat into a communist, it did not *per se* require him to interpret communism as the fulfilment of history. Nor did Feuerbach's humanism lead to such conclusions. It was Hegel who supplied the missing link. But for the heritage of German Idealism, the 'materialist conception of history' would never have come into being.

The apparent paradox is lessened when one reflects that what Marx shared with Hegel was after all simply the belief that there is an objective meaning in history. For Hegel this is constituted by the progressive evolution of the spirit towards freedom, while for Marx it is bound up with man's mastery over nature, including his own nature. Since for Hegel freedom and self-consciousness are united in the

---

[1] 'It requires no great penetration to realise that the materialist doctrines of original goodness, equal intellectual endowment, all-importance of experience, custom, education . . . etc., are necessarily connected with communism and socialism. If man derives all his knowledge . . . from the sensible world, and from his experience of the sensible world, it follows that the task consists in so ordering the empirical world that man encounters in it what is truly human . . . that he experiences himself humanly.' *The Holy Family*, MEGA I/3, p. 307. (Cf. the official English translation, Moscow, 1956, pp. 175–6, for a slightly different rendering.)

absolute idea, i.e., God, history becomes the autobiography of God, and this aspect of his system inevitably provoked a reaction which in some cases went all the way towards radical empiricism. Yet it is a misconception to suppose that Marx abandoned the attempt to see the historical process as a whole. History to him was the story of man's self-creation. It was a single process held together by an internal logic whose pattern lay open to discovery, once the idealist mystification had been cast off. It was *not* a record of events passively reflected in the mind, any more than it was the unfolding of the disembodied idea through time and space. Feuerbach's influence had enabled Marx to get rid of Hegel's neo-Platonic idealism which 'within the framework of empirical, exoteric history . . . introduces the operation of a speculative, esoteric history'.[1] It had not caused him to doubt that history possessed its own logic. Nor was he in the least inclined towards the sceptical nominalist position of writers for whom theory yielded not a true report of the inherent structure of reality, but merely a kind of intellectual shorthand. The logic of history was thoroughly objective and communicable. It could be grasped by the intellect, and at the same time—since it was the history of man—it was capable of modification as soon as men understood the nature of the process in which they were involved: a process whereby their own creations had assumed the aspect of seemingly external and inevitable laws. History therefore culminated not in the intellectual contemplation of the past, but in the deliberate shaping of the future. The modern age in particular was distinguished precisely by this realisation. The French Revolution in politics, and German philosophy in theory, were different forms of this incipient breakthrough. True humanism, i.e., socialism, was its consummation. The coming revolution represented not simply the negation of the existing social order, but the triumph of rationality over brute existence. In common with Feuerbach, and with the 'philosophic radicals' in general, Marx held that mankind had reached maturity. The creation of a rational society need no longer be relegated to the realm of utopia.[2]

---

[1] *The Holy Family*, London, 1957, p. 115; cf. Sidney Hook, *From Hegel to Marx*, New York, 1950, ch. I.

[2] Hook, op. cit., pp. 36 ff; Marcuse, op. cit., pp. 258 ff. It is a debatable question to what extent Hegel drifted away from his Aristotelean starting-point in the direction of neo-Platonism. There is less reason to be uncertain about Marx's attitude: plainly he is neither a nominalist like Hobbes, nor does he believe that universals subsist prior to their exemplification in concrete actuality, or in abstraction therefrom. In short, his standpoint is substantially that of Aristotle.

2

THE CRITIQUE OF SOCIETY

TO SAY THAT HISTORY is logical is to affirm that there is a logic of social development. For this conclusion Marx did not depend on Hegel: the decisive steps had already been taken by the theorists of the French Enlightenment, from Montesquieu to Linguet and Condorcet, and by the Scottish historians of the same period.[1] What Marx obtained from Hegel was the notion that history is the progressive self-creation of man, a process whose motor is practical social activity—i.e., in the last resort, human labour. Hegel had expounded this theme in his customary obscure fashion, but his meaning could be disentangled without too much trouble from his perverse habit of attributing the real movement of history to the unfolding of pre-existing categories. 'The great thing in Hegel's Phenomenology . . . is that Hegel conceives the self-creation of man as a process, regards objectification as . . . alienation and as transcendence of this alienation; and that he therefore grasps the nature of *labour* and comprehends objective man . . . as the result of his *own labour*.'[2] Man

---

[1] Adam Ferguson, *Essay on the History of Civil Society*, 1767; John Millar, *Observations Concerning the Distinction of Ranks in Society*, 1771. For Marx's view of Linguet cf. his comment on Proudhon, MESW I, p. 396.

[2] Marx, *Economic-Philosophical Manuscripts* (1844), hereafter cited as EPM; cf. MEGA I/3, p. 156 (Eng. transl., Moscow, 1959, p. 151); our version follows the German text.

41

produces both himself and his world, and he does so through practical activity which modifies his own nature, at the same time that it transforms external nature. '(Since) . . . for socialist man the whole of *what is called world history* is nothing but the creation of man by human labour, and the emergence of Nature for man, he therefore has the evident and irrefutable proof of his *self-creation*, of his own *origins*.'[1] There is a great deal more to the same effect in the Paris and Brussels manuscripts of 1844-6, some of which were only published in 1931-2 and are still insufficiently known.[2] Taking the *Economic-Philosophical MSS* (1844), the *Holy Family* (1845), the *Theses on Feuerbach* (1845) and the *German Ideology* (1845-6) as a whole, one can say that they combine a fully developed philosophy of history with a rudimentary sociology—the latter for the most part derived from the French Encyclopaedists and their nineteenth-century successors: the Saint-Simonians and the other schools of French socialism. What is misleadingly called the materialist conception of history represents a fusion of these elements: the social system viewed as a whole turns upon the historical process, and conversely the latter discloses its human, social essence as soon as man's 'nature' is seen to consist in his ability to produce the means of his existence, thereby transforming nature into 'human' nature. Anthropology is the key to history, as with Feuerbach; but whereas the latter had postulated an unchanging human essence, Marx emphasises that man should be viewed historically: what he makes of himself depends on the interaction of his forces with the environment—including the man-made institutions of society.[3] Nonetheless it will not do to make a positivist out of Marx, although the temptation is strong if one merely considers his criticism of the antiquated 'idealist'

[1] EPM, MEGA I/3, pp. 125-6. (Literally '. . . of his birth through himself, of his process of coming-to-be.' The official Soviet translation retains the involved Hegelian terminology at the cost of some obscurity.)

[2] Cf. Bottomore and Rubel, op. cit., pp. 1-48; the *Economic-Philosophical Manuscripts* are now available in the Soviet edition already cited, though with an inadequate preface. In addition there now exists a German edition (Cologne and Berlin, 1950) with a lengthy critical preface by E. Thier, based on the text in MEGA.

[3] 'Men can be distinguished from the animals by consciousness, by religion, or by anything else one may choose. They themselves begin to distinguish themselves from the animals as soon as they begin to *produce* their means of subsistence, a step which is determined by their physical constitution. In producing their means of subsistence, men indirectly produce their actual material life.' *The German Ideology*, MEGA I/5, pp. 10-11.

fashion of writing history.[1] However scientific and empirical in intention and in its methodical treatment of problems, his sociology rests ultimately upon a view of human nature which is philosophical. The Marxian critique of society is motivated by society's failure to realise man's potentialities. For while man actualises his being in social life, he is also hampered by it. Man is social by nature. One must '. . . above all avoid postulating "society" once more as an abstraction confronting the individual. The individual is a social being. . . . Individual life and the life of the species are not different things. . . .'[2] But precisely for this reason society can become a hindrance to the full development of man's faculties. The motor of this development is labour, which so far from being merely an economic category is the 'existential activity' of man, his 'free conscious activity', and his principal means of developing all the potentialities of his 'universal nature'.[3] Now man cannot develop fully unless he is free, but this must not be done at the expense of others, as in classical Antiquity where work was performed by slaves; for both parties to such a relationship are inevitably dehumanised. Freedom, to be genuine, must be universal, hence the individual is free only if all other men are free and able to develop as 'universal beings'. Only when this condition has been attained will the existence of individual men realise the potentialities inherent in the species.[4]

These terms relate back to the philosophy of history outlined by Hegel, as well as to the materialist anthropology of Feuerbach and the Saint-Simonians. The fusion operates at two levels. On the one hand, Marx introduces the Hegelian dialectic of subject-object, so as to eliminate the 'one-sidedness' of a 'mechanical' materialism which posits man as the passive receptacle of an unchanging nature. On the other hand, 'man's self-creation' is seen to involve the real needs of

[1] Cf. *German Ideology*, MEGA I/5, pp. 27–9. 'This conception of history therefore rests on the exposition of the real process of production, starting out from the material production of life itself, and on the comprehension of the mode of intercourse linked to and produced by this mode of production, i.e. civil society in its various stages, as the foundation of all history. . . . All earlier conceptions of history either neglected this real basis of history altogether or treated it as a secondary affair unconnected with the historical process. . . . Thus man's relationship to nature is excluded from history, and in this manner the antithesis of nature and history is established. . . . The Hegelian philosophy of history is the final . . . consequence of this entire German historiography.' 'Where speculation ends—in real life—real, positive science, the representation of practical activity, of the practical process of men's development, begins.' (Ibid., p. 16.)
[2] EPM, MEGA I/3, p. 117.   [3] Ibid., pp. 87–8.   [4] Ibid., p. 89.

empirical human beings, which Hegel had neglected. The conclusion demonstrates that man is truly himself insofar as he is able to recognise himself in the man-made universe which surrounds him.[1] The failure to attain this self-realisation is defined as 'alienation' (once more a concept derived from Hegel, who in turn had borrowed it from Rousseau), and the ultimate goal of the historical process which 'realises' all the potentialities of man's nature is described as the overcoming of alienation.[2] There are two comments to be made on this: first, the notion of such a consummation is metaphysical, and indeed ultimately religious: it represents the utopian element in Marx's thought, transmitted to him both via Hegel's philosophy of reason and Feuerbach's conception of human nature. Secondly, it evidently forms the counterpart of the Marxian 'union of theory and practice'. The latter is required to bring about that 'total' revolution in human affairs which philosophy by itself cannot provide, because being an intellectual activity in a world not really ruled by the intellect, it must of necessity come to terms with reality as it is.

Philosophy thus becomes an aspect of man's 'alienation', insofar as it represents an illusory realm of essences divorced from the world of material existence. Even a critical philosophy—the last refuge of the Young Hegelians—shared this radical defect, quite apart from the fact that with Bauer et al. it usually limited itself to a critique of theology. To realise its aims, philosophy must become practical, i.e., cease to be philosophy. It must become the theory of total revolution. For the 'realisation of philosophy' is not to be achieved without strife. In order to satisfy the needs which all men share in theory, it is necessary to proceed against some men in practice![3]

---

[1] EPM, MEGA I/3, pp. 85 ff.   [2] Ibid., pp. 114 ff.

[3] The literature on this theme threatens to submerge all other aspects of the Marxian system; perhaps the fullest critical discussion (from a Thomist standpoint) is to be found in Jean-Yves Calvez, *La Pensée de Karl Marx*, Paris, 1956, passim; cf. also Cottier, op. cit., pp. 153 ff; for an unorthodox analysis cf. Henri Lefebvre, *Pour connaitre la pensée de Karl Marx*, Paris, 1948; cf. the same author's *Problèmes actuels du Marxisme*, Paris, 1958; for recent German literature, cf. *Marxismusstudien*, passim; Heinrich Popitz, *Der entfremdete Mensch: Zeitkritik und Geschichtsphilosophie des jungen Marx*, Basle, 1953; Erich Thier, *Die Anthropologie des jungen Marx nach den Pariser oekonomisch-philosophischen Manuskripten*, Cologne, 1950. The philosophical writings published in Poland since 1955 by L. Kolakovski and others may be regarded as the counterpart of this growing concern with the humanist roots of Marxism. Cf. Kolakovski, *Der Mensch ohne Alternative*, Munich, 1960.

The sociology of Marx is the obverse of his philosophy of history. It is not detached from it, nor does it employ a historiographical foundation for the purpose of deducing generalisations, in the manner of positivism. In his writings between 1844 and 1846 Marx develops a critique of society whose theoretical character is not contradicted by its practical purpose. The concept of 'alienated labour' is used as an analytical tool to define the actual role of the working class in modern, i.e., bourgeois society. Labour likewise appears as a political category in the context of the revolution then preparing— which was of course destined to be a 'bourgeois' one, at any rate in Germany. It has been remarked with truth that the proletariat makes its first appearance in Marx's writings as the social force needed to realise the aims of German philosophy in its latest, Feuerbachian, stage: a class 'with radical chains' was needed to bring about a radical change in (German) society.[1] This concept could still be interpreted in traditional 'Jacobin' fashion as looking towards the democratic revolution which France had undergone, and which Germany was destined to miss; and presumably it was so interpreted by the liberal Hegelian Arnold Ruge, under whose auspices Marx's writings then (1844) appeared.[2] But Marx was already beginning to move away from both Ruge and Feuerbach. If his political standpoint in 1844–6 is still democratic, his critique of society increasingly sounds the socialist theme. And it is precisely this critique which causes him to see society as a whole, i.e., to develop a theory of how it functions. Feuerbach had sought the secret of 'alienation' in anthropology; Marx seeks it in sociology, or rather, he is obliged to sketch out a rudimentary sociology in order to account for phenomena—religion, class division, the state—which had remained incomprehensible as long as radical thinkers failed to grasp their historical and social character. Feuerbach was the prototype of all such thinkers. 'Insofar as he is a materialist, history does not exist for him, and insofar as he treats of history, he is no materialist.'[3]

Two conditions are necessary: society must be viewed historically, and it must be viewed as a whole. To do so is to realise that the

[1] MEGA I/1, p. 619.

[2] Cf. Franz Mehring, *Karl Marx: Geschichte seines Lebens*, Leipzig, 1933, pp. 82 ff (Eng. tr. London, 1936, pp. 58 ff); *Gesammelte Schriften von Karl Marx und Friedrich Engels 1841–50*, ed. Mehring, Stuttgart, 1913, vol. I, pp. 331 ff.

[3] *German Ideology*, MEGA I/5, p. 34; cf. also the third 'Thesis on Feuerbach' (original in *Marx-Engels Archiv*, Moscow-Frankfurt, 1926, vol. I, pp. 227 ff; cf. MEGA I/5, pp. 533–5).

social system is propelled by internal contradictions which are essential to its functioning and cannot be legislated out of existence, though they can be overcome 'at a higher level', i.e., after history has reached the stage of the classless society. For the time being, class antagonisms are the motor of historical (social) development. Progress depends upon them. At the same time they are responsible for the failure of humanist philosophy—and its counterpart, utopian socialism—to alter the conditions under which men are compelled to live and work. This failure has a theoretical and a practical side. Theoretically it expresses itself in the inability of materialist-humanist doctrine to give an account of the actual social process; practically it is demonstrated by the impotence of reform movements which start from the supposition that society is the plastic material of the critical intellect (commonly thought of as being embodied in the educated classes which constitute 'public opinion').

The materialist doctrine concerning the alteration of circumstances and education forgets that circumstances are changed by men, and that the educator must himself be educated. It is therefore obliged to divide society into two parts, of which one is superior to the other. The coincidence of the transforming of circumstances and of human activity, or self-transformation, can only be conceived and rationally apprehended as revolutionary practice. (*Praxis*.)[1]

Here the union of theory and practice is seen to entail nothing short of revolution. But even where Marx theorises about the given social structure, as in his later writings, the theory of society is always integrated with a radical critique of the existing order. This is not to say that a politically neutral and 'value-free' sociology cannot be deduced from Marx's utterances, but he himself clearly did not believe that this could be done systematically until the social order had been transformed. Before social relations could become sufficiently transparent for a genuine science of society to be feasible, men would have to achieve conscious control over their circumstances. Indeed, this aim was the very essence of socialism:

The standpoint of the old materialism is 'civil society'; the standpoint of the new materialism is human society or socialised humanity.[2]

---

[1] Bottomore and Rubel, op. cit., pp. 67 ff; for the original text cf. *Karl Marx—der historische Materialismus*, ed. S. Landshut and J. P. Mayer, Leipzig, 1932, vol. II, pp. 3 ff. Engels's version of the *Theses* departs in some instances from the original; cf. Ryazanov, *Marx-Engels Archiv*, vol. I, pp. 205 ff.

[2] 'Tenth Thesis on Feuerbach', loc. cit.; cf. also EPM, MEGA I/3, p. 121:

The customary mistranslation of the Hegelian term 'civil society' (literally *buergerliche Gesellschaft*) as 'bourgeois society' tends to obscure the fact that Marx is here polemicising against both Feuerbach and Hegel. The latter had employed this term to designate the sum total of social relations which bind the individual to the community. The 'philosophic radicals' on the other hand—including both Bentham and his French forerunners—were obsessed with the 'intelligent self-interest' of the individual: a concept which played a key role in their systems. Ultimately, political theory reduced itself for them to interest psychology, while for Hegel it culminated in an authoritarian doctrine of the state, for whose sake the individual was supposed to exist. In its West European, hedonist and utilitarian form, materialism was quite compatible with the political orthodoxy of its day. Indeed it supplied liberalism with much of its intellectual ammunition, both in the domestic struggle against the old order, and in its attempts to dissolve authoritarian structures on a world scale. In the 1840's it was not yet clear that Germany would by contrast become identified with conservative, romantic, and authoritarian world-views, but the issue had already been stated, in an ideological form at least, by Hegel and his conservative followers in the Prussian bureaucracy, and the radicals badly needed a counterideology. In going beyond Feuerbach, Marx also indicated his conviction that the radical movement ought to steer clear of the 'old materialism' in its vulgarised Benthamite form, since to accept it was to sink below the theoretical level attained by the German critics of utilitarianism: it was impossible to dislodge Hegel by appealing to Bentham—or for that matter to Owen. The heritage of idealist metaphysics must be transcended, not discarded; and the first step consisted in realising that Hegel had been right to reject the dualism of empirical fact and normative aim. Values are incarnate in history, and their realisation depends on historical activity. Man transforms his own nature through labour, and history is the record of this transformation. Human solidarity is achieved by dissolving the social barriers erected in this process. To Marx this was not an 'ideal' in the Kantian sense: he held that a stage had been reached where men could build a genuine community and thus overcome the alienation

'The resolution of *theoretical* contradictions is possible only through *practical* means, only through the practical energy of men. Their resolution is thus by no means only the task of the understanding, but is a real problem of life which philosophy was unable to accomplish precisely because it conceived the problem as *purely* a theoretical one.'

imposed upon their own existence by the previous effort to master external nature. Precisely for this reason the old interest psychology, which treated human nature as a datum, could be relinquished: if human nature was a social category, it too was capable of being transformed. Such a transformation, however, could not operate in a society disrupted by class antagonisms—a society, moreover, in which those who did most of the work were excluded both from political power and from the official culture. 'Socialised humanity' was inconceivable without genuine solidarity; hence a socialist society must be one without classes. The philosophy underlying this conclusion is spelled out in the Paris manuscripts. The following is a brief summary of the main argument, though without any attempt at systematisation.[1]

Political economy, though ostensibly concerned with abstractions such as capital, labour, or land, has for its real (though unacknowledged) subject the relationship of man to the man-made world of objects within which he moves and which reflects his essence as a generic being (*Gattungswesen*). It is the *nature* of man to surround himself with a man-made universe. In so doing he loses himself. 'Labour's realisation is its objectification.' This loss can become so extreme as to involve the annihilation of the creator. 'So much does labour's realisation appear as loss of reality that the worker loses reality to the point of starving to death.' 'So much does the appropriation of the object appear as estrangement that the more objects the worker produces the fewer can he possess, and the more he falls under the dominion of his product, capital.' This circumstance exemplifies a more general law. 'It is the same in religion. The more man puts into God, the less he retains in himself.' In society, this dialectic becomes more pronounced to the extent that the individual is estranged from his own creation, so that 'the life which he has conferred on the object confronts him as something hostile and alien.' Political economy, far from clarifying this state of affairs, obscures it by treating capital, labour, etc., as independent realities, instead of recognising

---

[1] For the following cf. EPM, Moscow, 1959 edn., pp. 67 ff. The text of this translation has not been followed in all particulars. Thus, e.g., 'Gattungswesen' is rendered as 'generic being' rather than 'species being'. It may be worth remarking that the German term 'Wesen' can be translated either as 'being' or 'essence', depending on the context and on the philosophy of the writer. In his early writings, down to and including the Paris manuscripts of 1844, Marx is still sufficiently under Hegel's influence to mean 'essence' or 'essential being' when he speaks of 'Wesen'.

them as manifestations of human activity. 'Political economy conceals the estrangement inherent in the nature of labour by not considering the direct relationship between the worker (labour) and production. It is true that labour produces for the rich wonderful things, but for the worker it produces privation. It produces palaces—but for the worker, hovels. . . . It replaces labour by machines—but some of the workers it throws back to a barbarous type of labour, and the others it turns into machines. It produces intelligence—but for the worker, idiocy, cretinism.'[1]

Alienated labour also interferes with man's generic nature as a being who spontaneously produces objects in which he mirrors himself. 'For he . . . contemplates himself in a world that he has created. In tearing away from man the object of his production, therefore, estranged labour tears him from his generic existence . . . and transforms his advantage over animals into the disadvantage that his inorganic body, nature, is taken from him. Similarly, in degrading spontaneous activity, free activity, into a means, alienated labour transforms man's generic existence into an instrument of his physical existence.'

The alienation of man from his own product involves his estrangement from other men. 'Hence within the relationship of alienated labour, each man views the other in accordance with the standard and the position in which he finds himself as a labourer.' In this resides the germ of class division. 'Every self-estrangement of man from himself and from nature appears in the relation in which he places himself and nature to men other than and differentiated from himself. Thus the religious alienation necessarily appears in the relationship of the layman to the priest, or again to a mediator, etc. . . . In the real, practical world, self-estrangement can become manifest only through the real practical relationship to other men. The medium through which alienation takes place is itself practical . . . Through estranged, alienated labour, then, the worker produces the relationship to this labour of a man alien to labour and standing outside it. The relationship of the worker to labour engenders the relationship to it of the capitalist, or whatever one chooses to call the master of labour. *Private property* is thus the product, the

[1] Op. cit., p. 71. Strictly speaking one ought to distinguish between *Entfremdung* (alienation or estrangement) and *Entaeusserung* (objectification)—the process whereby man externalises his being. But the distinction plays a larger role in Hegel's thinking than in that of Marx, where both terms are often employed as synonyms; cf. Cottier, op. cit., pp. 34 ff.

result, the necessary consequence of *alienated labour*, of the external relation of the worker to nature and to himself.'[1]

Private property in the means of production, and class rule by a propertied and privileged minority, are historically connected; they represent two sides of the same coin. Private property subordinates the producer to the non-producer (and incidentally turns woman into the slave of man). Communism, by simultaneously abolishing class rule and human exploitation, thus appears as 'the positive transcendence of private property, of human self-alienation, and therefore as the real appropriation of the human essence by and for man'. 'Communism is the riddle of history solved, and it knows itself to be this solution.' It is able to attain this standpoint because it represents not a mere ideal, but an actual process inherent in the nature of things. Modern society, in creating the proletariat, has finally compelled men to take note of the fact that the reality underlying all their strivings is the alienation of labour. Under modern conditions this relationship is bound up with the division of society into mutually hostile classes. 'The division of labour is the expression in political economy of the social character of labour within the alienation.' Under capitalism, labour itself—the precondition of human existence—becomes a commodity, and the workman a proletarian who owns nothing and is in fact (though not in form) owned by someone else. The split in society mirrors that in the individual who has been estranged from the products of his toil, i.e., from his own nature. Private property—as a form of self-alienation—produces communism as its necessary antithesis. Its supersession therefore signifies the ending of social conflict and the restoration of man's harmony with his own nature. On these grounds it is possible for Marx to assert that communism represents both the realisation of freedom and 'the resolution of the conflict between man and nature'. A society in which men are no longer estranged from themselves is also the first that can be described as truly human.[2]

---

[1] EPM, pp. 74-6, 77-80. Cf. Proudhon, *Système des contradictions économiques*, vol. I, pp. 388-9: '*Dieu* en religion, *l'Etat* en politique, la *Propriété* en économie, telle est la triple forme sous laquelle l'humanité, devenue étrangère à elle-même, n'a cessé de se déchirer de ses propres mains.'

[2] EPM., pp. 102 ff, 115 ff, 129 ff.

3

THE DOCTRINE OF REVOLUTION

AFTER WHAT has been said it is scarcely surprising that one should have to revert from sociology to Hegelian philosophy—and from France to Germany—in tracing the doctrine of revolution, unfolded in Marx's writings on the eve of 1848: the date of the *Communist Manifesto* and of the abortive European democratic rising. It has become customary to treat the *Manifesto* as the theoretical expression of that 'proletarian revolution' which is supposed to have triumphed in Russia in 1917 after some hopeful preparatory experiments on French soil between 1848 and 1871. More will have to be said about the link between the French and the Russian experience. For the moment the question is what 'the revolution' signified for Marx (and for Engels) on the eve of 1848. And here the first point to be noted is that they were primarily concerned with Germany. This may seem obvious, seeing that they were in the forefront of the German radical movement which briefly occupied the stage in 1848–9. But it is frequently overlooked; all the more reason for emphasising it.

The only revolution possible in Germany at that stage was a 'bourgeois-democratic' one, a fact quite obvious to Marx and Engels (though not to all their associates) by 1847 at the latest.[1] With the

[1] Cf. Engels, *On the History of the Communist League*, MESW II, pp. 306–23. The urgency of such a revolution from the viewpoint of the German middle

51

wisdom of hindsight it is easy today to perceive that in actual fact the revolution never emerged from the theoretical sphere, but in the 1840's this outcome was not easily predictable. In retrospect one can also discern a difference of emphasis on this point between Marx and Engels, the former being less inclined to hope for a successful demo-cratic rebellion against the absolutist regime, preparatory to a normal development on Western lines. Indeed Marx never seems to have believed that such an outcome was likely on German soil, while Engels frequently insisted that it was inevitable, and moreover that it was the duty of the Communists to promote it and not let themselves be deflected by the anti-capitalist and anti-liberal tirades of those 'true socialists' whose sentimental longing for a partnership between the monarchy and the working class merely served to prolong the death agony of the old regime.[1] Where both men agreed was in holding that *if* there was to be a successful revolution in Germany, it would need to mobilise the masses; but this left open the question who was to direct it. That the German middle class was quite incapable of promoting a radical break with the past did not become apparent for some years, and when it had, the theoretical and tactical differences between Marx and Engels automatically ceased to be relevant.

But this is to anticipate. In 1844–7, and *a fortiori* before he had formed his lifelong partnership with Engels in the autumn of 1844, Marx was occupied with the problem of fitting the imminent German revolution into the conceptual framework he had just elaborated, and here his reading of recent French history suggested a possible solu-tion. Paradoxically, the very backwardness of Germany made it seem plausible to suppose that the Germans would not content themselves with the kind of revolution that Western Europe had undergone.

class is emphasised in Engels's 'Der Status Quo in Deutschland' (MEGA I/6, pp. 231–49), written in March 1847, but not published before 1932. In view of the stress laid in this important essay on the need to promote a bour-geois revolution in Germany, for the sake of the country's national develop-ment, it is not surprising that modern Communist literature tends to be silent about it.

[1] Engels, 'Der Status Quo in Deutschland', MEGA I/6, p. 233; cf. also the relevant passages in the *Communist Manifesto*, MEGA I/6, pp. 549 ff (Eng. tr. in MESW I, pp. 57 ff). A textual comparison shows that those passages which stress the progressive character of a capitalist development in Germany, and the reactionary nature of all counter-tendencies, including socialist ones, are taken over from Engels's unpublished manuscripts of 1847, including his *Grundsaetze des Kommunismus*, of which more later. For Engels's sus-tained hostility towards Hess, Grün, and the 'true socialists' generally, cf. MEGA I/6, pp. 33–116.

True, in many respects Germany had only just reached a stage already attained in France or Britain, notably in economics.[1] But precisely because his native country was so far behind, Marx thought that the coming revolution might be all the more radical. It would then transcend the socio-political level reached in Western Europe and for the first time place the proletariat upon the stage of history:

It is not the *radical* revolution, *universal human* emancipation, which is a utopian dream for Germany, but rather the partial, merely political, revolution, which leaves the pillars of the building intact. What is the basis of a partial, merely political, revolution? Simply this: *a part of civic society* emancipates itself and attains *general* domination, a particular class, from its *particular situation*, undertakes the general emancipation of society. . . . But in Germany every class lacks not only the consistency, the incisiveness, the courage, the ruthlessness required to turn it into the negative representative of society, but also that generosity needed to identify itself, if only for a moment, with the popular mind. . . . The middle class hardly dares to conceive the idea of emancipation from its own standpoint, and already the development of social conditions, and the progress of political theory, declares this standpoint to be antiquated or at least problematical.

In France, partial emancipation is the basis of complete emancipation. In Germany, universal emancipation is the *conditio sine qua non* of any partial emancipation. In France it is the reality, in Germany the impossibility, of a step-by-step emancipation which must give birth to complete liberty. . . . Where then is there the *positive* possibility of German emancipation? In the formation of a class with *radical chains* . . . a class which is the dissolution of all classes, a sphere of society which has a universal character because its sufferings are universal, and which claims no *particular right* because the wrong committed against it is not a *particular wrong* but wrong *as such.* . . . When the proletariat declares the *dissolution of the existing social order* it does no more than proclaim the *secret of its own existence*, for it constitutes the *effective* dissolution of this order. . . . As philosophy finds its *material* weapons in the proletariat, so the proletariat discovers its *intellectual* weapons in philosophy, and once the lightning-flash of the idea has penetrated this naïve popular soil, the emancipation of the *Germans* to *manhood* will become reality. . . . The emancipation of the *German* is the emancipation of *man*. *Philosophy* is the *head* of this emancipation, and the *proletariat* its *heart*. Philosophy cannot realise itself without abolishing the proletariat, and the proletariat cannot emancipate itself without realising philosophy.[2]

This famous passage is commonly cited as proof that in 1844 Marx was not yet a Marxist: in other words, that he had not yet developed the 'materialist' outlook which after 1850—and in particular from

---

[1] 'Zur Kritik der Hegelschen Rechtsphilosophie' (1844), MEGA I/1, p. 611
[2] Ibid., pp. 617–21.

the 1870's onward—was to become the hallmark of orthodoxy. This seems a curious way of approaching the subject. Whatever may be said about the evolution of doctrine, there is no 'Marxism' apart from Marx's own writings, and the above passage is certainly one of his most characteristic early statements. Moreover, so far from being a passing aberration, it represents the very essence of his pre-1848 theorising about the coming revolution. It is true that in later years he took a less exalted view of the part which thought had to play in transforming the world, just as the concept of a social revolution which would transcend philosophy by 'realising' its aims, disappeared from his writings; but it was never repudiated, nor could it have been, for it is precisely what he meant by the 'union of theory and practice'. Without this central idea, Marxism is just another species of materialist determinism, and this is indeed what the later socialist movement largely succeeded in making out of it. But the transformation was never complete; at the core of the system, however much it might be watered down by its own author and others to suit the positivist fashion of the later nineteenth century, there remained something resembling the original vision of a world made new by a unique event fusing thought and action, theory and practice, philosophy and the revolution, into a creative drama of human liberation. It is literally true that apart from this quasi-metaphysical *tour de force* the whole subsequent history of the Marxist movement must remain incomprehensible.

It is worth noting that while in his essay of 1844 Marx stood Hegel's conservative philosophy of the state on its head, he did so by carrying to its furthest extreme Hegel's own rationalist mode of thinking. Although the language of the lengthy passage just quoted is reminiscent of Feuerbach—notably the emphasis on the 'emancipation of man'—the logic behind it is Hegelian: the present order of things stands condemned because it is irrational. Elsewhere in the same essay the existing state of affairs is declared to be 'beneath the level of history' and 'beneath criticism', from which it follows that its dissolution is both imminent and urgent. No more than Hegel did Marx doubt that what was irrational was also unreal. The most irrational, and consequently the least real, of all possible phenomena was a state of affairs such as that in pre-1848 Germany which, unlike the *ancien régime* of 1789, could not even claim to represent the traditional social order, but was a pure anachronism due to the backwardness of Germany and its lack of social development. To criticise this state of affairs—to lay bare its contradictions—was to demonstrate why such a condition of things could not be maintained much longer.

But in order to become effective, criticism had to abandon its purely theoretical status and turn into an instrument of revolution. If the youthful Hegel had in a general manner developed the notion that Reason must go out into the world and, as it were, work for its living in order to come to itself, Marx goes so far as to postulate a theoretical critique which makes an end of philosophy—in the traditional sense of the term—by 'realising' its aims. Such a critique is indeed no longer philosophy, if by that term is meant contemplation, and on these grounds it has sometimes been said that Marx at this point ceased to be a philosopher. This suggestion fails on two counts: in the first place, Marx had never written anything but critiques, though it was only in 1844 that he extended his criticism of institutions to the point of fusing theory and practice; secondly, this fusion was no less philosophical—indeed metaphysical—for being directed against the ruling ideas of the age. To say that the coming revolution would make an end of philosophy by fulfilling its ultimate aims—liberty and equality—was to make as grandiose a claim as any that had been put forward since German Idealism was launched by Hegel and Schelling in the 1790's. Where Marx breaks away from the idealist scheme is in placing thought within a material context: philosophy by itself cannot transform the social order simply by holding up a scheme of perfection or a conceptual image of 'true' reality; it needs an ally, and can find it only in a class whose existence proclaims 'the effective dissolution of this order'. This is a radical inversion of the idealist conception, but hardly a repudiation of philosophy as such. The 'critical theory' of 1844 is still philosophical in essence; its criterion of judgment is the irrationality of religion—lengthily developed in the same essay—and the deeper irrationality reflected in the need for religious consolation. At no point is it suggested that the coming revolution is to be welcomed simply because it is inevitable. Rather its inevitability is deduced from the intolerable conflict between the demands of reason and the unreasonableness of the *status quo*.

These general considerations find their counterpart in a doctrine of revolution behind which it is not difficult to perceive the general model of Jacobinism, as modified and brought up to date to suit the theoretical requirements of the 1840's. The 'critical theory' is intended as the theory of a political revolution patterned on that of 1789–94, but with this difference: instead of 'the people' we now— almost for the first time—encounter 'the proletariat'.

The essential precondition of the hoped-for German revolution is defined as 'the formation of a class with *radical chains* . . . a class which is the dissolution of all classes'. Marx as good as admits that as yet no such stratum exists east of the Rhine, though it is beginning to form, thus raising backward Germany to the West European level. Its inevitable growth is expected to furnish 'philosophy', i.e., the radical intellectuals, with the instrument required to overturn the existing order. That of course was substantially what had occurred in France in 1789, with the important difference that in the meantime the industrial proletariat had taken over from the traditional urban plebs. By the same token, the question why the French Revolution had in the end failed to achieve the ultimate aims of its most advanced spokesmen could now at last be answered in the light of recent socialist-communist literature: the Jacobins had been unable to transcend the framework of bourgeois society. Yet 'partial emancipation' (the downfall of the *ancien régime*) had been secured, and 'complete emancipation' (socialism) was sure to follow. In backward Germany, still lagging far behind, this order had to be reversed: only the revolutionary proletariat, led by the intellectual vanguard, could accomplish even the 'partial emancipation' implicit in the 'merely political' revolution already victorious in France; only a class whose inhuman condition proclaimed 'the dissolution of the existing social order' could enable 'philosophy' to realise its aims. Because that class was bound to reject the social order root and branch, 'philosophy finds its material weapons in the proletariat'. The coming revolution would be total because its aim was nothing less than the radical transformation of man's being in the world.

For all its utopian overtones—not to mention the strained conjunction of Hegelian and Feuerbachian concepts—Marx's essay of 1844 discloses a clear enough realisation that the German bourgeoisie would not in fact make the revolution which in his view was required to bring Germany up to the West European level. And if it failed, the task necessarily devolved upon the class which was already forming in the womb of bourgeois society, but had not yet found political expression. Hence the revolution, though 'bourgeois' in origin, would have to be led by the proletariat! Three-quarters of a century later a similar mode of reasoning served to fortify Lenin in his faith that the hour had struck for Russia to proclaim the world revolution: not *although* but *because* she was the most backward of the great European nations! In so doing he was compelled to repudiate not only Social-Democratic orthodoxy, but post-1850 Marxism as well; he was not, however, being untrue to the spirit of the early Marx, though reflection might have prompted doubt whether philosophical manifestos are meant to be taken literally and used as political guide-posts. In 1844 Marx had not yet emancipated himself from either Feuerbach or Hegel, and even the *Communist Manifesto* of 1847–8 (though written with far greater comprehension of history and economics) presents far too sweeping a synthesis of philosophy and revolutionary strategy to be of use as a political textbook. All this, however, belongs to a different chapter. In the 1840's there was no real chance of anyone in Europe—least of all in Germany— taking such formulations literally. Indeed the German proletariat so confidently invoked by Marx scarcely existed. The actual historical *locus* of revolutionary politics was Paris, and in Paris the era of proletarian insurrections in the service of bourgeois democracy was drawing to a close.[1]

If the utopian extrapolation from Feuerbach's philosophy was to be abandoned—and by 1847, when the *Manifesto* was in preparation, Marx had already cast some of his youthful ideological baggage overboard—there arose a further difficulty: to say that the coming German revolution could only be a bourgeois one[2] was equivalent to saying that it would bring the liberals to power. This awkward conclusion could be qualified by asserting that the proletarian revolution would follow in the wake of this first upheaval;[3] but there remained the task of making these paradoxes plausible to those outside the narrow circle of the Communist leadership. Already there loomed the problem of inducing the 'masses' to follow the lead of a 'vanguard' which could afford to take the long view because it incorporated the science of revolution. In 1848–9 these preoccupations were to be drowned in a torrent of happenings that fell far short of accomplishing even the modest opening phase of the two-stage upheaval envisaged in the *Manifesto*. Subsequently the rise of Social-Democracy, and the virtual abandonment of the old strategy by Marx himself,

[1] Cf. Marx, *The Class Struggles in France 1848–50* (preface by Engels), MESW I, pp. 118 ff. After the failure of the 1848–9 movement, Marx gradually relinquished his faith in historical short-cuts, but the repudiation was never quite complete and overt. Engels went further, as we shall see.

[2] *Manifesto of the Communist Party*, MESW I, p. 65.   [3] Ibid.

served to obscure the significance of the solution with which the founders of Marxism had briefly toyed in those turbulent years. Here again it remained for the Russian Revolution to revive a dormant issue that Western socialists had long believed to be dead.

While the *Manifesto* skipped entire stages of the sacrosanct historical process in order to telescope two different revolutions into one, its authors could at least point to the example set by the French socialist and communist sects of the period. In common with them, Marx and Engels thought in terms of the revolutionary experience of 1789–94, when moderate factions were displaced by more radical ones, until the whole democratic movement had advanced far beyond its original starting-point. It was more difficult to justify the implicit assumption that European capitalism in 1847 was already outmoded and ripe for socialisation. This was to mistake the birth-pangs of the new order for its death-throes—a misunderstanding only possible in an age in which the memory of the French Revolution had accustomed people to expect the imminent collapse of the existing social order. That the latter was still largely pre-capitalist, hence in urgent need of radical *bourgeois* measures, was a circumstance not wholly lost upon Engels, who had seen enough of England to be able to correct any misconceptions Marx might have entertained on this point. Yet paradoxically it was Engels who in 1844–5 persuaded Marx to regard Britain as the laboratory of the first genuinely proletarian-socialist revolution.[1] By 1847, with the *Manifesto* in preparation, it became urgent to formulate the theoretical grounds of this forecast, and here again it was Engels who took the lead.

He did so in a document which has not received its due share of attention, despite the fact that Marx utilised it in drafting the final text of the *Manifesto*.[2] Taken together with his earlier writings it may be said to outline a conception of history and a doctrine of revolution

[1] Cf. Engels, 'Umrisse zu einer Kritik der Nationaloekonomie', in *Deutsch‾ Franzoesische Jahrbuecher*, 1844, MEGA I/2, pp. 379 ff. It was this essay which first drew the two men together. In the following year, Engels's *Condition of the Working Class in England* presented the socialist solution as the necessary outcome of the British situation—on the grounds that a revolution was preparing which would bring the Chartists to power and thus precipitate a social transformation.

[2] Engels, 'Grundsaetze des Kommunismus', MEGA I/6, pp. 503–22. The text was first published by Eduard Bernstein in 1913. Cf. also Gustav Mayer, *Friedrich Engels*, The Hague, 1934, vol. I, pp. 283–5, where it is briefly dismissed as a 'casual sketch'. For a thorough analysis of the document and its implications cf. H. Bollnow, 'Engels' Auffassung von Revolution und Entwicklung', in *Marxismusstudien*, Tuebingen, 1954, vol. I, pp. 77–144.

significantly different from that of Marx. That this is not an academic matter becomes evident when one compares these early writings with the works of the mature Engels, which from the 1870's onward became the theoretical foundation of German Social-Democracy. The internal consistency is striking; so is the persistence of certain guiding ideas which do not occur in Marx and in some respects even run counter to the general tendency of his thinking. Thus Engels makes considerable play with the 'industrial revolution'—a concept which Marx had not yet begun to employ.[1] In other respects too the tenor of his argument is a good deal more technocratic than that of the *Manifesto*. At the risk of some schematisation the difference can be described as that between a socio-political concept oriented on French political experience, and a doctrine derived from the contemplation of industrial strains in early Victorian England. Thus it is plain in reading Engels that he is mainly concerned with the role of the proletariat in the 'industrial revolution', and behind this theme there already looms the notion that the 'proletarian revolution' is destined to set free the 'productive forces' at present held back by the institutions of bourgeois society. Echoes of this technological enthusiasm recur in the *Manifesto*, as does the emphasis on the revolutionary role of capitalism in doing away with pre-industrial forms of society; but where Marx stresses the catastrophic character of the process, Engels is inclined to emphasise its liberating and progressive side: the emancipation of the productive forces already set in train by the 'industrial revolution' remains incomplete under capitalism because private property stands in the way. Communism represents its consummation, and the proletarian revolution is primarily envisaged as the act whereby *the industrial revolution escapes from bourgeois control.*[2]

If this idea was destined to become a key concept of Leninism, another aspect of Engels's thought turns up a generation earlier in the ideology of German Social-Democracy, namely his stress upon the inevitability of the coming socio-political transformation. The latter

[1] Engels, loc. cit., p. 503; cf. also Bollnow, loc. cit., p. 79.

[2] Engels, ibid., pp. 510-15. The terms 'Produktionskraefte' and 'Produktivkraefte' are employed indifferently by Marx and Engels in their early writings; in this they followed the example of the French economists of the period who commonly spoke of 'forces productives' or 'forces productrices'. Cf. Marx's use of these terms in the original French text of his *Poverty of Philosophy* (1847): *Misère de la philosophie. Réponse à la philosophie de la misère de M. Proudhon* (MEGA I/6, pp. 117–228).

being the necessary consequence of the industrial revolution in its relentless unfolding within the womb of bourgeois society, its tempo depended primarily upon the degree of economic development already reached under capitalism. The more industrialised a country, the more numerous its working class, and the nearer the date of socialisation, whether peaceable or violent. In 1847 Engels still thought that Britain would lead the way, with Germany far in the rear, and the backward agrarian countries waiting to be transformed by the example of the more advanced.[1] A generation later this perspective was extended to Germany, and then to Europe in general. Engels is thus in a very real sense the father both of Social-Democratic orthodoxy and of the Leninist faith in industrialisation. He could even be viewed as a distant precursor of Fabian socialism, were it not for his scepticism about the likelihood of a peaceful transition, and his dislike of the pre-1848 'socialists' who (unlike the 'communists') urged measures falling short of the abolition of private property in the means of production.[2] It may be that gradualism is not a necessary consequence of determinism. The prevalence of the latter in Engels's thinking is unquestionable, and helps to explain not merely some of his more obvious divergencies from Marx, but also the fact that in the subsequent development of the socialist movement it was Engels rather than Marx who supplied guidance at the tactical level.

As against the complex dialectic of existence and essence, reality and 'alienation', which Marx develops in his writings between 1843 and 1848, Engels sketches a simpler and more harmonious picture. Neither the *Condition of the Working Class* (1845) nor the fragmentary *Grundsaetze* (1847) are weighed down by philosophical ballast. In conformity with their author's lifelong adherence to the optimistic world-view of the Enlightenment,[3] the emancipation of society through 'communism' (i.e., through the abolition of private property in the means of production) is envisaged as a unilinear process in which modern man—man as formed by the industrial revolution and the attendant triumph of science over religious superstition—achieves complete self-realisation. In contrast to Marx, the accent falls upon the satisfaction of human needs rather than upon the transformation of (human and social) nature. The coming revolution is destined to

[1] Engels, loc. cit., p. 516.

[2] Ibid., pp. 519–21. In the 1840's socialism was commonly regarded as a philanthropic middle-class movement; hence the preference shown by Marx and Engels for the term 'communism'.

[3] Cf. Gustav Mayer, *Friedrich Engels*, passim; Bollnow, loc. cit., pp. 101 ff.

remove the barriers to freedom and equality; its inevitability arises from the conflict between the productive forces unleashed by the new technology, and the inadequacy of the existing institutions. The Marxian *complexio oppositorum* of bourgeoisie and proletariat has no real place in this picture; although duly mentioned in passing, it is external to the real purport of Engels's argument which operates with the concepts of the Enlightenment in its most recent, positivistic, phase. In close parallel with these methodical assumptions, the role of the 'subjective factor' is reduced almost to vanishing point: determinism rules throughout, the active agents of progress being disembodied entities such as technology, science, or the industrial revolution as such. Other abstractions prominently displayed include society, machinery, the productive forces, capital, industry, the class struggle, and finally the new society, in which all these factors will be combined in a new and superior harmony.[1]

On the eve of the 1848 upheaval, this optimistic and positivist doctrine was no more than an ingredient in the explosive theoretical mixture which Marx was preparing in the *Manifesto*. The time had not yet come for the socialist movement to step into the liberal inheritance. In 1848 most radicals commonly employed Jacobin terminology. For the tiny Communist League, then about to seize partial control of the radical stirrings in Germany, Marx's philosophy of total revolution, with its chiliastic overtones familiar to readers brought up in the Judaeo-Christian tradition, was more appropriate than the hopeful anticipations entertained by Engels. Not that the two men were conscious of important differences in outlook. When it came to drafting the *Manifesto*, Engels characteristically yielded to the unquestioned authority of his senior associate. The first published document of German Communism thus bore the imprint of revolutionary French thinking, down to points of style and phrasing whose Jacobin, or Babouvist, ancestry could not possibly be mistaken. Whatever the precise extent of Marx's debt to his Saint-Simonian and Fourierist predecessors—among whom Victor Considérant requires special mention on account of his *Manifeste de la démocratie au XIXème siècle* (1847) which anticipates some of the formulations of

[1] For the peculiarities of Engels's style, cf. Bollnow, loc. cit., pp. 105–14. That his sentence constructions disclose a distinctive manner of harmonising an optimistic world-view with a deterministic philosophy of revolution, must be apparent to anyone familiar with the original texts. It is scarcely accidental that this style (down to peculiarities of grammatical and syntactical construction) later recurs in Bernstein and Kautsky.

the *Communist Manifesto*—the latter is clearly as much a French as a German document, and its incomparable rhetorical power owes more to the synthesis of these two European traditions than conventional critics have been ready to concede. For the same reason it does not translate well into English. In this seemingly external and insignificant fact it is possible to discern the latent element of a problem which was to become important when Marxism ceased to be a Continental European doctrine and tried to accommodate itself to the traditions of the English-speaking peoples. In the age of the democratic revolution, which in Western Europe climaxed in 1848, it was natural for the first generation of socialists to think of the coming transformation in terms derived from their own political experiences. On the Continent of Europe, these experiences were determined by the struggle against absolutism which ran parallel to the new conflict of classes. The birth-pangs of the industrial revolution thus aggravated a tension which had no real counterpart in Britain, let alone North America. Notwithstanding the Chartist movement, the 'social revolution' meant different things to Continental democrats still struggling to throw off the inherited deadweight of autocracy, and to English radicals not burdened with this particular problem. 'Red republicanism' was confined to Europe, and within Europe it centred on France, where democracy's first battle had been fought and won in the streets of Paris. The Communist League of 1848 was the inheritor of this tradition, and the *Manifesto* spells out the implications of a world-view which owed more to reminiscences of 1789–94 than its authors would have been willing to admit.

PART THREE

THE TEST OF REALITY
1848–1871

1

THE GERMAN QUESTION

THE *Communist Manifesto*, as everyone knows, made its appearance on the eve of an upheaval in Europe—an abortive rising serving as the curtain-raiser for an era of war and revolution. In consequence there has been a tendency to see Marx as the 'man of 1848' and his doctrine as a response to problems peculiar to Central Europe. Although the plausibility of this view is somewhat diminished by the overwhelmingly 'French' character of the *Manifesto* (down to its style), and the irrelevance of its guiding ideas to the conditions then prevailing in Germany, there is some substance in it—provided one is not misled into supposing that the European turmoil of 1848–9 bore a close resemblance to the social revolution predicted, on the eve of these uprisings, in the *Manifesto*. This was not the case even in Paris, where the February revolution, and the subsequent proletarian insurrection in June, came nearest to fulfilling the conditions laid down by Marx for the seizure of power. There was no question of a real threat to the bourgeois order elsewhere in Europe—not even in the Rhineland to which the leaders of the Communist League repaired in the spring of 1848, hoping to get the nascent democratic movement under control. An event such as the February rising in Paris, which had driven Louis Philippe from his throne and proclaimed the Republic, was altogether beyond the horizon of the

German democrats—let alone the liberals. The principal concern of the latter, from the moment power had fallen into their lap as the result of popular insurrection in the spring of 1848, was to obtain the adherence of the princes—notably the King of Prussia—to the national cause.[1]

This early attempt on the part of the liberals to win the headship of the German national movement through a policy of compromise has customarily been treated as a sign of weakness already foreshadowing the subsequent capitulation of liberalism during the Bismarck era. While such an assessment is accurate enough it tends to simplify the complex of problems confronting Central Europe in general and Germany in particular. The region was one in which past historical failures had left a particularly rich legacy of unsolved problems. If liberalism failed in 1848, Lutheranism had done so three centuries earlier, not to mention the abortive medieval attempts to establish an effective central authority. The present enshrines the past; in the case of nineteenth-century Germany it enshrined a record of misfortune unparalleled in Europe.[2]

This background determined not merely the actual course of events in 1848-9, of which more later, but also the manner in which these events were perceived. From the threatened autocracies, through the liberal constitutionalists, to the national-democratic revolutionaries, and finally to the leaders of the embryonic Communist party, each group had its own formula for explaining the past and shaping the future. If ever there was a region where philosophies of history had immediate political relevance, it was Central Europe, for here everything depended upon a correct reading of the structural faults embedded in the political landscape. These structures plainly were of ancient origin and correspondingly brittle in texture.[3]

It is a mistake to suppose that Marx and Engels were unique in

---

[1] G. Barraclough, *Factors in German History*, Oxford, 1946, pp. 110 ff.

[2] G. Barraclough, *Origins of Modern Germany*, Oxford, 1946, passim. For an authoritative German account of the pre-1848 situation, written from a moderately conservative viewpoint, cf. F. Schnabel, *Deutsche Geschichte im Neunzehnten Jahrhundert*, 4 vols., Freiburg, 1948-51, especially vol. I.

[3] Schnabel, *Deutsche Geschichte*, vol. I, pp. 80 ff. Cf. Engels to Mehring, 14 July, 1893, in MESC, pp. 543-4; 'In studying German history—the story of a continuous state of wretchedness—I have always found that a comparison with the corresponding French periods produces a correct idea of proportions, because what happens there is the direct opposite of what happens in our country .. There, a rare objective logic during the whole course of the process; with us, more and more dismal dislocation.'

approaching their task with an arsenal of historical concepts in mind. The appeal to history was the common feature of conservative, liberal and radical theorists—not to mention the spokesmen of some two dozen submerged nationalities who in 1848–9 were suddenly and dramatically propelled into the political arena. Indeed the national question soon took precedence over all others, until rivalry among the European powers—and among the leaders of conflicting revolutionary sects—reduced itself to a search for the means of mobilising popular support for the redrafting of frontiers. The German question naturally held the centre of the stage, but Poland, Hungary, Bohemia, and Italy were not far behind. It was a foretaste of the greater cataclysm of 1918–19, and the yet more drastic rearrangements of 1945–8. Some of the unsolved problems then dramatised for the first time are still with us.

Germany conditioned everything else and in Germany the pivotal position was occupied by Prussia. Since the defeat of German liberalism was later to become the single most important element in the European picture, this subject requires some consideration.

In 1848 the Prussian autocracy passed through a crisis which foreshadowed its violent dissolution seventy years later, in the German pseudo-revolution of 1918. The opening stage was the Berlin insurrection of March 18–19, 1848, which pitted a rebellious population against the hated army, and compelled the King to temporise for a while with democratic demands. Behind this clash lay the gradual dissolution of the autocratic structure inherited from the eighteenth century and only superficially modified by the so-called reform era of 1807–19.[1]

After the upheaval of 1848–9 Prussia gradually transformed itself into a semi-constitutional state, but the change remained incomplete and the resulting patchwork of bureaucratic reforms and quasi-parliamentary institutions without real power involved the liberals in a series of compromises which in the end cost them both their self-respect and their popular following. Their discomfiture was completed in the 1860's when Bismarck unified Germany without them and against them. Liberalism never recovered from this moral catastrophe. The subsequent history of Germany, down to and including the disasters of 1918, 1933 and 1945, is in part determined by the failure of the 1848 revolution. This sequence, however, must be seen

[1] Gordon A. Craig, *The Politics of the Prussian Army 1640–1945*, Oxford, 1955, pp. 65–81; Schnabel, *Deutsche Geschichte*, vol. II, pp. 272 ff.

in the context of a national history which made a different outcome unlikely. To say that the Prussian liberals—and more generally the German liberals—failed in their task is merely to say that they followed in the footsteps of earlier generations who had not succeeded in creating political institutions on the West European model. From the viewpoint of a genuinely revolutionary party the resulting distortions were simply an additional handicap to be overcome in the democratic reconstruction of Germany; but such a party, though not wholly non-existent in 1848 or later, was far too weak to undertake this reconstruction unaided. The initiative lay with the liberals who then had the backing of most of the middle class and the peasantry; and the liberals, for reasons which soon became apparent, aimed at a compromise with the autocracy. The outcome—since the government had no intention of compromising on terms that endangered its control over the army and the administration—was a stalemate which lasted for some years, to be broken when Bismarck channelled the growing national flood into the reactionary camp.

In 1848 this termination of the constitutional struggle was still veiled. Liberalism and nationalism had been marching together for decades, and it seemed unlikely that the alliance would split apart. Indeed so confident were the Prussian liberals of their unshakeable hold over the national movement that during their brief triumph in the spring of 1848 they made no serious attempt to get the army under control. Even the royalist *coup d'état* of November 1848, and the subsequent imposition of a pseudo-constitution, did not shake their belief that time was on their side. It never occurred to them that the autocracy might in the end establish links with the nation over their heads, or that the army might gain a popularity which would enable it to dispense with parliamentary control.[1] These misconceptions were rooted in a situation which had no counterpart in Western Europe, though in more than one respect it resembled that in Russia. The defeat of the liberal constitutionalists cannot simply be put down to inadequate leadership. There was something about Prussia that baffled both its enemies and its defenders. In the end they could only take refuge in the assertion that the Prussian state was unique—as in a sense it was. Certainly for all the obvious parallels with Russia on the one hand and Sweden on the other, there was nothing quite like it in Europe.[2]

[1] Barraclough, *Factors in German History*, pp. 118 ff.
[2] F. L. Carsten, *The Origins of Prussia*, Oxford, 1954; W. O. Henderson,

The uniqueness of Prussia lay not simply in the preponderant role of the military, but in the fact that the kingdom exercised the leading political role in Germany on the basis of a social structure which was essentially East European. As far back as the fifteenth century the social destinies of Eastern and Western Europe had separated, and at this crucial juncture the territories which later formed Prussia had begun to follow the Russo-Polish pattern.[1] Nor was this trend effectively reversed at a later date. The eighteenth-century absolutism did not carry 'enlightenment' to the point of abolishing serfdom or tampering with the privileges of the landowning nobility which controlled the army and there reproduced the relationship between Junker and serf in the officer's despotism over the men.[2] Most remarkable of all, even the collapse of Prussia in the first war against Napoleon (1806–7) did not lead to a radical reconstruction. The modernisation of the government undertaken during the subsequent reform period stopped short of structural changes dangerous to the power of the landed gentry. The latter indeed obtained the principal benefit from the belated abolition of serfdom in 1807–10, the chief effect of the reform legislation being the creation of a landless agricultural proletariat. When something like genuine peasant emancipation finally came in 1848, it was too late. The mass of the peasantry had been ruined, and the Junker class, already in control of military and administrative power, now possessed an unchallengeable economic base as well.[3]

If peasant serfdom and the preponderance of the rural gentry were traits which Prussia shared with Russia and Poland, the Prussian military monarchy was genuinely unique. Poland had no effective

The State and the Industrial Revolution in Prussia 1740–1870, Liverpool, 1958; Walter M. Simon, *The Failure of the Prussian Reform Movement, 1807–1819*, Cornell, 1955.

[1] Carsten, op. cit., pp. 135, 147–8, 149–64.

[2] Carsten, p. 273. For the difference between Hohenzollern and Bourbon absolutism, cf. the same author's 'Prussian Despotism at its Height', *History*, London, February and June, 1955, pp. 42–67.

[3] J. H. Clapham, *The Economic Development of France and Germany 1815–1914*, Cambridge, 1951, 4th ed., pp. 37–49; cf. also Simon, op. cit., pp. 20–37, 88–104; Schnabel, *Deutsche Geschichte*, vol. II, pp. 291–5. The questionable character of the so-called reform legislation passed under Hardenberg and Schoen in 1810–19, so far as the smaller peasants and the landless labourers were concerned, was long veiled by the liberal legend which made the most of the Stein-Hardenberg myth in order to link the reform period with the anti-French national rising of 1813–15. This myth fabrication has only in recent years been dismantled in part, with the aid of conservative South German historians like Schnabel who have no interest in the perpetuation of the Prussian legend.

central government—hence its disappearance from the map in the late eighteenth century—and Tsarist absolutism lacked the bureaucratic efficiency which was the special mark of Prussian administration. It was the bureaucracy which enabled the Prussian monarchy during the Napoleonic period to survive defeat, and thereafter to substitute administrative improvements for a genuine political renovation. The reform legislation instituted after 1807 was the work of enlightened bureaucrats, and it was their conversion to economic liberalism that was responsible for the gradual adoption, from 1815 onwards, of tariff measures which facilitated the subsequent unification of Germany under Prussian leadership.[1] By 1848 these tendencies were sufficiently far advanced for the main body of middle-class opinion to favour a policy of building a unified Germany around Prussia. Yet the same bureaucratic efficiency which enabled Prussia to take the lead in economic development also gave the government a considerable degree of direct and indirect control over the economy, thereby strengthening the autocracy at the very moment when it came into conflict with the bourgeoisie.[2]

To grasp what happened in 1848–71 it is necessary to bear in mind that while the Prussian monarchy rested upon the twin pillars of the officers' corps and the civilian bureaucracy, control of the former was its real foundation and remained essential to its functioning. In every major crisis the government revealed itself as a military despotism in which the army took precedence over the civilian administration. In quiet times the latter carried sufficient weight to give Prussia the appearance of a quasi-constitutional state; but every challenge to the royal autocracy, or to the basic interests of the landed nobility and gentry which exercised control over the army through the Junker-dominated officers corps, brought into play a mechanism against which democratic opposition movements beat in vain. In 1848 these movements could still look to the territorial reserve army, the *Landwehr*, as a bulwark against complete Junker domination. Subsequently

---

[1] Henderson, op. cit., pp. 76–95.

[2] Ibid., xiii–xxiii. The Prussian bureaucracy never really abandoned the task of economic regulation and control, whereas in Western Europe the governments, after having pioneered in industrial development from about 1600 to 1750, gradually withdrew from the stage in favour of private enterprise. In Prussia the process was slowed by the country's poverty, but even more by the absolutist traditions of the government. Thus when the constitutional struggle came to a head in the 1860's (and was duly decided in favour of the bureaucracy) the latter could quite legitimately claim to have taken the major share in the country's industrial development.

its effectiveness was blunted, and the middle-class opposition lost its only shield. In exchange it obtained a pseudo-constitution and a parliament elected on a franchise which secured a permanent majority for the larger property-owners. Having won this inadequate foothold, the liberals thereafter devoted their major energy to urging a 'German' policy upon the government, i.e., a policy of using the unreformed Prussian army in the service of the national cause.[1]

The national question, in the form in which it came to dominate German, and ultimately European, politics down to 1933–45, was not at first intrinsically linked with the internal policies of Prussia. The fact that her territories were scattered across the five parallel streams which flow through northern Germany did indeed help to make Prussia the natural focus of the national movement, once it had become clear that Austria was incapable of unifying Germany on an alternative basis. But the choice involved some hesitation on the part of even the North German liberals, let alone the South German democrats who clung to the belief that a federal and/or republican solution, with or without Austria, was possible. The conflict over this question dominated the 1848–71 period and had a profound effect upon the outlook of the political parties then in process of formation, as well as the labour movement which by the 1860's had split (as had the liberals) into pro- and anti-Prussian factions. In 1848 all this was still hidden in the mists of the future. A democratic reorganisation of Germany seemed not impossible after the Vienna and Berlin insurgents had driven the army from the two great capital cities and forced the governments to hold parliamentary elections on a basis of universal suffrage (soon to be abrogated). It was plausible to suppose that the revolution might enter a republican phase, as it had done in France, or at least compel the various German governments to federate on a more or less democratic basis. The defeat of these hopes was shortly to bring about that fateful alliance between German nationalism and Prussian militarism from which all the subsequent misfortunes of Germany have sprung, but in 1848 the issue was still in the balance. It was soon to be decided in a fashion which deepened the antagonism between Germany and the Western world, without improving German relations with the Slavs.[2]

[1] For details of this fateful alignment cf. Craig, op. cit., pp. 65 ff; Simon, op. cit., pp. 197 ff.

[2] Barraclough, *Factors in German History*, pp. 110 ff; Craig, op. cit., pp. 106–35; Simon, op. cit., pp. 4–5; A. J. P. Taylor, *The Habsburg Monarchy 1809–1918*, London, 1948, pp. 57–82.

The complex interplay of nationalist and democratic movements throughout Central Europe in this period will have to be briefly considered in conjunction with the development of Marx's and Engels's views on the national question. Here it is pertinent to recall that in 1848 both men could publicly and privately associate themselves with the cause of German national unification, while remaining true to the principles laid down in the publications of the Communist League. Under German conditions, nationalism was an integral part of the democratic programme, to which the Communist group was committed since it represented the extreme left wing of the democratic movement. That movement was then engaged in what promised to become a struggle for the radical reconstruction of Central Europe, and the presence within its ranks of a small but energetic 'ginger group' caused neither surprise nor dismay. It was a situation which in later years was to have its counterpart in numerous democratic upheavals, with the important difference that the Central European experiment of 1848-9 was a failure, both from the standpoint of the radicals and in the opinion of those who stood further to the right. Both groups were united by the conviction that the national question demanded a democratic solution, though Marx and Engels had their own idea of what that solution would ultimately have to look like. After the defeat, when it had become obvious that the German middle class was incapable of leading a national-democratic revolution, these differences were accentuated by the growing readiness of most democrats to accept half a loaf, but in 1848 no one as yet thought in those terms. That a quasi-solution of the national question would be achieved under Prussian leadership, supported by the main body of middle-class opinion, seemed the least probable of all outcomes.

In retrospect it is apparent that all concerned underrated the strength of the Prussian position. Not only did Prussia possess the most efficient military organisation in Germany,[1] but her economic policies had secured for her the tacit support of the industrial bourgeoisie which was rapidly becoming the most important element in the movement for national unification. The protectionist and, by implication, anti-liberal tendencies of this group were already noticeable before 1848, as were its dislike of England and a certain veiled antagonism towards those liberal elements in German society who stood for free trade and the adoption of 'English institutions'. In the 1830's and 1840's such nationalist and protectionist tendencies

[1] Craig, op. cit., pp. 136-74.

were skilfully combined by influential propagandists like List into a coherent system which anticipated many of the subsequent features of the Bismarckian National Liberalism of the 1880's, though List himself was South German and *grossdeutsch*, i.e., intent on including the Habsburg lands. While a succession of political crises shook Germany, the Prussian government and the manufacturing interests in the North gradually moved towards a rapprochement, until the collapse of the liberal parliamentary opposition in 1866, and the subsequent Bismarckian unification of the *Reich*, enabled them to conclude a permanent union.[1]

It is typical of the confused alignments of the period that the opposition to this North German interest bloc ran all the way from the conservative South German 'particularists' to the embryonic Communist group led by Marx and Engels. Defence of 'states' rights' played a conspicuous part in the conflict over German unification which in the end all but deadlocked the National Assembly in 1848–9, while among the various interests who sheltered behind this convenient slogan the Catholic Church was by far the most powerful. Its adherents rarely came into the open, but were all the more active behind the scenes.[2] The cleavage between the Protestant North and the predominantly Catholic South divided Germany as effectively as the traditional clash of interests between agrarian Prussia east of the Elbe and the industrial Rhineland, where middle-class radicalism shaded off into revolution. To make matters worse, the Rhineland belonged formally to Prussia, and the Rhenish radicals—Marx and Engels among them—for all their dislike of the Berlin regime were compelled to operate within a political framework which saddled Prussia with the task of unifying, if not the whole of Germany, at least its northern half. The alternative was a radical reconstruction which would have done away with all the existing governments and reorganised the whole of Germany on a republican-democratic basis. But though such demands were voiced in 1848–9 by a sizeable fraction of the democratic party, they were not 'practical politics' in the

[1] Clapham, op. cit., pp. 97–102, 150–7; Henderson, op. cit., pp. 144–7; Simon, op. cit., pp. 229–40; Schnabel, op. cit., III, pp. 330–71. For List's anti-Semitism and his hostility to England, as well as to the 'Manchester school', cf. Schnabel, op. cit., pp. 346–51. The extent to which List anticipated tendencies later manifested in National Socialism is debatable. At any rate he may be said to have pioneered the nationalist view that commercialism, pacifism, philo-Semitism, and Anglophilia, invariably went together.

[2] Wilhelm Mommsen, *Groesse und Versagen des deutschen Buergertums. Ein Beitrag zur Geschichte der Jahre 1848–1849*, Stuttgart, 1949, pp. 172–9.

absence of a mass movement which never materialised outside the two capital cities (Vienna and Berlin) and a few isolated districts in the South-West. Least of all did such a movement have a chance of gaining power in Cologne, where the Communist League had its headquarters. Its leaders therefore wisely concentrated on 'permeation', the left wing of the democratic party in the National Assembly being the obvious field of manœuvre.[1]

To grasp what this strategy involved it must be borne in mind that adherence to the national-democratic cause in practice meant the *grossdeutsche* solution of the German question, i.e., the incorporation of the Habsburg territories in a unified *Reich*. The consequences of this alignment were to plague Marx and Engels for years; among others they were partly responsible for the quarrel with Lassalle in the 1860's and the failure to found a unified labour movement before 1875. Immediately the issue brought them into conflict with the Slav nationalists in Austria and with Bakunin; this was a trivial reflection of the far from trivial circumstance that German nationalism in 1848–9 celebrated its appearance on the European stage by declaring war upon the Western Slavs.[2] Like List, who in this respect was a typical South German democrat, the majority of the radicals in the Frankfurt Assembly were not only *grossdeutsch* but annexationist. If the Catholic conservatives disliked Prussia for religious reasons, and because their leaders preferred the Habsburgs to the Hohenzollerns, the democrats—with the saving exception of a small minority who genuinely adhered to the nationality principle—were carried away by a mixture of patriotism and archaic dreams of a restored *Reich* which in effect foreshadowed the *Mitteleuropa* of twentieth-century politics. By comparison, the moderate liberals, who merely wished to conquer Germany with Prussian help and then build a navy to overawe the Danes and impress the British, were models of realism and statesmanship.[3]

---

[1] Mommsen, op. cit., pp. 129–36; Mehring, *Karl Marx*, pp. 152–90. (Cited after the English edition, London, 1951.)

[2] Mommsen, op. cit., pp. 182–3, 208–11. For Marx's and Engels's views on the national question, see below. The complete text of their writings between March and December 1848 is available in MEGA I/7. These, however, do not include some of the more important utterances on the national problem.

[3] Mommsen, pp. 82–91, 210–11. Some of the democrats in the National Assembly anticipated the pan-Germanism of 1914. In addition to founding a *grossdeutsch* empire including the Habsburg territories (and Alsace-Lorraine), they intended to embark on a policy of expansion in Eastern Europe and the Balkans down to the Black Sea.

Behind this chauvinist immaturity lay a social cleavage between the democratic radicals, who on the whole represented the less enlightened elements of the provincial middle class, and the liberals, who stemmed from the cultivated upper stratum and consequently had less use for patriotic rhetoric. By upbringing and education Marx and Engels belonged to the latter group, while politically they stood far to the left of both. If they nevertheless maintained a tactical alliance with the democracy, while ridiculing both its slogans and its leaders, this was owing to their conviction that the liberals would not advance one step unless driven on by a popular movement. This proved true enough, but the Communist League nonetheless paid a heavy price for the involvement of its leaders with a party which first ruined the democratic cause by its rhetorical extravagance and political ineptitude, and then passed its *grossdeutsche* programme on to a generation that no longer believed in democracy. On the whole Marx and Engels probably had no choice, since the labour movement was as yet virtually non-existent; the alternative to the tactics they adopted would have been to abandon the arena altogether to the democrats—hardly a course to be expected from the authors of the *Communist Manifesto*. It can be argued that in urging a democratic revolution, alliance with the French Republic, the Italians and the Poles, and revolutionary war against Tsarist Russia, the *Neue Rheinische Zeitung* under their editorship did about as well as could have been expected in the circumstances (a few nationalist sallies by Engels on the Slav issue excepted); the fact remains that in 1848–9 the leaders of the Communist League (who had recently proclaimed the imminent end of all national politics) could obtain a hearing only by blowing the patriotic bugle as hard as possible. In later years they might defend these tactics on the grounds that the backwardness of Germany left them no choice, but the example had been set and could be followed by others.[1]

[1] Solomon F. Bloom, *The World of Nations: A Study of the National Implications in the Work of Karl Marx*, New York, 1941, especially pp. 134–50. For Engels's residual pan-Germanism in 1848–9, cf. Gustav Mayer, *Friedrich Engels*, vol. I, pp. 325–30. The two important articles on pan-Slavism published in the *Neue Rheinische Zeitung* in January and February 1849, and reprinted in vol. III of Mehring's *Nachlassausgabe* of 1902 (pp. 233–64), are known to have been written by Engels. (Cf. Mehring, op. cit., p. 269; Mayer, op. cit., vol. I, p. 326.) These articles contain most of the doctrinaire characterisations of the minor Slav nations—the Poles always excepted—which were explicitly abandoned in later Marxist literature; cf. Karl Marx and Friedrich Engels, *The Russian Menace to Europe* (P. W. Blackstock and B. F. Hoselitz eds.), London, 1953, pp. 246 ff.

2

NATIONALISM AND DEMOCRACY

ANY ATTEMPT to discuss the flow and ebb of revolution and reaction between 1848 and 1871 must inevitably concentrate on the interplay of domestic and external events. The era was particularly rich in revolutionary upheavals, and at the same time it witnessed the unification of Germany and Italy, and therewith the completion of the European state system of the nineteenth century. It has never proved possible to disregard the evident connection between these parallel series of happenings, and indeed once nationalism and liberalism had become respectable the dominant school of historiography took pride in establishing the thesis that the liberal middle class had stood in the forefront of the national struggle. Although at best a half-truth, this approach did serve as a guide-post to the analysis of national movements elsewhere. It also enabled the newcomers—principally Germany and Italy—to assert a definite political orientation, though in either case the national-liberal integration soon proved powerless to contain popular energies. In our present context it is relevant to enquire what effect these events had upon the consciousness of the newly emerging labour movement which was soon to come under the influence of Marxist doctrines. It has been noted that in 1848–9, and for some time thereafter, Marx and Engels operated within the radical wing of the democratic movement, which in Central Europe was still overwhelmingly 'bourgeois', in the sense of being non-socialist. If this suggests that they had a foot in each camp, this impression must now be corrected, at any rate to the extent of showing in what respect 'bourgeois democracy' in 1848–71 connoted something different from the term of abuse which it was to become in Leninist literature two or three generations later.

The revolution of 1848–9 was a genuine turning-point among others also in that it disrupted the alliance between the middle class, the peasants, and the urban workers, which had been the basis of the democratic movement in Europe since the French Revolution.[1] Once this rupture had occurred, liberalism and socialism were left to confront each other as enemies, and it became plausible (though inaccurate) to assert that bourgeoisie and proletariat were the only active agents of the historical process. Prior to 1848 such a statement would have sounded extravagant even in Paris, where the two classes were soon to meet on the barricades. Outside France, and more particularly in Germany, where two-thirds of the population were still engaged in agriculture and there was as yet hardly anything resembling modern industry,[2] such a doctrine lacked even the degree of persuasiveness it might have possessed for French socialists, had it come to their attention. Belief in the power of democracy to solve all social problems was still too deep, and democracy itself too radical a slogan, for anyone save a handful of Communists to suppose that the 'proletariat' could signify anything but the lower ranks of 'the people'—i.e., the burgher-peasant-worker coalition which had made the Great Revolution in France and now (in 1848) was expected to score an even greater triumph all over Europe. It was the failure of these expectations, and the consequent dissolution of the great democratic movement into a host of quarrelling sects, which for the first time caused a significant number of revolutionaries to doubt the efficacy of the ancient Jacobin (or Jeffersonian) panaceas.[3]

But before this disintegration had set in, the classical democratic coalition secured a final triumph: over large areas of Central Europe its victorious sweep in the spring of 1848 enabled the peasantry (or what was left of it) to get rid of the remnants of serfdom and become free property-owners. This done, the coalition dissolved, the peasants

[1] Arthur Rosenberg, *Democracy and Socialism*, London, 1939, pp. 13–15.
[2] Rudolf Stadelmann, *Soziale und politische Geschichte der Revolution von 1848*, Munich, 1948, pp. 9–28.
[3] Rosenberg, op. cit., pp. 125–33.

turning conservative; and the urban radicals were left to fight unaided, or aided only by the workers: not yet an industrial proletariat
in the modern sense, but for the most part a fluid mass of recently
pauperised artisans ready to fight democracy's battles; though there
was also a nucleus of genuine factory workers, who on the whole
tended to be more cautious and 'reformist'. Thus the political upheaval brought about a significant social realignment, of which bourgeois liberalism and labour socialism were to be the beneficiaries.[1]

Such an outcome, though gratifying to the liberals—who during
these years everywhere obtained a share of power—and in a measure
to the socialists, for whom it constituted proof of their doctrine of
class conflict, was far from pleasing to the democratic radicals. This
party had borne the heat of the day in 1848–9 and now found itself
everywhere defeated, persecuted, driven into exile, or dragged before
courts-martial, and in addition scorned by socialists and reactionaries
alike as the rump of a hopelessly discredited cause. This disintegration of European democracy (taking the term in its classical
sense) in 1848–9 has been succeeded and overlaid by so many bigger
catastrophes that there is some danger of overlooking its significance.
Immediately it meant the termination of all hope of reconstructing
Central Europe along democratic lines—possibly a utopian aim, but
one which had animated the intellectual elite before 1848. In the
somewhat longer perspective it supplied the chief motive force behind
the emerging Social-Democratic movement, which was largely the old
movement on a new social basis. It also compelled Marx and Engels
to break with their old democratic associates and shift the gravitational centre of their activity towards the labour movement. This
aspect has naturally attracted the attention of socialist historians, who
have frequently failed to notice that in the process the founders of
Marxism were obliged to jettison part of their theoretical baggage.
Neither the Marxian theory of democracy nor the Marxian view of
national evolution are fully comprehensible unless it is remembered
that they took shape on the morrow of the worst defeat democracy
and nationalism had yet suffered in Europe.[2]

[1] Stadelmann, op. cit., pp. 76–82; L. B. Namier, *1848: The Revolution of the
Intellectuals*, London, 1944, pp. 7–24. It is difficult to follow Namier in his
suggestion that in France and Germany the middle classes in 1848 'comprised
probably half the nation' (p. 7), unless one includes all the property-owning
peasants. The latter, however, stood altogether outside the framework of
middle-class politics.

[2] Rosenberg, op. cit., pp. 145–70; Gustav Mayer, op. cit., I, pp. 324 ff,
351–5, 362–8.

The informal but effective republican-democratic 'International' of 1830–48, with its unofficial headquarters in Paris, had been held together by loyalties and beliefs which in the last analysis went back to the crowning achievement of the French Revolution: the 'democratic dictatorship' of 1793–4. To the adherents of this tradition, republicanism and democracy meant neither more nor less than the realisation of the goals proclaimed in that crucial moment of history. In this sense the democratic party included not merely the socialist sects of the period, but also the left-wingers among the Chartists, and those national revolutionaries (e.g., the radicals among the Polish emigrés) who stood for a drastic solution of the agrarian problem. The Paris workers were regarded as the vanguard of the movement, for the good reason that they seemed most likely to bring about a successful uprising, but the revolution's aims were so defined as to leave room for 'liberal' and 'socialist' tendencies alike. If most of the radicals believed that democracy would automatically solve what was coming to be known as the 'social problem', those who disagreed (e.g., Marx and his associates, but likewise Proudhon and his followers in France and Belgium) did not on this account renounce their allegiance to the democratic movement which on the eve of 1848 drew together in the struggle against all existing authorities. Thus in 1847 Marx and Engels spent much of their time establishing contacts between the Chartists in Britain and what was generally known as the democratic-socialist party in France. The essential unity of this 'International' was well demonstrated when on November 29, 1847, the anniversary of the Polish insurrection of 1830 was celebrated by the 'Fraternal Democrats' in London at a meeting attended by English, French, Polish, German, Swiss, etc., delegates, at which Marx addressed the gathering on behalf of a corresponding society in Brussels—in effect the local chapter of the German Communist League.[1]

It is noteworthy that even then the bulk of those who in 1848–9 were to be known as democrats in Central Europe—i.e., the left wing of the Frankfurt Assembly and their followers in Austria and Southern Germany—stood outside the democratic 'International' so defined. 'Jacobinism' had few followers in Germany, and those mainly among the illegal socialist sects. The country as a whole was

[1] Rosenberg, op. cit., pp. 73–5. For an account of the meeting (originally published in the *Northern Star*, the Chartist organ, on December 4, 1847, under the title: The Polish Revolution. Important Public Meeting), cf. MEGA I/6, pp. 625–31.

too backward, and the democratic opposition too conservative and philistine, to encourage a form of popular radicalism with socialist overtones. But these distinctions were fluid, and it seemed likely that Germany too would be drawn into the movement, as indeed happened to some extent in 1848–9 under the impact of events. 'Red republicans' who appealed to peasants against landowners—then the most extreme type of revolutionary activity possible in Central Europe, outside a few great cities—could and did pave the way for Social-Democrats who in the next generation turned to the industrial workers. But the changeover took some decades to accomplish, and it was precisely this interim period which witnessed the defeat of democratic hopes.[1] In the subsequent development of the European socialist movement it became the fashion to blame the outcome of the 1848–9 uprising on the weakness and shortsightedness of the middle class which had sold its political birthright for a mess of pottage. Marx and Engels set the tone,[2] and their followers repeated that the German middle class had failed where the French bourgeoisie had succeeded in 1789, and the English a century earlier. This analysis still lacked the edge which its authors gave it in later years, after further reflection had caused them to revise their earlier estimate of the liberal bourgeoisie as a 'revolutionary' force. By the 1860's Engels was ready to write liberal democracy off as a lost cause and to describe Bonapartism as 'the real religion of the modern bourgeoisie'.[3] Marx did not go quite so far, if only because he was committed to the view that the democratic republic was the normal form of bourgeois political organisation, and Engels eventually adopted the same position, though largely on the grounds that democracy had now (in the 1890's) become a conservative safeguard against socialism and the proletariat.[4]

In all this it is possible to trace an equivocation which was to

[1] Rosenberg, op. cit., passim; Stadelmann, op. cit., pp. 83–99. It is worth remembering that the *Communist Manifesto*, though published early in 1848, had actually been drafted in the preceding autumn, i.e., before the outbreak of revolution.

[2] Cf. Marx, 'The Bourgeoisie and the Counter-Revolution', MESW I, pp. 66–9. (Full text in MEGA I/7, pp. 484–530); see also Mehring, *Nachlass*, vol. III, pp. 206–29.

[3] Engels to Marx, April 13, 1866, cf. MESC, pp. 214–15: 'It is becoming ever clearer to me that the bourgeoisie has not the stuff in it for ruling directly itself, and that therefore where there is no oligarchy to take over, for good pay, the management of state and society in the interests of the bourgeoisie, a Bonapartist semi-dictatorship is the normal form.'

[4] MESC, pp. 454–7, 534–5.

become the source of considerable theoretical and practical confusion in later years. The 'bourgeois revolution' referred to in the *Manifesto* is the radical-democratic revolution on the Jacobin pattern of 1793–4, in which the middle class seizes political power with the help of an emancipated peasantry and the urban working population. By contrast, the 'bourgeois republic' of Marx's and Engels's later writings relates to political institutions such as the Third Republic in France after 1871. Lastly, there were countries, e.g., Bismarckian Germany, where in the absence of a powerful bourgeois-democratic party it fell to the labour movement to promote those aims which had once been the common property of liberal and socialist radicals. This was assumed to be the chief task of Social-Democracy until it had won power, when it would be able to introduce socialist measures with the backing of the majority. In Marx's and Engels's scattered observations on the subject these concepts are clearly distinguished, but the distinctions were never systematised, and the resulting ambiguities played their part in enabling rival groups to claim the inheritance of orthodoxy.

The significance of these disputes for the nascent European labour movement will be considered later against the background of French experience from 1848 to 1871, i.e., from the 'June days' to the Paris Commune. For the moment we must retrace our steps in order to determine the link between democracy and nationalism in the thought pattern developed by Marx and Engels (with some assistance from Lassalle) in the 1850's and 1860's. Consideration of this theme involves a geographical shift from Western to Central Europe—except for Italy whose belated national unification in 1859–70 gave it an equivocal position midway between the German and the French experience. Italy, unlike France, was not yet a nation, but unlike Germany it was not saddled to the same degree with the imperial curse. Its national movement could thus develop along fairly straightforward lines, while German nationalism was deflected from its true aim by the mirage of the medieval *Reich* and the consequent tension between genuinely national and spuriously imperial aims. Also, unlike their German counterparts (with the unimportant exception of the small group of Rhenish radicals), the Italian nationalists were for the most part neither hostile to France nor oblivious of the fact that the French Revolution was the source of almost all progressive currents in Europe. In this respect, too, they maintained the underlying unity of West European liberalism, against which the nascent German national movement of Napoleonic and post-Napoleonic days was consistently in revolt.[1]

It has been noted that the emerging split between liberalism and democracy in the German revolution of 1848–9 corresponded to the dividing line between North and South—and thus in part to the religious cleavage, although some regions in the South were both Protestant and liberal. It also reflected the growing social antagonism between the modern industrial and commercial bourgeoisie, which increasingly supported the 'Prussian solution', and the mass of burghers, artisans and peasants in areas not yet touched by the industrial revolution. The social homogeneity of this Southern environment provided the democracy in 1848 with an élan which rendered it irresistible so long as it did not overstep its regional boundaries. Had the whole of Germany resembled the agrarian South-West, the national-democratic movement would doubtless have carried the day and unified the entire country under the black-red-gold banner. That it proved incapable of attaining this quite reasonable aim was due not simply to the provincial philistinism of its leaders, but—in the estimation of Marx and Engels anyhow—to its class character: while the liberal party, with its North German backing and its growing identification with the industrial bourgeoisie, attracted all the more influential elements in German society and eventually spread to the South to become genuinely nation-wide, the democracy remained bound by its agrarian origins and consequently dwindled into a permanent opposition group. National unification, whether *grossdeutsch* or *kleindeutsch* (i.e., excluding Austria), could only succeed on an industrial basis, and once the liberal bourgeoisie had made up its mind to back the Prussian solution, the democratic cause was doomed: doubly so because its adherents tended to be either pro-Habsburg or pro-French (depending on whether their leaders were conservatives or radicals), while the Protestant North, for sound economic as well as political reasons, looked to England. The British system had become the admired liberal model: it excluded the majority of the population from power, while satisfying its material needs and promoting a rate of economic development unheard of in the remainder of Europe.[2]

---

[1] Mommsen, op. cit., pp. 215–26; H. Holldack, 'Probleme des Risorgimento', *Historische Zeitschrift*, Munich, June 1952, pp. 505 ff; Schnabel, *Deutsche Geschichte*, II, pp. 234 ff.

[2] For the pro-British and anti-French bias of North German liberalism between 1830 and 1870 cf. Schnabel, op. cit., II, pp. 181 ff. For the clash between

It is typical of Marx's sombre realism—itself a *grand bourgeois* trait incomprehensible to an associate like Wilhelm Liebknecht who stemmed from the South German democracy—that the moment he grasped this situation he resolutely severed the remaining links which bound his group to the dying democratic cause. Henceforth, whatever he and Engels might think of Prussia's political record, they accepted not merely the Prussian solution of the German question, but its corollary: the defeat of democracy in its old form and the consequent necessity of imposing upon the embryonic German labour movement the backbreaking task of transforming Bismarck's empire into a nation on the Western model. Whatever one may think of the manner in which the Social-Democratic movement subsequently discharged this duty, its spiritual fathers cannot be accused of having set their aims too low. If anything they erred in the other direction.[1]

These experiences went far towards shaping the considered view which Marx—and following him Engels—took of democracy and the nation-state. Nothing that had occurred since the *Manifesto*'s publication as yet pointed away from its definition of 'the executive of the modern state' as 'a committee for managing the common affairs of the whole bourgeoisie'.[2] If anything, the course of events in France after the fall of Louis Philippe (whose regime had originally been intended in this description) seemed to confirm its truth. Though the Bonapartist dictatorship after 1851 based itself directly on the army, and indirectly on the peasants, its principal social function plainly was the defence of property against the have-nots.[3] The plaudits showered upon the regime throughout Europe left no doubt that it was precisely this feature which rendered it acceptable even to liberals,

liberalism and democracy in 1848 cf. Mommsen, op. cit., pp. 149 ff. There was an ideological element in the Protestant solidarity displayed by British and German liberals, as well as by the conservative forces in Prussia who felt drawn to the British monarchy and the Tories; but the relevant fact is that the spread of National Liberalism in Southern Germany during the 1860's was accompanied by a movement away from France. The democrats might differ over Republicanism and Bonapartism, but their enduring pro-French orientation betrayed a social bias in favour of an agrarian order and a prosperous peasantry, as against the liberal concern with tariffs and manufactures; cf. H. Gollwitzer, 'Der Caesarismus Napoleons III. im Widerhall der öffentlichen Meinung Deutschlands', *Historische Zeitschrift*, Munich, February 1952, pp. 23 ff passim.

[1] Gustav Mayer, *Friedrich Engels*, vol. II, pp. 160 ff; Marx-Engels correspondence, July 25–7, 1866, August 15, 1870, September 1, 1870 (cf. MESC, pp. 219–21, 297–301); Marx-Engels 'Circular Letter', September 17–18, 1879, (MESC, pp. 388–95). [2] MESW I, p. 36.

[3] Marx, *The Eighteenth Brumaire of Louis Bonaparte*, MESW I, pp. 243 ff.

despite its militarism and the dubious character of its leading figures.[1] At the same time the increasing affection shown by the middle class in Germany for Prussia, and the eventual capitulation of the National Liberals to Bismarck,[2] pointed in a similar direction. As for Britain, the parliamentary franchise still excluded the working class, and when in 1867 its upper layer was admitted, this was done on the express grounds that since the collapse of Chartism in the 1850's labour's aims no longer represented a threat to the social order. If there was any doubt about the bourgeois character of the British government, it sprang rather from the fact that the aristocracy had managed to hold on, through the House of Lords, to a disproportionate share of power. In Marx's view this was largely owing to its stranglehold on Ireland, 'England's first colony', and among the aims suggested by Marx and Engels to their English associates—Chartists and trade unionists alike—the promotion of Irish self-government and land-reform consequently stood high on the list.[3]

In contrast with Britain and France, the Central European picture was complicated by the fact that the nation-state had not yet come into being, while the middle class showed no desire to promote democratic institutions even to the limited extent already taken for granted in Western Europe. This same middle class, moreover, was just then splitting up into antagonistic sections, its economically stronger wing drifting towards compromise with the authoritarian regime, while the retrograde mass of petty traders, peasants, and artisans clung to a Rousseauist, or Jeffersonian, concept of demo-cracy that was plainly outdated—if they did not seek salvation in Bonapartism. A modern labour movement scarcely existed as yet, and its first stirrings were accompanied by the usual utopian schemes for by-passing the reality of industrial capitalism by way of pro-ducers' co-operatives. It is not surprising that Marx and Engels had to expend considerable ingenuity on the task of maintaining contact

---

[1] Cf. Gollwitzer, loc. cit., passim. [2] Craig, op. cit., pp. 174–9.
[3] MESC, pp. 234–7, 244–5, 256, 276–81. Cf. Marx to Kugelmann, November 29, 1869, MESC, p. 277: '*The prime condition* of emancipation here—the over-throw of the English landed oligarchy—remains impossible because its position here cannot be stormed as long as it maintains its strongly entrenched outposts in Ireland.' Having with some reluctance adopted the view that national emancipation in Ireland must precede democratic revolution in England, and not *vice versa*, Marx continued to advocate a federal relationship between the two countries rather than complete separation. This later became the standard Social-Democratic approach to nationality questions and even found a dim echo in Leninism.

with this primitive movement (whose chances they did not rate high). Indeed for a number of years they were almost isolated.[1]

This deadlock was broken in the 1860's by the American Civil War, the founding of the First International, and Lassalle's agitation in Germany, which established the nucleus of something like an independent labour movement. Pending these events, the two exiles relied for their contacts on Italian, Polish, and Hungarian nationalists among the refugees, rather than on their fellow-socialists. Of these three movements, only the Italian could lay claim to liberal-democratic orthodoxy. The Polish national movement was democratic without being liberal; the Hungarian—a rebellion of the landowning gentry against Vienna—was neither. Its only merit, from the revolutionary viewpoint of 1848-9, lay in its resolute fight against the Habsburg monarchy and in the fact that it had been put down by Russian arms. The Poles, whose political outlook was more advanced, for a while became Marx's and Engels's favourite revolutionaries, as indeed they were foremost in all domestic battles on the Continent, down to the Paris Commune of 1871. Their romantic nationalism formed a suitable counterpart to the utopian French socialism which dominated the period. Neither survived the catastrophe of 1871, when France finally became a bourgeois republic after abjuring its revolutionary past in an orgy of bloodletting that eclipsed even the June days of 1848.[2]

These attachments remained episodic. Neither Poland nor Hungary could supply a substitute for the great democratic army, now defeated and scattered all over the globe. Already in 1850 Marx considered that the fate of their struggles for national independence had been settled by the crushing of the proletarian insurrection in the streets of Paris. 'The Hungarian shall not be free, nor the Pole, nor the Italian, as long as the worker remains a slave!'[3] While this became a favourite theme of the new Social-Democratic internationalism which slowly developed from 1864 onward, it did not immediately suggest a revision of political concepts already formed in 1848. Meanwhile Engels refused to retract his unfavourable opinion of the Western Slavs, though he and Marx gradually became more hopeful of the Russians.[4]

---

[1] Mehring, *Karl Marx*, pp. 238–88; Gustav Mayer, op. cit., II, pp. 42 ff.

[2] Namier, op. cit., pp. 57 ff; Taylor, op. cit., pp. 51 ff; MESC, pp. 114–16, 173–4, 183.

[3] *Class Struggles in France*, MESW I, p. 163.

[4] S. F. Bloom, *The World of Nations*, pp. 39 ff; cf. Ryazanov, 'Karl Marx und Friedrich Engels über die Polenfrage', *Archiv für die Geschichte des*

From a theoretical viewpoint the chief gain from the confused polemics of this period lay in a slight clarification of the 'national class' concept vaguely thrown out by Marx in the *Manifesto* and then left in the air. Since this aspect of his theorising was to acquire major importance with the victory of Leninism and the subsequent spread of Russian Communism to backward countries, it justifies some consideration, the more so since in Western literature it has been neglected in favour of some of the more sweeping, but less operational, notions adumbrated in the *Manifesto*: notably the well-known statement that the workers have no fatherland. This was just the sort of thing that young men influenced by French socialism were fond of saying on the eve of 1848. It made a splendid slogan (it also enshrined an important idea quite unrelated to actual facts) but it had absolutely no significance, save as a protest against the alienation of the industrial proletariat from society. By contrast, Marx's concept of the 'national class' is altogether original and extremely relevant to the theory and practice of modern Communism. Rather surprisingly, it has been ignored.[1]

To grasp what is involved it is necessary to recall the paradox inherent in the four decisive texts in which Marx formulated his doctrine of class conflict: *The Communist Manifesto* (1847-8), the *Class Struggles in France* (1850), the *Eighteenth Brumaire* (1852), and the *Civil War in France* (1871). All four are determined by French experience and French political thinking, yet they aim at something like a general theory of the state. The strain thereby thrown on the conceptual framework was only slightly lessened by the assumption that France was the model European nation and that its politics presented in chemically pure form what elsewhere was still partly confused or veiled by medieval survivals. Unlike the majority of German political theorists of his age, notably the liberals,[2] Marx regarded England rather than France as the exception from the general European rule. France was the 'classical' case: just as in medieval times

---

Sozialismus und der Arbeiterbewegung, VI, pp. 175 ff. While Engels (like Lassalle) remained an opponent of Austro-Slavism, he was ready enough to predict that the South Slavs would one day shake off the Turkish yoke and form a 'free, independent, Christian (sic) state on the ruins of the Moslem empire in Europe'. ('What is to become of European Turkey?', *N.Y. Tribune*, April 21, 1853; cf. *Gesammelte Schriften von Marx und Engels, 1852-62*, ed. Ryazanov, Stuttgart, 1920, vol. I, pp. 165-70.)

[1] Bloom, op. cit., pp. 57 ff.

[2] Cf. Schnabel, op. cit., II, pp. 184 ff; Mommsen, op. cit., pp. 21 ff; Stadelmann op. cit., pp. 35 ff.

it had been the centre of feudalism, so now its national life provided the clearest possible view of the class conflicts which were splitting society apart, even though economically Britain was further advanced along the same road. But France was also the 'model' in that its political institutions had been refashioned by the greatest and most successful of 'bourgeois revolutions'. Here more than elsewhere it was evident that the bourgeoisie had once functioned as the 'national class', i.e., the class which represented the interest of the whole of society against its retrograde members.[1] Now for the proletariat to aim at political power meant that it must prove its ability to take over the bourgeoisie's role as the socially progressive class, and to this end it must take the lead in reorganising society. Failure to rise to this level would count as evidence that the working class was not yet ready to play the part for which history had cast it.[2]

In the quasi-Jacobinical form which Marx gave to this doctrine in 1848–50, the 'dictatorship of the proletariat' was the obvious reply to the (real or assumed) 'dictatorship of the bourgeoisie'. This conclusion did not necessarily follow from the concept of the 'national class', and Marx subsequently modified it to take account of the rise of Social-Democracy. The core of the doctrine was not affected by this development, for whether or not the transition to socialism was pictured as peaceful and democratic, Marxism always implied that the rise to power of the working class would bring about a total reorganisation of society. The assumption was that the labour move-

---

[1] 'The Prussian bourgeoisie was not, like the French in 1789, the class which represented the whole of modern society against the representatives of ancient society: the monarchy and the nobility. It had degenerated to a kind of estate, as much opposed to the crown as to the people . . .' MESW I, p. 69. This post-revolutionary judgment contrasts sharply with the assessment of the German bourgeoisie's potentially revolutionary role in the *Manifesto*. On the eve of the 1848 upheaval, Marx still regarded the German bourgeoisie as the 'national class'.

[2] *Class Struggles in France*, MESW I, p. 162. 'The Paris proletariat was driven into the June insurrection by the bourgeoisie. This alone sufficed to mark its doom. Its immediate, avowed needs did not drive it to engage in a fight for the violent overthrow of the bourgeoisie, nor was it equal to this task. The *Moniteur* had to inform it officially that the time was past when the Republic felt it necessary to pay tribute to its illusions, and only defeat persuaded it of the truth that the smallest improvement in its position remains a utopia within the bourgeois republic, a utopia that becomes a crime as soon as it attempts to transform itself into reality.' (Text after the original, 'Die Klassenkaempfe in Frankreich', *Neue Rheinische Revue*, 1850; cf. *Karl Marx und Friedrich Engels, Ausgewaehlte Schriften*, East Berlin, 1952, vol. I, p. 145. The MESW translation is both lifeless and inaccurate.)

ment represented a higher form of social organisation, rendered possible by the development of the productive forces beyond the point compatible with capitalism. For society (the nation)[1] was not merely split into antagonistic classes: it also incorporated antagonistic modes of production, some of them inherited from the past, others in process of emerging. At this point the class concept cut across that of the nation. The 'national class' was that stratum which embodied the forward-looking tendencies, i.e., those which at a given moment made it possible for society to raise itself to a higher technological, economic, and social level. The bourgeoisie had once been such a class, but Marx considered that its historic role was now nearing its term. In the *Manifesto* it was even asserted that this fact was evident from the growth of pauperism, from which it followed that 'the bourgeoisie is unfit any longer to be the ruling class in society'.[2] This extravagant assertion—a typical rhetorical product of the 'hungry forties'—was later quietly abandoned by Engels, after Marx had already watered it considerably in *Capital*. But the underlying argument retained its importance not only for Marx but for his followers: in particular for those among them who were not troubled by concern for the preservation of 'bourgeois democracy'.

Now it is evident that the 'national class' concept can be given a conservative interpretation. It can be employed to defend a social order which, though class-ridden and undemocratic, is distinguished by rapid economic growth. It can also be turned into a politically neutral instrument of sociological analysis, once it is realised that co-operation among social classes is at least as frequent and normal a phenomenon as conflict. Nonetheless the idea does have revolutionary implications, since national leadership by a rising new class may be of crucial importance when a country stands at the crossroads of national unification and/or industrialisation. And it is precisely this sense which Marx intended when he tried to apply his 'French' doctrine to Germany in 1848–71. For the German middle class had not followed the example of its Dutch, English, American, and French predecessors. Instead of trying to conquer political power it had contented itself with capturing the market, leaving the exercise of governmental authority to others. Nor was the German labour movement able to supply the lack. Germany nonetheless became a modern country, but it did so with a difference which was to prove crucial

[1] Marx employs both terms interchangeably; cf. Bloom, op. cit., pp. 17 ff.
[2] MESW I, p. 45.

when in the following generation its rulers embarked upon a course of rivalry with the Western powers. Marx did not live to see the outcome, but he left a doctrinal legacy which both democratic Socialists and Communists could interpret as they chose.

To say that the roots of this historic divergence are to be found in the above-mentioned Marxian texts is a meaningful statement only when it is remembered that these writings are themselves part of a tradition reaching back to some of the most critical episodes of the Great Revolution: the Jacobin dictatorship of 1793–4, the Thermidorian reaction of 1794–5, and Babeuf's abortive rebellion (1796) against the newly consolidated bourgeois regime. Marx generalised from circumstances profoundly marked by the political and intellectual heritage of this brief but crucial period. The inheritors of the Jacobin-Babouvist tradition in the France of 1848–71 were the Blanquists, and Auguste Blanqui (1805–81) was both the unquestioned leader of the conspiratorial underground and the most important link between the 'old' and the 'new' revolutionary movement. Marx never concealed his admiration for Blanqui, without altogether sharing his faith in the providential role of Paris as the capital of the revolution. Yet he was aware that the German situation differed profoundly from the French. It would have been ludicrous to speak of a 'revolutionary proletariat' in the Germany of 1848, and no German city—not even Vienna, let alone Berlin—resembled Paris in strategic importance for the revolutionary movement, whether middle-class or proletarian. Significantly, Marx's pamphleteering in 1848–52 for the most part dealt with France, not Germany. He left it to Engels to describe—in a series of articles in the *New York Tribune* which appeared over Marx's signature—the tragi-comedy of the abortive German revolution.[1]

---

[1] For the socio-economic background of French politics cf. Jean L'Homme, *La grande bourgeoisie au pouvoir 1830–1880*, Paris, 1960. For Blanqui cf. Alan B. Spitzer, *The Revolutionary Theories of Louis Auguste Blanqui*, New York, 1957, passim. For the history and the general significance of Babouvism, cf. Talmon, *Origins*, pp. 167 ff. Babeuf's principal associate, Philip Buonarroti (1761–1837), survived the catastrophe of Babouvism and became the 'grand old man' of the radical sects in the 1820's and 1830's. The continuity of the revolutionary tradition was maintained by the link between Buonarroti —at one time (1794) the colleague of his countryman Bonaparte—and the youthful Blanqui: the last Jacobin and the first Communist.

3

SOCIALISM AND THE
LABOUR MOVEMENT

WITH THE CONCLUDING remarks of the previous chapter the theme
has insensibly shifted towards Social-Democratic strategy in the
liberal age, and away from the issues uppermost in the minds of both
conservatives and radicals in 1848-9. This fact in itself provides a key
to the understanding of the era which opened in the 1860's and closed
in 1914. In the main, its problems will concern us later, in connection
with the rise of a Social-Democratic movement which was at least
nominally Marxist. Here it is worth noting that this fusion represented
something like a shotgun marriage. Social-Democracy was older than
Marxism, and its first manifestations did not gain the plaudits of
either Marx or Engels. A perusal of their correspondence is enough
to show what an unflattering opinion they held of its leaders and
programmes. Even the term 'Social-Democrat' irritated them; it
reeked not only of reformist socialism, but of lower-middle-class
respectability, and there was nothing they disliked more.[1] Moreover,
the roots of the whole movement—according to Marx anyhow—lay
in the defeat which the proletariat had suffered in the Paris insurrection of June 1848, and in the subsequent reconciliation of the democratic opposition party (the 'Montagne') with the revolutionary

[1] Cf. Engels to Marx, November 16, 1864, MEGA III/3, p. 203.

working-men's clubs. This democratic-socialist coalition, in which the bourgeois democrats took the lead, had in its turn failed to bar Louis Bonaparte's road to power.[1] The legacy it left—an alliance of democracy and the workers under the banner of reformist socialism—was not to his taste. Its temporary success in 1849 he attributed to the peculiarities of the French situation: the triumphant reactionaries, having cast off the republican politicians who dominated the government and parliament after the fall of Louis Philippe, had felt free to give vent to their monarchist longings: 'The cry "long live the Social-Democratic Republic" was declared unconstitutional; the cry "long live the Republic" was prosecuted as Social-Democratic.'[2] This sufficed to invest the new party with a revolutionary aura which did not properly belong to it. Moreover, France was economically backward compared with England, and this circumstance vitiated its politics:

'In England—and the biggest French manufacturers are petty bourgeois compared with their English rivals—the manufacturers, a Cobden, a Bright, are encountered at the head of the crusade against the Bank and the stock-exchange aristocracy. Why not in France? In England industry predominates; in France agriculture. In England, industry requires free trade, in France protection, national monopoly alongside other monopolies. French industry does not dominate French production, hence the French industrialists do not dominate the French bourgeoisie. In order to secure the promotion of their interests as against the other factions of the bourgeoisie, they cannot, like the English, head the movement and simultaneously push their class interest to the fore; they are obliged to follow in the wake

[1] Marx, *Class Struggles in France*, MESW I, pp. 164 ff. 'The social and the democratic party, the party of the workers and that of the petty bourgeoisie, united to form the Social-Democratic party, that is, the Red party' (ibid., p. 191). In Marx's view this redness was deceptive, and the panic which the party inspired among the conservative sections of French society was attributable to the propaganda of its enemies rather than to its real aims.

[2] Marx, op. cit., p. 203. It is well to remember that in 1848–50 the followers of Blanqui were not alone in identifying republicanism with dictatorship. Thus in August 1848 three disciples of Comte presented to the Positivist Society a project for a revolutionary dictatorship to be installed in Paris. Yet the Comteists were far from being socialists, let alone communists. On the contrary, no more zealous defenders of private property and free enterprise existed. They merely shared with the Blanquists—and not with them alone—the traditional view that it was for Paris to determine the political fate of the country. For the historical roots of this attitude, cf. Talmon, *Origins*, pp. 209 ff.

of the revolution and serve interests which are opposed to the common interest of their class. . . . In France the petty bourgeois does what normally the industrial bourgeois ought to do; the worker does what normally should be the task of the petty bourgeois; and who accomplishes the task of the worker? Nobody. It is not accomplished in France, it is proclaimed in France. It is nowhere solved within the national walls; the class war within French society turns into a world war in which the nations confront one another. The solution begins at the moment when the world conflict pushes the proletariat to the forefront of the nation which dominates the world market—England.'[1]

With this concept in their minds it is understandable that Marx and Engels were far from enthusiastic when the only radical movement in Germany—that founded by Lassalle—in 1864 chose a name which in 1849 had sounded revolutionary only after the defeat of the real revolution. It was as good as an announcement that 'proletarian revolution' and 'communism' were ruled out, in the interest of an alliance between the nascent labour movement and what was left of the democracy after the defeats and disappointments of the 1850's. That this was indeed the purpose of the new movement became obvious before long, even after it had split into rival groups, one of which was headed by men who regarded themselves as disciples of Marx and Engels. To the latter this relationship was scarcely obvious. The only explanation they could find for the ensuing muddle was that Germany was even more backward than France. But then England, which was economically most advanced, could not, after the final collapse of Chartism in the 1850's, even boast a labour party on the Continental model, merely a trade-union movement. In the circumstances there was nothing for it but to work through all existing organisations, in the hope that the pre-socialist remnants would gradually be sloughed off: a process which was to take almost a generation and whose completion Marx did not live to see.[2]

The immediate problem was how to cope with the effect of Lassalle's

[1] Marx, op. cit., p. 211. (Text after the German edition, Berlin, 1952, vol. I, pp. 191–2.) At first sight this assessment seems difficult to square with the picture of France as the political model, but it was possible to get around this by arguing that France posed the social problem in its most naked form, though the solution must be left to economically more advanced nations.

[2] Mehring, *Karl Marx*, pp. 316 ff; Mayer, vol. II, pp. 120 ff; Rosenberg, op. cit., pp. 145 ff. For Lassalle's writings during this period, cf. *Ferdinand Lassalle, Auswahl von Reden und Schriften*, ed. Karl Renner, Berlin, 1923. (The reference to Mehring relates to the English edition of his work.)

agitation in Germany which focused on the popular demand for a democratic franchise in Prussia, and at the same time sought to draw the emerging labour movement away from the middle-class liberals who were then engaged in another of their periodic bouts of pseudo-opposition to the Prussian government.[1] The story is fairly familiar in its broad outlines, though frequent emphasis on the personal antagonism between Marx and Lassalle has tended to obscure the issue. It was not a question of 'reformism' versus 'revolution'—Lassalle was if anything more inclined than Marx to force the pace, and in any case neither man dealt in such childish banalities. The dispute concerned the role which the fledgling workers' movement was to play during the next phase of Germany's national-democratic revolution, i.e. the attempt to transform Germany from a congeries of petty states into a modern nation. There could be no question of ignoring the political struggle, but it was by no means clear that the tactics of 1848–9 could be revived. In those days the embryonic Communist group had functioned as the extreme left wing of a broad coalition which in principle included the liberal bourgeoisie. Lassalle now proposed to break away from this policy. Instead of trying to drive the liberal opposition forward, he decided to by-pass it. The workers' movement—led by himself—was to take the lead in the political struggle with a view to extracting a broader franchise in Prussia. Eventually the movement was to become both national and democratic: war and revolution being Lassalle's recipe for the unification of Germany. On the other hand, its socialist aims were to be realised—in part at least—by the Prussian government: notably through state aid to producers' associations. Lassalle seems to have thought that he could unleash a mass movement which would force Bismarck to introduce universal suffrage as the only means of gaining popular support. Meantime the evident impossibility of unifying Germany by peaceful means, and the unwillingness of the bourgeois opposition to adopt a revolutionary programme, gave him a chance to accuse the liberals of treason to the national cause.[2]

[1] Rosenberg, op. cit., pp. 156 ff; *Ferdinand Lassalle*, pp. 10 ff; Kurt Brandis, *Die deutsche Sozialdemokratie bis zum Fall des Sozialistengesetzes*, Leipzig, 1931, pp. 9–26; Horst Lademacher, 'Zu den Anfaengen der deutschen Sozialdemokratie 1863–1878', in *International Review of Social History*, Amsterdam, 1959, vol. IV, part 2, pp. 239 ff; part 3, pp. 367 ff; Thilo Ramm, 'Lassalle und Marx', *Marxismusstudien*, III, pp. 185–221.

[2] *Lassalle*, ed. Renner, pp. 31 ff. Lassalle is one of those people who are the despair of historians. As the founder of German Social-Democracy he is obviously an important figure. He can also claim some interest on account of his

In judging these tactics and the effect they had on Marx and Engels it is necessary to bear in mind that Lassalle understood the situation in Prussia much better than they did. He would not have fallen into the mistake Engels made in 1866, when on the eve of Prussia's decisive military triumph over Austria he confidently predicted an Austrian victory and a rebellion in the Prussian army.[1] In retrospect it is also clear that he was right in refusing to credit the liberals with the capacity or the desire to lead a popular movement for the democratisation of the Prussian franchise, or indeed for the defence of the constitution following Bismarck's flagrant disregard of parliament in 1862-6. One can go further. It is, after all, a fact that Bismarck introduced universal suffrage in the Reich (though not in Prussia) after Lassalle's death in 1864, and that this extension of the franchise enabled the Social-Democrats to become the largest (though scarcely the most influential) German political party. Finally, in 1918 Bismarck's successors were compelled to efface themselves before the heirs of Lassalle. It is thus tempting to conclude that Lassalle's political judgment in 1863-4 was altogether superior to that of the two theorists in England.[2]

The trouble with this argument is that it ignores what to Marx and Engels was most important, namely the effect which Lassalle's tactics were likely to have on the long-term outlook of the labour movement.

personal involvement with most of the characteristic movements of his time— from literary romanticism (he was among others an unsuccessful dramatist) to Hegelianism. Yet his voluminous political writings, though extremely effective as propaganda, do not add up to a coherent whole, while as an economist he is not merely insignificant: he does not exist. The reader who doubts this is invited to consult his speech on indirect taxation and the condition of the working class, October 12, 1863, in *Lassalle*, ed. Renner, pp. 221 ff.

[1] Engels to Marx, May 25, 1866; MEGA III/3, p. 335; for his more strictly military writings cf. *Engels as Military Critic*, ed. Chaloner and Henderson, Manchester, 1959, pp. 121 ff.

[2] Cf. Mehring, *Geschichte der deutschen Sozialdemokratie*, Stuttgart, 1897, vol. I, pp. 520 ff. Mehring's treatment of this contentious subject is conditioned by his concern for party unity. His belief that Lassalle's national-democratic agitation was really quite compatible with the strategy advocated by Marx and Engels does not stand up to examination. The fact is that the only revolution Lassalle ever had in mind was a democratic one which was to give the working class *equality of rights*; while the principal issue which divided his followers from the rival 'Eisenach' labour group organised by W. Liebknecht and Bebel in 1869 arose from the latter's commitment to democratic *republicanism* and hatred of Prussia; in short, the national question was decisive on both sides, for it was their anti-Prussian alignment which made Liebknecht and Bebel advocate an alliance with the liberal-democratic opposition in the South. Cf. Brandis, op. cit., pp. 25 ff.

To draw the workers away from the liberals was one thing; to enter into an unholy partnership with Bismarck was quite a different matter, and potentially demoralising for a movement whose political character was still unformed. Lassalle's fantasies about state aid to producer co-operatives were bad enough, but what really made Marx and Engels increasingly hostile was his silence, and that of his followers after his death, about the means whereby the Prussian nobility and gentry maintained their hold over the countryside.[1] Lastly, the Lassallean tactics smacked of *Realpolitik*, i.e., subordination of principle to expediency, and it was Marx's considered view that this kind of opportunism had been the ruin of the democratic opposition in 1848. To revive it now, on the plea that it was possible to obtain concessions from Bismarck, seemed to him the height of folly.[2] It was an aggravating circumstance that both Bismarck and Lassalle seemed to be toying with Bonapartism. This was not simply Marx's belief. Lassalle's German contemporaries too sensed that he was drifting in this direction.[3] At first Marx merely poked good-natured fun at Lassalle for being an 'enlightened Bonapartist'.[4] Later he came to suspect that Lassalle would have sold out completely had not his sudden death intervened.

By a coincidence this event occurred a few weeks before the inaugural meeting of what was to become known as the First International. Some months later, Marx's old enemy Proudhon died, thus relieving him of another worry. Thus 1864–5 is a turning-point in the story: for the first time Marx was able to exert direct influence over the international labour movement. If the rise of Marxist Social-Democracy must nonetheless be dated from 1871 rather than 1864, this is because as yet neither the British trade unions nor the French-socialist movement had felt the need to revise their indigenous traditions.

[1] Marx to Engels, February 18, 1865, MESC, pp. 198 ff; Marx to Kugelmann, February 23, 1865, MESC, pp. 202 ff.

[2] Cf. Marx to Kugelmann, loc. cit., pp. 205 ff: 'I think that Schweitzer and the others have honest intentions, but they are "practical politicians" (*Realpolitiker*). They want to take *existing circumstances* into consideration. . . . They know that the workers' press and the workers' movement in Prussia (and therefore in the rest of Germany) exist solely by the grace of the police. So they want to take things as they are, and not irritate the government, just like our "republican" practical politicians who are willing to swallow a Hohenzollern *emperor*. . . . It is the sort of practicality (*Realpolitik*) which places Germany so far behind all other civilized countries.' (Ibid., text after the original.)

[3] Cf. Gustav Mayer, *Bismarck und Lassalle*, Berlin, 1928, passim.

[4] Marx to Engels, July 30, 1862; cf. MEGA III/3, p. 83.

The 1860's were a turning-point in other respects as well. Down to 1848 the 'social problem' in Central Europe had been virtually synonymous with the land problem.[1] To an extent this was true even in France, though here the peasants had already turned conservative, a fact noted by Marx in his analysis of Bonapartism.[2] In consequence, democratic movements had to satisfy peasant demands, and where they failed to do so—notably in Hungary and Poland, where the movement was dominated by the landowning gentry, but also to a degree in Italy—they were in danger of being undercut by the governments.[3] On the eve of 1848 the radical wing of the movement, which subsequently became the nucleus of Social-Democracy, would have denounced as an evident absurdity any attempt to differentiate between peasant and worker interests: both classes were being exploited by the 'moneyed aristocracy' and oppressed by the governments under its control.[4] By the 1860's this naïve view had given rise to a more sophisticated but less hopeful analysis: the peasants were now rated a conservative force, while the pauperised artisans who manned most of the barricades in 1848-9 had either despaired of democracy, emigrated to America, or become factory workers. Only in the latter case were they suitable recruits to the nascent Social-Democratic movement. Insofar as they still hoped to remain independent of the industrial-capitalist nexus, they were more likely to back conservative, clerical, or utopian, chimeras than to give their support to the new socialist movement.[5]

The latter therefore had to begin by explaining to the newly proletarianised masses of the industrial regions that the economic revolution could not be reversed: however much the disappearance of the old independent artisanate might be regretted, the chicken could not be put back into the egg. This was in line with the prevailing liberal orthodoxy, but it did not render a political alliance with liberalism

[1] Clapham, op. cit., pp. 1-5, 29 ff; Stadelmann, op. cit., pp. 22 ff; Namier, op. cit., pp. 17 ff.

[2] *The Eighteenth Brumaire of Louis Bonaparte*, MESW I, pp. 333 ff.

[3] Cf. MESC, pp. 69-71, for Marx's view of Mazzini's tactics.

[4] Mehring, *Geschichte der deutschen Sozialdemokratie*, vol. I, pp. 36 ff. So influential a leader of the German Social-Democratic movement as Wilhelm Liebknecht stemmed ideologically from the agrarian struggles of the 1830's in his native Hesse; cf. Mehring, op. cit., p. 63.

[5] Mehring, op. cit., vol. I, pp. 440-1, 455 ff; vol. II, pp. 1-17. Lassalle's followers at first opposed trade union activity, since their master had taught them that the 'iron law of wages' could not be modified by collective bargaining; but such doctrinaire certitudes (which confirmed Marx in his belief that the Lassalleans were a hopeless sect) were not maintained for long.

any easier, for conditions in Central Europe were now beginning to approximate that social cleavage between bourgeoisie and proletariat which Marx had postulated some years earlier in the *Manifesto*. If Lassalle was careful not to quote Marx in public, he was nonetheless his pupil and aware of what was happening. At the same time he was enough of a political realist to frame his programme in terms which made an appeal both to the new industrial workers and to pauperised artisans who still hoped to escape the factory. It was this feature of his agitation which so irritated Marx. On theoretical grounds he had a good case, but Lassalle had the better political instinct. State aid to producer co-operatives might be economic nonsense (in Bismarck's Prussia it was also political nonsense), but it was exactly what the somewhat amorphous working-class movement in Leipzig, Frankfurt and other German cities wanted to hear. Lassalle's original socialist pronunciamento of March 1, 1863, had perforce to be addressed to men who were 'utopian' socialists in the succession of Weitling, the first German communist—though himself still an artisan of the old school. Its instantaneous success was due to the fact that it combined the old radical fervour with newfangled talk about economic science —but the latter so interpreted as to turn its edge against the manufacturers and their liberal apologists. Intellectually it was just what his hearers required. A purely Marxian analysis would have been incomprehensible to them.[1]

With his appeal to the existing governments to help solve the social problem, Lassalle was likewise on traditional ground. Such an approach suited both the outlook of the Prussian bureaucracy and the intellectual climate of a country which had not cast off that veneration of the state which was Marx's principal *bête noire* in relation to Germany. Whenever Marx has occasion to vent his irritation on the state in general, and the Prussian state in particular, he sounds more like a liberal than a socialist; doubtless he would have denied that there was any basic conflict or contradiction—a view unfortunately no longer tenable.[2] Even Lassalle's agitation for universal suffrage

[1] Cf. Lassalle, 'Offenes Antwortschreiben etc,' in *Auswahl von Reden und Schriften*, ed. Renner, pp. 295 ff. The effect of this pamphlet has been compared to a bomb explosion. At any rate it touched off a political upheaval: within a few years nearly every capable labour organiser in Germany had turned his back on the liberals and subscribed to the cause of an independent workers' movement. For the link between Weitling's socialist agitation in the 1840's and the Lassallean movement in the 1860's, cf. Mehring, op. cit., vol. I, pp. 168 ff; vol. II, pp. 6, 17 ff.

[2] Cf. Marx, *Critique of the Gotha Programme*, MESW II, pp. 29 ff.

did not reconcile Marx to his tactics: conditions in Germany being what they were, he held that a broader franchise was more likely to promote Bonapartism than democracy. This did not entail support for the liberal programme of rule by a parliament elected on a narrow franchise weighted in favour of property-owners: a programme which gave Lassalle his best opportunity for denouncing the liberals as enemies of democracy and the working class. It did, however, imply that such denunciations should be coupled with a refusal to trade labour support of Bismarck for a broader franchise. But the notion of such a stratagem was Lassalle's trump card. On this point no understanding between him and Marx was possible.[1]

In later years, when Marx became involved in doctrinal disputes with the Proudhonists and with Bakunin over the nature of the state, he was compelled to formulate his views in a somewhat more systematic fashion, and he then did so with reference to France, more particularly after the Paris Commune of 1871: in his view the first 'proletarian dictatorship' in history. These issues did not enter into his quarrel with Lassalle, for the excellent reason that in Germany the only relevant question was how far the fledgling labour movement should go in support of the liberal opposition. This tactical problem solved itself when the liberals made it clear that, given a choice between authoritarian rule and democracy, they greatly preferred the former. A liberal-democratic movement—i.e., one which, though led by the middle class, genuinely backed the demand for a broad franchise—would have constituted a severe embarrassment not only for Lassalle but for Marx. But no such movement ever materialised. Universal suffrage was introduced by Bismarck in the North German federal parliament in 1867, after he had won his fight against the liberal opposition; and the latter made no attempt to press for a similar change in Prussia, where the old undemocratic franchise remained in force until the general collapse of 1918.

By a coincidence, 1867 was also the year in which the second Reform Bill gave the vote to the upper layer of the British working class, and since here Parliament had real power, trade union pressure on both political parties yielded practical results. It is evident from

---

[1] Mehring, op. cit., vol. II, pp. 68 ff; Ramm, loc. cit., pp. 208 ff. Mehring, who in general takes a favourable view of Lassalle, nonetheless notes that he shocked a sizeable part of his potential following by appearing to side with Bismarck against the liberals. In Berlin, where the elite of skilled workers supported the liberal opposition, his campaign was a failure, and what backing he had came from pauperised artisans.

Marx's comments on the subject that these developments laid the ground for his subsequent belief in the possibility of a peaceful British evolution towards socialism.[1] But then England had always had a mellowing effect on him. As early as the 1850's his reports on British parliamentary proceedings in American and German newspapers show him not merely conversant with the intricacies of the party game, but also inclined to believe that the British working class need only gain the franchise to obtain political power.[2]

It is important to note this gradual shift in Marx's attitude to democracy, for his involvement in the affairs of the International becomes incomprehensible on the stock assumption that there had been no change in his outlook since he contemptuously dismissed the first manifestations of democratic socialism in France, in 1849–52 as a 'coalition of petty bourgeois and workers' which by its nature could do nothing to eliminate the antagonism of capital and labour. The Marx of 1864 was the theorist of a *labour* movement and *therefore* committed to democratic socialism, however much this circumstance was clouded in his own mind by the continuing struggle to overthrow the old regime.

---

[1] G. D. H. Cole, *History of Socialist Thought*, II, pp. 92 ff.

[2] *Gesammelte Schriften von Karl Marx und Friedrich Engels 1852–62*, ed. Ryazanov, Stuttgart, 1920, vol. I, p. 9. 'For the British working class, universal suffrage means political power, for the proletariat forms the great majority of the population . . .' (Letter to the *New York Tribune*, August 25, 1852.) Chartism was already fading out when Marx wrote this, but after 1850 he never really abandoned the democratic position where England was concerned. Continental politics were a different matter.

4

THE FIRST INTERNATIONAL

IT IS CONVENIENT at this point to introduce some general observations before turning to the First International and the Paris Commune. At first sight neither has much to do with Marxism. The International emerged from an exchange of views among English and French labour leaders, while the Commune was directed by men who were either indifferent or hostile to Marx's theoretical standpoint.[1] But the Marxian doctrine of class conflict in its final form reflects the impact which these developments had on him, and conversely he helped to formulate the programme of the first international labour movement.[2] It is thus relevant to enquire what were the theoretical preconceptions with which he approached his task. The reply is by no means simple, for in dealing with an international movement centred on London—and later with a revolutionary outbreak located in Paris —Marx was in part guided by tactical considerations which enjoined caution in expressing his real views. He had to bridge the gap between

---

[1] Cole, op. cit., II, pp. 88 ff, 134 ff. The literature on both topics is too voluminous for even the barest bibliographical outline.

[2] Of which the German Social-Democrats at first did not form part: they were inhibited by legislation which forbade affiliation to international bodies, and anyhow Marx wanted no Lassalleans in 'his' International. This is another justification for treating the subject separately.

'bourgeois democracy' and 'socialist democracy', for the International was by no means committed to socialism, let alone revolution. He also had to clarify certain ambiguities in his own mind. It is this last point which concerns us here.

When Marx emerged from semi-obscurity in 1864 to take a hand in shaping the programme of the International,[1] he had spent fifteen years in London and become sufficiently familiar with British political life to appreciate that a strategy derived from Continental models would no longer do for England. This realisation, however, cut both ways. If it ruled out the possibility of anything like a revival of Chartism, it also suggested that the British labour movement might be able to by-pass some of the stages through which the Continental movement was going. Britain was both nationally homogeneous and highly industrialised—in fact the only genuinely capitalist country in Europe. Apart from Ireland there was neither a national problem nor a peasant problem to confuse the class line-up, and we have seen that Marx hoped for an agrarian revolution in Ireland which would relieve British democracy of the incubus still weighing upon it. This consideration, however, was linked to a circumstance which consistently baffled him, namely the fact that although British *society* was bourgeois, the British *government* was not: Parliament, though no longer the almost exclusive domain of the landed nobility, was still to a very large extent controlled by it—the House of Lords completely so. The immediate problem therefore was to drive the aristocracy from power—including the Whig aristocracy, which, though up to a point willing to execute bourgeois policies, was constitutionally incapable of really doing so, and indeed had recently displayed this incapacity during the Crimean war.[2]

In the early 1850's Marx still tended to regard Tories, Whigs and Peelites as parties belonging essentially to the past, whereas the Cobdenite free-traders and the Chartists represented the future.[3] It was therefore annoying that the Cobdenites failed to gain greater political power, while the Chartists steadily declined. Instead the Whigs gradually transformed themselves into the nucleus of the Liberal

---

[1] MESW I, pp. 377 ff; Cole, op. cit., II, pp. 91 ff.

[2] Cf. *Gesammelte Schriften*, ed. Ryazanov, vol. II, pp. 321 ff. Apart from the Whigs, the group Marx disliked most were the Peelites: they too were essentially bourgeois, yet helped to perpetuate the aristocracy's monopoly of political power. It is evident that he underrated the importance of this group; cf. Ryazanov's comment, op. cit., vol. I, pp. 447 ff.

[3] *Gesammelte Schriften*, vol. I, pp. 6 ff.

party, to which the Cobdenite group lent its reluctant support, while the trade unions brought up the rear. Even the Tories continued to exist, despite the abolition of the Corn Laws which Marx had regarded as fatal to their prospects (a view shared by Cobden). By the 'sixties this transformation had advanced sufficiently far to render illusory all hope of a middle-class revolt against the oligarchy—a threat which had loomed large in the 'hungry forties' and was almost revived for a moment by the national indignation over aristocratic mismanagement during the Crimean war. At the height of the resulting storm against the Ministry, Marx's hopes rose for a brief moment.[1] When the 'governing caste' muddled through, he lost interest in the subject and turned to other matters. By the 'sixties, with the International there to absorb his energies, he became reconciled to the thought that the historic alliance between aristocracy and bourgeoisie, which had characterised British society since 1688, was likely to continue; this, however, rendered all the more urgent the task of drawing the trade unions away from the nascent Liberal party. At the start, i.e., in 1864, this strategy looked quite hopeful, the more so since it was the Tories under Disraeli's skilful leadership who reaped most of the benefit in 1867, when the skilled workers got the vote. Later the tide began to run in the other direction: Marx's growing troubles with the General Council of the International from 1871 onward arose from the fact that the British trade union leaders, who until then had given him what amounted to a blank cheque, were becoming reconciled to the *status quo*, hence less inclined to associate with Continental socialists.[2] The latter were for the most part far from revolutionary—especially after the expulsion of Bakunin and his Anarchists from the International in 1872. But even the Social-Democrats now stood considerably to the left of the British union leaders, who had decided to throw in their lot with the reigning Liberal party at the very moment when on the Continent labour was moving towards a decisive rupture with liberalism.

Even without the Parisian cataclysm, a breach with the British

[1] Ibid., vol. II, p. 129. 'The governing caste, which in England by no means coincides with the ruling class, will be driven from one coalition to the next, until exhaustive proof has been furnished that it has lost its capacity for governing.' (Article in *Neue Oder-Zeitung*, February 8, 1855.) Of the existing parties Marx throughout this period preferred the Tories, who at least possessed the merit of being reliably anti-Russian: unlike Cobden and, of course, Palmerston, whom he even suspected of secretly favouring Russian expansion. (Ibid., vol. I, pp. 224 ff; vol. II, pp. 465 ff.)

[2] Cole, op. cit., II, pp. 104 ff, 132 ff.

trade unions would thus in the long run have been unavoidable. Marx could put up with liberals who shrank from breaking the political power of the 'governing caste', but he could not extend the same tolerance to labour leaders. The issue in Britain after all was simply one of parliamentary democracy: no one had proposed anything really drastic. For the middle class to pursue its traditional symbiosis with the ruling aristocracy was one thing; for the trade unions to enter into a similar relationship with the now politically dominant bourgeois-aristocratic coalition was, in Marx's view, equivalent to surrendering labour's birthright. Under his influence, and that of Engels, this became the prevailing view among European Social-Democrats during the following generation, and the resulting tension lasted until the British labour movement once more became politically active.[1]

Bearing all this in mind, it is remarkable that in 1864 the leaders of the British trade union movement committed themselves to a document which revived some aspects of the Chartist tradition and at the same time pointed forward to what was later called democratic socialism. The *Inaugural Address* is in a sense the Charter of Social-Democracy.[2] It sets out both a political and an economic programme, the theoretical side of which will have to be considered in connection with Marx's critique of political economy. Politically, it drew upon the traditions of the 1848–9 movement, i.e., the struggle for democracy. Radical democrats could and did take satisfaction from what the Address had to say about 'heroic Poland', then as later 'assassinated by Russia', and 'the immense and unresisted encroachments of that barbarous power whose head is in St. Petersburgh and whose hands are in every Cabinet of Europe'.[3] All this was familiar enough and straight in the democratic tradition of 1848–1849. The novelty lay in the emphasis upon the aims of organised labour, working through legislatures still dominated by the possessing classes, as well as through its own organisations. The Address reminded its readers that although Chartism had faded out, the British

[1] Cole, op. cit., pp. 379 ff; Rosenberg, op. cit., pp. 210 ff. For Engels's views on British labour in the 1880's cf. his remarks in a letter to Kautsky of September 12, 1882, MESC, pp. 422–3.
[2] Cf. *Inaugural Address of the Working Men's International Association.* MESW, I, pp. 377 ff. The text was drafted by Marx on October 21–7, 1864, and published by the General Council of the International in the following month, the organisation itself having been formally established at a public meeting on September 28, 1864, at St. Martin's Hall, London.
[3] Ibid., p. 384.

working class 'after a thirty years' struggle fought with the most admirable perseverance', had won a great victory (in 1847) by pushing the Ten Hours Bill through Parliament. Moreover, 'there was in store a still greater victory of the political economy of labour over the political economy of property', namely the co-operative movement.[1] 'The value of these great social experiments cannot be overrated.'[2] Still, even these triumphs were bound to remain incomplete, for nothing much was to be expected from a House of Commons dominated—as Palmerston had recently proclaimed in public—by landed proprietors. 'To conquer political power has therefore become the great duty of the working classes. They seem to have comprehended this, for in England, Germany, Italy and France there have taken place simultaneous revivals, and simultaneous efforts are being made at the political reorganisation of the working men's party.'[3] Here the language is fairly ambiguous, and no doubt Marx did not speak his whole mind.[4] Yet whatever his *arrière-pensées*, he had in fact outlined the basic programme of Social-Democracy. When the British trade unions a few years later shrank back from its implications, it was they and not he who abandoned the common platform, and eventually they were to return to it.

It has been remarked with some justice that neither Marx nor Engels ever quite understood the character of the democratic labour movement which came into being in Western Europe from the 1860's onward.[5] Both men had their roots in the pre-1848 revolutionary sects which aimed at a complete transformation of society, and they experienced some difficulty in adapting to the modern labour movement which was inevitably a good deal more reformist than the old Jacobin-Socialist 'International' with its dreams of a new heaven and a new earth. Yet somehow or other they managed to make the transition. In 1864 it was still possible to draw upon both the old and the new sources of radicalism, and Marx did so with remarkable skill, fusing the traditional democratic creed with the new upsurge of

[1] MESW I, pp. 382–3.
[2] Ibid., p. 383.
[3] Ibid., p. 384.
[4] Cf. Marx to Engels, November 4, 1864: 'It was very difficult to frame the thing so that our view should appear in a form acceptable from the present standpoint of the workers' movement. In a few weeks the same people will be holding meetings for the franchise with Bright and Cobden. It will take time before the reawakened movement allows the old boldness of speech . . .' MESC, p. 182.
[5] Rosenberg, op. cit., pp. 222 ff.

organised labour into a mixture which seemed explosive enough—though the only real explosion of the period, the Paris Commune, had nothing whatever to do with it.

The Commune in fact not only helped to wreck the International: it introduced an equivocation into the very heart of the movement, for under its influence Marx temporarily abandoned his realistic outlook of 1864 and reverted to the utopianism of the *Communist Manifesto*. Moreover, by enshrining the memory of the Paris rising in the greatest of his political pamphlets,[1] he imposed upon the growing Social-Democratic movement a political myth which stood in no relation to its daily practice. Hence in part the split personality which from 1871 onward came to plague all Socialist parties in Europe: they could not very well disown the Commune, but neither could they steer by the lurid light it cast. It remained a 'glorious event' and the sharpest possible point of difference with bourgeois liberalism, but its symbolic value far outweighed any political significance it possessed.

Even this qualified adoption of a revolutionary standpoint went far beyond what the staid leaders of the British trade unions were prepared to accept, and Marx's impassioned defence of the Commune helped to bring their association with the General Council to an end. Many of them had indeed never been altogether comfortable in the presence of so many foreigners, and only a very special combination of circumstances in the 1860's enabled them to place their weight behind the International. The story is complicated, and the more one studies it the more one is impressed by the importance which the continuing struggle for democracy possessed for the emerging labour movement.[2] The London Trades Council, which took the initiative on the British side, had indeed emerged from a major economic conflict.[3] But the Council was also behind the public meetings in support of the North in the American Civil War and the great demonstrations welcoming Garibaldi when he visited England in April 1864. Above all, its leaders were prominent among the signatories of an Address

---

[1] *The Civil War in France*, MESW I, pp. 499 ff.

[2] Cole, op. cit., II, pp. 102 ff. A succinct account, written from the Marxist standpoint but drawing upon the entire literature of the period, is given by Ryazanov, 'Zur Geschichte der Ersten Internationale', in *Marx-Engels Archiv*, vol. I, Frankfurt, 1926, pp. 119–202.

[3] The London building trades dispute of 1859–60, which lasted for over six months, has been described as a turning point in the history of British trade unionism; cf. Ryazanov, loc. cit., pp. 125 ff.

to their French colleagues on the subject of Poland which had nothing whatever to do with trade union matters, but all the more with the democratic crusade against Russia.[1] The Address itself was a sequel to a public meeting held at St. James Hall, London, on July 22, 1863, when British and French radicals and labour leaders for the first time protested jointly against Russian oppression of Poland, consequent upon the Polish insurrection in that year, and urged their respective governments to intervene.[2] At an earlier meeting, on April 28, where pressure was urged upon the British government—committed, like the French, to diplomatic protests on Poland's behalf—no French delegates had been present, but news of a parallel pro-Polish agitation among the Parisian workers suggested the advisability of proceeding jointly. Since the British and French labour leaders had already become acquainted during the London International Exhibition of 1862, there was no difficulty about making contact. The two governments could not well object: Napoleon III was then in his 'liberal' phase and besides the Polish cause—unlike the Italian—had Catholic support, so that he ran no risks from that quarter. British public opinion, i.e., liberal middle-class opinion, was likewise favourable, though its illusions about the British Cabinet's readiness to help the Poles were not shared by the more advanced union leaders. At the July 22 meeting, the future British delegates on the General Council of the International not only went all out in support of Poland, but also indicated that they did not expect Palmerston and his colleagues —who had recently distinguished themselves by supporting the South in the American Civil War—to lift a finger on behalf of the Poles.[3]

The whole movement must be seen in the context of the democratic upsurge of the 1860's which succeeded a decade of reaction. January

[1] 'To the Workmen of France from the Working Men of England', first published on December 5, 1863, in the *Beehive*, the official organ of the London Trades Council. Its editor, Hartwell, was a former Chartist, and the contributors included Frederick Harrison and E. S. Beesly—both leading Positivists, i.e. followers of Comte, and acquainted with Marx. (Cf. Ryazanov, loc. cit., pp. 133 ff.) For Marx's relations with the small but influential Positivist group, cf. Royden Harrison, 'E. S. Beesly and Karl Marx', *International Review of Social History*, Amsterdam, 1959, vol. IV, pp. 22 ff, 208 ff.

[2] Ryazanov, loc. cit., pp. 166 ff.

[3] 'He (Cremer) had no faith in it (sc. the government). He remembered how Palmerston had treated Hungary, and he believed he would sacrifice Poland in the same way, if the people of England permitted him to do so.' (*Beehive*, July 25, 1863, quoted by Ryazanov, loc. cit., p. 167.) Cremer, a leading member of the Trades Council, was to be among the most active British representatives on the General Council of the International.

1863—the date of the Polish insurrection which inflamed the old democratic hatred of Russia—was also the date on which Lincoln's Emancipation Proclamation went into effect, and the British union leaders were first drawn into the movement by way of the radical campaign to aid the North.[1] To these men the anti-slavery struggle in America represented substantially the same cause as the Italian and Polish national insurrections, the attempts of the French workers to organise themselves under the dictatorial rule of Napoleon III, and their own campaign for universal suffrage. The December 5, 1863, Address 'to the workmen of France from the workingmen of England', already referred to, characteristically opens not with a reference to industrial conflicts, but with a lengthy tribute to 'the cause of Poland'. After various uncomplimentary remarks about 'kings and emperors' who have 'their meetings and feasts' 'pleasing the frivolous and gratifying the fortunate', at the same time 'creating heavier burthens for the honest and industrious poor to sweat under', the Address states that 'as a means to check the existing abuse of power, we echo your call for a fraternity of peoples'; and after further lengthy references to Garibaldi, Mexico, Switzerland, and the 'cruel war with China' recently conducted by the British and French governments, the document concludes with yet another appeal for 'a united effort for the freedom of Poland', an appeal couched in the authentic language of the popular radicalism of the period.[2]

[1] At a meeting held in St. James Hall on March 26, 1863, in support of the Northern cause, Bright was succeeded on the platform by the leaders of the London Trades Council who subsequently took the initiative in campaigning for Poland. Howell and Cremer spoke, while Odger, Charles Murray, Robert Shaw, and Applegarth, sat on the organising committee. The incident made a deep impression on contemporaries who had never yet seen labour leaders in such a prominent role. These were the men who after 1864 sat on the General Council of the International, with Marx commonly acting as their spokesman. Cf. Ryazanov, loc. cit., p. 166; H. Evans, *Sir Randall Cremer*, London, 1909, pp. 26–30; A. W. Humphrey, *Robert Applegarth*, London, 1914, pp. 4–6.

[2] 'We say with you, let our first united effort be for the freedom of Poland; the justness of her cause demands it, treaty obligations make it imperative, and duty pursuits the way. . . . We must do this to prevent the intrigues of secret diplomacy (that scourge of nations) by which the devil's tragedy would be played over again, Poland's noblest sons be murdered, her daughters become the prey of a brutal soldiery, making that fair land once more a huge slaughterhouse to the everlasting shame and disgrace of the civilised world.' Signed on behalf of the working men of England by: Thos. Grant Facey, Painter, President; William Cremer, Joiner; C. Goddard, Bookbinder Committee; John Eglinton, Carpenter; George Odger, Shoemaker, Hon. Sec. (Cf. Ryazanov, loc. cit., pp. 173 ff.) During the subsequent dispute on the London Trades Council over the propriety of this intervention in foreign affairs, the

After this it is scarcely surprising to find the same men prominent in the 'Trades Unionist Manhood Suffrage Association' formally constituted in September, 1864, only a few weeks before the St. Martin's Hall meeting which launched the Working Men's International Association. When Marx, in the 'Inaugural Address' drawn up on their behalf, laid stress on the obstacles to social progress presented by the unreformed House of Commons, he was generalising from their recent experience and could be certain of their further support; for the next five or six years he was their spokesman in all dealings with the Continent, while at the same time he interpreted the Continental movement for their benefit. In particular it seems to have fallen to him to discourage the somewhat uncritical Francophilism of Comte's British followers, in whose eyes even Napoleon III benefited from the afterglow of the French Revolution.[1]

The counterpart of all this activity was the renascence of the French labour movement, which went on steadily during the 1860's, notwithstanding the fact that trade union activities remained at most semi-legal.[2] It is impossible here to pursue the dispute between those socialists in France who favoured a strictly non-political trade union movement, and their opponents who aimed at an organisation with broadly political aims. Both groups supported the International, but as time went on the 'politicals' grew stronger, and by 1870 they were in control of most sections—a circumstance which made the Commune possible, though hardly inevitable. The Parisian working-class leaders who brought their followers into the International—principally Tolain, Fribourg and Varlin—had begun as disciples of Proudhon, who for years had been preaching abstention from politics. This was not his only point of difference from Marx, and indeed Proudhonism remained Marx's principal worry throughout this period. In the later 'sixties the congresses of the International were largely dominated by somewhat academic debates over Proudhon's economic nostrums, while towards the end of the period a further element of confusion was introduced by Bakunin's intervention

Address was described by its critics as a 'red republican document' and its practical usefulness in promoting co-operation with French labour leaders was doubted—not perhaps without reason. Yet when in the following year the union leaders turned to Marx for the draft of the Inaugural Address, 'heroic Poland' once more figured in the text that won their approval.

[1] Marx to Engels, December 10, 1864, MEGA III/3, p. 214.

[2] Cole, op. cit., pp. 97 ff; Ryazanov, loc. cit., pp. 177 ff; Dolléans, op. cit., I, pp. 277 ff.

which merged with the Proudhonist issue, both men being hostile to state control and centralisation. All this makes a wearisome tale of complicated manœuvring in the pursuit of which much toil and virtue were consumed. The main outlines are nonetheless fairly simple. They must be recapitulated, though with extreme brevity, if the conflicts provoked by the catastrophe of the Paris Commune are to be placed in perspective.[1]

Except for being contemporaries Proudhon and Marx had little in common.[2] Fortunately for the International, their historic dispute over socialist theory in 1846–7 did not enter directly into the matter, for Proudhon had died in January 1865, four months after the movement got under way. Had he lived longer, its congresses would probably have been enlivened by some further acrimonious polemics, the more so since Proudhon did not share the general democratic enthusiasm for Poland and hatred of Tsarism. For his French followers, and generally for the labour movement in France, 1864 was an important date, for it witnessed something like the tacit legalisation of trade unions, as well as a revival of political interest among the Paris workers. The new mood was reflected in a manifesto published early in 1864 by Tolain and other labour leaders who were active on the French side in forming the International. Though strongly influenced by Proudhon, they differed from him in advocating participation in elections, and their growing impatience with abstentionism was probably a factor in causing Proudhon to reformulate his views in his posthumously published work, *De la capacité politique des classes ouvrières* (1865), in such a way as to make it possible for his French disciples to retain their ideological purity and yet take part in the International, side by side with men who took an altogether different view of the connection between the economic and the political struggle.

The 'Manifesto of the Sixty' (published in the *Opinion Nationale* on February 17, 1864) was signed by most of the men who subsequently played the leading role in the International as representatives

---

[1] The dissension between Proudhon's 'mutualist' followers and the 'collectivist' group around Varlin is documented in Dolléans, op. cit., pp. 306 ff.

[2] For Marx's considered view of Proudhon, cf. his letter to J. B. Schweitzer, January 24, 1865, MESC, pp. 184 ff. This is a shorter and more satisfactory introduction to the subject than his well-known polemic against Proudhon in *The Misery of Philosophy*, MEGA I/6, pp. 117 ff. Cf. also Erich Thier, 'Marx und Proudhon', *Marxismusstudien*, vol. II, pp. 120 ff. Proudhon's numerous writings cannot enter into consideration here, not even his *Système des contradictions économiques, ou Philosophie de la misère* (Paris, 1846, new edn. Paris, 1923) which provoked Marx's well-known rejoinder.

of Proudhonism. Its publication preceded by a few months the law of May 25, 1864, which placed trade unionism in France on a semi-legal basis, though with many restrictions; and it was immediately followed by Tolain's unsuccessful candidature in a Paris by-election— the first time that a representative of the workers had come forward in a parliamentary election under the Second Empire. The 'Manifesto' itself is an extremely moderate document which eschews not merely all revolutionary activity, but even the idea of organising strikes. Labour's aims are defined as 'La liberté du travail, le crédit, la solidarité'. Politically, the nomination of workers' candidates is described as a means of 'fortifying, by completing it, the action of the liberal opposition'. This was a far cry from Lassalle, but also from Proudhon, who had previously counselled abstention from elections. The reference to 'credit', on the other hand, was a tribute to Proudhon's favourite panacea—a credit bank to finance workers' co-operatives.

From Marx's viewpoint these developments were vastly more important than the subsequent quarrel with Bakunin. France was one of the two main pillars of the movement, England being the other, and the French labour movement was the principal force whose reawakening promised to undermine the stability of the Second Empire. He therefore took good care not to let doctrinal differences with the Proudhonists interfere with his direction of the General Council, though he was not sorry when their influence declined as control of the French sections increasingly passed to their 'collectivist' rivals, among whom Eugène Varlin (1839–71) gradually assumed the leadership. What Varlin described as 'anti-authoritarian communism' was the nearest thing to his own viewpoint then possible in France. The 'collectivists' were likewise in the forefront of the attempt to give a genuinely political character to the French labour movement. Yet Varlin was opposed to the Blanquists, who for their part took no interest in the International. He represented a new type: the politically educated labour leader who had emancipated himself from sectarian fanaticism and conspiracy-mongering. In 1871 he was to become one of the central figures of the Commune, and the principal 'Internationalist' on its directing body.

In view of what was to follow it is worth bearing in mind that for Marx these French issues were quite unconnected with the subsequent rift caused by Bakunin. A personal element entered into the matter. Marx had a high regard for Blanqui, whom he more than once characterised as 'the head and the heart of the proletarian party in France';[1] he was also prepared to take Proudhon seriously, although he disliked him. In contrast he seems to have regarded Bakunin's intervention as nothing more than a squalid nuisance.[2] It was one thing, in his view, to dispute theoretical questions with a man like Proudhon, who though self-taught was something of an economist; or to differ over tactics with Blanqui, the most stoically enduring of revolutionary martyrs. It was an altogether different matter to have one's work disrupted by someone like Bakunin, who not only spread confusion wherever he went, but who in his spare time preached pan-Slavism.[3] Personal issues apart, the revolutionary movement in France, and the handful of Russian exiles in Geneva, could scarcely be said to inhabit the same political universe: in the 1860's and for some time thereafter, Marx saw no reason to take Russian emigrants seriously.

[1] For Marx's relations with Blanqui, cf. Spitzer, op. cit., pp. 115 ff; Auguste Cornu, *Karl Marx et la Révolution de 1848*, Paris, 1948, pp. 62–3. There are a number of friendly references to Blanqui in the Marx-Engels correspondence. On March 1, 1869, Marx informed Engels that Lafargue had transmitted a cordial message from Blanqui (cf. MEGA III/4, p. 159).

[2] Cf. his mordant account of Bakunin's personality and record in *Ein Complott gegen die Internationale Arbeiter-Assoziation*, Braunschweig, 1874: the German version of the pamphlet he circulated after Bakunin's expulsion from the International.

[3] Ibid., pp. 91 ff. Cf. also *L'Alliance de la Démocratie Socialiste et L'Association Internationale des Travailleurs*, London, 1873. This was the sequel to an earlier pamphlet: *Les prétendues scissions dans l'Internationale*, Geneva, 1872; reprinted in *Le mouvement socialiste*, No. 253/4, 1913; German text now in Karl Marx—*Politische Schriften*, ed. Lieber, Stuttgart, 1960, vol. II, pp. 958 ff. For details of Marx's personal involvement in the resulting split within the International and his share in the composition of these pamphlets, see *Karl Marx—Chronik seines Lebens in Einzeldaten*, Moscow, 1934, pp. 322 ff.

THE COMMUNE

COMMUNISM IS A TERM which in the course of time has acquired a variety of meanings. In the 1840's it was associated with the conspiratorial *Société Communiste* in which old Montagnards and youthful plotters came together on a common platform.[1] In the 1870's it signified the Paris Commune of 1871. There is irony in the fact that the Commune's leadership did not include a single communist in the modern sense of the term, and at best one delegate who could be called a Marxist: not untypically he was a refugee from Hungary.[2] After its fall Marx was to impose the heritage of the Commune upon the Social-Democratic movement. This was a remarkable *tour de force* even in France, where the massacre perpetrated by the forces of 'order' in May 1871 blended easily with memories of the slaughter of Parisian workers by the Army and the National Guard in the June 1848 insurrection.[3] Beyond the borders of France it was scarcely possible to see in the Commune anything but the final catastrophe of the old romantic French socialism. This was how Marx himself came to view the matter a decade later, when passions had cooled. But by then a myth had been established.

The Paris Commune of March–May, 1871, in one of its aspects,

[1] Dolléans, op. cit., I, pp. 174 ff. [2] Cole, op. cit., II, pp. 148 ff.
[3] Marx, *The Civil War in France*, MESW I, pp. 536 ff.

was the last of the revolutionary convulsions through which the Republic consolidated itself after 1789. While aware of this circumstance, Marx held that it was also the first major rebellion of the modern industrial proletariat. This view had for its corollary the belief that France was setting the pace for the struggle between capital and labour. But Marx himself had observed that France was economically and socially lagging behind England, and that its political struggles reflected this backwardness.[1] After the failure of the Commune he saw more clearly that the repeated proletarian rebellions were evidence of political immaturity, and towards the end of his life he said as much—in a letter which was published much later.[2] He thus came close to echoing the advice Proudhon had given the French workers twenty years earlier: not to let themselves be drawn into political uprisings which did not benefit their class. Yet in the 1860's Marx had favoured Blanqui rather than Proudhon, though neither he nor Engels had any illusions about the antiquated character of Blanqui's doctrine in which France figured as the pre-destined leader of humanity. Characteristically, the Blanquists took no interest whatever in the International. Nor was it possible for Marx to hold with Blanqui that Paris was the *véritable représentation nationale* in all circumstances—even if the rest of the country repudiated its leadership: 'Paris, the true representative, the concentrated essence of the nation, dominates the assembly (i.e., the legislature) which is only its material and nominal emanation.'[3] To Marx this was precisely the kind of old-fashioned Jacobin romanticism which the Paris workers would have to outgrow.[4]

These contradictions were subsequently enshrined in the official ideology of Marxist Social-Democracy—itself a term of dubious ancestry, since Social-Democracy originally signified a coalition of workers, peasants and the urban lower middle class (collectively known as 'the people') against 'the aristocracy': the latter including

[1] *Class Struggles in France*, MESW I, p. 211.

[2] Marx to F. A. Sorge, November 5, 1880. 'This (the recent formation of socialist groups in France who had adopted a "reformist" programme drawn up for them by Marx) . . . is *the first real labour movement in France*. Up to the present time only sects existed there, which naturally received their slogans from the founder of the sect, whereas the mass of the proletariat followed the radical or pseudo-radical bourgeois and fought for them on the decisive day, only to be slaughtered, deported, etc., on the very next day by the fellows they had hoisted into the saddle.' MESC, pp. 404–5.

[3] Blanqui, Unpublished MSS, 9581, pp. 93, 121; quoted by Spitzer, op. cit., p. 167.

[4] Bloom, op. cit., pp. 126–33.

both the old landed nobility and the 'aristocracy of money', to employ the significant term much in vogue in the 1840's. In this traditional sense it could perhaps be held that the Paris Commune had been a Social-Democratic enterprise, for had it not claimed to represent the entire people, and were there not among its leaders old-fashioned Jacobin republicans, alongside Proudhonist socialists, Blanquist 'communists', and newfangled Internationalists? This is as much as to say that the Commune belonged to the old world of the 'bourgeois revolution', or at most that it represented a transitional phase; which is precisely what Marx and Engels came to suggest in later years, thereby salvaging 'scientific socialism' from the utopian shipwreck. But before casting anchor on this new shore they felt constrained to pay tribute to the older deities on which they, no less than the Parisian workers, were reluctant to turn their backs.[1]

These Parisian workers were not, in 1871, 'factory hands' in the English sense, any more than they had been in 1848. The majority were employed in small establishments, and indeed were craftsmen rather than industrial proletarians.[2] This state of affairs (as Marx knew perfectly well and never ceased to deplore) explained the influence of Proudhon, since his schemes for establishing producers' co-operatives were calculated to fit the interests (and the illusions) of artisans not yet drawn into the industrial maelstrom. In the *Inaugural Address* of 1864 Marx had made his bow to tradition by explaining that co-operative production demonstrated the possibility of socialism;[3] though he had also emphasised that 'co-operative labour ought

---

[1] The Blanquists of course held that it was the duty of Paris to legislate for the rest of France; but this conviction was shared by their allies in the Commune, including the disciples of Auguste Comte, who were on principle opposed to socialism. They too believed that the workers, 'belonging to the most numerous class, their views have the greatest generality; having interests which are least implicated in local affairs, (they) display the greatest disinterestedness; finally, being the hardest pressed by the need for social reconstruction, they are the most . . . revolutionary section. On all these counts, it is just that political power in France should belong to Paris; and on all these counts, too, power comes to the proletariat.' (E. Sémerie, '*La République et le peuple souverain,*' *Mémoire lu au Club Positiviste de Paris, April 3, 1871.* Quoted by R. Harrison, 'E. S. Beesly and Karl Marx', loc. cit., p. 210.)

[2] Clapham, op. cit., p. 71: 'The number of concerns employing more than a hundred people in 1848 was so small that they could not much affect the average for the whole country. Outside mining and metallurgy they hardly existed . . . More than twenty years later, out of 101,000 people in Paris classed as *fabricants,* 62,000 worked alone or with only one assistant . . .'

[3] 'The value of these great social experiments cannot be overrated. By deed, instead of by argument, they have shown that production on a large scale, and

114

to be developed to national dimensions, and consequently . . . fostered by national means', which in turn depended upon the conquest of political power by the working class.[1] This fell short of the socialisation of the means of production—a slogan which Marx could not at this stage have incorporated into the programme of the International without antagonising the bulk of the French delegates.[2] For not only Tolain and his group, but the majority of French socialists in the 1860's, were 'mutualists' and hostile to 'collectivism': the society to which they looked forward was one in which every man would own property and receive the full fruit of his labour, either personally or through a co-operative producers' association: the latter to be financed by 'gratuitous credit'—i.e., interest-free loans—advanced to them by a People's Credit Bank, which was to be an autonomous public institution, written into the constitution, but in no sense under government control.[3]

To Marx all this was the merest fantasy. He had, however, no wish to engage in a doctrinaire dispute over co-operation and socialisation: not merely because it would have been tactically unwise, but because he did not in fact regard it as an urgent issue. It was no part of his scheme to induce the existing governments to take over the control of industry. Only a state controlled by the workers could be trusted to participate in the socialisation of production. On this point, as it happened, both Proudhonists and collectivists were in agreement with him, while in England the issue of state aid had been dead since the early days of Owen: the co-operative movement here was developing on a purely voluntary basis.[4] Moreover, the real drive within the International came from the trade union movement which pitted the industrial workers against the employers, i.e., followed what Marx considered the best way of curing the workers of their residual illusions about class harmony. In this respect he had been able until 1870 to feel that time was on his side. Hence the confusion caused by Bakunin's propaganda from 1868 onward seemed to him essentially trivial. If Bakunin and his followers thought fit to argue that the International should go on record against the existence of God, the authority of the state, or the morality of inheritance, they

in accord with the behests of modern science, may be carried on without the existence of a class of masters employing a class of hands; that to bear fruit, the means of labour need not be monopolised as a means of domination over, and extortion against the labouring man himself . . .' *Inaugural Address of the W.M.I.A.*, MESW I, p. 383.   [1] Ibid., pp. 383–4.
[2] Cole, op. cit., II, p. 94.   [3] Ibid.   [4] Ibid., p. 97.

were to his mind merely introducing a childish irritant which the labour movement could be trusted to outgrow.[1]

All this was changed in an instant by the catastrophe of the Paris Commune. Not only did this political earthquake revive all the old Jacobin-Blanquist illusions about the revolutionary dictatorship of Paris over the rest of France: it also fused the issue of co-operation versus collectivisation with the Proudhonist-Bakuninist hostility to the state. Nearly all the leading Communards had been opposed to centralisation and in favour of reorganising France, after the defeat of 1870–1, on the basis of a federation of free communes. Even a 'collectivist' like Varlin, who in the 1860's had moved steadily away from 'mutualism' and craft unionism, was a confirmed 'federalist': the France he looked forward to was not a centralised Republic on the Jacobin model, but a federation of autonomous communes, with the authority of the central power reduced to a minimum. In short, the state was to 'wither away'. If the Jacobins and the Blanquists, who together formed the majority on the elected council of the Commune, were opposed to such a wide delegation of authority, they did not for the moment make an issue of it, the more so since all parties were agreed that Paris must take the lead in the revolution.[2]

The isolation of the Commune from the remainder of France meant that these issues could not be put to the test, while in Paris the brief experience of quasi-socialist rule only resulted in a few innocuous measures which had nothing to do with socialism in either its Proudhonist or its Marxist form.[3] What made the Commune important were not its achievements (which were derisory), or

[1] Marx to Engels, March 5, 1869, MESC, pp. 265–6.

[2] Cole, op. cit., pp. 140 ff; Spitzer, op. cit., pp. 154 ff. Of the labour leaders prominent in the International, Tolain took no part in the rising. Varlin was shot after the fighting, along with an estimated 20,000 prisoners who were massacred by the Versailles forces. To make matters more confusing, the Internationalists—chiefly Varlin and the Hungarian Leo Frankel, who escaped —were among the outstanding moderates when it came to reprisals, while the terrorist wing was led by the Blanquists and the old-style Jacobins. The latter included Arthur Ranc, who later became an associate of Gambetta and one of the more prominent figures of the Third Republic.

[3] Cole, op. cit., pp. 157 ff. Leo Frankel, who was in charge of Labour and Industry, did his best to get workshops abandoned by their owners re-opened as co-operatives; he also abolished night baking. That was about the sum total of the social reforms introduced during the two months of the Commune's existence. In part its activities were financed by the Bank of France, which went on operating all through the revolution, on the understanding that it was to be left alone if it provided enough funds to help the authorities carry on with their daily work.

116

the clamour of some of its leaders for a revolutionary war against 'the Prussians' (which was an exercise in old-fashioned Jacobinism), but the fact that despite its evident harmlessness it was drowned in blood by the Versailles government, spurred on by a frenzied legislature in which rural monarchists and clericals predominated. Confronted with this display of savagery, against which bourgeois liberalism raised only the most muted protest, it was impossible for the nascent Social-Democratic movement to remain silent. Moreover, the official hysteria had transmitted itself to the bulk of middle-class opinion all over Europe, with the result that the International—which had next to nothing to do with the outbreak—was held responsible for all the real or imagined outrages of the Communards. Even had they wished to do so, Socialists belonging to it could not have dissociated themselves from the disaster that had befallen their comrades. If any doubts persisted they were stilled by Marx's impassioned defence of the Paris rising, whose tragic defeat he represented as 'the glorious harbinger of a new society'.[1]

The immediate consequence of the Paris upheaval was to wreck the International—not so much because it was persecuted by the European governments, but because the British trade unions withdrew, while its Continental followers were disrupted by the conflict between the factions led respectively by Marx and Bakunin.[2] This is often represented as a struggle between Social-Democracy and Anarchism; it is more accurately described as the occasion for the formation of these two rival movements. In 1872–4, when the conflict was at its height, there were only shades of difference in regard to what was later assumed to be the main issue, i.e., the role of the state. For all Bakunin's diatribes against the 'authoritarian doctrine' of Marx, the latter had embodied the substance of the Proudhonist 'federal' scheme in his manifesto on the Commune:[3] much to the indignation of the Bakuninists who accused him of having done so merely in order to 'annex' the memory of the martyrs to his own cause. On this issue most of Marx's French supporters after 1871 were Blanquist refugees—but they could not be described as adherents to his doctrines, their only point of agreement with him being belief in the need for a temporary dictatorship during the revolution.[4]

[1] *The Civil War in France*, MESW I, p. 542.
[2] Cole, op. cit., II, pp. 174 ff.
[3] *The Civil War in France*, loc. cit., pp. 519 ff.
[4] Cole, op. cit., II, pp. 198 ff; Spitzer, op. cit., pp. 157 ff.

Marx had no use for their conspiratorial tactics, their belief in leadership by a self-appointed vanguard, and their over-estimation of the role of Paris; to say nothing of their antiquated vision of France as the revolutionary Messiah among the nations—a tradition they shared with the old-style Jacobins who had been their allies during the Commune. And they in turn could make nothing of his concern for trade union organisation and the self-emancipation of the working class. The surviving Proudhonists were equally unhelpful, most of them eventually joining Bakunin. The only French labour leader who had ever come close to Marx's position in these matters was Varlin; and Varlin was dead.[1]

What made the whole issue so confusing was that while the Commune had largely been run by the Jacobin-Blanquist majority—plus a handful of Internationalists in direct touch with the General Council in London (i.e., with Marx)—its proclaimed goals were Proudhonist: 'federalism', i.e., the replacement of bureaucratic centralisation by local self-government, being foremost among its aims. There were no 'state socialists' among its leaders—even Varlin urged workers' control of industry, rather than state ownership of the means of production.[2] What then did communism mean? To the Jacobin-Blanquist majority it evidently meant the revolutionary dictatorship of Paris over the rest of France, on the model of 1793, though exercised in the name of the proletariat: and this was how Thiers and the rural conservatives in the National Assembly at Versailles saw the matter, whence their determination to drown the rebellion in blood. Yet the Commune had been democratically elected and could legitimately claim to be the properly constituted government of Paris. From a legal viewpoint it was simply the municipal government—though a municipality on which socialists for the first time held power. It could not well be described as a

---

[1] Michel Collinet, *La Tragédie du Marxisme*, Paris, 1948, pp. 143 ff; Cole, op. cit., II, pp. 204 ff; Bloom, op. cit., pp. 130 ff. For Marx's and Engels's view of Jacobin-Blanquist revolutionary nationalism, cf. MESC, pp. 216-17, 294-5. For Blanqui's patriotic attitude during the siege of Paris in 1870, cf. Spitzer, op. cit., pp. 116 ff. It was difficult for Marx to criticise the line Blanqui took, since he agreed with him in believing that the French bourgeoisie had systematically sabotaged the defence of Paris, preferring defeat to a victory won with the help of popular revolution. (Cf. Marx to Kugelmann, February 4, 1871, MESC, pp. 311-12.) Marx was in fact throughout this period torn between his dislike of French chauvinism and his desire for a French victory—but not one that would endanger Germany's recently established unity.

[2] Collinet, op. cit., p. 144.

'proletarian dictatorship', for not only had it been duly elected, but its political composition ran all the way from middle-class republicans to socialists of the most varied hues. But for the panic flight of a large number of propertied citizens it probably would have had a bourgeois-republican majority. Even so its armed defenders included considerable numbers of men who represented the traditional republicanism of the French middle class.

In his pamphlet, which was to become one of the canonical texts of Social-Democracy, and later of Communism—though each gave it a different interpretation—Marx straddled these issues in a manner which to this day has enabled adherents of both schools of thought to claim him for their master. Reviving his 1848–52 polemics against the 'parasitic growth' of bureaucracy in France, he drew a picture of the 'centralised State power, with its ubiquitous organs of standing army, police, bureaucracy, clergy, and judicature—organs wrought after the plan of a systematic and hierarchic division of labour'.[1] This 'ready-made State machinery' the working class could not 'simply lay hold of . . . and wield it for its own purposes'.[2] Already in 1848 this truth had been dimly felt, and now at last the Commune had clarified it. 'The direct antithesis to the Empire was the Commune. The cry of "social republic" with which the revolution of February (sc. 1848) was ushered in by the Paris proletariat, did but express a vague aspiration after a Republic that was not only to supersede the monarchical form of class-rule, but class-rule itself. The Commune was the positive form of that Republic.'[3]

The Commune, moreover, had been both an elected body and a true representation of the working class. It was 'formed of the municipal councillors, chosen by universal suffrage in the various wards of the town . . . The majority of its members were naturally working men, or acknowledged representatives of the working class.'[4] Marx regarded this as 'natural' because after all the majority of the population belonged to the working class; yet the industrial proletariat properly so-called was a minority even within the general working population. The pamphlet goes on to declare that 'the Commune was to be a working, not a parliamentary body (sic), executive and legislative at the same time':[5] a formula which was later to become a Leninist shibboleth. Lastly, 'the Paris Commune was of course to serve as a model to all the great industrial centres in France. The

---

[1] *The Civil War in France*, loc. cit., p. 516.   [2] Ibid.
[3] Ibid., pp. 518–19.   [4] Ibid., p. 519.   [5] Ibid.

communal regime once established in Paris and the secondary centres, the old centralised Government would in the provinces, too, have to give way to the self-government of the producers.'[1] That indeed was what the 'federals' had believed, but it is odd to find Marx lending his support to this amiable piece of wish-fulfilment.

Was he justified in terms of contemporary opinion? The local commune was indeed the traditional unit of administration. France was made up of communes, and every opponent of the monstrous centralised state apparatus tended to think of his local commune as the focus of popular resistance to the government—a government which the industrial workers had come to identify with an oppressive ruling class. Yet the Paris Commune had represented 'the workers' only because the propertied classes had fled, and outside Paris the towns were islands in an agrarian sea. What was to be the relationship of the reorganised urban centres to the country population—a population still under the sway of the local nobility and clergy, and only too ready, as soldiers, to carry fire and sword through the proletarian suburbs of the great cities? In 1871 Marx seemed to have thought that he held the answer. As he formulated it, it was a conclusion curiously resembling the vision of his old enemy Proudhon:

It is generally the fate of completely new historical creations to be mistaken for the counterpart of older and even defunct forms of social life to which they may bear a certain likeness. Thus this new Commune, which breaks the modern State power, has been mistaken for a reproduction of the medieval Communes which first preceded and afterward became the substratum of, that very State power . . . The Communal Constitution would have restored to the social body all the forces hitherto absorbed by the State parasite feeding upon and clogging the free movement of society. By this one act it would have initiated the regeneration of France . . . the Communal Constitution brought the rural producers under the intellectual lead of the central towns of their districts, and thus secured to them, in the working men, the natural trustees of their interests.[2]

It may readily be granted that this was an ultra-democratic vision; for this very reason it was also a utopian one. It was likewise new for Marx to say nothing about the establishment of a centralised revolutionary government, and to usher in the reign of liberty without further preliminaries. On this point he seemed in 1871 to have come close to Proudhon. Yet when in his *Critique of the Gotha Programme* four years later he referred to the 'dictatorship of the proletariat', he did not mention the example of the Commune! Apparently, then, the

[1] Ibid., p. 520. [2] Ibid., p. 521.

'federal' solution was suitable for France alone, and perhaps on second thoughts not even for France.[1]

Nor was he consistent in defending the rightness of the decision to rise in arms, under the eyes of the victorious Prussian army which stood ready to back the Versailles government. In 1871 he had been emphatic in declaring that even should the rising be crushed, it was 'the most glorious deed of our party since the June (1848) insurrection'.[2] Yet a decade later he told a Dutch correspondent that 'a socialist government does not come into power . . . unless conditions are so developed that it can immediately take the necessary measures for intimidating the mass of the bourgeoisie sufficiently to gain time —the first desideratum—for permanent action'. And he went on:

> Perhaps you will refer me to the Paris Commune; but apart from the fact that this was merely the rising of a city under exceptional conditions, the majority of the Commune was in no way socialist, nor could it be. With a modicum of common-sense, however, it could have reached a compromise with Versailles useful to the whole people—the only thing that could be attained at the time. The appropriation of the Bank of France alone would have been enough to put a rapid end to the rodomontades of the Versailles crowd, etc.[3]

This was to be Marx's final verdict on the Commune, and in time it became the settled judgment of those Socialists who felt that in following him they had forever broken with the utopian tradition preserved by the Anarchists. In practice this meant the Social-Democratic movement in Western Europe and the United States. It did not then occur to its representatives—most of whom had meanwhile assumed the habit of describing themselves as Marxists—that the issue would one day be revived.

[1] Collinet, op. cit., pp. 144 ff; cf. *Critique of the Gotha Programme*, MESW II, p. 30.

[2] Letter to Kugelmann, April 12, 1871, MESC, pp. 318–19. 'After six months of hunger and ruin, caused by internal treachery more even than by the external enemy, they rise, beneath Prussian bayonets, as if there had never been a war between France and Germany and the enemy were not still at the gates of Paris! History has no like example of greatness! . . . Compare these heaven-storming Parisians with the heavenly slaves of the German-Prussian Holy Roman Empire . . .'

[3] Marx to F. Domela-Nieuwenhuis, February 22, 1881, MESC, p. 410 (Text after the original, in *Ausgewaehlte Briefe*, Berlin, 1953, pp. 406–7).

6

THE PERMANENT REVOLUTION

IT IS TIME for a summing-up. We have seen how Marx and Engels anticipated the revolutionary upheaval of 1848 with the publication of the *Communist Manifesto*, and how in 1871 Marx reacted to the catastrophe of the Paris Commune with a qualified restatement of the traditional revolutionary standpoint in his pamphlet *The Civil War in France*. In between these two important dates, the founding of the First International in 1864 had quietly inaugurated the appearance on the scene of a new political force: the modern labour movement, committed to democratic socialism. Marx stood at the centre of these currents; the streams of history converged in his person. In 1871 he enshrined the memory of the Commune in a pamphlet whose grandiose rhetoric rang down the curtain on an epoch, yet at the same time he managed to keep alive the heritage of revolutionary utopianism. In the following year he drove Bakunin's adherents from the International, and for good measure affirmed his own belief in the possibility of a peaceful transition to socialism wherever democracy was far enough advanced.[1] Ever since then it has been possible

---

[1] In an address to a meeting in Amsterdam, on September 8, 1872, following the conclusion of the congress which expelled Bakunin; cf. B. Nicolaevsky and O. Maenchen-Helfen, *Karl Marx: Man and Fighter*, pp. 363–4 (hereafter cited as Nicolaevsky).

for Social-Democrats and Communists alike to appeal to his authority; and for good reason. The contradictions latent in his outlook were fused into a doctrine which Janus-like confronted the beholder whatever his angle of vision.

The roots of the dilemma are traceable to the earliest and least understood chapter in the history of Marxism: the role of Marx and Engels in the secret Communist League of the late 'forties and early 'fifties.[1] It was here that the founders of modern socialism first encountered the workers' movement, and this circumstance inevitably left its mark, long after they had broken with conspiratorial politics in general and the League in particular. For the League was not merely a secret society—that was something it had in common with half the revolutionary movements of its time, including some whose political aims were tamely liberal. It was the repository of the communist dream in its original Messianic form. Those who joined it had by that very act broken with the existing world and committed themselves to aims not realisable as long as society was organised into classes, held together by the state, and synonymous with the nation. The new vision not merely invalidated these traditional concepts: it declared them to be superfluous and on the point of being superseded by the proletarian revolution, which would usher in a society without classes, without exploitation, and—most remarkable of all—without national affiliations. It was precisely this vision which distinguished the communists of the 1840's from the socialists: doctrinaire reformers who merely wished to place society on a stabler basis.

But the League was also the extreme wing of the 'bourgeois' revolution then preparing in Germany, and when that revolution broke out, its leaders found themselves involved with a democratic movement whose aims, so far from being communist, were not even socialist: there was as yet in Central Europe no labour movement to

[1] Cf. Engels, *On the History of the Communist League*, MESW II, pp. 306 ff; Nicolaevsky, op. cit., pp. 107 ff. Engels's brief sketch leaves many details unexplained, but brings out the Blanquist and Babouvist roots of the organisation, as it grew out of the earlier 'League of the Just' founded in Paris in 1836 by radical German workmen influenced by French doctrines. '. . . the League was at that time actually not much more than the German branch of the French secret societies, especially the *Société des Saisons* led by Blanqui and Barbès . . .' (Engels, loc. cit., p. 307). This situation changed in the 1840's, but the link with the French societies, notably with Blanqui and his group, was never entirely severed. For an historical sketch of these conspiratorial sects, cf. E. J. Hobsbawm, *Primitive Rebels*, Manchester, 1959, pp. 150 ff.

lend real weight to such tendencies; indeed there was hardly an industrial working-class. The revolution, moreover, was not merely 'bourgeois' but 'national', its immediate aim being the unification of Germany. The only 'internationalism' possible in this situation was one which had little in common with that of the Communist League, but could be justified on traditional Jacobin lines: a revolutionary alliance of French, German, Polish, Italian, and Hungarian democrats against the powers of the Holy Alliance. In the circumstances of 1848–9 this programme made excellent sense, and the League did its best to propagate it. But it was not specifically communist, and it entailed support for every national movement that revolted against its ancient oppressors. Marx's repeated assertions in 1848–9 that 'the revolution' would win once the Paris proletariat had triumphed over its oppressors[1] established only the slenderest kind of link between the 'bourgeois' and the 'proletarian' components of the League's ideology—and only as long as the revolutionary intoxication lasted. After 1850 the hope of an impending social transformation faded, and with it the conviction of Marx's associates that their role in it would be that of the Jacobins in the 'old' revolution.[2]

What this role would have involved, had the opportunity for it occurred in Western Europe, may be gathered from a document which received little attention during the heyday of Social-Democracy after 1871, but was given due prominence by Leninists from 1917 onward: the *Address of the Central Committee to the Communist League* drawn up by Marx and Engels in March 1850, i.e., at a time when they believed another revolutionary outbreak on the Continent to be imminent. Here is to be found the entire compendium of Communist tactics in a bourgeois-democratic revolution: from the 'united front' strategy to the systematic undermining of one's allies, and the establishment of 'proletarian dictatorship'.[3] Even a hint of terrorism is not lacking: Marx was then under the influence of Blanqui and—

[1] Cf. the article entitled 'Neujahr 1849' in Mehring ed., *Gesammelte Schriften von Karl Marx und Friedrich Engels*, III, pp. 230–2.

[2] Mehring, op. cit., pp. 80 ff; Nicolaevsky, op. cit., pp. 155 ff. It has often been noted that the leaders of the Communist League ran their organ, the *Neue Rheinische Zeitung*, as a 'bourgeois-democratic' vehicle and took virtually no interest in the nascent labour movement, which was altogether 'reformist'. These tactics led to violent conflicts with rival groups in Germany, and after 1850 they were decisive in bringing about the dissolution of the whole organisation.

[3] MESW I, pp. 106 ff. For an analysis of this remarkable document, cf. Nicolaevsky, op. cit., pp. 206 ff.

not for the last time—in a tactical alliance with the Blanquist emigrants in London. The latter even persuaded him to join a super-secret international society, which seems to have quietly faded away after a few months. Nothing came of all this in the short run, the less so since Marx soon concluded that the revolutionary era was over. Yet he never quite repudiated his activities during this period, just as on the other hand he never regretted having advocated a purely 'bourgeois-democratic' strategy for Germany in 1848–9: on the latter point he had even been ready to break with close associates.

The long-term significance of these experiments was to be considerable. They were never quite forgotten, and when the revolutionary movement came to a head in Russia around 1905 their spirit was revived by Lenin. By that time the West European movement had become democratic, and Marxism itself now signified the theoretical justification of peaceful and 'reformist' tactics, as against the antiquated revolutionism of Bakunin's anarcho-syndicalist progeny. But the *Communist Manifesto* and the *Address of the Central Committee* could still be quoted, and these documents breathed a very different spirit. Western Social-Democrats might dismiss these writings as relics of a bygone age. Even in France, Blanquism no longer counted after 1871, now that the Republic was firmly established and the labour movement had begun to evolve on democratic lines; while in Germany, henceforth the main stronghold of Marxist Social-Democracy, the *Manifesto* and the *Address* were not taken seriously even by the most orthodox Marxists.[1] Their assumptions had been abandoned: tacitly by Marx himself, explicitly by Engels and his German followers. They presupposed a pattern of events which experience had shown to be no longer possible in Europe— or indeed in any advanced country. But the obverse also applied: where the pre-1848 situation still existed, the fire that had gone out in the West might still burst into flames.[2]

It is not clear to what extent Marx himself perceived the significance of his brief Jacobin-Blanquist aberration in 1850. Six months after

---

[1] Cf. Mehring's treatment of the subject in his *Karl Marx*, pp. 200 ff.

[2] In his *History of the Communist League*, Engels skims over this point, with a brief remark to the effect that 'The Address . . . is still of interest today, because petty-bourgeois democracy is still the party which must certainly be the first to come to power in Germany as the saviour of society from the communist workers on the occasion of the next European upheaval now soon due.' This hardly squared with the actual theory and practice of German Social-Democracy at the time when he was writing, i.e., in 1885. But what was irrelevant for Germany might become important for Russia.

drafting the *Address* he broke with the majority of his German associates, among others on the grounds that they were trying to force the pace. 'While we say to the workers: you have fifteen or twenty or fifty years of war and civil war to go through, not just to alter the existing circumstances, but to change yourselves and make yourselves fit for political power—you on the contrary say: we must obtain power at once. . . . While we draw the workers' attention to the undeveloped state of the German proletariat, you outrageously flatter the national sentiments and social prejudices of the German artisan. . . . Just as the democrats made a sacred entity of the word "people", so do you with the word "proletariat". . . .'[1] There was here a hint of a new attitude, but no specific recognition that the day of Blanquist *coups* might be over for good.

By the 1870's this realisation had sunk in, and even the Paris Commune—though for a moment it revived the old revolutionary fervour—did not permanently dislodge Marx from his mature standpoint. As the modern democratic labour movement took shape, it became evident that its aims and methods were essentially different from those of the "old" revolutionary movement: now seen to belong to a bygone age, at any rate in Western Europe. The strategy of the Communist League was now paradoxically revealed to have fitted the circumstances of a 'bourgeois' revolution rather than the needs of the emerging labour movement. The latter, where it was able to develop in more or less democratic conditions, adopted what it could from the corpus of Marxist doctrines, but took no interest in the slogan which in 1848–50 had seemed to the leaders of the Communist League to sum up its purpose as well as its strategy: 'The Revolution in Permanence!'

In 1850 this slogan possessed a perfectly clear operational meaning. As Marx put it in the *Address*, it was the task of the workers to arm themselves during the first stage of a democratic upsurge against the old regime, and having acquired arms with the benevolent connivance of their bourgeois-democratic allies, 'to dictate such conditions to them that the rule of the bourgeois democrats will from the outset carry the seeds of its downfall, and their subsequent extrusion by . . . the proletariat . . . be considerably facilitated. . . . Above all, the workers must . . . compel the democrats to carry out their present terrorist phrases. . . . Alongside of the new official government they must establish simultaneously their own revolutionary workers'

[1] Mehring, *Karl Marx*, p. 206.

government, whether in the form of . . . municipal councils, or workers' clubs or workers' committees, so that the bourgeois-democratic authorities . . . from the outset see themselves supervised and threatened by authorities backed by the whole mass of the workers. . . .' This was the Blanquist strategy in a nutshell. As practised in France—or rather in Paris—by Blanqui's followers in 1848-9, it was both a foretaste of the 1871 Commune and a throwback to the Jacobin-Babouvist risings of 1793-6. After all it was not for nothing that Buonarroti had been the teacher of Blanqui and indeed of an entire generation of youthful rebels who won their spurs in the 1830 rising. The aged 'Nestor of the Revolution' was the progenitor of the conspiratorial *Société des Saisons* from which in the 1840's the German Communist League had branched off.

The only trouble was that all this had extraordinarily little to do with the actual circumstances in which the handful of German Communists were placed after 1850. As soon as Marx realised this—it did not take him long—he dissolved the League, turned his back upon the Blanquist emissaries (though not upon Blanqui himself), and for the remainder of his life adamantly refused to engage in revolutionary conspiracy. Moreover, he renounced—at least by implication—the entire perspective sketched out in the confidential 1850 circular. This new orientation was to culminate in the doctrine laid down in the *Inaugural Address* of 1864. Western Europe having turned the corner and acquired democratic institutions, however inadequate, the ancient revolutionary model was clearly out of date. It was not formally repudiated, merely allowed to drop out of sight. This attitude became the corner-stone of Social-Democratic Marxism from 1871 onward. It took the first Russian revolution of 1905 to introduce a new political line-up.

But this is to anticipate. The point to note here is that Marx's tacit renunciation of Blanquism also entailed the abandonment of the vanguard concept. In the brief but crucial history of French revolutionary socialism between 1830 and 1870 this concept had implied at once the dictatorship of Paris over the rest of France, and the dictatorship of the proletariat over the rest of society. Both had suffered shipwreck in the Commune. Both were now discredited, along with the entire Jacobin-Babouvist tradition on which French republicanism, and subsequently French socialism, had fed since the Great Revolution. There was of course no corresponding tradition in Germany, nor did its profoundly unrevolutionary labour movement require to be told that insurrections were out of date: Bismarckian Germany was already launched on its own course of development, and German Social-Democracy shared little more than the name with the survivors of the Commune. In German eyes the adoption of Marxism signified that the era of romantic revolution was closed.

The issue could be revived only if a situation corresponding to that in France before 1871 arose in Eastern Europe. For here the old regime was still intact, and an effective challenge required at the very least the active participation of the workers in the struggle for democracy. Because this was to become the key issue in the history of Russian socialism, it is important to state exactly what it was that distinguished Marx's attitude from that of Blanqui on the all-important subject of political leadership. Both men, as we have seen, were largely in agreement—at any rate down to 1871—on the necessity of a temporary dictatorship under circumstances such as those which had repeatedly arisen in France. But whereas Blanqui was all his life fundamentally indifferent to the labour movement, Marx eventually came to adopt the view that working-class activity provided the only yardstick by which the progress of socialism could be measured. In practice this meant that the character as well as the tempo of political action had to be regulated by the spontaneously formed aspirations and beliefs of authentic labour leaders—not by the preconceived notions of a self-appointed vanguard for the most part composed of intellectuals. Here was a genuine cleavage of the most fundamental kind. Blanqui's indifference to the real workers' movement; his tendency to lump all the 'toilers' together under the comprehensive label of 'the people'; his old-fashioned Jacobin chauvinism and his worship of conspiracy—all marked him off as a representative of the 'old' revolutionary creed. It was a necessary consequence of his outlook that popular movements not controlled by a conspiratorial elite of 'professional revolutionaries'—the type, though not the term, was already in existence—should incur his hostility or indifference. In this respect Leninism was later to demonstrate a remarkable resemblance to the Blanquist model; whereas Marx—for all the personal sympathy he repeatedly expressed for the old conspirator—had never (save for a brief moment in 1850) seriously considered adopting his strategy. The only 'vanguard' he was prepared to trust was one composed of authentic labour leaders; and the only thing he demanded of them was that they should recognise the *political* character of labour's protracted struggle for emancipation: as Varlin and his group had finally done in the late 1860's, when they broke with Proudhon's teaching and came round to the view that the working class must gain political power. Because this was the basic test he applied to the workers' movement, Marx in the end evolved a political outlook which fitted the requirements of the modern age. In this mature conception, labour's conquest of power represents an aspect of the struggle for democracy. Capital and labour now confront one another as rivals within a political setting whose nature determines the form—and to a considerable degree the content—of their struggle for predominance. Democratic socialism takes its place alongside democratic liberalism as the universally recognised expression of labour's slow rise to maturity and power. If Marx never expressly repudiated the 'Jacobin' model enshrined in the *Manifesto*, he did not in practice allow it to hamper him. The pragmatic theorist who guided the uncertain steps of the First International, and who preserved its heritage after the catastrophe of the Paris Commune, had finally outgrown the man of 1848.

PART FOUR

THE THEORY OF BOURGEOIS SOCIETY 1850–1895

1

THE VICTORIAN WATERSHED

IN ATTENDING TO the course of events in Europe, down to the Paris Commune and the dissolution of the First International, the preceding part necessarily left an important gap in respect of Marxist theory properly so called. In particular, very little has so far been said about Marx's economic studies, and nothing about *Capital*, the bulk of which took shape in the 1860's. The resulting white spaces on the map must now be filled, and to this end we are obliged to retrace our steps in time by some twenty years, reckoning back from the catastrophe of 1871 which marked the close of the revolutionary era in Continental Europe. This brings us to 1851—the date of the great Industrial Exhibition which provided Victorian England with a suitable opportunity for celebrating the peaceful conquests of free trade. When the first volume of *Capital* was published in 1867, the liberal era was at its height; the 1890's by contrast witnessed a significant slackening of the characteristic Victorian optimism, side by side with a revival of socialist tendencies in Britain. The biographical data—Marx returned to his economic studies in 1851, and the concluding volume of *Capital* was published by Engels in 1894, a year before his death—fit easily into this framework, which has the additional merit of clarifying the connection between liberal and socialist economics, while rendering somewhat more comprehensible the internal logic of the

133

Marxian system. As we shall see, that system has much in common with other creations of the Victorian age. If there are general grounds for describing Marxism as 'essentially a product of the bourgeois mind',[1] this description applies with special force to those writings of Marx and Engels which represent, as it were, the critical counter-point to the almost perpetual Victorian celebration. At times indeed the critics themselves joined the chorus:

We now turn to America. The most important factum here . . . is the discovery of the Californian goldfields. Even now, after barely eighteen months, one can foresee that this discovery is due to have even more grandiose results than that of America itself. For three hundred and thirty years the entire trade between Europe and the Pacific has . . . revolved around the Cape of Good Hope, or around Cape Horn. All projects for a shortcut via the Panamanian isthmus were wrecked by the narrow-minded jealousy of the trading nations. The Californian goldmines were discovered eighteen months ago, and already the Yankees have started a railway, a major highway, a canal from the Gulf of Mexico; already steamers ply the routes from New York to Chagres, from Panama to San Francisco; already the Pacific trade centres on Panama, and Cape Horn is left behind. A coastline extending for thirty longitudes, one of the most beautiful and fertile in the world, hitherto almost uninhabited, visibly transforms itself into a wealthy, civilised country, thickly populated by people of all races, from the Yankee to the Chinese, from the Negro to the Indian and Malayan, from Creoles and Mestizos to Europeans. The gold of California pours in torrents over America and the Asian shores of the Pacific, dragging the most obscurantist and barbarous nations into world trade and civilisation (sic). For the second time, world commerce changes course. What Tyre, Carthage and Alexandria were for the Old World, what Genoa and Venice were in the Middle Ages, what London and Liverpool were until now—the emporiums of world trade—that New York and San Francisco, San Juan de Nicaragua and Leon, Chagres and Panama, are about to become. The gravitational centre of world commerce—in the Middle Ages, Italy, in more recent times, England—is now to be found in the southern half of the North American continent. Old Europe's industry and trade will have to make tremendous efforts if they are not to fall into the decay of Italian trade and industry since the sixteenth century, if England and France are not to become what Venice, Genoa and Holland are today. . . . Thanks to the gold of California and the tireless energy of the Yankees, both shores of the Pacific will soon be as populous, as open to trade, as industrial, as the coast from Boston to New Orleans. The Pacific will become what the Atlantic is today, and what the Mediterranean was in Antiquity and in the Middle Ages—the great highway of world commerce; while the Atlantic will decline to the status of an inland sea similar to the Mediterranean today. The sole chance for the civilised European countries to avoid the industrial,

[1] J. A. Schumpeter, *Capitalism, Socialism and Democracy*, 3rd edn., London and New York, 1950, p. 6.

commercial and political dependence which has befallen Italy, Spain and Portugal lies in a social revolution which—while it is yet time—transforms the modes of production and transport in conformity with the technological requirements of modern production, thus releasing fresh productive forces, securing the superiority of European industry and cancelling the disadvantages of the geographical situation.[1]

This unabashed hymn to industrial progress under capitalism, barely two years after the publication of the *Communist Manifesto* (which, however, contained similar passages), was quite in accordance with Marx's—and especially Engels's—outlook, but it must have grated upon the less sophisticated members of the Communist League and hastened the dissolution of that organisation. The years 1850–2 were in fact marked by a growing cleavage within the League most of whose adherents were unwilling to follow Marx and Engels in taking the long view. Already by the end of 1850 Marx had come to the conclusion that European politics pivoted on Britain, which was just then entering upon a period of industrial prosperity that had the effect of stabilising the existing order. 'The original process always occurs in England; it is the demiurge of the bourgeois cosmos. On the Continent, the various phases of the cycle periodically traversed by bourgeois society occur in secondary or tertiary form.'[2] Political revolutions on the Continent hence lacked ultimate significance unless they reacted upon the centre of the 'bourgeois cosmos': Victorian England. 'Violent eruptions are naturally more likely to occur in the extremities of the bourgeois organism than in its heart, since here countervailing tendencies are more effective. On the other hand, the degree to which Continental revolutions react back upon England represents the measure in which these revolutions genuinely impinge upon bourgeois conditions of life, or merely upon their political forms.'[3] As it happened, the revolutionary cycle which had begun in 1847 and reached its apogee in 1848–9, was now nearing its close, and the opening of another cycle was contingent upon the future outbreak of an economic crisis in Britain:

[1] Cf. Mehring, *Nachlassausgabe*, III, pp. 443–4; full text in *Neue Rheinische Zeitung: Politisch-oekonomische Revue*, London, 1850; reprinted in book form, Dresden, 1955, p. 120. The (unsigned) article from which the above passage has been extracted, appears to be mainly the work of Engels, with editorial emendations by Marx. It was published, together with other material, in the February 1850 issue of the monthly journal (hereafter cited as *Neue Rheinische Revue*) which had taken the place of the defunct Cologne organ of the Communist League, the *Neue Rheinische Zeitung*.

[2] *Neue Rheinische Revue*, May–October 1850, loc. cit., p. 317.   [3] Ibid.

With this general prosperity, during which the productive forces of bourgeois society develop as luxuriantly as bourgeois conditions permit, there can be no question of a genuine revolution. Such a revolution is possible only in periods when these *two factors—modern productive forces* and *bourgeois forms of production*—are in conflict. The squabbles currently engaged in by the various factions of the Continental party of order . . . so far from promoting fresh revolutions, are on the contrary possible only because the social foundation is momentarily so stable and—what the reactionaries don't understand—so bourgeois. It will repel all reactionary projects intended to stem bourgeois development as surely as it will repel the moral indignation and the enthusiastic manifestoes of the democrats. *A new revolution* is possible only as the sequel of a new crisis. *It is, however, equally certain.*[1]

As if to underline the change in perspective, the projected Industrial Exhibition of 1851 is expressly described in the same article (published in the fall of 1850) as the British bourgeoisie's rejoinder to the 'merely political' revolutions on the Continent:

This exhibition was announced by the British bourgeoisie, with admirable calm, already in 1849, at a time when the entire Continent still dreamed of revolution. In it (the bourgeoisie) summons all its vassals, from France to China, for a great examination, when they must show how they have spent their time; and even the almighty Russian Tsar is constrained to order his subjects to present themselves before the examiners. This great world congress of products and producers has an altogether different significance than the absolutist congresses of Bregenz and Warsaw which induce such nightmares in our Continental democratic philistines. . . . With this exhibition the world bourgeoisie erects its pantheon in the new Rome, where it proudly places on show the deities it has fabricated. . . .[2]

Victorian England, though regrettably immune to revolution and refractory even to ordinary democracy, was likewise too bourgeois to provide a suitable soil for aristocratic and clerical manipulations. The death of Peel in 1850 gave Marx and Engels an opportunity to note that 'the statesmanship of this leader of the landed aristocracy, who himself stemmed from the middle class, consisted in the realisation that nowadays the only remaining aristocracy is the bourgeoisie'.[3] Even Catholic Emancipation and the controversy over Papal influence—a major issue of British politics in 1850—are brought in to underline the point:

The most recent event to attract attention in England is the appointment of Mr. (sic) Wiseman to the post of Cardinal-Archbishop of Westminster,

---

[1] Ibid., pp. 317–18. (Italics in the original.)
[2] Ibid., pp. 310–11.   [3] Ibid., p. 319.

and the Papal decree which divides England into thirteen Catholic bishop-rics. This step . . . which came as a considerable surprise to the Church of England, provides fresh evidence of the illusion entertained by the whole reactionary party on the Continent, viz., that the victories they have recently gained in the service of the bourgeoisie must necessarily entail the restoration of feudal absolutism with its entire religious panoply. Catholic-ism finds support in England among the two extremes of society, the aristo-cracy and the mob (*Lumpenproletariat*). The latter, the Irish mob . . . is Catholic by descent. The aristocracy toyed with Puseyism while it was fashionable, until it became the fashion to join the Catholic Church. At a time when the struggle with the advancing bourgeoisie impelled the English aristocracy to emphasise its feudal character, it was natural that the reli-gious ideologists of the aristocracy, the orthodox High Church theologians, in conflict with the middle-class Dissenters felt compelled to draw the logical conclusion from their semi-Catholic dogmas and rites, so that cases of reactionary Anglicans joining (the Catholic Church) became more fre-quent. These insignificant events produced the most sanguine hopes . . . in the minds of the Catholic clergy. . . . For the bourgeoisie, the whole comedy is significant only insofar as it provides it with a chance for fresh attacks upon the High Church and its universities. . . .[1]

Britain for Marx and Engels was the rock on which the revolu-tionary wave of 1848–9 had been dashed to spray, but only insofar as the movement had for a time attempted to transcend the bourgeois order. Its purely political aims were compatible with British interests, and had been frustrated chiefly because the conservative forces were able to fall back upon the great bulwark of European reaction: Tsarist absolutism. The question then was whether the two great con-servative powers—Russia and England—would fall out, and when they did so in 1853–6, over the Straits and Constantinople, Marx's only fear was that the Crimean war might end in a draw. His writings and letters of the period are full of sardonic comments on the inability of the British and French governments to press the war to a successful conclusion. For the rest he expected little in the way of new political stirrings. Engels at first was more optimistic. Reasoning on Hegelian lines he terminated an appraisal of the political situation in 1853 with the words: 'However, it is a good thing that the revolution this time

[1] Ibid., pp. 319–20. The unsigned passage is unquestionably by Engels. Quite apart from the fact that the subject was not one in which Marx took much interest, the emphasis upon the progressive role played by the middle class in getting rid of 'feudal barriers' to enlightenment and progress is quite in accor-dance with Engels's habitual outlook. Historians of socialism unfamiliar with the German background have commonly overlooked the debt Engels owes to Heine and other writers of the group originally known as 'Young Germany'. Anti-clericalism was part of the radical attitude; so was the rapturous welcom-ing of technical progress.

encounters a sturdy opponent in the shape of Russia, and not such feeble scarecrows as in 1848.'[1] When his hopeful expectation of 'an aristocratic-bourgeois revolution in Petersburg, and an ensuing civil war within the country'[2] came to nothing, he cheerfully switched his attention to Germany, where trouble was brewing between Austria and Prussia. Viewed from a British vantage-point these tensions in Eastern and Central Europe had much in common. Insensibly, the two exiles were drawn towards the standard Victorian attitude to Continental affairs: whatever shape events in Europe might take, England was certain to follow her own course. There was no true community of destiny linking the Venice of the Ocean—then nearing the zenith of its power and splendour—with the semi-agrarian military monarchies of the Continent. Even France was no longer taken quite seriously, though the next *political* outbreak was certain to occur in Paris. In this respect, as in others, Engels and Marx from about 1850 onward came to adopt the representative Victorian outlook. In time they even developed a faintly supercilious attitude towards Continental revolutionaries who attached undue importance to purely political convulsions in the 'extremities of the bourgeois organism'. Democracy and the labour movement might still have to fight major battles on the Continent, but from an economic viewpoint England stood out as the cradle of the modern world and the centre of bourgeois society. Until it was drawn into the general movement, socialism would remain parochial.

Here then was a paradox: while Continental socialism grew in strength from the 1860's onward, there was no corresponding development in Britain until the 1890's, when Marx had already left the scene. For the greater part of the period, Marx and Engels had before them the spectacle of a Britain where the free-trade boom had seemingly made an end of class conflict in its old form. Chartism was forgotten. Already in 1850 the prospects of that once great movement appeared dim, the more so since 'the petty-bourgeois elements who still adhere to the party, together with the aristocracy of labour, have formed a purely democratic faction whose programme is limited to the People's Charter and a few other petty-bourgeois reforms'.[3] True, 'the mass of workers who genuinely live under proletarian conditions belong to the revolutionary wing of Chartism',[4] but their

[1] Engels to J. Weydemeyer, April 12, 1853, MESC, p. 91.
[2] Ibid., p. 90.
[3] *Neue Rheinische Revue*, loc. cit., p. 320.   [4] Ibid.

leaders, Julian Harney and Ernest Jones, failed to come up to the expectations they had briefly aroused in Marx and Engels. Even Owenism was dying out;[1] and the ambiguous attitude of the trade unions towards the International has already been noted.

The long Victorian peace thus constitutes a watershed between two phases in the socialist movement: that which climaxed briefly in 1848-9, and the revival of the 1890's. During this lengthy interval no forward move was possible in England; consequently the emphasis had to fall on the purely political part of the Social-Democratic programme, and even this was too radical for the British labour movement. Insofar as they did not blame this unsatisfactory state of affairs on the Irish imbroglio, Marx and Engels attributed it to the free-trade boom and Britain's temporary near-monopoly of world trade in manufactures.[2] Behind this passing configuration, Marx, as was his habit, discerned a deeper historical logic:

We cannot deny that bourgeois society has experienced its sixteenth century a second time—a sixteenth century which will, I trust, sound its death-knell, as the former thrust it into life. The real task of bourgeois society is the establishment of the world market, at any rate in outline, and a productive system based on this foundation. Since the globe is round, this seems to have been achieved with the colonisation of California and Australia, and the opening up of China and Japan. The difficult question for us is this: on the Continent the revolution is imminent and will immediately assume a socialist character. Will it not of necessity be crushed in this little corner, since over a much vaster terrain the movement of bourgeois society is still in the ascendant?[3]

In pondering such utterances it is worth remembering that for Marx 'bourgeois society' was synonymous with what his liberal contemporaries termed 'civilisation', save that he took a more sombre view of its merits and prospects: it signified both a social whole and a stage in history. That much indeed was common ground at the time. On liberal principles there was no cause to suspect that 'civilisation'—having at long last emerged from barbarism, feudalism, militarism, and various attendant evils—might itself be no more than a

[1] Cole, op. cit., II, p. 381: 'Co-operation . . . had cut its Socialist connections at any rate by the 1860's.'

[2] Cf. Engels to Marx, October 7, 1858, MESC, pp. 132-3. 'For the rest it seems to me that Jones's new move . . . is really bound up with the fact that the English proletariat is actually becoming more and more bourgeois, so that this most bourgeois of all nations apparently aims . . . at a bourgeois aristocracy and a bourgeois proletariat alongside the bourgeoisie. For a nation which exploits the whole world this is of course justifiable up to a point.'

[3] Marx to Engels, October 8, 1858; cf. MEGA III/2, p. 342; MESC, p. 134.

passing phenomenon. On the contrary, now that liberal society had finally come into full bloom there was every reason to expect that it would spread over the whole globe. To Marx of course this kind of faith simply represented further proof that the liberals were incapable of telling the difference between the substance of historical reality and its transitory forms. In contrast to their optimism he held that bourgeois society had already exhausted its *raison d'être* in giving birth to forces (the world market and modern industry) which socialism stood ready to inherit. With the growth and development of the labour movement, at any rate in Europe, this outcome could now, in the mid-nineteenth century, safely be taken for granted, though it raised awkward problems in relation to the more backward regions of the globe: an interesting anticipation of issues which were to arise in a rather different context a century later.

But this same society, whose ideologists so plainly mistook temporary success for genuine permanence, possessed a past as well as a future. How had it come into being, and what kept it going? Its first flowering in the Renaissance of the sixteenth century, as well as its present Indian summer, were rooted in historical circumstances now lost from view. Moreover, there was the unsolved problem of its location: why had it come into existence only in Europe? If the historical aspect of Marx's theory was to be integrated with his analysis of capitalism, these questions demanded an answer. In *Capital* it is taken for granted that the industrial revolution is associated with a particular stage of Western society. But before the economist felt able to work on this assumption, the historian in Marx had to come to terms with the evidence and relate it to his vision of the social process; the theory of society had to account for a particular problem: the genesis of bourgeois society.

2

HISTORICAL MATERIALISM

TO APPRECIATE the Marxian conception of history it is necessary to remember that its author belonged to an age which recognised no limitations to the range of knowledge available to a single mind. Historical generalisations of the most far-reaching and universal kind were not merely admired but expected. In this regard Marx was a true Victorian, for faith in general theories was by no means confined to Central Europe, though German writers were among its foremost exponents. Taine, Tocqueville, and Gobineau in France, Mill and Spencer in England, were as productive of sweeping hypotheses as any German. Nowadays the fashion has changed, and a committee of experts sitting on the problem would doubtless have little difficulty in showing that these writers piled up errors of fact all over the place. But the committee would have to be numerous and well-staffed: no single scholar today commands the erudition and breadth of vision characteristic of the Victorians; to say nothing of the confidence with which they approached their several tasks.

The particular problem with which Marx was concerned, though closely related to the investigations of his contemporaries, had a character of its own, by reason of his peculiar philosophical training. For writers like Taine or Tocqueville it was enough to describe the historical links connecting successive stages of society, e.g., to trace the causal sequence of events leading from the rise of feudalism in medieval Europe to the *ancien régime* in its finished form, and thence to the French Revolution. To Marx this was not an altogether satisfactory procedure, although he did not disdain it and indeed relied for his factual research on historical investigations of just this kind. They were not, however, what he was really after. For his own purpose it was essential that the pattern of events should display the kind of internal logic where each successive stage is seen to arise as a matter of necessity, and not just of fact. Thus processes such as the development of feudalism out of primitive tribalism, or the growth of bourgeois society within the feudal system, had to be related to changes inherent in the logic of the anterior stage. Unless this could be done, the study of history, for all the scholarly precision of the historians, was bound to remain a merely empirical enterprise—hence pre-scientific.

In relation to modern society this problem exhibited two different aspects: why had bourgeois society come into being in Europe, and how had it arisen out of medieval feudalism? On the customary view these were distinct questions, the province respectively of two independent disciplines. For Marx they were two sides of the same coin, since to him bourgeois civilisation was both an organic whole and a particular stage in the general process of world history. Failure to grasp this connection was in his eyes proof of theoretical incompetence, or subjection to 'the bourgeois ideas-treadmill'.

The Marxian theory of early capitalist development will be discussed in the next chapter. What concerns us here are Marx's hypotheses regarding the genesis of European feudalism, and more generally the Marxian doctrine of historical stages. What is known as the 'materialist conception of history' is best understood in this context. Indeed it is arguable that outside the range of this particular set of problems it is not really a definite theory at all.

Marx fell in with the general run of nineteenth-century writers by postulating the primarily military character of the feudal system.[1] The question then was how this particular form of society had come into being, and how it had managed to maintain itself after its original military function had been usurped by other agencies. This problem

---

[1] It is, however, not quite accurate to say that he 'substantially accepted the bourgeois view that feudalism was a reign of force'. (Schumpeter, *Capitalism, Socialism, and Democracy*, p. 17.) As we shall see the matter is more complicated.

is much more troublesome for Marxists than the rise of capitalism, which can be explained in fairly straightforward fashion as a consequence of technological change: the bourgeois mode of production gradually proving its superiority, thereby enabling its agents, the capitalists, to accumulate first wealth and finally political power. By contrast, the origins of feudal society plainly have to do with military conquest, while the resulting system of landlordism in turn conditioned the structure of society, including its technology. This looks at first like a very awkward poser for the Marxian conception of history, and scholars who otherwise sympathise with at any rate the general model of historical materialism have been inclined to argue that it works only for a single case: the genesis of capitalism.[1] In fact, as we shall see, Marx did have a theory of feudalism which is consistent with his general doctrine and requires no auxiliary hypotheses, though for various reasons it did not gain wide currency. Engels in particular paid little attention to it, while advancing his own, much less interesting, explanation.[2]

The first rudimentary sketch of the Marxian theory of class society appears in the opening section of the 1845–6 manuscript known as the *German Ideology*, while a fuller version was inserted in the original draft of *Capital*, composed in 1857–8 but not published during Marx's lifetime.[3] The fact that some of these writings remained unknown for many years undoubtedly helped to cloud a discussion which was anyhow confused by partisanship. From our viewpoint the relevant fact is that the 1845–6 draft already contains a brief sketch of the Marxian theory of society, with particular reference to classical

[1] Schumpeter, ibid.

[2] Cf. his remarks on the sources of political power in *The Origin of the Family, Private Property, and the State* (hereafter cited as *Origin of the Family*), MESW II, pp. 239 ff.

[3] For the *German Ideology*, cf. MEGA I/5, pp. 10 ff; the full text of the 1845–6 MSS was first made public in 1932. The 1857–8 draft of *Capital* appeared in print for the first time in 1939–40, in a two-volume version edited by the Marx-Engels-Lenin Institute in Moscow, and was subsequently republished in one volume under the title *Grundrisse der Kritik der politischen Oekonomie (Rohentwurf)*, Berlin, 1953. The work, which runs to well over a thousand pages, includes the material published in 1859 by Marx under the title *Zur Kritik der politischen Oekonomie*, with the well-known preface giving a brief summary of what is now customarily referred to as the materialist conception of history. Hereafter, the 1857–8 draft will be cited as *Grundrisse*, the 1859 publication as *Kritik*. Quotations from the latter refer to the German edition; an English translation first appeared in 1904 under the title *Critique of Political Economy*, including some material not contained in the original 1859 edition and first published in *Neue Zeit*, 1902–3.

Antiquity and the European Middle Ages. The guiding ideas are deduced from the standard histories of the period, a good deal of emphasis being laid on the growth of latifundia in late antiquity and the emergence of primitive serfdom in early medieval times. But these conclusions are subsumed under a general notion which Marx had worked out for himself, namely that 'the various stages of development in the division of labour represent so many forms of property; i.e., the particular stage reached in the division of labour determines likewise the relations of the individuals towards each other with regard to the materials, instruments and product of labour'. Tribal ownership is described as the 'original form' of property, corresponding to a social order defined as 'an extension of the family: patriarchal tribal chiefs, below them the members of the tribe, lastly slaves. The slavery latent in the family develops only gradually with the increase of population and necessities, and with the extension of external intercourse, whether commerce or war.'[1] Next, on a higher historical and social level, we encounter 'the communal and public property of Antiquity, resulting especially from the union of several tribes into a city, either by agreement or by conquest, and which is still accompanied by slavery. Alongside communal property, mobile and later also immobile private property begins to develop, but as an abnormality subordinate to communal property. It is only as a community that the citizens hold power over their labouring slaves, and for this reason alone they are tied to the form of communal property. . . . Hence the social order established on this basis, and with it the power of the people, decays in proportion as real private property develops.'[2] The 'third form' of property is feudal and pertains to the European Middle Ages. Though its origins are linked to fortuitous historical circumstances—the decay of the Roman Empire, the barbarian conquest, the decline of the towns, etc.—Marx considers that feudalism displays a social logic which relates it back to the earlier 'forms' from which it sprang. 'Like tribal and communal property it likewise rests on a community, but one which confronts not the slaves, as in Antiquity, but the peasant serfs as the directly producing class. . . . This feudal hierarchy, just like the antique community, was an association against the subject class of producers, though owing to differences in the conditions of production, the forms of association, and the relationship towards the direct producers, were different.'[3]

[1] *German Ideology*, MEGA I/5, pp. 11–12.   [2] Ibid., p. 12.   [3] Ibid., p. 14.

Though only briefly sketched out, this rudimentary scheme already discloses the characteristic Marxian urge towards fusing historical and social logic. In the bulky 1857–8 draft manuscript the historical sketch of pre-capitalist society reappears in a much more detailed version which provides the clue to a good many otherwise puzzling Marxian utterances on the subject of class. In the meantime, however, Marx had—jointly with Engels—come across a fresh problem. His stay in England, and especially his study of the British Government's involvement with India and China, had made him aware that Oriental society posed a difficulty for his scheme. Hitherto he had virtually ignored non-European cultures and contented himself with drawing upon the known history of classical Antiquity and the Middle Ages. From 1850 onward we find him engaged in an increasingly systematic attempt to bring Oriental society within the compass of his general theory, until with the emergence of a revolutionary movement in Russia this subject acquired immediate political importance, as well as posing an intricate theoretical problem, of which more later.[1]

The first fruits of these studies were some newspaper articles on India and China in which 'Asiatic society' makes its appearance, together with a suggestion that 'climate and territorial conditions' made extensive canalisation 'the basis of Oriental agriculture', while social conditions unfavourable to 'voluntary association' brought about 'the interference of the centralised power of the government'.[2] This hesitant entry into a new theoretical field was preceded by a correspondence between Marx and Engels[3] which went some way towards clarifying the subject in their minds, the chief conclusion being (in Marx's view) that earlier writers were correct in considering 'the basis of all phenomena in the East . . . to be the absence of private property in land. This is the real key, even to the Oriental heaven.'[4] This theme in turn leads to some sceptical remarks on the

---

[1] Cf. Karl A. Wittfogel, *Oriental Despotism*, Yale, 1957, especially pp. 372 ff. The majority of Marx's and Engels's utterances on the subject of China and India are scattered through their writings in the *New York Daily Tribune* (hereafter cited as NYDT), of which only part have been edited, chiefly by Ryazanov (cf. supra). For the rest, their views on the subject of Oriental society have to be pieced together from their correspondence, and from such inadequate and tendentious selections as those made by R. P. Dutt (*Articles on India*, Bombay, 1951) and Dona Torr (*Marx on China 1853–60*, London, 1951).

[2] NYDT, June 25 and August 8, 1853. Cf. MESW I, pp. 345–60.

[3] MEGA III/1, pp. 471, 475–7, 480–7; MESC, pp. 95–104.

[4] Marx to Engels, June 2, 1853, MEGA III/1, p. 477; MESC, p. 99. Cf. also Engels to Marx, June 6, 1853, MEGA III/1, p. 480; MESC, p. 99. 'But how

role of the self-governing Indian village community. 'I believe one cannot imagine a more solid foundation for a stagnant Asiatic despotism. And however much the English may have Hibernicised the country, the breaking-up of these primitive stereotypes was the *sine qua non* of Europeanisation.'[1]

In contrast to Asian despotism, feudalism appeared to be a socio-historical formation outside the Oriental context. Marx seems not to have concerned himself with Japan, but his thesis regarding the nature of the 'Asiatic mode of production' does not exclude the possibility of exceptions from the general pattern. So far as Europe was concerned, feudalism clearly was linked to an *historical* fact: the decline of classical Antiquity. On the other hand, its social roots appeared to lie in the military chieftainship of the barbarian tribes who had overrun the Roman Empire, and this tribal structure did not differ from the organisation of the primitive Indo-Germanic peoples who, some two millenniums earlier, had become the ancestors of the Graeco-Roman civilisation. Why then had feudalism not developed in Greece and Rome out of this earlier wave of conquests, which in fact led to the city-state of classical Antiquity? And conversely, why did not the city-state in due course give birth to something like modern capitalism, instead of collapsing and making way for a more primitive form of social organisation? Marx was as much bothered by these questions as were later sociologists, and it is noteworthy that the theory he sketches out has much in common with the conclusions subsequently reached by the greatest of his critics.[2] Both explanations turn on the role of slave labour, and both also have this in common that they treat slavery as an *organic* feature of the society which found its political form in the Greek *polis*, thereafter in the Roman Republic, and finally in the Roman Empire.

Since this theme is closely linked with the Marxian theory of capitalist development no apology is needed for devoting some space to it. Apart from their intrinsic interest for sociologists and historians,

does it come about that the Orientals did not arrive at landed property, even in its feudal form? I think it is mainly due to the climate . . . An Oriental government never had more than three departments: finance (plunder at home), war (plunder at home and abroad), and public works (provision for reproduction). The British Government in India has administered (1) and (2) in a rather narrow spirit and dropped (3) entirely, so that Indian agriculture is being ruined. . . .'
    [1] Marx to Engels, June 14, 1853, MEGA III/1, p. 487; MESC, pp. 103–4.
    [2] Cf. Max Weber, 'Die sozialen Gruende des Untergangs der antiken Kultur', *Gesammelte Aufsaetze zur Sozial- und Wirtschaftsgeschichte*, Tuebingen, 1924, pp. 289–311.

Marx's observations on the subject—duly edited and purged of their real theoretical content—have become the foundation of an ideology which has replaced other modes of thought over a third of the globe. This alone should be sufficient to ensure some attention for his views. But there is the further consideration that his scattered remarks, when properly understood and related to each other, are by no means favourable to the standard interpretation current in the Soviet orbit: they could even be described as potentially subversive of much that currently passes for orthodoxy in those parts.[1] In a lesser degree this also applies to Engels's subsequent popularisation of the Marxian conception, notably in his *Origin of the Family* (1884), though here one comes up against the difficulty of having to cope simultaneously with the Morgan-Engels view of pre-history, which is not strictly germane to our subject. It is perhaps worth noting that the Marxian hypothesis (as drafted in 1857–8, i.e., before Marx had read Morgan) does not depend on any particular anthropological data other than the most general notions about tribal society then current among European scholars.

Marx begins by asking what a society is like in which the producers own the instruments of production, and he replies that historically such a state of affairs is exemplified by peasant proprietorship. For 'capital' and 'labour' to come into existence as separate and independent factors, the labourer must cease to be the owner of the material resources on which production depends. 'Thus above all separation of the labourer from the soil (earth) as his natural laboratory—hence dissolution of free petty proprietorship in land, as well as of collective landownership resting on the Oriental commune. Under both forms the labourer confronts the objective conditions of his work as their owner; this is the natural unity of labour with its material preconditions.'[2] The transformation of this independent (individual or collective) producer into a landless labourer is the outcome of a lengthy historical process whose early phases reach back to primitive tribal society. At this stage, 'the earth is the great laboratory,

---

[1] Cf. Wittfogel, op. cit., pp. 380 ff. It is hardly surprising that contemporary Russian and Chinese writers should have been reluctant to develop the suggestions thrown out by Marx and Engels on the subject of Oriental despotism: some of their remarks are uncomfortably close to the bone. Conversely, Western scholars, even when not hampered by political blinkers, can scarcely be said to have made the most of Marx's interesting—and, for his time, astonishingly advanced—ideas on the subject of early European history.

[2] *Grundrisse*, p. 375.

the arsenal, which provides both the implements and the materials of labour, as well as the seat, the basis, of the commonwealth. . . . Each individual is an *owner* or *proprietor* only . . . as a member of this commonwealth. The real *appropriation* through the process of labour occurs under these *preconditions*, which are themselves not the *product* of labour, but appear as its natural or *divine* presuppositions'.[1]

Historically, this primitive society takes two different roads of development: the Oriental and the Occidental. In the former (elsewhere described by Marx as the social counterpart of the 'Asiatic mode of production', founded on centrally controlled canalisation and other public works) the tribal community forms the basis of a unitary system whose unifying function is represented, and ultimately usurped, by the *despot*, while its ideological reflex appears in the *deity*. The primitive unity of the small tribal community—by now only one among many—appears 'realised in the despot, as the father of the many communities', who also appropriates the surplus product.[2] Having become sedentary, the scattered village communities continue to be the real owners of their land, notwithstanding the juridical fiction which makes the king (or the god) the sole owner. But 'part of their surplus labour belongs to the higher unity which at last exists as a *person*, and this surplus labour finds expression both in tribute and in joint (common) labours glorifying the unity either of the real despot or of the imaginary tribal personality, the god.'[3] The king and the god are both historical creations: they are projections of the tribe, with the difference that the former represents its real unity in warfare against other tribes, the latter its illusory existence as an entity different from and independent of its members. The social organism may be more or less democratic, depending on the degree to which common tasks are performed freely or under central direction. Where the major economic operations of society come under central control—as in the Asian societies with their extensive waterworks—these socially necessary operations 'appear as the work of the higher unity—the despotic government suspended above the small communities'.[4]

As against this 'Oriental' pattern (which however is also traceable 'in Mexico, Peru, among the ancient Celts, (and) some Indian tribes')[5]

---

[1] *Grundrisse*, p. 376.
[2] Ibid., pp. 376–7. Cf. also *Capital* (1960 edn.), vol. III, p. 772: 'The state is then the supreme lord. Sovereignty here consists in the ownership of land concentrated on a national scale.'
[3] *Grundrisse*, p. 377.   [4] Ibid.   [5] Ibid.

a 'second form' of development, 'the product of a more varied historical life (affecting) the destinies . . . of the original tribes', leads to a social organisation centred on an urban seat of government. Here the occupants of the land reside in town and 'the soil appears as the territory of the city; not the village as a mere appendage of the land'.[1] In the absence of a central power these tiny urban republics collide frequently with one another, with the result that warfare becomes endemic. 'The difficulties encountered by the commonwealth can only result from other commonwealths, which either have already occupied the soil or disturb the community in its occupation. War is therefore the great common task, the great joint effort required to occupy the objective conditions of living existence, or to guard and perpetuate their occupation. Hence the community, composed of families, originally has a warlike, military, organisation, and this is one of the conditions of its proprietorship. The urban concentration of dwellings is the foundation of this military organisation.'[2]

In this Occidental society—typified by Greece and Rome—communal property, 'as state ownership, *ager publicus*', appears separate from private (landed) property, which now becomes the basis of a new type of civilisation. The individual develops into an independent landowner, i.e., into a farmer, while 'the community—as the state—represents on the one hand the interconnection of these free and equal private owners, their union against the outside world, and also its guarantee. The community is here as much dependent on the status of its members as working farmers, as the independence of the latter rests on their interconnection as members of the community, (and) the securing of the *ager publicus* for common needs and common glory.'[3] Yet the peculiar circumstances imposed upon these tiny warlike commonwealths tend constantly to burst their narrow bounds. The perpetuation of the community requires the possession of a minimum of land by all its members and 'their reproduction as self-sustaining peasants, whose surplus time belongs to the commune, i.e., to the labour of war, etc.'[4] Hence the essence of ancient citizenship is military; only constant warlike expansion can guarantee landed property to all citizens, and conversely farming is rated highly as a school of the soldierly virtues. The socio-economic organisation of the community thus implies a definite political structure: only landowners are full citizens, while trade and industry are left to foreigners

[1] *Grundrisse*, p. 378.　　　　　　　　[2] Ibid., p. 378.
[3] Ibid., pp. 378–9.　　　　　　　　[4] Ibid., p. 380.

and freedmen, artisanship not being regarded as an occupation suitable for a citizen. 'The history of classical Antiquity is the history of cities; but of cities founded on land ownership and agriculture.'[1]

These societies eventually succumb to their own logic. 'In order that the community be able to go on existing in the ancient manner, its elements must be reproduced under the objective conditions which are presupposed. Production itself, the growth of population (this too is an aspect of production) necessarily does away with these preconditions, destroys them instead of reproducing them, and thus the commonwealth disappears together with the forms of property on which it was founded . . . In particular, the effect of war and conquest, which e.g. in Rome was among the essential economic preconditions of the community, eliminates the real tie binding it together.'[2] The basis of the whole process is always to be sought in 'the reproduction of . . . more or less natural . . . or . . . traditional relations of the individual to his community, and a *certain predetermined, objective* form of (individual and social) existence'. The form of the process is thus determined by limiting factors which impose a barrier to progress beyond a certain point of growth, and this is one side of the matter. On the other hand, the gradual removal of these primitive conditions—e.g., in the case of Rome, by way of military expansion, slave labour, latifundia, etc.—leads to the dissolution of the old commonwealth. 'Within a certain orbit, major developments are possible. The individuals may appear as great. But no free and full development of the individual or the society is possible, since such a development is in conflict with the original relationship.'[3]

The cycle of growth and decay is thus predetermined by the primitive social nexus. There is no escape from its logic. 'If the individual alters his relationship to the community, he thereby alters the community and has a destructive effect upon it and upon its economic base; on the other hand, the change in the economic base is brought about by its own dialectic, impoverishment etc.'[4] The manner in which the agrarian commonwealth is organised precludes the development of the productive forces beyond a certain point. 'Among the Ancients we never encounter an enquiry as to which form of landed property is the most productive, the most wealth-creating. . . . The question is always what form of property is conducive to creating model citizens. As an end in itself, wealth appears only among the

---

[1] *Grundrisse*, pp. 381–2. [2] Ibid., p. 386.
[3] Ibid., pp. 386–7. [4] Ibid., p. 386.

few commercial peoples—monopolists of the carrying trade—who live in the pores of the old world. . . . Hence the antique viewpoint which makes man—under whatever restricted national, religious, or political definition—the end of production, appears very lofty in comparison with the modern world, where production appears as the end of man, and wealth as the aim of production. But in fact, when the narrow limiting bourgeois form has been discarded, what is wealth but the universality of human needs, potentialities, enjoyments, productive powers of the individuals? The full development of man's control over the forces of nature . . . and over his own nature? . . . Hence on the one hand, the childish old world appears as the higher stage. It is so if we look for self-contained harmony, form, limitation. It represents satisfaction from a narrow standpoint; while modernity gives no satisfaction, or, where it does so, appears vulgar (*gemein*). . . .'[1]

But this primitive harmony has for its foundation the warlike solidarity of the commonwealth against its neighbours, and the solidarity of the citizens against their own slaves, who in the end are left to do almost all the productive work, while their owners monopolise public life—i.e., war and politics based on war.[2] The restriction of citizenship (or property, which comes to the same) to members of the conquering tribal nation leads straight to the enslavement of vanquished and despoiled enemies. 'Slavery and serfdom are thus only further developments of the form of property resting on a tribal foundation.'[3] Conversely, colonisation and war are made necessary by the growth in the number of citizens. 'Hence slavery and extension of the *ager publicus*, and therewith the patricians who represent the commonwealth. Hence the maintenance of the commonwealth leads to the destruction of the conditions on which it is based. . . . If it be argued that productivity could be raised within the same area by developing the productive forces etc., (which in the case of traditional farming takes longest of all) this would necessitate new forms of organising labour . . . thus once more doing away with the old economic conditions of the commonwealth. The act of reproduction alters not merely the objective preconditions . . . but the producers themselves change, in that they develop new qualities . . . new forces

[1] *Grundrisse*, pp. 387–8.

[2] 'War is therefore among the oldest labours of each of these primitive commonwealths, both for the safeguarding of property and for the acquisition of additional property.' *Grundrisse*, p. 391.

[3] Ibid., p. 392.

and ideas, new forms of communication.'[1] 'A certain stage in the development of the forces of production of the labouring subjects, corresponding to definite relations among themselves and towards nature. . . . Reproduction until a given point. Then . . . dissolution.'[2]

Historically, this dissolution of the 'childish old world', in which man exists as a citizen only insofar as he is not a slave, appears as the decline and fall of classical Antiquity. When Marx describes 'Asiatic, ancient, feudal, and modern bourgeois modes of production' as 'progressive epochs in the economic formation of society'[3] he takes the unilinear view of history common to his age; that is to say, he assumes that slavery, feudalism, and capitalism are definite phases in the development of Western society, unknown to the Orient whose historical stagnation is viewed as the consequence of the dominant 'Asiatic mode of production'. In this context, in which classical Antiquity stands for one particular form of social organisation, medieval and modern Europe represent at least two: feudalism and capitalism; and possibly three, since Marx considered that Europe had become ripe for socialism. Apart from occasional worries over the political constellation he does not seem to have questioned the ability of European civilisation to rejuvenate itself through periodic social transformations. Since it had already undergone the change-over from medieval feudalism based on peasant serfdom, to modern capitalism founded on free labour, there seemed to be no reason why it should not take the further step of transcending the bourgeois framework—notwithstanding that 'over a much vaster terrain the movement of bourgeois society is still in the ascendant'.[4]

But while his general scheme is unilinear, Marx does not altogether share the prevailing optimism in respect of 'progress'. There are hints that every advance has to be paid for by the relinquishment of achievements possible only under more primitive conditions. Thus

---

[1] *Grundrisse*, pp. 393–4.

[2] Ibid., p. 395. It is noteworthy that the class antagonism plays only a subordinate part in this construction. The ruling class of the Roman Republic (the patricians) are expressly described as representatives of the whole commonwealth. It is the intrinsic nature of the latter, rather than the class interest of the oligarchy, which brings about its dissolution. (Cf. Weber, loc. cit., for a similar view of the economic factors responsible for the decay of classical antiquity, with special reference to the latifundia and the growth of a primitive form of serfdom under the later Empire.)

[3] *Zur Kritik* (1958 edn.), p. 14; for the standard translation cf. MESW I, p. 363.

[4] MESC, p. 134.

the civic virtues of the Romans were inseparable from the quasi-military nature of their original republican commonwealth. Thus, too, with certain spiritual creations:

> In the case of art it is well known that certain flourishing periods are not by any means proportionate to the general development of society, hence to its material foundation, the skeleton, as it were, of its organisation. For example, the Greeks compared with the moderns, or Shakespeare. In the case of certain art forms, e.g., the epos, it is even recognised that they cannot be produced in their epoch-making, classical form once artistic production as such has begun; hence that within the artistic realm certain important formations are possible only in an undeveloped stage. . . .[1]

There is here perhaps an echo of Hegel's pessimism concerning the fate of art in an increasingly rational and scientific world. At any rate Marx, in this instructive passage of his original draft for *Capital*, goes on to raise the awkward question whether 'an evolution of society which excludes all mythological attitude(s) towards nature' may not in the long run turn out to be the death of art! Material progress has to be paid for. To say that on these assumptions socialism is bound to evolve as the 'synthesis' of primitive tribal communism and its opposite, private property, would evidently be nonsense; no such perspective is inherent either in the above historical sketch, or in the 'materialist conception' generally. It could even be argued that the entire scheme is politically neutral. In any event Marx himself—unlike some of his followers—deduced the necessity of socialism not from any general theory of history, but from the analysis of the 'capitalist mode of production' and its social counterpart: bourgeois society.

[1] *Grundrisse*, p. 30; *Zur Kritik, etc.*, p. 268.

3

BOURGEOIS SOCIETY

AT FIRST GLANCE it may seem surprising that this topic should be discussed under a separate chapter-heading, instead of being included in the theory of capitalism. Alternatively it might well be thought that the two have little to do with each other. On this view capitalism denotes certain purely economic arrangements, and the question of its genesis as a social system is quite irrelevant to its functioning. This is the customary approach, and if the present study were concerned with any doctrine but Marxism it would be quite feasible to treat the subject in this manner. But it will not do in the case of Marx, for the good reason that he admitted no such distinction. For him (as indeed for some non-Marxists) capitalism and bourgeois society were intrinsically linked together: not as topics of 'research', but as historical realities; and the notion that capitalist production might have arisen under any other circumstances was just what he was trying to demolish. On his view, bourgeois society had given rise to capitalism, just as capitalism in turn had given birth to the industrial revolution: the entire process culminating in the dissolution of the social system which had cradled it.[1]

---

[1] For a somewhat similar view, cf. Schumpeter, *Capitalism, Socialism and Democracy*, pp. 121 ff. There are of course differences, e.g., in the role allotted to entrepreneurship, but basically there is the same insistence that capitalism

154

Of the three terms relevant in this context—bourgeois society, capitalism, the industrial revolution—the first refers to a state of society which allows capitalist 'relations of production' to become dominant. The distinction was important to Marx, the more so since academic economists had in his day already acquired the habit of treating 'capitalism' as an extension of 'capital', and the latter as synonymous with the use of tools. This made a capitalist of the savage—possibly also of the orang-utang—while it obscured the circumstances under which capital was accumulated until it became the determining factor in society. On the Marxian view this process culminates in the rise of industrialism, after going through a phase in which merchant capital predominates.[1] Hence the 'industrial revolution' comes last, instead of being placed first, as became the fashion in the later nineteenth century. Modern industry emerges from the nexus of bourgeois relationships, and thus represents the final achievement of the entire bourgeois-capitalist era. Insofar as it necessitates large-scale production, hence concentration of capital, industrialism tends to disrupt bourgeois society while the 'capitalist mode of production' is still in full flower.[2]

What then is this bourgeois society which is neither synonymous with modern capitalism, nor, as we have seen, traceable in the East (or in Antiquity), notwithstanding the presence of urban centres and commerce? The only possible answer is that it represents the particular form of society which grew up in Europe since the late Middle Ages. So far from being a variant of a universal type, it is historically unique. Classical Antiquity sprouted cities and a form of commercial capitalism, but it never developed a society which was genuinely bourgeois, i.e., based upon autonomous urban corporations dominated by independent artisans, traders, and manufacturers, who in time accumulated sufficient capital to become the socially dominant stratum. The bourgeoisie has grown from small beginnings, starting with a hole-and-corner existence in the interstices of feudal society. This is a theme to which Marx recurs frequently. It will not do, however, to rest content with citing his early and rather general utterances

as an *economic* system can only function within a uniquely determined *social* environment.

[1] Cf. *Capital*, vol. III, pp. 324 ff (1960 edn.).

[2] Cf. the well-known passage on the destruction of capitalist private property through 'centralisation of the means of production', in *Capital*, vol. I, p. 789 (London, 1938 edition). In the *Communist Manifesto* these distinctions do not yet appear with full clarity.

on the subject, before he had delved deeper into historical studies.[1] As time went on he refined his concepts and became more adept in distinguishing various stages in the process, starting with the municipal movement in early medieval times. His comments e.g., on Thierry's *Histoire de la formation et du progrès du tiers-état* (1853) already show a considerable advance beyond the brilliant but sketchy generalisations of the *Manifesto*, let alone the philosophical abstractions of his early Hegelian phase.[2]

In general Marx distinguishes three stages in the process: (1) the growth of urban centres in the later Middle Ages, still as it were within the pores of feudal society; (2) the great expansion of world trade in the sixteenth and seventeenth centuries, which stimulated the development of commercial capital and at the same time induced small manufacturers to accumulate capital and take to trade;[3] and (3) the modern age properly so called in which *industrial* capital predominates. To some extent these phases overlap. Thus trade is already important in the first stage, while on the other hand capitalist production in manufactures provides the basis for the world-wide commercial expansion characteristic of the Renaissance. Nonetheless each stage is associated with a particular dominant form: artisanate, commerce, industry. The first and third phase in turn are linked by the circumstance that handicrafts proved more important than commerce in laying the foundations of manufacturing industry. Commerce stimulated the general development of the economy and, together with colonial expansion in Asia and America, helped to

---

[1] Cf. *Manifesto of the Communist Party*, MESW I, p. 35: 'From the serfs of the Middle Ages sprang the chartered burghers of the earliest towns. From these burgesses the first elements of the bourgeoisie were developed.'

[2] Cf. Marx to Engels, July 27, 1854, MESC, pp. 105-8. 'From his account it can be excellently demonstrated how the class arises, while the different forms in which its centre of gravity lies at different times . . . break down. . . . Unfortunately, in dealing with the *maîtrises, jurandes*, etc.—with the forms, in short, in which the industrial bourgeoisie developed—he has confined himself almost entirely to general . . . phrases. . . . What he develops and emphasises well is the conspiratorial and revolutionary character of the municipal movement in the twelfth century. The German emperors . . . issued edicts against these "communiones," "conspirationes," and "conjurationes," quite in the spirit of the German Federal Diet. . . . This policy of the German emperors was utilised by the French kings to give secret support to the "sworn confederacies" and "communes" in Lorraine, Alsace, Dauphiné, Franche Comté, Lyonnais, etc., and detach them from the German Empire. . . . It is often comical to see how "communio" was employed as a term of abuse, as communism is today. . . .'

[3] *Capital*, III, pp. 327-8 (1960 edn.).

disrupt the feudal system. 'Nevertheless, the modern mode of production, in its first period, the manufacturing period, developed only in places where the conditions for it had already been created in the Middle Ages. Compare for instance Holland with Portugal. And when in the sixteenth, and partly in the seventeenth century, the sudden expansion of commerce and the creation of a new world market had a determining effect on the decline of the old mode of production and on the rise of the capitalist mode, this occurred on the basis of the already existing capitalist form of production . . .'[1]

At first sight all this looks like ordinary economic history, and indeed it is the common view that Marx was really an economic historian who unfortunately coupled his investigations with a doctrinaire theory of economics properly so called. Large stretches of his chief work can in fact be subsumed under the general heading of economic history, notably those sections of *Capital*, vol. I, where he goes into the genesis of what he termed 'primitive accumulation'. Nonetheless one cannot really separate Marx the historian from Marx the economist, for the good reason that his definition of capitalism as a working system is itself historical. Not only did he stress its roots in bourgeois society, but he insisted—perversely, in the opinion of his critics—that 'capital' and 'labour' were historical factors, in the sense that a major socio-historical revolution was needed to bring them into being. The proletariat and the bourgeoisie—the latter term referring to the capitalist stratum which took the place of the medieval guild artisans and small-scale manufacturers—had come into being through a process in which the majority of producers were forcibly separated from their tools. 'Primitive accumulation' thus constituted a social revolution. 'The capitalist system presupposes the complete separation of the labourers from all property in the means by which they can realize their labour.'[2] There is no need to go into details: the chapter on 'primitive accumulation' in *Capital*, vol. I, is among the best-known of Marx's voluminous writings. Its general thesis has never been seriously disputed, and perhaps the only thing remaining to be said is that Western economists have been strangely reluctant to make use of it in analysing the imposition of industrialism under non-capitalist regimes. For it is of course obvious that everything Marx has to say about the forcible dispossession of peasants and

---

[1] Ibid., pp. 327–8; the citation follows the German text, 1949 edn., p. 365.
[2] *Capital*, I, pp. 737–8. Cf. also *Theories of Surplus Value* (ed. Bonner and Burns, London, 1951), pp. 45 ff.

artisans, and the artificial creation of wage labourers at the mercy of a new ruling class, applies with equal force to planned and centralised industrialisation under conditions of despotic state control. While it is hardly surprising that Soviet economists have been disinclined to fit the cap to their ears, the embarrassed silence on this topic in other quarters perhaps reflects a certain reluctance to have this particular skeleton pulled from the closet.

From a theoretical standpoint the significant question is whether Marx was successful in linking the economic logic of the process to its historical environment. What *caused* 'primitive accumulation' to take a form that resulted in full-fledged capitalism establishing itself in Western Europe? It has been suggested that on the Marxian view 'it is essential for the *logic* of capitalism, and not only a matter of *fact*, that it grew out of a feudal state of society'.[1] At first sight this seems borne out by Marx's observation that 'the economic structure of capitalist society has grown out of the economic structure of feudal society. The dissolution of the latter set free the elements of the former.'[2] This statement, however, is immediately preceded by another one which does not sound like a generalisation: 'The so-called primitive accumulation, therefore, is nothing else than the historic process of divorcing the producer from the means of production. It appears as primitive because it forms the pre-historic stage of capital and of the mode of production corresponding with it.' This leaves it uncertain whether Marx regarded the rise of capitalism, where and when it occurred, as more than the outcome of a special combination of circumstances. As has been noted, Marx and Engels held that the Orient had not evolved anything corresponding to private property in land: unquestionably one of the preconditions of genuine feudalism. Neither were there any self-governing manufacturing towns elsewhere but in Europe. The whole development therefore constituted a very special case and its roots lay in a definite period: the later Middle Ages. Marx says expressly that 'although we come across the first beginnings of capitalist production as early as the fourteenth or fifteenth century, sporadically, in certain towns of the Mediterranean, the capitalist era dates from the sixteenth century. Wherever it appears, the abolition of serfdom has long been effected, and the highest development of the Middle Ages, the existence of sovereign towns, has long been on the wane.'[3] It is only in this context that the immediately preceding passage—'The starting-point of the

[1] Schumpeter, op. cit., p. 17.   [2] *Capital*, I, p. 738.   [3] Ibid., p. 739.

development that gave rise to the wage-labourer as well as the capitalist was the servitude of the labourer. The advance consisted in a change of form of this servitude, in the transformation of feudal exploitation into capitalist exploitation'—assumes the character of a generalisation. The whole argument clearly is not intended to do more than summarise what in Marx's opinion had actually taken place. Moreover, he goes on to say that the process occurred in its 'classic' form only in England, though elsewhere similar tendencies were at work.[1]

On the whole then it would appear that he was not, in this part of his work, trying to lay down a general law. Certainly there is no suggestion in his mature writings that the feudal system is bound, from a kind of inner logic, to sprout capitalist tendencies. Such a notion would in fact have run counter to the historical cast of his thinking. The conclusion cannot be avoided that Marx regarded European capitalism as a unique social formation. Its rise was 'historic' in the sense that it had taken place 'under definite conditions', which presumably accounted for the absence of similar developments under less favourable circumstances. This line of thought is open to criticism, but it does not support the suggestion that the transitional stage is simply wrapped in mystery.[2] What it amounts to is an emphasis on the uniqueness of those formative processes which had given rise to a new type of social organisation: in this case 'the pre-historic stage of capital', i.e., the stage which antedates the establishment of the 'capitalist mode of production' properly so called. What lies before this unique occurrence is 'pre-historic' in the sense that 'capital' has its own 'history', which is of course primarily an economic one: the history of its transition from commercial to industrial capitalism, and beyond the latter to the point where 'centralisation of the means of production and socialisation of labour . . . become incompatible with their capitalist integument'.[3]

So far as the factual side is concerned, economic historians since Marx have for the most part been content to elaborate upon his general ideas. If this leaves the genesis of capitalism partly in the dark, the reason is that we still do not know enough about the manner in which early bourgeois society grew up in the interstices of the feudal system. Concerning the latter Marx held views which are not intrinsically related to his theory of capitalist development, since this deals with the manner in which 'simple commodity production' by

[1] Ibid., p. 739.　　[2] Schumpeter, op. cit., pp. 17–18.　　[3] *Capital*, I, p. 789.

artisans and peasants is transformed into capitalist production carried on by wage-labourers. It is therefore not a strictly relevant question whether Marx (or Engels, who took more interest in the subject) had a satisfactory theory of how feudalism came to develop in the European middle ages. The general explanation they favoured—that it was an outgrowth of military conquest which disrupted the old tribal pattern by turning the hereditary chiefs into reigning sovereigns—is clearly no more than an approximation.[1] In any case it is irrelevant to the problem of accounting for the modest beginnings, and the triumphant culmination, of the bourgeois epoch. So far as Marx was concerned, this epoch opens with the formation of sizeable urban centres in the later Middle Ages, i.e., at a time when the 'feudal mode of production' had barely reached its apogee. Thus the two stages overlap, and the interconnection between them appears at first only in the circumstance that some kind of commodity production—and trade based on this production—had to be carried on even at the very low level of economic activity characteristic of the Middle Ages.

That this happened when it did is simply an historical circumstance which as such enters into any history of economics, whether socialist or liberal. One cannot even say that there is anything specifically Marxian about the notion that the revival of urban manufacture and commerce was bound to have a disruptive effect upon feudal society, since this was a commonplace among the writers from whom Marx obtained his own notions on the subject, and has not been questioned by economic historians since his day.[2] The stress laid by Marx on the disruptive character of the process is, however, connected with his general theory, because it enables him to challenge the conventional stress upon the 'harmony of all legitimate interests'. Before the market economy could come into being, a violent revolution had to operate upon the institutional framework of a society characterised, on the one hand, by peasant farming and, on the other, by small-scale commodity production. The 'bourgeois economists' who concentrated on the operation of the market and the price system

[1] Cf. Engels, *Origin of the Family*, etc., MESW II, p. 274: 'We know that rule over subjugated people is incompatible with the gentile order. Here we see it on a large scale. The German peoples, masters of the Roman provinces, had to organise their conquest; . . . Thus the organs of the gentile constitution had to be transformed into organs of state. . . . The moment had arrived for transforming military leadership into kingship.'

[2] Cf. H. Pirenne, *Economic and Social History of Medieval Europe*, London, 1936, pp. 50 ff; M. Dobb, *Studies in the Development of Capitalism*, London, 1946, pp. 33 ff.

were, in his view, oblivious of the historical ground on which they stood, or else apologetically employed in glossing over the reality of class conflict. The rise of capitalism involved the creation of the modern proletariat; its functioning depended upon the confrontation of 'capital' and 'labour', under conditions where 'labour' was synonymous with non-ownership.[1]

If these terms were reshuffled so as to give 'labour' control over 'capital', the system would cease to operate, or change into something else. It was of course Marx's purpose to help bring this about, but he also believed that the process had its own logic: 'labour' would become the dominant factor because its constantly growing productivity made it unnecessary to operate the economy within a framework of class rule. Capitalism itself was laying the foundations of the new order by developing the productive forces of society beyond the point where they could still be contained by the existing social arrangements. When that point had been reached, the 'political economy of labour', i.e., socialism, would take over from the 'political economy of capital'. The shape of the new order was not sketched out very distinctly, and the same obscurity was allowed to envelop the character of the transition period. Presumably it would depend on circumstances. But whether it was slow or rapid, peaceful or violent, the change-over would necessarily involve the disappearance of a society based on private ownership of the means of production. The latter were in any case due to be progressively centralised and 'socialised' by the very logic of the capitalist system—a system fatal to the institutions that had once given birth to it.[2]

[1] 'Capital therefore presupposes wage-labour; wage-labour presupposes capital. They condition each other; each brings the other into existence.' *Wage Labour and Capital* (1849), MEGA I/6, p. 485. 'Capital too is a social relation of production. It is a bourgeois relation of production, a relation of production of bourgeois society.' Cf. MESW I, pp. 90–2.

[2] 'This does not re-establish private property for the producer, but gives him individual property based on the acquisitions of the capitalist era: i.e., on co-operation and the possession in common of the land and of the means of production.' (*Capital*, I, p. 789.) The distinction between 'private' and 'individual' ownership is not made very clear, but the citizens of the co-operative commonwealth are in any case expected to own *something*. From a general viewpoint it is noteworthy that in his mature writings Marx no longer treats every kind of individual ownership as a form of 'self-estrangement', but rather tends to assume that it is a precondition of such limited, but real, freedom as is possible in society.

4

POLITICAL ECONOMY

HAVING REACHED this point it might seem reasonable to proceed straight to the Marxian theory of how the capitalist system operates, once it has come into existence as the result of the process described by Marx as 'primitive accumulation'. Instead we are obliged to undertake a detour into methodology. There are two reasons for this: first, Marx originally developed his doctrine in the form of a critique of what was then known as 'political economy', and his reasoning cannot be adequately understood outside this context. Secondly, his critique of current doctrine implied a theoretical approach which 'places' him as an economist belonging to the so-called classical school. Since the 'revision' of Marxist theory at the end of the nineteenth century coincided with the displacement of this school from the position it had hitherto occupied in the official teaching of economics, the classical view needs to be considered alongside the Marxian with which it shares certain basic assumptions. Unless this is borne in mind it is difficult to understand why and how the Marxian position continued to be defended after 1895 (i.e., after the death of Engels) by writers who had before them a clear choice between two alternative models, of which the Marxian by that time looked distinctly old-fashioned. It can of course be held that the choice was motivated by non-scientific considerations, but even if this is accepted it is important to see what it was that the Marxist school thought worth preserving.[1]

At the lowest level of abstraction relevant to the discussion of economics, the problem which presented itself to Marx may be set out as follows: it is assumed that the organisation of society has a determining effect upon the division of the social product among the various classes; it is likewise assumed that economic theory must throw light on macro-economic processes bound up with the class structure. We have seen how in Marx's model this mechanism operates to bring about the accumulation of capital in pre-bourgeois and bourgeois society. This was something to which economists before his time had not given much attention. For Marx it was, in every sense, the starting-point. At the very outset of his career he had protested that the economists ignored the social foundations on which the market system was based.[2] Almost a quarter of a century later, after he had himself become a professional economist (though not an academic one), he still maintained that the socially determined division of labour ought to be the starting-point for any rational explanation of how the economic system operated:

Every child knows that a country which ceased to work, I will not say for a year, but even for a few weeks, would perish. Every child knows too that the mass of products corresponding to the different needs require different and quantitatively determined masses of the total labour of society. That this *necessity* of *distributing* social labour in definite proportions cannot possibly be done away with by the *particular form* of social production, but can only change its *mode of appearance*, is self-evident. . . . And the *form* in which this proportional distribution of labour operates, in a state of society where the interconnection of social labour is manifested in the *private exchange* of the individual products of labour, is precisely the *exchange value* of these products.[3]

[1] Cf. for the following E. Roll, *A History of Economic Thought*, London, 1938, pp. 140 ff; M. Dobb, *Political Economy and Capitalism*, London, 1937, pp. 34 ff; P. M. Sweezy, *The Theory of Capitalist Development*, London, 1946, pp. 11 ff; R. L. Meek, *Studies in the Labour Theory of Value*, London, 1956, pp. 18 ff; R. Schlesinger, *Marx: His Time and Ours*, London, 1950, pp. 103 ff. All these writers are in the Marxist tradition, and their treatment of the classical heritage differs from that found in the standard academic textbooks. This seems as good a reason as any for referring to them in what is intended as a brief summary of the Marxian viewpoint.

[2] 'Political economy begins with the fact of private property; it does not explain it. . . . Political economy provides no explanation of the . . . distinction of labour from capital, of capital from land . . . what should be explained is assumed.' EPM (1844), MEGA I/3, pp. 81–2.

[3] Letter to L. Kugelmann, July 11, 1868. (Text after the amended translation in MESC, pp. 251–2.)

On the Marxian assumption, commodities exchange in proportion to their values, i.e., in proportion to the amount of labour embodied in them. This is the celebrated 'law of value', described by a critic as 'the economic expression of the fact (that) socially productive labour (constitutes) the basis of economic existence'.[1] As such the formula is really no more than a restatement of the materialist conception of history, which is meant to hold for all forms of society. Engels, however, goes on to suggest that the 'law' determines economic processes in a capitalist system, despite the fact that average prices no longer correspond to the embodied 'values' of commodities, as they had done under 'simple commodity production'.[2] This discrepancy of course was not unknown to Marx; on the contrary, he regarded it as the chief riddle of economic theory, but a riddle that could be solved, provided the ultimate determination of all economic exchanges by the embodiment of socially necessary labour was kept in mind:

> The scientific task consists precisely in working out *how* the law of value operates. So that if one wished at the very start to explain all the phenomena which apparently contradict the law, one would have to present the science *before* the science. The vulgar economist has not the faintest notion that the actual every-day exchange relations cannot be directly identical with the magnitudes of value. The essence of bourgeois society consists precisely in this, that *a priori* there is no conscious social regulation of production. The rational and naturally necessary asserts itself only as a blindly working average.[3]

It is important to be clear about the meaning of this passage. Economic sociology did not require Marx to go beyond asserting that the historically constituted division of labour in bourgeois (or capitalist) society[4] was the determining factor in causing the system to operate in certain ways, e.g., to remunerate owners of means of production (capitalists) in proportion to their capital rather than their

---

[1] W. Sombart, with some reservations approvingly quoted by Engels; cf. supplement to vol. III of *Capital* (Moscow, 1960, edn.).

[2] Ibid., pp. 871 ff.   [3] Letter to Kugelmann, MESC, p. 252.

[4] Strictly speaking there is no such thing as capitalist society, at least if one adheres to the Marxian scheme. Capitalism refers to the economic relations characteristic of *bourgeois* society, which as a matter of historical fact has never existed outside Western Europe and the Americas, though in a rudimentary form it was beginning to develop in Eastern Europe before 1917. For obvious reasons, Leninist writers are not anxious to stress this distinction, which is, however, inescapable if one adopts Marx's conceptual apparatus. In the following, capitalism denotes the *economic system* characteristic of *bourgeois society*, the latter being the fully developed form of *Western civilisation*.

managerial (or entrepreneurial) function. These and other points were indeed important to him, as they were to socialists who did not share his interest in the 'law of value'; but they did not concern him primarily as an economist. In the latter capacity he thought it necessary to affirm, not just that bourgeois 'relations of production' (*Produktionsverhaeltnisse*) represented an institutional framework of great importance for the functioning of the system, but that it was possible to construct a theoretical model with reference to one particular factor of outstanding importance, namely, labour. It followed that the prime task of economic theory consisted in deriving market prices from this factor.

It is worth trying to understand how Marx came to regard such an operation as both possible and necessary. Nothing is explained by saying that a commitment to the labour theory of value was implicit in the socialist critique of capitalism. This sort of explanation may be adequate when applied to the early Ricardian socialists, but it becomes positively absurd in dealing with Marx. For him there had to be conclusive intellectual arguments in favour of pursuing a line of reasoning which even in Ricardo's day had not gone without criticism.[1] To say that he was essentially a Ricardian who saw every problem through the eyes of his predecessor, hardly represents a satisfactory explanation. Moreover, one must not overlook the important difference between Ricardo's theory of value and Marx's: Ricardo introduced the labour-quantity theorem as a means of explaining the actual movement of exchange values (prices), but otherwise attached no significance to it, and would have been perfectly willing to drop it if another explanation had suggested itself. This was not the case with Marx.[2] For the moment, however, we must leave Marx and turn to the broader question how classical political economy came to concern itself with the value problem in the first place.

Although theorising about economic phenomena is older than either capitalism or the science of economics, it is indisputable that the latter developed alongside the former, as a systematic clarification of problems inherent in the growth of a market economy. 'Political economy', as it came to be known after having outgrown medieval canon law, had for its immediate subject those social relations and

---

[1] Schumpeter, *History of Economic Analysis*, pp. 588 ff; Blaug, *Ricardian Economics*, pp. 52 ff.
[2] Schumpeter, op. cit., p. 596.

economic processes which were about to give rise to merchant capitalism.[1] This involved a gradual shedding of concepts inherited from an earlier age, when a certain amount of rudimentary theorising about exchange relations took place under the aegis of scholasticism.[2] From an analytical standpoint the medieval prohibition upon the taking of interest is of less interest in this connection than the scholastic attempt to formulate the concept of a 'just price', since this entailed a distinction between the 'value' of commodities (defined in terms of cost to the producer, who was normally an artisan or trader) and the price his goods might fetch in the market. Any discrepancy between cost and reward that failed to repay the seller—in respect of labour invested, but also risk undertaken, costs of transport, etc.— was regarded as an infringement of commutative justice, and as such would incur moral censure. Ideally, and to some extent actually, cases of this sort fell under the jurisdiction of the authorities who would normally apply commonsense criteria in judging whether costs and rewards were proportionate. Under conditions of 'simple commodity exchange' (to employ the Marxian terminology) this usually sufficed to secure *both* an acceptable measure of distributive justice *and* a means of defining the relationship between values (=costs) and prices, there being no great theoretical or practical difficulty about comparing average costs and average rewards in a society where trade was at a minimum and the producers normally operated under roughly comparable conditions and with similar tools.[3]

The disruption of this simple equilibrium through the growth of merchant capital meant among other things that it was no longer practicable to equate 'value' with producers' costs. Instead attention shifted to the manner in which goods were priced under more or less competitive conditions, and it came to be recognised that the 'just price' might be equated with the current market price, wherever the latter was not distorted by artificial price-fixing or monopoly. Thus the estimation of the market was accepted as valid, and if the producer did not recover his original outlay, that was his bad luck.

[1] Roll, op. cit., p. 22; Dobb, op. cit., pp. 34 ff; Meek, op. cit., pp. 12 ff.

[2] Schumpeter, op. cit., pp. 92 ff.

[3] Schumpeter, op. cit., p. 93; cf. also R. H. Tawney, *Religion and the Rise of Capitalism* (Pelican edn., London, 1937, pp. 46–9). Whether this justifies the suggestion that the 'true descendant of the doctrines of Aquinas is the labour theory of value. The last of the Schoolmen was Karl Marx' (Tawney, ibid., p. 49), is another matter.

Conversely, if he obtained more for his produce than it was 'worth' to him (under the old reckoning), this might be justified on the grounds that it was evidently 'worth' more than its costs *to his customers*. The valuation placed by the buyer upon the commodity thus introduced a new criterion, which in due course made it possible to drop the cost approach and equate 'value' with subjective usefulness to the buyer. Alternatively, 'value' could be identified with actual market price, the latter being regulated by supply and demand. This was the final step, and not surprisingly it was taken by the mercantilist writers who generalised the practice of the merchants. By the seventeenth century, therefore, 'value' in economic literature had generally come to signify price, its determination being left to the market; though it was generally understood that there was also something called 'intrinsic value' or usefulness—this being the material foundation, so to speak, of the exchange mechanism. Exactly how exchange value could be said to arise from usefulness was left unclear.[1]

The next turn of the wheel introduces a different conception of value, which (in common with the medieval canonists) once more lays emphasis upon production costs, and it is here that our analytical difficulties begin. For this period—the so-called classical one—is associated both with the rise of industrial capitalism, and with the emergence of the labour theory of value, in the form in which Marx inherited it from A. Smith and Ricardo. This circumstance alone shows that the subject has to be approached historically. From the late seventeenth century onward, 'political economy'—now beginning to acquire definite shape—aspires to become a science and at the same time gropes towards a theory of costs based upon a new evaluation of the importance of human labour. This is one of the watersheds separating the mercantilist from the industrial era, and quite properly it is graced by the emergence of a fresh set of theoretical generalisations. Among their authors mention must briefly be made of Locke,

[1] The writers of this period, though pre-classical in the academic usage of the term, include some economists whom Marx reckoned among the founders of 'political economy', e.g., Petty in England and Boisguillebert in France, both mercantilists in the fullest sense. It is worth bearing in mind that for Marx 'political economy' starts with these seventeenth-century authors and culminates in Ricardo, after reaching an earlier peak with Quesnay in France and A. Smith in England. This approach differs significantly from the standard liberal account, which has the middle of the eighteenth century for its starting-point, and describes as 'classical' some nineteenth-century writers (e.g., Senior) whom Marx classed among the 'vulgar economists'.

since he can be said to have anticipated Smith in suggesting that labour is the principal source of (use) value.[1] Throughout this period, the new emphasis upon the wealth-creating power of production rather than trade (as with the mercantilists) clearly reflects the growing importance of manufacturing industry. This is true at any rate of England. In France the later eighteenth century witnessed the rise of the physiocratic school, which rather perversely sought to place manufactures among the 'sterile' occupations, reserving the honorific term 'productive' for agriculture; though here too the emphasis was upon the productivity of labour when applied to natural riches.[2]

The next step was taken by A. Smith, who summed up what had gone before, notably with regard to value theory. This intellectual inheritance included some striking suggestions thrown out by the anonymous author of a pamphlet to which Marx referred on some occasions and which may be conjectured to have influenced Smith when he came to formulate his views; for here we encounter a labour-quantity theory which substantially anticipates that of the classical school, even to the extent of stating, in regard to 'the Necessaries of Life', that 'the Value of them, when they are exchanged the one for the other, is regulated by the Quantity of Labour necessarily required, and commonly taken in producing them; and the Value or Price of them, when they are bought and sold, and compared to a common Medium, will be govern'd by the Quantity of Labour employ'd'.[3] There is an echo of this in the *Wealth of Nations* (Book I, ch. VI), though the notion that quantity of labour regulates the exchange of products is limited by Smith to 'that early and rude state of society which precedes both the accumulation of stock and the appropriation of land'. It is questionable whether this in itself constitutes more than the skeleton of a labour theory, since for the situation envisaged by

---

[1] Cf. Locke, *Of Civil Government* (Everyman edn.), pp. 136–7. Locke does not seem to have distinguished between use value and exchange value, and the importance he attributes to labour in the production of wealth clearly has to do with the former. As a distant forerunner of the labour theory he can be said to qualify only insofar as he apparently suggested something like it to Smith. But his moral support was doubtless welcome.

[2] For a recent discussion of the physiocratic school cf. R. L. Meek, 'The Physiocratic Concept of Profit', in *Economica*, vol. XXVI, No. 101, February 1959.

[3] *Some Thoughts on the Interest of Money in General* (probably 1738), quoted by Meek, op. cit., pp. 42 ff.

Smith it is equivalent to saying that labour is the only available factor of production: in which case the whole proposition comes close to being a tautology.[1] But the Smithian formulation does something else: it fixes attention upon the social relationships which determine the share-out of the total product. Smith (possibly influenced by Locke) went on from there to restate the Natural Law doctrine that 'the produce of labour constitutes the natural recompense or wages of labour'. In the original state of things 'the whole produce of labour belongs to the labourer. He has neither landlord nor master to share with him.'[2] Affirmations of this sort were too vague (and too much in tune with current opinion) to occasion either surprise or resentment when they were first uttered, though this attitude was to change later on, after the socialists had learned to make use of them. In any case such propositions were not germane to economic analysis, which even in the days of A. Smith operated at an altogether different level of abstraction. But they did something else: they set political economy firmly on the road towards a general theory of society.

In treating the division of labour as the central mainspring of economic activity, Smith went beyond economics in the technical sense of the term. His theory of value, such as it is, grows out of his analysis of social relations, as does his enquiry into the division of the social product. Nothing is gained, however, by pretending that his discussion of value theory is satisfactory from a theoretical viewpoint. His utterances on the subject are ambiguous and confused, several different strands of thought being interwoven in his treatment of the value concept, so that it became possible for later writers to claim him for the subjectivist school, while other elements of his thinking were developed by Ricardo and his pupils.[3] For a genuine labour-quantity theory, which makes labour the regulator of exchange-value (price), as well as the source of use-value (wealth), one has to turn to Ricardo; while the only consistent attempt to work out the implications of the labour theory was made by Marx.

Before leaving Smith, however, it is worth noting that his defective formulation of the value concept does not necessarily invalidate his factual analysis; the latter is not logically dependent upon the labour theory in the form in which he stated it, or failed to state it. When he

[1] Schumpeter, op. cit., p. 310.
[2] *The Wealth of Nations* (Modern Library edn., New York, 1937), p. 64.
[3] Schumpeter, op. cit., pp. 308 ff; Roll, op. cit., pp. 158 ff; Meek, *Studies* pp. 60 ff.

suggested a rudimentary doctrine of surplus value,[1] he did so not with reference to any speculative derivation of market prices from values, but on the basis of observable facts which few contemporaries would have been willing to question. Moreover, he did not pass censure upon the arrangements he described. A system based on the appropriation of surplus value by landowners and manufacturers appeared to him the only possible one, if not perhaps the best possible in some philosophical (Natural Law) sense. The point is worth making because it has frequently been affirmed that moral condemnation of surplus-value appropriation, from the standpoint of Natural Law ethics, is the essence of socialism. This holds good, with some reservations, for the Ricardian socialists around 1830; for Proudhon and his followers in France; and for Rodbertus, who can fairly be described as the spiritual father of German *Kathedersozialismus*; but it is absurd when applied to Marx, who spent much of his time criticising the 'utopian socialists' for interpreting the labour theory to mean that the whole produce of labour ought to accrue to the immediate producer. This was impossible, as he took pains to point out, even under full socialism;[2] and it certainly did not provide the socialist movement with a practical orientation. The labour theory was indeed bound up with a social philosophy which placed 'relations of production' in the centre of the picture. But by itself it did not commit its adherents to any particular programme. For proof of this contention one need look no farther than the work of Ricardo (1772–1823) who was the first writer to formulate the labour theory in a manner that made it relevant to theoretical economics.[3]

What Ricardo meant by political economy—and it is this meaning which Marx took over from him, and which the Marxian school has conserved—is indicated in the very first sentence of the preface to his great work: 'The produce of the earth—all that is derived from its

---

[1] Cf. *Wealth of Nations*, Book I, ch. VIII. Rent and profit are here described as 'deductions' from the 'produce of labour' which in the 'original state of things' belongs wholly to the labourer. 'In all arts and manufactures the greater part of the workmen stand in need of a master to advance them the materials of their work, and their wages and maintenance till it be completed. He shares in the produce of their labour, or in the value which it adds to the materials upon which it is bestowed; and in this share consists his profit.' (Ibid., p. 65.)

[2] Cf. *Critique of the Gotha Programme*, MESW II, pp. 20 ff.

[3] Schumpeter, op. cit., pp. 469–80, 590 ff; Blaug, op. cit., passim; Roll, op. cit., pp. 175 ff; Meek, op. cit., pp. 82 ff. There is a vast literature on Ricardo, but for our purpose only his version of the labour theory need be considered, since it served Marx as a starting-point for his own doctrine.

surface by the united application of labour, machinery and capital—is divided among three classes of the community; namely, the proprietor of the land, the owner of the stock or capital necessary for its cultivation, and the labourers by whose industry it is cultivated.' After noting that 'in different stages of society, the proportions of the whole produce of the earth which will be allotted to each of these classes, under the names of rent, profit, wages, will be . . . different . . .' he goes on to declare that 'to determine the laws which regulate this distribution, is the principal problem in Political Economy'.[1] The theory of value was a means to this end. There were moments when he wavered on the question of the practical use to which 'the doctrine of value' might be put in analysing 'the proportions in which the whole produce is divided between landlords, capitalists and labourers';[2] but these doubts were voiced in his private correspondence, not in his published work. The latter is dominated by the quest for an invariable standard of value applicable to the measurement of the social product; and in this search for an unchangeable standard he was led (following Smith) to the famous statement which introduces and sums up the first chapter of the *Principles*: 'The value of a commodity, or the quantity of any other commodity for which it will exchange, depends on the relative quantity of labour which is necessary for its production, and not on the greater or less compensation which is paid for that labour.'[3] Utility, he added, 'is not the measure of exchangeable value, although it is absolutely essential to it'. These affirmations may not represent 'the heart of the Ricardian system', which has to do with the rent of land and its effect on the rate of profit,[4] but they are all that need concern us, for they form the starting-point of Marx's attempt to formulate a satisfactory theory of value after Ricardo's immediate followers had abandoned the attempt.[5]

That the enterprise was so soon relinquished was principally due to Ricardo's failure to account for the discrepancy between embodied labour ratios and actual exchange ratios—a difficulty he tried to meet by introducing 'modifications' which undermined his general principle. In his analysis of wages, too, he came up against an obstacle

[1] David Ricardo, *Principles of Political Economy and Taxation*, ed. P. Sraffa and M. Dobb, Cambridge, 1953, p. 5.

[2] Ibid., p. xxxiii.

[3] *Principles*, p. 11.

[4] Cf. Blaug, op. cit., p. 3.

[5] Blaug, pp. 46 ff; Meek, op. cit., pp. 110 ff.

which had already baffled Smith: the exchange of commodities was supposed to represent an exchange of equal quantities of embodied labour, but this equivalence disappears when capital and labour are exchanged, for the wages paid to the labourer possess a smaller exchange value than the output which he produces for the capitalist. In other words, the theory failed to account for the phenomenon of profit.[1] It was this theoretical puzzle which led Marx to formulate his doctrine of surplus value, of which more later. Here it remains to be noted that the social and political implications of Ricardo's general model were plainly unfavourable to landowners, but in no sense favourable to industrial workers.[2] It is true that the 'Ricardian socialists' were able to draw their own conclusions from the suggestion that labour is the only value-creating factor of production. This, however, required no great ingenuity, and if the notion of surplus value had amounted to no more, it would have been lost from view so far as economic theory was concerned. That this did not occur was due to the intervention of Marx who gave a new formulation to the concept. Surplus value and exploitation are both inherent in the Ricardian system, but Ricardo did not himself draw such conclusions, let alone anticipate their later use.

Compared with the Ricardian version of the labour theory, the Marxian is distinguished by greater logical coherence, though this does not necessarily rescue it from the charge of being irrelevant to the proper business of economic analysis. At any rate Marx was the only Ricardian who ever went through with the labour theory of value. To do this he was obliged to reformulate it. He started from the proposition—already laid down by Smith and elaborated by Ricardo—that a commodity which is to serve as the standard of exchange value must itself be invariable.[3] He also accepted Ricardo's statement that such an invariant measure of value was to be found in the unit of labour embodied (subject to unimportant qualifications) in commodities. On this hypothesis, all that was needed to obtain an invariant measure was to imagine a commodity which always embodied the same quantity of labour. By means of this intellectual operation, commodities acquired inherent (objective) values which could be compared—the very thing that was impossible as long as exchange *value* simply meant exchange *ratio*. But Marx went further

[1] Roll, op. cit., pp. 182–4.
[2] Schumpeter, op. cit., p. 553; Blaug, op. cit., pp. 6 ff.
[3] Schumpeter, op. cit., pp. 591 ff; Blaug, op. cit., p. 16; Dobb, op. cit., p. 10.

than Ricardo. The latter had treated embodied labour as the regulator of exchange values, but had not troubled to define the concept of value itself. For Marx, the quantity of labour incorporated in products does not merely determine their value; it *is* their value; commodities *are* congealed labour. This difference had practical consequences. Ricardo—and even more so his followers, notably James Mill and McCulloch—had been baffled by the discrepancy between actual exchange ratios and imputed labour costs; this seemed to make nonsense of the principle that (under certain assumed conditions) the exchange values (prices) of commodities are proportional to the quantities of labour embodied in them. It would be an absurdity to say that for Marx this problem did not exist, since it formed the starting-point of his theorising; but it did not constitute any reason to modify his value theory, for on his supposition 'value' was always identical with embodied labour, whatever might be true of relative prices. The problem rather consisted in showing how these absolute (objective) values came to be 'realised' in such a way that commodities—while still retaining their values—were sold at market prices *not* proportional to these values. For Ricardo, values and prices were ultimately the same thing; for Marx they were not. Hence he was able to carry the notion of an absolute value to its logical conclusion, though at the cost of creating what in the end turned out to be the insoluble problem of relating the two calculi to each other. Given the original assumption, there is no logical flaw in the Marxian system, for we may *define* 'value' in whatever manner we please; whether the operation yields results commensurate with the intellectual labour invested in it, is another matter, on which Marxists and non-Marxists have continued to differ.[1]

In judging Ricardian and Marxian economics from a modern standpoint it is important to disentangle their problems from their attempted solutions, and the solutions from the methodical assumptions that went into them. The latter included a labour-cost theory of value which ultimately went back to the Natural Law proposition that all riches are produced by human toil.[2] General notions of this kind in turn served as a pointer towards the solution of genuinely technical problems, e.g., the problem of discovering an invariant measure of value. These procedures have to be judged on their merit,

---

[1] Schumpeter, op. cit., pp. 597–8. For a defence of the Marxist position cf. Dobb, op. cit., pp. 12 ff; Meek, op. cit., pp. 116 ff.
[2] Cf. Ricardo, *Principles*, ed. Sraffa, pp. 284–5.

and cannot be validly defended (or criticised) on philosophical grounds alone. In the lengthy debate around the labour theory this was frequently overlooked. It became a commonplace of academic criticism that Ricardo, and following him Marx, had been induced by non-scientific considerations to adopt a value theory which was irrelevant to the task of economic analysis. On the other side, the defenders of the labour theory clung to the notion that the expenditure of human energy (labour) somehow constituted a unique cost element which in the long run *must* regulate prices. This was not necessarily an irrational approach to the problem of identifying an objective standard of measurement lying outside the field of price-variables; whether the search was successful is a question which has nothing to do with one's philosophical or political preferences.

It is also worth noting that the abandonment of the classical cost approach does not necessarily entail a diminution of interest in the problem it was intended to clarify. The central issue posed by Ricardo and elaborated by Marx, namely the relative shares of capital and labour in the total product and their connection with the rate of capital formation, has certainly not lost its relevance. The classics were guilty of many confusions, but they never overlooked the fact that 'political economy' had to do with the operation of the system as a whole, not merely with the determination of prices. In technical language, they tried to build a macro-economic model; their successors had less ambitious aims in view and were generally more successful in attaining them. Whether at the level of abstraction at which they chose to operate it was still possible to see the economic problem in realistic terms, is another matter.

Even the labour theory of value was not simply the empty general notion its critics professed to see in it. Among the distinctions established by classical political economy was that between 'riches' and 'value': the point being that while nature, as well as the expenditure of human physical energy (labour), went into the creation of wealth, 'value' by contrast represented a social relationship. Its origin was held to lie in costs, and the latter in turn had to be measured by a particular scarcity factor, namely labour. These distinctions belong properly speaking to the realm of economic sociology, and it is arguable that in applying a labour-cost theory of value derived from primitive social conditions to an economic model belonging to a higher stage, the classics were guilty of confusing different levels of

174

abstraction.[1] Instead of becoming unduly concerned over this logical blunder (if that is what it was), one should bear in mind that their attention was fixed on processes having to do with the size and distribution of the social product. Ultimately, what concerned them was 'the wealth of nations', and the social conditions under which human effort went into the production of riches. To this Ricardo added the division of the total product among the major classes of society, and thus laid the basis for the Marxian synthesis of sociology and political economy. Marx's formulation of the so-called materialist conception of history ('In the social production of their life, men enter into definite relations that are indispensable and independent of their will, relations of production which correspond to a definite stage of development of their material productive forces')[2] implicitly defines the subject of his economic doctrine, inasmuch as it was his aim to lay bare the 'law of motion' of bourgeois society by analysing its economic mechanism. This meant welding into a whole sociology and economics, both conceived historically. Technical economic analysis entered into the synthesis as an indispensable element, no more. The basic conception of an immanent economic process whose logic transforms bourgeois society into something else, retains its significance even in the absence of proof that the process is regulated by the operation of the 'law of value' under the particular conditions created by capitalism: conditions which for Marx were characterised by the failure of the participants to perceive the essentially social nature of their actions. This approach is arbitrary, but no more so than a doctrine which starts from the experiences of Robinson Crusoe. To the extent that he based his economics on a comprehensive vision of society, Marx stands in the central tradition of political economy. Paradoxically, he can be described as the last, as well as the greatest, of the classical economists.[3]

---

[1] The reference here of course is to the classics of 'political economy', e.g., the physiocrats, A. Smith, and Ricardo, plus his immediate followers, down to John Stuart Mill. In current academic parlance, 'classical' economics has a different connotation.

[2] *A Contribution to the Critique of Political Economy. Preface.* MESW I, pp. 362–3.

[3] Schumpeter, op. cit., p. 441; Sweezy, op. cit., pp. 41 ff; for the Marxist critique of equilibrium analysis cf. *inter alia* Paul Sering, "Zu Marschalls neuklassischer Oekonomie', in *Zeitschrift für Sozialforschung*, Paris, 1937, vol. vi, no. 3, pp. 522–40.

5

MARXIAN ECONOMICS

IT REMAINS to summarise as briefly as possible Marx's theory of economic development and its relevance for his sociological analysis. After what has been said about his views on the historic relationship of capitalism to bourgeois society, there is no need to emphasise that Marx's strictly economic theorising operates at a level of abstraction much higher than—and in any case quite different from—his sociology. In the end both are brought together by his theory of capitalist development, which purports to show that the inherent logic of the system imposes insuperable barriers to its functioning beyond a certain point. But this conclusion is arrived at by way of a very elaborate process of reasoning which systematically abstracts from all save strictly economic relations. In this part of his work Marx proceeds like any other classical economist, though this fact is obscured by his terminology. Where he differs from his predecessors is not in being more abstract, but in abstracting from other matters. The analysis of rent in Ricardo's work had been related to its author's concern with the conflicting interests of industry and agriculture. Marx in turn emphasised the capital-labour relationship as being central to the functioning of capitalism in its fully developed phase. The starting-point of his analysis is the purchase of labour-power by the capitalist, and large sections of *Capital* (vol. I) are devoted to a discussion of the capital-labour relationship in an 'isolated' or 'abstract' form, other social relations being temporarily ignored, to be reintroduced later. This is standard procedure and does not entail the impossible notion that there are only two classes in society. Marx considered that capital had become 'the all-dominating power of bourgeois society', from which it followed that industrial production (rather than agriculture, which historically comes earlier) was the logical starting-point for an analysis of the system.[1]

Since even the briefest outline of *Capital* would fill a volume, we must content ourselves with elaborating a few points which are relevant to our theme. Perhaps the most general formula serviceable in this context would be to say that Marx was trying to show how the 'law of value' operates under capitalism, and how in the long run it determines the allocation of capital and labour to the various branches of production, with the economic consequences (including periodic crises) resulting therefrom. Such a formulation, of course, does no more than outline a very general programme, which it took Marx several volumes of theoretical work (for the greater part not published in his lifetime) to accomplish. Throughout, the link between economics and sociology is maintained by reliance upon the law of value, as a principle of exchange relations between commodities, as well as a determinant of the manner in which the social product is distributed among the major classes. Since it is assumed that under any social system the organisation of production 'determines the (forms of) consumption, distribution, exchange',[2] the task consists of showing how the particular organisation of capitalist production (in which the immediate producers possess only their labour-power) determines the exchange of commodities so produced. This involves the theoretical problem of explaining how and why exchange ratios continue to be a function of embodied labour ratios, although in appearance they diverge. Failing such a demonstration it might still be asserted on general (historical) grounds that relations of production ultimately determine relations of exchange (this is the simplest way of summing up the materialist conception of history, if anything so involved can ever be reduced to a formula); but proof of the assertion would be lacking, at any rate for the case of capitalism. That is why the labour

[1] Sweezy, op. cit., pp. 16 ff. The quotation is from the English (Kerr) edition of the *Critique of Political Economy*, p. 302. For the following, in addition to Sweezy, cf. Dobb, op. cit., pp. 55 ff; Roll, op. cit., pp. 265 ff; Schlesinger, op. cit., p. 110; Meek, op. cit., pp. 144 ff. Critical views will be considered later.

[2] *Critique of Political Economy*, p. 291.

theory is relevant to Marxist sociology, while the strictly economic analysis embodied in *Capital* can, with some ingenuity, be rendered independent of it. Of course if one happens not to be interested in Marx's doctrine beyond its contribution to 'economics' in the technical sense, the whole problem falls to the ground.

The analysis begins with a reformulation of the familiar classical distinction between use value and exchange value. The former is ruled out as a determinant of (long-term equilibrium) prices, though the grounds for dismissing it are not fully stated and had to be rather laboriously rediscovered by Marx's followers in the next generation.[1] Exchange value is defined as a historical category pertaining only to commodities produced for a market.[2] Under capitalism, where the producers no longer own their tools (as distinct from 'simple commodity production', where they do) exchange value acquires a further connotation: it now signifies that the social division of labour, which gives rise to the phenomenon of commodity exchange, is at the same time a division between classes. For purposes of simplification it is assumed that production takes places under conditions where all essential operations are performed by hired workers, while those who control the means of production figure simply as owners of capital and hirers of labour-power. This is the general economic model discussed in *Capital*, vol. I. Like all such models it is sufficiently abstract to yield formulations of the type required by any theory that aims at more than a simple enumeration of empirical data. On the same principle it is assumed that all the labour performed is 'socially necessary', i.e., in accordance with prevailing technical standards and normal conditions of production; as well as homogeneous, i.e., expenditure of one uniform labour-power.[3] The difficulties inherent in these assumptions were not overlooked by Marx, but he probably underestimated their seriousness.

The next step consists in accounting for the phenomenon of profit on the (classical) assumption that labour is the only source of value.

[1] Cf. R. Hilferding, *Böhm-Bawerk's Criticism of Marx*, ed. Sweezy, New York, 1949, pp. 123 ff. (Originally published under the title 'Böhm-Bawerk's Marx-Kritik', in *Marx-Studien*, vol. I, Vienna, 1904.)

[2] *Capital*, vol. I, p. 60. 'From that moment the distinction becomes firmly established between the utility of an object for the purposes of consumption, and its utility for the purposes of exchange.' For a fuller treatment of the subject cf. *Theories of Surplus Labour*, London, 1951, pp. 107 ff.

[3] *Capital*, I, p. 6. Marx draws a distinction between 'concrete' and 'abstract' labour, but we cannot go into this here, although the point is relevant for the understanding of his value concept.

This concept had been modified by Marx in order to bring it into line with his definition of labour as the *measure* of value. Clearly, if labour was the invariant measure of the exchange value possessed by commodities, it could not itself have value. But under capitalism, labour appeared on the market as a commodity and thus must be assumed to possess exchange value. Moreover, if the exchange value of a product equalled the labour time contained in it, the exchange value of a day's labour must be equal to its product, i.e., the wages of labour must equal the product of labour, which plainly was not the case. Marx solved the puzzle—which to non-Marxists must appear artificial—by introducing a distinction between labour and labour-power, the latter signifying the working capacity of human beings, i.e., their store of physical and nervous energy. Under given conditions this general human faculty appears as the particular qualification of free individuals who have nothing else to sell. Labour-power having become 'alienated' as something that could be bought and sold like any other commodity, *its* value was determined by its own 'costs of production', i.e., by what was needed to maintain its owner. The difference between this minimum (which, however, represented the full value of what it bought), and the productive capacity of the labourer when applied at work, appeared in the form of surplus-value. Hence profit was accumulated by those who owned the means of production, not because capital (or ability) was a scarce factor which commanded a special premium, but because the productivity of labour under normal conditions exceeded what was necessary to maintain the labourer. The appearance of such a surplus was characteristic of all stages of society, but its appropriation under capitalism in the form of profit was conditioned by the fact that human labour-power was purchased as a commodity by those who owned the means of production. Under earlier forms of society, e.g., under feudalism, the productive surplus (or part of it) had simply been appropriated by the possessing class (which was also the ruling class) without further ado; but under capitalism, where all relations assumed a value-form, there was no visible surplus product to be withheld from the producer, only a surplus-*value* which had been generated by the social relation in which workers stood towards employers. Given this institutional arrangement, the requirements of the law of value were satisfied by the purchase of labour-power at its current market rate. That this particular commodity had the special faculty of generating a surplus over and above what it cost to reproduce, was no one's

179

fault, and no one was to blame if this surplus later made its appearance as a profit realised upon the investment of capital.

The exchange value of commodities so produced consists of two separate elements: the value transferred to it by the machinery and raw materials (constant capital) consumed in the process of production, and the additional value created by the application of labour-power for which payment is rendered in wages (variable capital). A given proportion of this newly created value is required to reproduce the labour-power expended in the process, i.e., to maintain the worker (and his family), while the balance represents surplus-labour whose value constitutes the source of profit. The ratio between these two magnitudes determines the rate of surplus-value, or rate of exploitation (reckoned upon the wage fund, or variable capital) while the ratio of surplus-value to the total (constant plus variable) capital represents the rate of profit. In this theoretical model prices are supposed to be regulated directly by values, and profits are made to depend on the proportion of variable capital (wages) to the total (since living labour alone creates an additional value, over and above that embodied in material means of production). The whole construction is necessarily abstract and not meant to apply to empirical reality without serious qualifications, which are developed in *Capital*, vol. III. Nonetheless Marx maintained that the principles laid down in volume I, though not applicable to each individual case, still determine the exchange value of commodities in the aggregate, as well as the rate of profit.

The crucial difficulty here is the relation of values to prices. It has already been pointed out that for Marx the value of a commodity is *defined* in terms of embodied labour; this disposes of the question whether or not his value theory is 'wrong'—a pseudo-problem on which both his followers and his critics subsequently wasted a good deal of effort. The relevant question is whether on his assumptions it is possible to account for the movement of (long-range equilibrium) prices and profits; and the candid answer must be that, though not impossible in principle, the operation is so involved, and requires so many auxiliary hypotheses, as to be very nearly self-defeating in practice.[1]

[1] Cf. Schumpeter, *Capitalism, Socialism and Democracy*, pp. 23 ff; Joan Robinson, *An Essay on Marxian Economics*, London, 1942, pp. 11 ff; Böhm-Bawerk (ed. Sweezy, op. cit.), pp. 9 ff. The literature on this subject is immense; some of the standard arguments and rebuttals will reappear in the course of our survey. Here it is intended to cite only the most general considerations.

Marx sets out by laying down the general rule that commodities tend to exchange at prices which correspond to their (embodied) values. 'Price is the money-name of the labour realised in a commodity.'[1] Temporary deviations from this rule are to be regarded as infractions of a general law which determines the exchange of commodities. In volume III[2] this principle is qualified by the admission that—account being taken of different capital-labour ratios in different industries, as well as the prevalence of a uniform rate of profit established by competition—commodities do not in fact exchange in accordance with embodied labour values, but rather according to 'prices of production', i.e., monetary costs plus an average profit. Whether one treats this admission as a fatal contradiction of the basic law laid down in volume I (as did Böhm-Bawerk and others), or whether one regards it as a sensible qualification of a theoretical 'first approximation' whose significance is not diminished thereby, must ultimately depend on what one expects a theory of value to do. If one's interest is focused on a sociological explanation of the genesis and operation of capitalism, there is no particular reason why one should not employ the Marxian apparatus, since its conceptual tools are evidently suited to an approach which treats the accumulation of capital as the central main-spring of the entire process. If one believes that a theory of value must justify itself by enabling economists to derive prices from values, it is hard to see what useful purpose is served by trying to salvage a theoretical model which makes such an operation impossibly difficult. Nothing that Marx has to say about the sociology of capitalism is invalidated by his adherence to a traditional standpoint which treats labour as the only value-creating factor of production. On the other hand, the convoluted mazes of sophistry developed by his orthodox disciples in order to bring the labour theory into harmony with the formal requirements of economic analysis, undoubtedly helped to give the whole system a more bizarre appearance than is really warranted.[3]

---

[1] *Capital*, I, p. 74.

[2] Which, though not published until 1894, was substantially completed by the time vol. I had appeared (1867), so that one cannot treat its formulations as a 'contradiction' of the abstract model developed earlier.

[3] For an account of the consequent debates within and without the Marxist camp (written from an orthodox standpoint) cf. Sweezy, *The Theory of Capitalist Development*, passim, where reference is also made to the 'Bortkiewicz corollary' concerning the relation of values to prices in the Marxian system. For a critical (though equally Marxist) view of Sweezy's position cf. Schlesinger, op. cit.,

At the risk of becoming enmeshed in a controversy which has now gone on for over half a century, an attempt must still be made to indicate briefly *why* Marx thought it necessary to maintain an approach whose difficulties were certainly apparent to him and which did nothing to facilitate his strictly technical work as an economist—work whose significance has become more apparent as interest has shifted from a static to a dynamic conception of the economic process.

Part of the explanation clearly has to do with the fact that the labour theory of value was an important constituent of an intellectual heritage to which every major classical treatise from the *Wealth of Nations* (1776) to John Stuart Mill's *Principles of Political Economy* (1848) had paid homage. In a sense the true question is not why Marx employed this conventional approach, but why he did not abandon it. The answer is that the concept of value defined the subject of economics in a manner which was both traditional and rational, if what was wanted was a model applicable to secular changes in the growth and distribution of society's output; while the concept of surplus-value was required to account for the phenomenon of profit. In the Marxian model surplus-value arises from the difference between the value of commodities (treated as an aggregate) and the value of labour-power, the latter representing not simply a cost element of production (as is necessarily the case under every form of society), but the source of an unearned increment appropriated by the purchasers of labour-power, i.e., the capitalists. The trouble with this construction is that it introduces a constant derived from pre-capitalist conditions (value determination by embodied labour) as an explanation of what happens under capitalism, where this determination no longer applies. The advantage Marx gained from this procedure was that it gave him a theoretical standpoint outside the capitalist nexus, and thus enabled him to treat the whole system as a passing historical phase, where other economists naïvely identified it with the market economy, commodity production, monetary relations, or some such unhistorical abstraction. As against this greater sociological realism he paid the price of having to account, in terms

pp. 119 ff. The orthodox position is once more upheld (with some qualifications) by R. L. Meek, op. cit., pp. 201 ff, following a line of reasoning suggested earlier by M. Dobb, op. cit., pp. 68 ff. For the representative Keynesian critique of Marx's approach cf. Joan Robinson, op. cit., pp. 20 ff. A viewpoint rather more critical of Marx than of Ricardo is set out by Blaug, op. cit., pp. 231 ff. For the alleged contradiction between vols. I and III of *Capital*, cf. Schumpeter, op. cit., p. 29.

of 'value', for what was occurring in the domain of prices and profits. He also entangled himself in serious methodological troubles by trying to settle the relation of skilled to unskilled, and of productive to unproductive, work. Some of these difficulties can be resolved with the aid of auxiliary concepts, but only at the cost of introducing fresh assumptions no longer grounded in the original ones.

Perhaps the only summing-up which might commend itself equally to adherents and critics of the Marxian approach would be to say that it represents an attempt to relate the sociology of capitalism (as a set of institutions involving the appropriation of surplus wealth) to a theory of how the social product is allocated by way of the price mechanism. This leaves unanswered the question whether the statement that all products cost society an effort of labour is a suitable starting-point for an analysis of exchange values (prices) in terms of labour costs. But even if the complicated transformation of values into prices which Marx effects (at considerable cost to himself and to the reader) in the third volume of *Capital* be regarded as a circuitous way of arriving at a predestined result, there remains the sociological core of the argument: to say that total prices equal total (labour) values implies a restatement of the classical doctrine that profits are derived from labour (whether living or stored up in the form of capital); from which it follows that mere ownership of capital *per se* is not a productive activity which can be adduced to explain the phenomenon of profit. This is not of course equivalent to saying that manufacturers and entrepreneurs are claimants without function: the Marxian 'capitalist' is an abstraction who enters his theoretical scheme only for the purpose of clarifying the capital-labour relationship. Where Marx has to deal with concrete historical problems, e.g., the genesis of the capitalist mode of production, he drops this approach and reintroduces the actual historical agents—farmers, manufacturers, merchants, etc.—whose activity causes the whole process to get under way.

In passing it may be observed that the treatment of profit in terms of class income had been a commonplace since the later eighteenth century. It was Smith, not Marx, who described profit as the income of those who employed hired labour: the third of the 'three great, original and constituent orders of every civilised society, from whose revenue that of every other order is ultimately derived'.[1] Moreover,

---

[1] *Wealth of Nations* (ed. Cannan, Modern Library edn., New York, 1937), p. 248.

Smith was careful to distinguish profits on 'stock' from wages of management, thus by anticipation exposing the fallacies of a line of reasoning whose prevalence in mid-nineteenth-century literature explains, if it does not wholly excuse, the language Marx occasionally employed about other economists.[1] Smith, like Ricardo, was as complacent about the role of entrepreneurs as Marx was hostile to them, but it would not have occurred to him to suppose that profits could be explained on the hypothesis that possession of wealth confers upon its owners a particular 'reward of abstinence'; or alternatively that capital by itself, i.e., stored-up equipment lying ready for use, has a magical capacity for generating that part of the national income which flows into the pockets of employers. Explanations of this kind had to await the coming of a more sophisticated breed of economists, who had eliminated all trace of empirical realism from their formulations. By now the wheel has come full circle, and academic scholars in the purest tradition of pre- and post-Keynesian economic analysis, though indifferent to the very concept of value (whether derived from costs or utility), are nonetheless reverting to the classical treatment of the subject, down to the measurement of output in terms of labour time.[2]

Instead of pursuing the value problem through the ramifications of Marx's analysis in volumes II and III of *Capital*, let us turn briefly to his theory of capitalist development as motivated by the accumulation of capital, and the consequent problem of keeping all the factors of production employed at a level which will enable accumulation to go forward without serious and worsening trouble.

[1] Ibid., p. 48. 'The profits of stock, it may perhaps be thought, are only a different name for the wages of a particular sort of labour, the labour of inspection and direction. They are, however, altogether different. . . . They are regulated altogether by the value of the stock employed, and are greater or smaller in proportion to the extent of this stock.'

[2] Cf. Joan Robinson, *The Accumulation of Capital*, London, 1958, p. 121. 'This is in some ways the most significant way of measuring capital, for the essence of the productive process is the expenditure of labour time, and labour time expended at one date can be carried forward to a later date by using it to produce physical objects (or to store up knowledge) which will make future labour more productive, so that capital goods in existence today can be regarded as an embodiment of past labour time to be used up in the future.' 'Looking at the matter in a philosophical light, the reason why there is no meaning to be attached to the marginal product of "capital" is that, from a long-run point of view, labour and natural resources are the factors of production in the economy as a whole, while capital goods and the time pattern are the means by which the factors are employed.' (Ibid., p. 310.) For the notion that profits are the reward of 'abstinence', see the same author's comment, op. cit., p. 393.

By common consent this is the most important part of Marx's theory, judged in terms of present-day significance: both with regard to the issue of full employment in industrially developed countries, and in relation to the scarcely less imposing problem of getting the process of capital accumulation started in areas still dominated by peasant farming or by primitive forms of pre-industrial capitalism. The Marxian theory of crises on the one hand, the Marxian view of capitalism as a dynamic system which generates its own steam (and its own 'internal contradictions') on the other, have acquired a topicality denied to most nineteenth-century intellectual constructions. These aspects of the system will recur at later stages of our discussion. Here it is merely intended to present a brief outline.

Marx's emphasis on capital accumulation as the factor which propels the whole economic process forward through time was, like other elements of his theory, an inheritance from the classics.[1] It consequently shared the fate which overtook the classical system in the latter part of the nineteenth century—that of being abandoned in favour of 'equilibrium analysis' of relative prices within a static system which was no longer expected to throw light on long-term processes of growth. Such an approach, however appropriate to a situation where economic expansion could be assumed, had the decided disadvantage of leaving blank all those spaces on the economic map where no such expansion had as yet got under way. In consequence economic theory ceased to be relevant to the problem of industrialisation and capital accumulation, despite the fact that over very large areas of the globe these were still unfulfilled desiderata.[2] What Marx had to say about these subjects mapped out territory into which few academic economists had yet penetrated, though a spirited debate was carried on in Russia, from the 1880's onward, over the question whether capitalist development was inevitable: a debate for which Marx's followers were partly responsible and which in the end they managed to monopolise. For the rest, it has taken the more recent global upheaval to stir academic interest in the problem of

[1] Cf. W. Arthur Lewis, 'Economic Development with Unlimited Supplies of Labour', *The Manchester School*, May 1954, pp. 139 ff. 'The classics, from Smith to Marx, all assumed, or argued, that an unlimited supply of labour was available at subsistence wages. They then enquired how production grows through time. They found the answer in capital accumulation, which they explained in terms of their analysis of the distribution of income.'

[2] Lewis, loc. cit., 'Asia's problems . . . attracted very few economists . . . (even the Asian economists themselves absorbed the assumptions and preoccupations of European economics . . .)'

economic development under conditions of surplus labour. The Marxian apparatus in this field—mostly developed in vols. II and III of *Capital*, which were not widely read—looks crude compared with some current models, but Marx's general approach in terms of capital-labour ratios, and the relation of capital accumulation to the growth of the labour force, provides the kind of theoretical framework that is needed to bring the whole complex of investment, industrialisation, and planning, into focus. This is now widely recognised, and it only remains to be said that, until the recent change in fashion, socialists were not markedly more concerned than liberals to invest intellectual surplus labour in this area.

There were of course good reasons for this neglect. Leaving aside the natural tendency to concentrate on one's own troubles,[1] there was every warrant for regarding the Marxian theory as important chiefly from the viewpoint of the full-blown capitalist economy already established in the advanced industrial countries. Marx himself gave the lead in this direction, and among his followers only the Russian Marxists—and not all of them—took systematic account of the altogether different set of problems connected with industrialisation. In the eyes of most Western socialists as well as their opponents, the Marxian doctrine had to be judged in terms of its ability to give an account of how capitalism functioned under modern conditions. These included the cyclical expansion and contraction of what Marx termed the 'industrial reserve-army', i.e. mass unemployment, but that was an altogether different matter from the kind of surplus population which went with pre-industrial stagnation. It is worth emphasising that the Marxian critique of capitalism had absolutely nothing to do with the latter question, though Marx did incidentally provide the analytical tools which later enabled sociologists and others to study the complex problem of 'underdevelopment'. Marxian socialism, during the fifty years between the publication of the first volume of *Capital* (1867) and the Russian upheaval of 1917, had for its central theme the performance of capitalism in the most highly developed countries of the world. Marx's own analysis was expressly designed for this purpose, though for historical reasons it maintained the continuity of the classical tradition, and therefore came into its

[1] E.g., during the 1930's, when Western economists were perforce occupied with other matters. But even so the irrelevance of the 'Keynesian revolution' to the issue of long-range development sparked by capital accumulation need not have been so completely overlooked; cf. Lewis, loc. cit., p. 140.

own again when public attention in the industrialised countries turned once more to the problem of long-range development.

In the light of these considerations, the relevance of Marxian thinking can be briefly considered under three main headings: (1) technological change and the alleged fall in the rate of profit; (2) the share of labour and the 'pauperisation' issue; (3) cyclical crises and the prospect of permanent breakdown. For people who still believe that Marx left a unified system whose totality is involved in every one of its parts, these issues are simply so many aspects of the 'crisis of capitalism'. Those who see the matter in another light will be more concerned to ask whether there is any necessary connection between the theorems in question, and to what extent they are capable of being reformulated.

That there was a long-run tendency for the rate of profit on capital to fall, was generally accepted by economists in Marx's time.[1] His originality consisted in linking this prospect with changes in what he termed the organic composition of capital, i.e., the ratio of constant (non-wage) to variable (wage) capital. Competition among capitalists, he held, would, via technical progress and capital accumulation, necessarily tend to enhance the proportion of embodied to living labour, or in different terms: raise the amount of capital per man employed; and since constant capital produced no additional surplus value, there would be a tendency for the share of profit to fall, assuming the rate of surplus-value (or rate of exploitation) to remain unchanged. Marx took due note of countervailing tendencies such as increasing productivity of labour, but seems to have felt that on balance these could only slow down the fall in the ratio of surplus value to embodied value. Thus a gradual decline in the rate of profit was postulated as an abstract tendency (or 'absolute law'), while the question to what extent it could be temporarily counteracted by forces working in the opposite direction was left open. Such forces might include a higher rate of exploitation which raised the amount of surplus value in proportion to capital; while technical progress and increasing productivity might 'cheapen the elements of constant capital' by reducing the value of machinery and raw materials, thus altering the 'organic composition of capital' in a direction running

---

[1] Schumpeter, *History*, pp. 651 ff; Robinson, *Essay*, pp. 41 ff; cf. also Dobb, *Political Economy and Capitalism*, pp. 94 ff, for a qualified defence of the Marxian theorem; and Schlesinger, *Marx*, pp. 144–9, for a critique, though delivered from a Marxist standpoint.

counter to the main trend. In this case the *value* of capital per worker employed might remain unchanged though productivity rose. The whole conception is clearly abstract and depends (even if one accepts the Marxian proposition about surplus-value) on a balance of conflicting tendencies which might equally well operate in the other direction; and the most one can say of the theorem is that it has not been (and probably cannot be) positively disproved. So far as the statistical evidence goes, it has been estimated that in Britain capital equipment per worker almost doubled between 1870 and 1940, while in the United States since 1870—with the not very surprising exception of the decade of the 1930's—capital has consistently grown faster than the labour force: in some decades almost twice as fast. But since productivity per worker rose during this period by approximately the same amount in Britain, and at an even faster rate in the USA, capital per worker did not grow in *value* terms, hence there was no reason why (on the Marxian assumption) profits should have declined. In fact they appear to have remained fairly constant, and where a drop has occurred the cause seems to have been labour's growing share in the total product.

A possibility overlooked by Marx in this context is that, under given social conditions, the ratio of surplus-value to variable capital (or rate of exploitation) might remain more or less constant, though profits showed a tendency to fall. With increasing productivity, real wages then must rise. This conclusion can easily be demonstrated, and it is surprising that Marx should have neglected the matter.[1] If labour receives a stable proportion of the net national income (which is the commonsense meaning of the statement that the rate of exploitation remains constant while capital accumulates), real income per head *must* go up, even if the share taken by wages does not alter. This is in fact what has been happening in all advanced industrial countries, once technical progress and the rate of accumulation have brought about an expansion of output sufficient to absorb the whole labour force. It is of course assumed here that the balance of forces in the labour market keeps the rate of exploitation (or rate of surplus value, which comes to the same thing) fairly constant; it is also

[1] Cf. Robinson, op. cit., pp. 42–3; Schlesinger, op. cit., p. 147. Marx assumes as a matter of course that capitalists will try to intensify exploitation in order to offset the fall in the rate of profit; there would then be no rise in real wages, though productivity improved. There is nothing wrong with the logic of this argument, but it does not fit the observable facts under modern conditions, given the growth in organised labour's bargaining strength.

assumed that there is no mass unemployment, and that the labour force does not increase faster than the national income: the latter being the typical situation of backward ('underdeveloped') countries. Given these conditions—which are present in all advanced countries where trade unions have adequate bargaining power and something like full employment prevails—real wages *must* rise. This is so obvious that adherents of the pauperisation (or 'immiseration') thesis have had to fall back on increasingly unreal assertions regarding the growth in the rate of exploitation (or fall in the share taken by wages in total output), in order to salvage the proposition that living standards are bound to decline, or at any rate cannot rise above a bare minimum whose constancy is ensured by the operation of the system.

In actual fact pauperisation plays no great part in the Marxian argument, apart from those passages where it is invoked to show what happens at the bottom of the social pyramid, where a 'reserve army' of more or less permanently unemployed is 'accumulated' by the mechanism of technological change operating upon a competitive economy. There is no warrant for the assertion that Marx expected real wages to fall until the entire working class was at, or below, subsistence level. The point of his argument is rather that real wages cannot permanently rise very much above this level, since their encroachment on profits would cause investments to decline. The 'reserve army' keeps wages stable and ensures that the rate of profit does not fall as rapidly as capital accumulation by itself (or technical progress, which comes to the same) would tend to imply. The argument is ingenious; the only trouble is that it does not reckon with the actual rise in wages which is likewise a function of technological progress—given certain not unreasonable assumptions about population growth, employment, and the balance of forces in the labour market. This is not to say that a situation corresponding to the Marxian hypothesis is not perfectly possible under capitalism. It is indeed characteristic of the early stages of capitalist development, and is still to be found in societies which have not broken through the 'sound barrier' of rapid technical and social advance. But it cannot be described as a 'general law' of development. At most it represents an abstract tendency which asserts itself only in the absence of counteracting forces. Such forces are not extraneous to the system; they are inherent in the kind of capital-labour relationship characteristic of a high degree of industrialisation and a high rate of progress. Only stagnation, or a series of worsening crises, could produce a situation akin to that envisaged by Marx in those passages of his work where he seems to imply that there is an actual historical tendency for conditions to deteriorate in such a manner that the accumulation of capital goes parallel with the growth of wealth and misery at opposite poles of society.[1]

Although Marx does not state in so many words that the relative share of wages in the total product is bound to decline, such an inference is implied in his contention that the 'organic composition of capital' changes over the long period so as to increase mechanical equipment per worker. Even so it does not follow that real wages are bound to fall or remain close to the subsistence level, and in fact the belief that they will tend to do so is linked in Marx's theory to a quite extraneous assumption—namely that the 'industrial reserve army' of unemployed, or irregularly employed, will keep wages down as capital accumulation proceeds. Something like this would doubtless happen if the system operated *in vacuo* and if there were no socially determined balance of forces in the labour market; but under present-day conditions this is no longer a reasonable supposition. The second strand of the argument—the tendential fall in the rate of profit—is developed at a level of abstraction where offsetting factors, e.g., technical progress, can always be said to be irrelevant to the long-run tendency. An assertion of this kind is inherently secure against disproof; but even at this level of theorising it is apparent that Marx did not allow sufficiently for growing productivity and its effect on the formation of surplus-value (to stay within his terminology).[2]

[1] *Capital*, I, pp. 786 ff. Elsewhere Marx makes due allowance for countervailing tendencies, ranging from trade-union pressure to the 'national or social element' embodied in current wages. Cf. *Wages, Price and Profit* (MESW I, p. 442): 'Besides this mere physical element, the value of labour is in every country determined by a traditional standard of life. It is not mere physical life, but it is the satisfaction of certain wants springing from the social conditions in which people are placed and reared up.' This might be treated as an additional explanation of why people will revolt against pauperisation, or against being held down to a subsistence level; but from a theoretical viewpoint it represents a damaging qualification of the principle that the value of labour-power (here described as the 'value of labour', since Marx was trying to popularise his argument for the benefit of his audience) is uniquely determined by the cost of reproducing the labourer.

[2] Cf. Robinson, *Essay*, p. 46: 'Productivity may rise without limit, and if real wages are constant, the rate of exploitation rises with it.' Conversely, of course, real wages must rise if with growing productivity the rate of exploitation remains constant. In either case the result hardly squares with the expectation of 'increasing misery'.

The falling rate of profit makes its appearance also in the Marxian theory of economic crises, this time as a short-run phenomenon whose connection with the alleged long-run tendency for profits to decline is rather tenuous.[1] In fact it can be questioned whether such a connection is implied by the logic of Marx's argument, though it clearly enters into the genesis of his thinking about crises. This circumstance is easily explained. What is today called the industrial cycle was still a fairly novel phenomenon when Marx first came to the study of economics, and the majority of those who busied themselves with this particular aspect of economic reality were either conservative opponents of industrialism or socialist critics of income distribution. In either case—i.e., whether they reasoned along lines suggested by Malthus or by Sismondi—they tended to interpret crises as symptoms of a fundamental disorder rooted in the nature of the new mode of production. Though Marx rejected the naïve arguments put forward by the 'under-consumptionists'—arguments which in the case of Malthus issued in a defence of landowners and rentiers, while Sismondi drew the conclusion that the workers ought to obtain a larger share of the social product—he was sufficiently impressed by their style of reasoning to link his own explanation of the trade cycle to his general theory of capitalist development. Hence the periodic rise and fall of profits which accompanies (and possibly generates) the decennial cycle, had to be related to the assumed long-range fall in the rate of profit. Fortunately for his analytical work Marx did not rest content with this dubious hypothesis, but went on to investigate the specific nature of the cycle, and in doing so managed to anticipate certain conclusions which academic economists reached by a different route only at a much later date.[2]

To avoid the confusion which customarily attends the discussion of this topic, it is important to realise that Marx's tentative explanation of the decennial production cycle is not logically dependent upon his hypothesis concerning the long-range prospects of capitalism, though such a connection doubtless existed in his own mind. Failure to appreciate this has frequently caused the discussion to revolve around extraneous issues, e.g., whether on the Marxian assumption there is a tendency for cyclical depressions to become more acute until the whole system breaks down or grinds to a stop.

[1] *Capital*, vol. III, pp. 242 ff (Moscow, 1960, edn.).
[2] Schumpeter, *History*, pp. 747 ff; Robinson, *Essay*, pp. 50 ff; Dobb, op. cit., pp. 79 ff.

This question was always important to Marxist economists, and we shall have to refer to it in dealing with the general development of Marxist theory from the 1890's onward; but it is not strictly relevant to the trade cycle as a phenomenon peculiar to the functioning of the market economy.[1] Unlike other socialists of his time, Marx took the view that periodic crises represent a mechanism whereby the system restores its equilibrium—though at considerable cost to the workers, and even at some cost to individual capitalists. From this it followed (a) that crises are necessary and not to be regarded as superficial phenomena caused by credit fluctuations; and (b) that as long as they occur, the peculiar automatism of the system can be said to be fully operative. This approach has more in common with the classical view than with the 'underconsumptionist' fallacies of Sismondi or Rodbertus, though Marx also assailed the conventional reliance on the 'law of markets', i.e., the proposition that output creates its own demand. The whole subject is much too complex to be dealt with in a few pages, but at the cost of extreme compression the following summary can perhaps be justified:

A. At the most general level at which Marx develops his argument he is concerned to show that the basic features of capitalism are potential causes of such cyclical disturbances as do in fact occur.[2] Fundamentally, capitalist accumulation is regulated by the search for profit, while the satisfaction of wants comes in only incidentally. Production is thus divorced from consumption, and though the two are brought together by the mechanism of the market, the latter operates in such a haphazard way as to ensure equilibrium between supply and demand only at the cost of periodic upheavals, in which 'superfluous' capital is destroyed and large numbers of uncompetitive firms are driven to the wall. Since purchases are divorced from sales, the 'law of markets' represents an abstraction to which nothing corresponds in reality, unless it be the recurrent trade cycle with its violent equilibration of prices and profits to 'values'.[3]

---

[1] Cf. Sweezy, op. cit., pp. 190 ff; Schlesinger, op. cit., pp. 165 ff. The so-called 'breakdown controversy' erupted around 1900 in connection with quite different problems, and its further development owed more to historical evidence pointing to an impending crisis of European capitalism than to theoretical considerations. It was only in the 1930's that some Marxists thought the factual evidence warranted the assertion that the ultimate breakdown postulated (or held possible) by Marx was actually about to take place.

[2] Cf. *Theories of Surplus Value*, pp. 368 ff.

[3] Cf. *Capital*, vol. I, p. 87: 'Nothing could be more childish than the dogma that because every sale is a purchase, and every purchase a sale, therefore the

B. The bare notion of 'potential causes' does not of course explain why crises do in fact occur, far less why they take the form of periodic disturbances within a recurrent cycle. The 'anarchy of production' is no more than a general precondition of what Marx regards as the characteristic movement of industrial growth under capitalism. The operative term is 'growth'. In a static system there would be no crises —at least none of this sort—while under capitalism the crisis is a factor within the general dynamic of a system propelled forward by the motor of accumulation. Within this system, the 'decennial cycle' represents a way of overcoming the built-in 'internal contradictions', though in a catastrophic manner and never more than temporarily. Each revolution of the system—taking the term 'revolution' in its original sense—raises it to a higher level, thus storing up the elements of new and more violent crises, alongside the accumulation of greater riches and an enlarged fund of technical knowledge.

C. The general preconditions of disequilibrium reappear in the actual causation of periodic crises, inasmuch as the latter are brought about by a sudden contraction of the market in relation to the mass of commodities produced at the height of the boom. Overproduction always relates to current prices and profits. The market could absorb all the commodities produced at lower prices, but in that case the original capital invested would not be replaced with the customary average profit. Fresh investment (accumulation) therefore grinds to a temporary halt, thus initiating the opening phase of a downward cycle which normally continues until prices and wages have dropped so low, and capital has become so abundant, that investment is once more profitable—at any rate for the more efficient entrepreneurs (the others having meantime been eliminated). Since 'constant capital' (the productive apparatus) has run down towards the end of the depression, there is a pent-up demand for fixed installations, the satisfaction of which provides the basis for a revival in the production-goods industries. In consequence the demand for labour grows, the 'reserve army' contracts, consuming power expands, and investment

circulation of commodities necessarily implies an equilibrium . . . If the split between the sale and the purchase becomes too pronounced, the intimate connection between them, their oneness, asserts itself by producing—a crisis.' Incidentally, this is a good instance of Marx's employment of Hegelian logic to illustrate a perfectly valid argument which few modern economists would dispute. It may be claimed that his logical training was helpful in enabling him to establish the point, but at any rate the argument cannot be said to *depend* on what he may have learned from Hegel. This of course is just what most of his followers, and some critics, would deny.

193

in the consumption-goods industries once more becomes profitable. Thus another upward phase of the cycle is inaugurated, and so on until the next crisis, which typically occurs at the very height of the boom, when profits are at their peak and wages have risen above the depression level, so that the preconditions for steady 'expanded reproduction' *appear* to be present—just when they are about to evaporate. It is evident that this schema is only very tenuously—if at all—connected with such general notions as the tendential fall in the rate of profit.[1] What relation does it bear to the other pillar of Marxist doctrine as popularly interpreted: the contradiction between unlimited capital accumulation and limited demand for consumption goods?

The difficulty with this question is that Marx failed to supply an unambiguous answer. Instead he may be said to have given several ambiguous ones. On the one hand, he rejected the ordinary 'underconsumption' explanation as superficial and tautological.[2] On the other hand, he said just enough about the barriers to progress imposed by 'the consumptive demand of a society in which the majority are poor and must always remain poor'[3] to render a more sophisticated version of such explanations plausible. Add to this the fact that his observations on the subject are scattered through his writings, and that the concluding volume of his major work was left unfinished, and it is not surprising that there are almost as many interpretations of his theory as there are interpreters.

Matters are not eased by Marx's habit of developing separate, though parallel, lines of reasoning on different levels of generality, so that a description of the basic features of capitalism which condition the possibility of recurrent crises, turns up in a part of his (unfinished) work where an explanation of the particular *form* of

[1] Profits are typically at their peak when the boom bursts, as are prices and wages. Of course there is a way of getting round this difficulty: it can be argued that though the *mass* of profits has grown (because of the demand for extra labour and other temporary factors), the *rate* of profit nonetheless has declined through changes in the capital-labour ratio. But the actual drop in profits at the peak of a boom requires no such explanation, which is indeed wholly implausible. On this point cf. Robinson, op. cit., pp. 44 ff.

[2] *Capital*, vol. II, pp. 475–6 (p. 410 of the Moscow, 1960, edn.): 'It is sheer tautology to say that crises are caused by the scarcity of effective consumption, or of effective consumers. The capitalist system does not know any other modes of consumption than effective ones, except that of *sub forma pauperis*. . . . That commodities are unsaleable means only that no effective purchasers have been found for them . . .'

[3] Ibid., p. 363 (p. 316).

such crises would be in order. Thus it has been possible to cite formulations of a very general kind as though they represented specific
observations on the mechanism of the trade cycle, e.g., the much-
quoted statement: 'The last cause of all real crises always remains the
poverty and restricted consumption of the masses as compared to
the tendency of capitalist production to develop the productive forces
in such a way that only the absolute power of consumption of the
entire society would be their limit.'[1] Or again: 'Crises are always
momentary and forcible solutions of existing contradictions, violent
eruptions which restore the disturbed equilibrium for a while.'[2] 'The
real barrier to capitalist production is *capital itself*; namely the fact
that capital and its realisation appear as the starting-point and the
conclusion, the motive and the aim of production: that production is
only production for *capital*. . . .'[3] Such pronouncements, whatever
their general import, evidently do not take us very far in explaining
the periodicity of crises, or indeed their necessity. Moreover, the
'underconsumptionist' bias of some of these utterances is contradicted by other passages. It is now generally recognised that Marx
did not develop a unified theory of crises, although his fragmentary
writings on the subject include analytical work of a very high order
which has retained its significance not only for the further development of Marxist theory, but for economics in general. Some of his
formulations, notably the model of 'simple and expanded reproduction' developed in the second volume of *Capital*, anticipate the kind
of thinking that has become academically respectable only in recent
decades. Space forbids even a summary treatment of this subject,
which to professional economists probably represents the most interesting part of his work.[4]

[1] *Capital*, vol. III, p. 568. Cf. also *Theories of Surplus Value*, p. 368. 'But the
whole process of accumulation resolves itself above all into *expanded production*, which on the one hand corresponds to the natural increase of the population, and on the other hand forms an immanent basis for the phenomena which
become manifest in *crises*. The measure of this expanded production is *capital*
itself—the actual level of the conditions of production and the boundless urge
of the capitalists to enrich themselves and increase their capital—and not in any
way *consumption*. The latter is limited from the outset, as the greater part of the
population, the working population, can only increase its consumption within
very narrow limits, while to the same degree as capitalism develops, the demand
for labour decreases *relatively*, although it increases *absolutely*.'
[2] *Capital*, vol. III, p. 292.   [3] Ibid., pp. 293–4. (Cf. 1960 edn., p. 245.)
[4] Schumpeter, op. cit., pp. 748–50; Robinson, op. cit., pp. 51–60; Dobb,
op. cit., pp. 99 ff. The topic is lengthily explored by Sweezy, op. cit., pp. 156 ff,
but as so frequently happens in controversies over the meaning of Marx's

It is, however, scarcely possible to abandon this theme without indicating very briefly wherein the difference lies between the Marxian and the Keynesian type of crisis explanation. Leaving aside the dispute among Marxists over the relative importance in Marx's scheme of statements pointing to overproduction (or underconsumption); and assuming that the more technical parts of his analysis are not *logically* dependent on long-range (and unprovable) hypotheses about the rate of profit, we are left with the question whether the fragmentary doctrine sketched out in volumes II and III of *Capital* is capable of development along lines which at least need not conflict with Keynesian theorising. The short answer would seem to be that this is indeed the case, though any such further development will have to abandon certain notions dear to orthodox Marxists, e.g., the dependence of the trade cycle on the alleged fall in the rate of profit, or the tendency for wages to take a smaller share in the national income. Part of Marx's argument can be reformulated in terms acceptable to modern economics; in other respects it appears safe to conclude that 'Marx does not develop a full theory of the trade cycle, or of the long-run movement of capitalism, but he points the direction in which a theory can be found.'[1]

Unfortunately, however, this does not exhaust the issue. Though Marx anticipated a good deal of modern thinking, he also introduced long-range considerations which cut across every type of theorising that treats the economic structure as 'given'. For him, crises are ultimately traceable to built-in contradictions inherent in the capitalist mode of production, while in modern liberal, i.e., Keynesian, economics, crises represent a failure of the mechanism to operate in accordance with its own basic principles. These differences of approach can be argued in technical terms, but ultimately they relate to different visions of the economic process. The Marxian view of capitalism as an unstable system which periodically solves its inherent problems only by setting up even more formidable barriers to further progress, is incompatible with any doctrine which treats the social structure as merely a 'given factor' of a total economic situation. In the end this is perhaps no more than to say that liberal and socialist economics necessarily take different views of the future of bourgeois society.

more abstract theorems, his conclusions are rejected by other Marxists: cf. Schlesinger, op. cit., pp. 169 ff. For a more recent exposition which seems to lay somewhat excessive stress on the pauperisation issue, cf. John Strachey, *Contemporary Capitalism*, London, 1956, pp. 82 ff.

[1] Robinson, op. cit., p. 56.

It is time to cast a backward glance upon the development of Marx's thinking on economics. In the light of what has been said earlier we can now note the underlying consistency of his approach, from the Paris manuscripts of 1844 to the final volumes of *Capital*. Some of the early formulations were indeed tacitly abandoned; thus the notion of 'estrangement' or 'alienation', which is central to the 1844 manuscripts, and still plays an important part in the *Grundrisse* of 1857-8, leads only a shadowy existence in *Capital*, where it reappears briefly as the 'fetishism of commodities'. Other concepts were diluted to take account of changing circumstances. Nonetheless a comparison of the earlier and the later writings discloses a fundamental unity of outlook. If in the Paris manuscripts it is stated that the accumulation of wealth goes parallel with that of misery, the same assumption underlies some of the more striking passages of *Capital*. In 1844 Marx already held that 'the worker becomes all the poorer the more wealth he produces'. In a certain fundamental sense this idea still haunts the sophisticated pages of his major work. If actual pauperisation is no longer much stressed, relative impoverishment—through the growth of the proletariat and especially the 'reserve army of labour'—receives all the more emphasis, as the necessary counterpart of capital accumulation at the other pole of society. Whatever his concessions to empirical evidence, Marx never renounced his Ricardian heritage.

The same reluctance to dispense with the intellectual apparatus of the classical writers is evident in the altogether disproportionate significance Marx allotted to the value theory he had taken over from Ricardo. After what has been said on this point it is scarcely necessary to emphasise that an exploitation theory could have been deduced without much trouble from the capitalist monopoly of ownership and the claim to unearned income that goes with it. In strict logic, a theory of this type is not dependent on the notion that labour is the unique source of value generated in production. Exploitation is present when the capitalist monopolises the gains which accrue from employment of capital, whether or not the value-creating quality is uniquely imputed to labour, or allotted to all the 'factors of production'. In a sense Marx recognised this when he made ownership of the means of production central to his argument. The labour theory of value, in the form he gave it, is not really essential to this part of his argument, and the excessive reliance he placed upon it created quite needless difficulties for his followers. The reasons which impelled him to adhere to the Ricardian approach have been indicated;

they were partly of an historical nature and in part related to the urge for intellectual systematisation. If the resulting construction, for all its undeniable grandeur, has acquired a distinctly old-fashioned look, that is a drawback it shares with other attempts to erect a comprehensive system upon the foundation of a few apparently self-evident propositions.

In the perspective of Marxism as a school of thought, this stress on systematic unity and completeness, coupled with faults in analysis due to the inadequacy of the labour theory, was to have far-reaching consequences. The publication by Engels in 1894 of the unfinished third volume of *Capital* (with the ingenious but unconvincing 'transformation' of imputed labour values into market prices) proved a turning-point. If it supplied the Marxist school with a firm foundation, it also helped to give rise to the 'revisionist' movement in theory. A few years after Böhm-Bawerk had opened the academic attack on Marx's solution of the value-price problem, the 'revisionists' in the Socialist camp were beginning to echo his arguments. This was not indeed the end of the matter: from about 1904 onward, the neo-Marxist school, with Vienna as its centre, began to rebut the 'marginalist' and 'revisionist' assault. Value derivation from utility and consumer choice—the core of marginalism—were dismissed as a shallow evasion of the problem, and the classical approach received fresh emphasis; though in practice the neo-Marxists operated less and less with deductions from the labour theory, and more and more with empirical results obtained by generalising Marx's views on the concentration of capital and the trend towards larger units. In this way the Marxian theory of capitalism merged insensibly with the neo-Marxian doctrine of imperialism as the expression of a new stage of economic development. By 1910 the old controversy over prices and values was giving way, at least in Central Europe, to a new and more topical disputation over economic rivalry among the European powers and the long-term viability of capitalism as a world system. The 1914–18 war speeded this process, and by 1930 the debate over methodological fundamentals seemed to have ended, when it was suddenly and dramatically revived by the world economic crisis and its theoretical sequel: the Keynesian revolution in academic thinking. Since this went hand in hand with the belated discovery of Marxism by American and British economists, recent years have witnessed something like a revival of the controversy which shook the Socialist movement in Europe around 1900.

From a purely theoretical standpoint this post-1930 debate has many attractions. Its general level was remarkably high, and it impinged directly upon two of the most dramatic developments of the period: the world economic crisis of 1930–3 and the planning experiment in the USSR.[1] The trouble, from the historian's viewpoint, is that the discussion coincided with the final dissolution of the Marxian school properly so called, whereas the 'great debate' of 1895–1905 took place at the peak of the preceding era—the one that was brought to a violent end in 1914. In consequence we are now once more obliged to retrace our steps and enquire into the fortunes of the Socialist movement during the age of its most rapid expansion. This is the proper procedure if one wants to know what happened to Marxism, and why. Mere theoretical exegesis will not supply the answer. Somewhere between 1870 and 1914–18, Marxism became the doctrine of European Socialism, and its fortunes from that moment were closely tied to the practical and ideological requirements of a mass movement. Even Lenin's theory of imperialism is not explicable simply in terms of what he had learned from Kautsky and Hilferding. One must also know why he regarded the 1914–18 war as confirmation of the orthodox thesis on capitalist development. This question is properly an historical one; it cannot be eluded.

Even if one stays within the framework of Marxian theory it is important to ask what effect *Capital* (notably the later volumes edited by Engels after the death of Marx in 1883) had on the developing theoretical consciousness of the Socialist movement from the 1890's onward. The inconvenience of this approach is indeed plain when one considers that the resulting doctrinal disputations—both among Marxists, and between Marxist and 'bourgeois' economists—were frequently conducted in terms which by current standards are somewhat antiquated, as well as being related to political issues that no longer concern us. But this cannot be helped. It is one of the penalties of approaching the subject from the historical side. Thus the so-called 'breakdown controversy', i.e., the argument over the supposed

---

[1] For details of the debate cf. the essay collection *Collectivist Economic Planning*, London, 1935; O. Lange and F. M. Taylor, *On the Economic Theory of Socialism*, Minneapolis, 1938; H. D. Dickinson, *Economics of Socialism*, Oxford, 1939; F. A. Hayek, *Individualism and Economic Order*, London, 1947. The last-named author's better-known tract entitled *The Road to Serfdom*, London, 1944, may perhaps be regarded as a polemical by-product of a discussion in which neither side pulled many punches. For a Marxist contribution cf. M. Dobb, 'The Question of Economic Law in a Socialist Economy', in *Political Economy and Capitalism*, 1937, pp. 270 ff.

tendency for economic crises to become more violent, was closely connected with the debate over imperialism, which became so important a part of Socialist thinking in the first quarter of the present century; and the same applies to the disputes which from the 1880's onward raged among Socialists in Russia over the inevitability or otherwise of capitalist development. Though neither of these controversies can be traced in detail, they must somehow be integrated into the general picture if the relevance of Marxism—indeed its very nature as a doctrine *and* a movement—is to be clarified. We therefore at this point drop our consideration of Marxian economics, which was merely intended as a general sketch, and return to the subject of Socialist theory (and practice) in the age of what came to be known as orthodox Marxism. This means *inter alia* giving attention to a particular chapter in the history of Central Europe. Why this is so ought to become apparent in the measure in which it is made clear what Marxist Socialism stood for between, roughly speaking, 1870 and 1918. These dates are not chosen at random; in our context they signify, among others, that Marxism as a movement took its shape from the historical environment which it attempted to transform. And here it may be said by way of anticipation that the ideological cleavage which from about 1905 increasingly divided the Socialists of Eastern Europe from those of the Western half of the Continent already foreshadowed the political line of division which after 1918 came to run between Communists and Social-Democrats; ultimately this rift made possible, even if it did not directly provoke, the partition of Europe in the wake of the Second World War. Political upheavals often have their harbingers in what at first appear to be obscure wrangles among academic theorists. In the march of events leading from 1848 to 1948—from the first formulation of the Communist programme to its institutional embodiment in Soviet Communism—the fact that Marxism was originally a German doctrine has always counted for more than a mere coincidence. It was through Germany that Russia, and the whole of Eastern Europe, were put in touch with the modern world during this period, and it was in Germany that this world impinged upon a complex of unsolved problems—national, social, spiritual—which came to a head in two European wars. There is no paradox involved in saying that the catastrophe of Germany as a nation between 1848 and 1948—when its eastern half was incorporated in the Soviet orbit—forms as much part of the history of Marxism as does the authorship of *Capital*.

PART FIVE

MARXIAN SOCIALISM
1871–1918

1

GENERAL CHARACTER
OF THE PERIOD

THE CLOSER we are to an epoch, the more difficult it is to comprehend its essential traits: we know at once too much and too little. While innumerable details elude us, enough information is available to make us wonder whether our principle of selection is not arbitrary and irrelevant. With periods lying in the remoter past this difficulty is lessened: we know—or think we know—what gave them their particular character; what it was, vulgarly speaking, that made them tick. Our immediate ancestors are at once more familiar and less comprehensible. The fact that within limits we are able to enter their universe illuminates, but also distorts, for the categories we bring to the task of understanding our predecessors are partly those by which their own world was organised; not surprisingly they seem to fit their object. Yet the disappearance of that world also involves the rearrangement of those intellectual principles with whose aid the chaos of phenomena was at one time reduced to order. Thus we cannot enter even briefly into the history of the liberal age (which was also the age of Marxian socialism) without becoming aware that its unifying concepts are no longer quite the same as our own.

The period under review saw a vast expansion of Western—particularly European—influence, together with the first stirrings of a counter-movement which was to gather strength from 1918 onward. It also witnessed a rapid, though uneven, economic expansion, with the industrialised countries in the van of reaping the corresponding benefits, but the remainder toiling not too far behind. In purely economic terms the United States and Germany were the chief gainers, but industrialisation was rapid in Russia, Japan, Italy and some of the overseas areas settled by Europeans. France maintained a slow tempo of growth, mainly from internal causes having to do with the social structure and the policies of successive governments, as well as the territorial losses suffered in 1871, when part of Lorraine was annexed by Germany.[1] The slowness of industrial advance translated itself into a significant failure to modernise social relations, so that French socialism after 1870 became the political expression of a relatively weak labour movement and gradually relinquished the leadership it had hitherto exercised. What France lost, in this as in other domains, Germany gained. There was no corresponding shift in favour of Britain, which now began to rank as a competitor of Germany rather than as the dominant world power. Intellectually and politically, liberalism continued to centre on the United Kingdom, while Germany and Austria became the rallying-points of agrarian-conservative and labour-socialist currents hostile to liberal ideas and policies. This polarity became marked from the 1880's onward and gradually helped to shape new alignments which in the end involved a rearrangement of international relations as well.[2]

Britain's economic difficulties began in the 1870's, when progress slackened in comparison with the preceding period of extremely rapid growth.[3] Until 1870 or thereabouts industrial production had been increasing at an annual rate of approximately four per cent; thereafter it averaged less than half that figure, while other countries forged ahead more rapidly. Between 1873 and 1913 the annual rate of growth in industry averaged 4·8 per cent for the United States, 3·9 per cent for Germany, 3·7 per cent for the world as a whole, and only 1·8 per cent for the United Kingdom. The main cause of this relative stagnation is now generally attributed to unfavourable changes in the export markets on which Britain had become unduly dependent

[1] Clapham, *Economic Development of France and Germany*, pp. 232 ff.

[2] Schumpeter, *History*, pp. 759 ff.

[3] For the following cf. Clapham, *An Economic History of Modern Britain*, vol. II, Cambridge, 1932, passim; H. M. Lynd, *England in the Eighteen-Eighties*, New York, 1945, pp. 23 ff; W. A. Lewis, *Economic Survey 1919–1939*, London, 1949, pp. 74 ff.

during the Victorian free-trade boom, when she captured a share of the total which she could not possibly hope to hold. There may have been some slowness in adapting to new industrial processes, but the industrialisation of overseas countries was probably the main factor.[1] At first real wages continued to rise—though mainly due to falling prices—but from about 1900 there is evidence of stagnation in wage purchasing power. Not surprisingly the period witnessed a gradual growth of socialist influences, though the small Marxist groups failed to profit from this trend and eventually lost out to their Fabian rivals.[2]

The significance of this gradual shift in Britain's world position was not limited to balance-of-power relationships; it affected the prestige of liberalism and therewith the outlook of the entrepreneurial middle-class, which on the whole was still the most influential— though not everywhere the ruling—group. From the 1880's onward the trend in Europe was away from free-trade and *laissez-faire*, towards protectionism, state control, labour legislation—and militarism. The forces behind these departures from liberal orthodoxy were manifold, but the outcome was uniform. Agrarian protectionists, heavy industries in need of tariffs, Socialist or Catholic labour unions, bureaucracies anxious to mediate social conflicts, nationalist and imperialist movements in search of *Lebensraum*, had different aims in view and frequently conflicted with each other; where they agreed was in promoting the gradual abandonment of liberal ideas and policies, notably in economics. The drift was slowest in England, though here too bourgeois self-confidence no longer matched the optimism of the mid-Victorian era. It was rapid in Central Europe, where liberalism had already been politically defeated before it came into conflict with the new economic and social trends. In Russia the issue scarcely arose: liberalism existed primarily as an aspiration in the minds of a minority among the intellectuals; virtually everyone else was hostile to it, the ruling bureaucracy as much as the agrarian conservatives and the socialist sects.[3]

---

[1] Lewis, op. cit., pp. 75 ff. Between 1876/80 and 1911/13, Britain's share of world manufacturing exports slipped from 38 to 27 per cent.

[2] Cole, *History of Socialist Thought*, vol. III, part I, pp. 104 ff; M. Beer, *History of British Socialism*, 1953 edn., vol. II, pp. 226 ff; H. M. Pelling, *The Origins of the Labour Party*, London, 1954; E. R. Pease, *History of the Fabian Society*, London, 1916, revised edn. 1925.

[3] Rosenberg, *Democracy and Socialism*, passim; R. C. K. Ensor, *England, 1870–1914*, Oxford, 1936, pp. 269 ff.

Some of these changes did not immediately disclose their long-range import. The relative stagnation of British industry, for example, was barely visible to wage-earners, whose real income may have risen by as much as 50 per cent between 1880 and 1900.[1] On the other hand, the trade unions could not help noticing that unemployment had become chronic. This did more than merely promote the growth of the 'new unionism' from the late 1880's onward, or the spread of Fabian ideas among radical intellectuals; it also lent strength to protectionist and imperialist tendencies. Sometimes the two went together. It would have been difficult to say what was more attractive to British voters in Joseph Chamberlain's 'unauthorised programme' of 1885 and in his subsequent activities: his imperial sentiment or his toying with the vocabulary of collectivism.[2] Elsewhere too the advocates of protectionism and of 'social reform' were often the same people, and in coming together they invariably caused the surviving defenders of liberal orthodoxy to look old-fashioned and a trifle foolish; though only in Central Europe did liberal parties actually collapse at the polls as early as the 1880's. In general the trend was gradual until the very end of the period under review, and in some areas of predominantly Catholic influence it was altogether neutralised by the liberal-socialist alliance against the Church, which pushed all other issues into the background. But such circumstances were exceptional, and even where they occurred the political advantage did not lie wholly with one side. As time went on it became apparent that 'Christian-Social' movements could refloat themselves by making common cause with trade unionism, agrarian protectionism, or anti-Semitism, depending on local conditions. In general, conservative forces did not yield much ground during the period; what they lost in one direction they generally recovered in another, their gradual expansion paralleling the more dramatic growth of the socialist movement. The losers were the liberal parties and the business classes that supported them.

Socially, all this was quite compatible with a considerable improvement in working-class standards and in the relative status of

[1] Schumpeter, op. cit., p. 759; cf. also Lynd, op. cit., p. 49, for a less favourable estimate. The relevant point in any case is that real wages rose because prices fell, which in turn was largely due to the adverse terms obtained by the primary producers—another factor which hampered the growth of Britain's overseas trade. There was hardly any rise in money wages, and after 1900 no improvement in real terms.

[2] Lynd, pp. 180 ff.

organised labour. The period in fact witnessed a significant growth of trade union organisation, and concurrently a gradual, unsystematic, but fairly uniform expansion of welfare legislation. Together with the rise in real wages, which was not confined to England, and the shortening of working hours, these factors brought about a social climate in Western Europe which enabled the Social-Democratic movement to rid itself of Anarchist competition and gain working-class support for what was on the whole (rhetorical extravagances apart) a programme of democratic reform. Sheer despair over the condition of the industrial proletariat gave way, from the 1870's onward, to a growing conviction that labour could better its status by organisation and collective bargaining. 'Reformism' was not confined to the British trade unions; after the Anarchist split of the 1870's and 1880's it underlay the activity of the Continental Socialist parties, for all their revolutionary phraseology. Of course all this applies only to Western Europe and, with some qualifications, to Germany and Austria-Hungary. In Eastern and Southern Europe the impact of early industrial capitalism during the same period reproduced all the horrors of the earlier West European phase in an aggravated form. The important point to note is that this lag was already felt as such. Where democratic liberalism obtained a second wind, as it did in England with the advent of the Liberal-Labour alliance after 1900, it was clearly perceived that the more backward European countries were going through a process which the industrialised nations had already left behind. Hence the sudden popularity of the term 'industrial revolution'. In Britain—not to mention the United States, which had escaped some of the worst horrors of the transition period and accordingly tended to adopt a somewhat patronising attitude towards Europe—the governing classes now felt able for the first time to draw breath and take credit for the achievements of the past. In this more relaxed climate the 'social problem' no longer signified—as it had done for the early Victorians—the inevitability of widespread pauperism, but rather the need to bring backward countries, and 'under-privileged' classes, up to a more civilised level.

The material foundation of this new attitude has often been linked to the rapidity of economic expansion which is supposed to have characterised the epoch; this explanation is unconvincing. World trade was anything but flourishing between the mid-seventies and the mid-nineties, when most of the changes here described took place;

and when a new period of rapid expansion opened around 1900, real wages in Britain remained stagnant.[1] Moreover, the pace of industrial growth after 1900 was fastest (apart from the United States) in Russia and Japan: not exactly areas of political maturity. In reality it was the social climate which had changed, and this because in Western Europe the industrial revolution had been absorbed. In its formative phase this revolution had involved the disruption of so large a part of the accepted social texture that class war was never far below the surface. Even where it did not, as in France, explode into civil war, the conflict of classes which accompanied the great economic gear-shift was heightened to a degree which has ceased to be comprehensible to the inhabitants of fully industrialised countries. Socialist and Anarchist doctrines of revolution were extrapolations from a state of affairs which a few decades later came to be thought of as characteristic of 'backward' countries. The same is true of working conditions and working-class standards of life. The environment reflected in Socialist literature between 1830 and 1870 was that of 'primitive accumulation' as depicted in the descriptive passages of *Capital* and in Engels's studies of the 1840's. It represented a unique condition of social barbarism characteristic of a period in which the newly emerged class of small industrial entrepreneurs was compelled to accumulate capital by every possible means, and naturally tried to extract the maximum working potential from the labour force at its disposal. With the gradual maturation of industrial capitalism—including the rise of larger and stabler units, and the disappearance of untrammelled competition—labour conditions became less barbarous and tensions abated. Relative rates of growth had little or nothing to do with it.

The paradox in all this from the liberal standpoint was that the movement away from free-trade policies occurred precisely at the time when the fruits of *laissez-faire* were beginning to be harvested.[2] Of course this is a somewhat partisan way of stating the matter. It could equally be said that liberalism had unleashed forces it could not control; much as Britain, after cradling the industrial revolution,

[1] And very likely in Continental Western Europe too; cf. Clapham, *Economic Development of France and Germany*, p. 406: 'There was some evidence, in the years 1901–14, of a slight deterioration in standards of living. ... The policies of the armed peace and economic self-sufficiency had to be paid for both in France and Germany.'

[2] Schumpeter, op. cit., pp. 766 ff; for the significant, and in the long run perhaps decisive, change in the intellectual climate of the era from 1890 onwards, cf. H. Stuart Hughes, *Consciousness and Society*, New York, 1958, passim.

failed to maintain the leading position she had occupied during the third quarter of the nineteenth century. There is truth in both state ments, though in relation to Central and Eastern Europe it would be more accurate to say that liberalism had failed. The peak of political influence was reached by liberal parties in Germany and Austria-Hungary around 1870, and what they had by then achieved fell considerably short of introducing parliamentary government—not to mention democracy—in these areas; though they did manage to implant the rule of law. Here if anywhere are the roots of the subsequent growth of Social-Democracy to a position not equalled by labour movements in Western Europe until much later. Conversely, the still predominantly agrarian character of Central and Eastern Europe—which provided their governments with a conservative basis, hampered political reform, and drove the emerging labour movement sharply to the left—also limited the prospects of democratic socialism by setting peasants against city workers. This was to become the principal tactical problem of Social-Democratic parties from the 1890's onward.

In Western Europe the gradual waning of liberal influence from the 1880's onward could for the most part not be camouflaged by external circumstances. There were no further bulwarks of autocracy to be stormed, though clerical pressures and peasant electorates retained importance in France and Italy, not to mention Spain where the modern world had not really penetrated. If liberal parliamentary majorities failed to usher in the golden age, other explanations had to be found. In a measure this is also true of England, where the successful completion of the Liberal programme was blocked, almost down to the eve of 1914, by the House of Lords, the Irish imbroglio, and Tory exploitation of the unholy trinity: protectionism, nationalism, imperialism. But imperialism was making successful inroads into the Liberal camp as well, and even had its adherents among Socialists.[1] In Germany the transition from the agrarian-cum-industrial protectionism of the 1880's to the rampant colonialism, navalism and imperialism of the Wilhelminian era encountered little opposition, and

[1] Cf. Bernard Semmel, *Imperialism and Social Reform*, London, 1960, passim. It is always possible to detect counter-currents, but it seems a little far-fetched to read anti-imperialist significance into the Liberal party's election victory of 1906 (as is done, e.g., by Schumpeter, op. cit., p. 767). After all, the Liberal Government of 1906–14 conducted a foreign policy which hardly differed from that of its predecessor. British Liberalism was anti-protectionist, but not in the main anti-imperialist: an important distinction. The pure logic of free-trade economics came to a halt where defence of overseas investments was concerned.

none at all from the dominant National-Liberal wing of middle-class liberalism. This was not (as German historians of the period tried to make the public believe) because Germany's mercantile interests demanded such a policy, but rather because the mercantile centres lacked the power to impose a rational attitude upon the Imperial Government. But the effect was the same, in that Germany drifted away from the policies which in the preceding generation had kept Europe more or less at peace.

These events had their counterpart in the intellectual sphere. It seems advisable to employ this cautious formula instead of insisting that certain changes in the mental climate were the 'ideological reflex' of an altered situation. The new outlook in philosophy, science and literature derived in part from a weakening of the liberal faith, and this can be related to the dwindling self-confidence of the middle class, faced with its own creation and no longer certain that the world of industrial capitalism corresponded to the optimistic anticipations of the Enlightenment. But it can also be held that the liberal movement faltered in the face of resistance from the old, unshaken world of conservative traditionalism. On this reading of the situation, the breakthrough originally associated with the French Revolution and the American Revolution had now been absorbed, and bourgeois society had become conservative. If this was a correct assessment, it fell to the socialist movement to resume the forward march from the point where middle-class radicalism had come to a halt. In summary form this may be described as the typical socialist analysis of West European reality after 1880. There were of course alternative ways of looking at the matter. In the United States, radical democracy, as represented by Henry George in economics or by W. J. Bryan in politics, implied agrarianism, not socialism. Even in England it was still possible in the 1880's for Chamberlain's associates to couple a programme of industrial welfare legislation with promises—admittedly utopian—of 'three acres and a cow' for landless labourers. There was some theoretical foundation for land nationalisation schemes in the views on rent which Ricardo had transmitted to his followers, down to and including John Stuart Mill; and Mill at least took this inheritance seriously enough to interest himself in practical land reform proposals. But by the time the Liberal party had fallen under the spell of Lloyd George, on the eve of the first world war, the traditional attack on the landed oligarchy was losing its power to stir the electorate, compared with the new 'collectivist' schemes for coping with urban misery and unemployment. Naturally the old slogans were not abandoned—they still meant a great deal to many Liberals, if not to social theorists in sympathy with the party's general aims; but their glamour was beginning to fade. By contrast, welfare legislation was attracting more interest. For a movement which once had rested firmly on the support of the middle-sized entrepreneur, the Liberal party on the eve of 1914 had come dangerously close to toying with 'collectivism'.[1]

Mention of Mill indeed serves as a reminder that there were conflicting ways of interpreting his heritage. In what follows some attention will perforce have to be devoted to the dispute between 'radical' and 'revisionist' tendencies in Continental Europe, while Fabianism will of necessity disappear from the picture. Yet the Fabian sources of much that was later called 'revisionism' in Germany and elsewhere were plain to see, while it was equally obvious that in England there was no longer a clear dividing-line between liberalism and 'collectivism'. Since adherents of both schools were in the habit of invoking Mill, it is not irrelevant to enquire where he stands in the matter. To students of his writings this is not really such a difficult question, and any remaining uncertainty is adequately settled by the reflection that the British labour movement probably knew what it was doing when it incorporated the substance of Mill's teachings in its social philosophy. Briefly, these teachings amount to an acceptance of socialism as both the *probable term* and the *desirable goal* of modern civilisation.[2] This attitude, however, was not based on a pessimistic assessment of capitalism's future performance, but rather upon the belief that the 'problem of production' had largely been solved, from which it followed that society could now begin to occupy itself with the infinitely more agreeable 'problem of distribution'. Of course if one takes the Marxian view that 'relations of production' are paramount, such notions will seem hopelessly unscientific; but we are not obliged here to take sides. The relevant point is that a doctrine of evolutionary socialism could with the

---

[1] Lynd, op. cit., pp. 108 ff; Beatrice Webb, *Our Partnership*, ed. B. Drake and M. Cole, London, 1948, pp. 105 ff. The early history of the Fabian Society has been chronicled by some of its founders, but for an inside view of the Society's achievement in 'permeating' liberal opinion, Mrs. Webb's diaries remain the classic source—quite apart from the fact that they give a fascinating picture of British politics and society.

[2] Cf. in particular the preface to the third edition of the *Principles* (1852), and the emendations in the text of Book IV, ch. 7.

greatest ease be derived from Mill's writings. And it was so derived: the philosophy which underlies the original *Fabian Essays* is plainly that of Mill; and in this sense the critique of capitalism put forward in that seminal work can be described as a gigantic footnote to the *Principles*. There is nothing surprising in this; after all, Marx and Mill had both started from Ricardo. If the industrial revolution was viewed in terms of its effect on society as a whole, and not merely on the entrepreneurs, then concern with matters such as class, income and social inequality followed naturally; and it was just this which formed the bridge from liberalism to evolutionary socialism. Of course this relationship was not visible to anyone save intellectuals; but then intellectuals were bound to take the lead in the socialist—as in any other—movement. If there was a difference between Fabian (or Millian) socialism and rival schools, it lay not in the social ancestry of their respective supporters—for the tiny Marxist and Anarchist sects in Britain were likewise dominated by intellectuals—but in the respective influence they exerted on public opinion and the emerging labour movement.

A situation of this kind could arise only in a country which was already fully industrialised and where liberalism had effectively conquered. Once this is grasped it also becomes clear why German 'revisionism' was bound to fail. But there is another side to the matter: on Millian (or Fabian, which comes to the same) principles it was assumed—even if not always clearly stated—that the gradual advent of socialism entailed the 'socialisation' of *all* strata, in that they would all have to adapt themselves to a more collectivist way of life, with the public authorities—the state—taking over large sectors of activity hitherto left to private initiative. This was an accurate forecast and also an interesting essay in applied sociology— as indeed much of the success of Fabian propaganda was due to its near-monopoly of sociological thinking, in an environment still dominated by pre-scientific forms of theorising about social wholes.[1] But it was likewise a conclusion which ran counter to the original impetus of liberal-radical thinking, and for this reason was bitterly resented by some people who might otherwise have sympathised with

---

[1] Cf. *Fabian Essays* (first published 1889, new edn., London, 1950), passim. The whole matter is put very clearly in Sidney Webb's introduction to the 1920 reprint, but Shaw's preface to the 1908 edition is already outspoken enough. Of course the Fabians never said in so many words that they regarded themselves as the nucleus of a new governing elite; they would have been foolish to do so. But nonetheless that is what their approach implied from the start.

the new movement. Since we shall not encounter either Mill or the Fabians again, it remains to be said that this particular variant of socialism has proved entirely suitable to an environment such as England provided. In all probability it represents the typical form in which socialism outgrows its liberal ancestry, under conditions where liberalism may be said to have accomplished its task. In a situation of this kind the only question that finally remains is how a planned economy can be made to work; and to this question Fabian socialism supplied at least one possible answer, though there were others. For in one of its aspects Fabianism turns out to have been an anticipation of what is now variously known as the age of planning, the rise of technocracy, or the managerial revolution. This should inspire one with fresh respect for the realism of its founders, but it likewise remains a fact that this particular brand of modern socialism is *defined* as the outcome of a situation in which radical aims are no longer compatible with liberal solutions. Had this circumstance been better understood, a good deal of scholastic disputation over the respective merits of Marxian and Fabian doctrines could have been avoided.

Two related subjects must be briefly discussed before this introductory account is concluded: the growth of imperialist tendencies from about 1880 onward, and the gradual emergence of certain intellectual attitudes which pointed to a disintegration of some traditional liberal certitudes: notably the rise of what has been called 'Social Darwinism'. Whether or not these currents had a common source, they certainly displayed a marked affinity for each other, and in the end their confluence produced a distinctive world-view which had scarcely anything in common with classical liberalism. In the period under review these stirrings had only begun to take shape; the final crystallisation was to occur after 1918, but most of the elements that went into the new synthesis were already present before the first world war.

So far as imperialism is concerned, its post-liberal emergence after 1870 is evidently all that matters. There is not much point in going into the history of so ancient a phenomenon. For our purpose what counts is that the free-trade era did *not*—as its protagonists had firmly expected—culminate in the dissolution of the old protectionist-colonialist-militarist nexus, but on the contrary laid the foundation for a tremendous new outcrop of such tendencies from the 1880's onward, following some preliminary rumblings in the preceding decade. *That*, and not the continuance of old-fashioned 'power politics' in Eastern and Central Europe—governed as before by auto-cratic, or semi-autocratic monarchies—was what shook confidence in the power of liberalism to dissolve the traditional political struc-tures. It made no difference whether liberals adapted themselves to the new trend (as for the most part they did) or whether they conducted an unsuccessful rearguard action against it. In either case they were obliged to concede defeat; and that in fact is what happened.[1]

The new movement, for obvious reasons, was cradled in late Vic-torian England; and its emergence as a political factor, also not sur-prisingly, coincided with the after-effects of the great economic crash of 1873 which inaugurated a new mental climate in Western Europe.[2] For the Conservative party it was a question of recovering its in-fluence and drawing the electorate away from Gladstonian Liberalism. 'Tory democracy' and 'social reform' were part of the mixture, but imperialism became the chief ingredient, and thereafter for many years provided a unifying concept which reconciled the voters to the ruling oligarchy—indeed made any other attitude seem unpatriotic:

It was put in the form of 'Imperial Federation'. The colonies—of which Disraeli in 1852 had written: 'These wretched colonies . . . are a millstone round our necks' . . . these same colonies were to become autonomous members in a unified empire. This empire was to form a customs union. The free soil of the colonies was to remain reserved for Englishmen. A uniform defence system was to be created. The whole structure was to be crowned by a central representative organ in London, creating a closer, living, connection between the imperial government and the colonies. The appeal to national sentiment, the battle-cry against 'Liberal' cosmopolitan-ism, already emerged sharply, just as they did later on in the agitation sponsored by Chamberlain, on whom fell Disraeli's mantle. Of itself the plan showed no inherent tendency to reach out beyond the 'Empire', and 'the Preservation of the Empire' was and is quite a good description of it. If we nevertheless include the 'Imperial Federation' plan under the heading of imperialism, this is because its protective tariff, its militarist sentiments, its ideology of a unified 'Greater Britain' all foreshadowed vague aggressive

---

[1] The literature on this subject is immense; but J. A. Hobson's study *Imperialism* (first published London, 1902, revised edn., 1938) is still the classic critique of imperialism from the standpoint of old-fashioned Cobdenite liberalism; cf. also J. A. Schumpeter, *Imperialism and Social Classes*, ed. Sweezy, 1951. Marxist writers will be considered later.

[2] 'The election campaign of 1874—or, to fix the date exactly, Disraeli's speech in the Crystal Palace in 1872—marked the birth of imperialism as the catch-phrase of domestic policies.' Schumpeter, op. cit., p. 12; cf. also Ensor, op. cit., p. 31.

trends that would have emerged soon enough if the plan had ever passed from the sphere of the slogan into the realm of actual policy.[1]

For Britain there were ways of reconciling liberalism and imperialism, if the latter meant no more than official promotion of overseas investments and a colonial policy which did not shut out competitors altogether; and in the end some such uneasy solution was adopted by the dominant 'liberal imperialist' wing of the Liberal party. There was a precedent for this in the earlier compromise which had kept the Whig-Liberal coalition together in the 1850's, despite the mutual detestation of Palmerston and Cobden; and perhaps, going further back, in the lasting effect of the Whig tradition, which was mercantilist and colonialist to the hilt, though it also groped towards the freeing of imports. But then the notion that mercantilism and protectionism are synonymous is a German delusion. The founders of the second British Empire—the one that succeeded the loss of the American Colonies—knew better. It was *after* this awful shock (and the concurrent rescue of Canada) that Huskisson—a Tory but a convert to free trade—warned his countrymen: 'England cannot afford to be little. She must be what she is, or nothing.'[2] In this perspective, which envisaged empire as an extension of overseas trade, imperialism and liberalism could be reconciled, so long as there was no drive to erect a tariff wall around the empire and defend the protected enclosure by force of arms against all comers. This latter aim ultimately became the Tory concept of empire. It was also what the German apologists of imperialism in the Wilhelminian era meant by it; but even before their brief hey-day, German economic historians like Bücher and Schmoller (following the lead given by List a generation earlier) had recast the concept of mercantilism so as to render it synonymous with industrial protectionism or economic nationalism: policies which Bismarckian Germany actually introduced in the

[1] Schumpeter, op. cit., pp. 12–13. The rather question-begging concluding sentence is perhaps attributable to the fact that at the time of writing (1919) it seemed important to the author to stress the difference between the 'liberal imperialism' of the pre-1914 British Government and the far from liberal ideologies and policies of the Central Powers in the first world war, then just concluded. Few modern historians would maintain with the same degree of confidence that Disraeli and Chamberlain failed to convert their countrymen to their viewpoint, at any rate temporarily. Cf. Semmel, op. cit., passim; A. P. Thornton, *The Imperial Idea and its Enemies*, London, 1959; for the liberal imperialists cf. J. Gallagher and R. Robinson, 'The Imperialism of Free Trade', *Economic History Review*, vol. vi, no. I, 1953.

[2] C. R. Fay, *English Economic History*, Cambridge, 1940, p. 7.

1880's. These men were the contemporaries of Marx and Engels, and it was in conscious opposition to their views that the leaders of German Social-Democracy adopted a more or less consistent free-trade orientation, at any rate from the 1890's onward. In this they were guided by Engels's gradual abandonment of his original sympathy for List's advocacy of nationalism and protectionism, and his adoption of Marx's uncompromising adherence to free trade. Such an attitude was not welcome to all sections of the German labour movement, but while it prevailed it made a bond between that movement and the dwindling liberal opposition.[1]

For the European labour movement of the 1890's and the decade preceding the war, the rejection of imperialism—though not necessarily of protectionism—was part of the struggle for democracy. The latter implied at least that the electorate should be the final judge of its own interests, which were not likely to be furthered by unregulated capital investment in the colonies, let alone by wars conducted for the sake of such investments. A conviction that governments or legislatures dominated by the great financial interests were likely to pursue warlike policies spread slowly but persistently from the 1880's onward, when the joint Anglo-French intervention in Egypt and the partition of Africa confronted the public with the spectacle of overseas rivalries reacting upon traditional national animosities at home. This of course was nothing new to the governing oligarchies who had always been aware that European tensions were likely to be aggravated by the clash of interests abroad. But it was a disagreeable discovery for the liberal-minded part of the middle-class public, which had been taught to believe that the dark ages of mercantilist struggles over 'spheres of interest' were over for good. The disillusionment was particularly bitter in England, where the liberal intellectuals had somehow managed to persuade themselves that their political creed —including the hedonist calculus which underpinned it—had genuinely become the credo of the industrialists (though not of the landowning oligarchy, which could not be expected to share such enlightened sentiments). The awakening, which began with the Boer War of 1899–1902, was violent enough to drive whole sections of the

[1] Alexander Gerschenkron, *Bread and Democracy in Germany*, University of California Press, 1943, pp. 33 ff. Originally there had been a noticeable difference between Marx's and Engels's attitudes on the issue of protection, but by the 1870's this had ceased to matter because the 'infant industry' argument no longer carried much weight in relation to German conditions; cf. Engels, *Briefe an Bebel*, Berlin, 1958, pp. 48, 62–3.

old radical movement into the socialist camp, though until the eve of 1914 democratic radicalism for the most part still adhered to the left wing of the Liberal party. Here the first world war marked the great divide: after 1914–18 radical opposition to imperialism no longer had a place within the Liberal fold.[1]

What such radical Liberals were reacting against was in the first place a certain temper of mind which, broadly speaking, can be described as hierarchical and authoritarian. In social terms it signified that the upper strata of the middle class—notably those connected with the military services and the colonial administration—had become infected with the ruling-class ethos. In its origins this attitude reflected a society in which class relations depended on status rather than contract and were cemented by veneration for a social hierarchy dominated by the landed aristocracy. When applied to the more fluid world of big business, whose title-deeds rested on personal achievement rather than hereditary status, the ruling-class ethos took on a different colour, but it remained authoritarian and anti-democratic. Its central idea was the need for a self-conscious elite to manage the common business of society. Where the aristocracy still exercised important governing functions, as it did in Victorian and Edwardian Britain, such notions drew strength from tradition, while their spread among the middle class was powerfully assisted by the imperial nexus. It was natural that an aristocratic Whig like Rosebery should for a while have become the most prominent spokesman of the Liberal Imperialist school. For him and his like, the Empire was no ordinary thing:

How marvellous it all is! Built not by saints and angels, but the work of men's hands; cemented with men's honest blood and with a world of tears, welded by the best brains of the centuries past; not without the taint and reproach incidental to all human work, but constructed on the whole with pure and splendid purpose. Human and yet not wholly human, for the most heedless and the most cynical must see the finger of the Divine.[2]

Such lyrical flights were not untypical, for if democratic radicals

---

[1] Cf. *Beatrice Webb's Diaries 1912–24*, ed. M. Cole, London, 1952, passim; R. B. McCallum, *Public Opinion and the Last Peace*, London, 1944, pp. 86 ff. The process which brought growing numbers of radical Liberals into the Labour party—by way of pacifist revulsion against the war and its aftermath—is well described in this work.

[2] Rosebery, quoted by G. Bennett, *The Concept of Empire*, London, 1953, pp. 326–7; for a less exalted view of the subject cf. John Strachey, *The End of Empire*, London, 1959.

gravitated increasingly towards pacifism, and finally towards social-ism, their opponents likewise had to seek new ground to stand on. From the 1880's onward imperialism, in addition to being so to speak a normal ingredient of governmental policy, gradually became an ideology and as such a rival of the democratic creed. This was in itself an inverted tribute to democracy, for apart from the framework of public discussion and popular elections such a development would have been quite incomprehensible. If left to themselves, the governing classes would have been quite content to follow their traditional objectives—which of course included the preservation, and if possible extension, of imperial possessions—without enlisting the help of an ideology; but in the age of democracy it was not enough to pursue an expansionist line: there had to be a creed to buttress it, especially if the policy was one that did not rhyme too well with majority in-terests. Hence imperialism now became the focus of a brand-new ruling-class ideology, and anything that looked like being helpful—from Natural Selection to Eugenics—was pressed into service.[1] Racialism and 'Social Darwinism' in particular were effectively con-scripted and made to perform various non-combatant duties in the counter-attack against democracy. There was indeed nothing new about the belief that certain groups were endowed by nature or history with particular talents for commanding others and generally getting the world's work done with the maximum despatch and efficiency; but such notions could now be paraded with all the authority of 'science' to back them up. The fact that they also did useful service in persuading governments and parliaments not to enact too much welfare legislation, naturally endeared them to businessmen, and to that extent weakened the attachment of the middle class to the older egalitarian liberalism. It became common form to maintain that those at the bottom of the social pyramid were there because they were unfit to rise higher, and that changes in environment or education could not do much to alter this state of

---

[1] Schumpeter, *History*, pp. 788 ff. One must not exaggerate the responsibility of either Darwin or Spencer for the use that was made of their ideas. But it is a fact that Darwin himself employed racial concepts to illustrate his methodi-cal scheme. Cf. the abbreviated edition of the *Life and Letters* (1887), ed. Francis Darwin, 1892, new edn., New York, 1958, p. 69: 'The more civilised so-called Caucasian races have beaten the Turkish hollow in the struggle for existence. Looking to the world at no very distant date, what an endless number of the lower races will have been eliminated by the higher civilised races through-out of the world.' These were not Tory sentiments: Darwin considered himself a Liberal.

affairs. For obvious reasons such notions did not commend themselves to the labour movement, which thus found itself practically compelled to assume the heritage of the traditional radical belief in perfectibility. This, if nothing else, helps to explain why in the period under review socialism became the chief repository of every hopeful scheme for the improvement of mankind. Not that socialists had a monopoly of the reforming spirit: it is only necessary to mention feminism and pacifism to demolish such a notion. But on the Continent at least such currents tended to coalesce increasingly with the Social-Democratic movement and even to affect its fundamental outlook upon society. The feminine strain in particular grew rather marked as time went on, and probably helped to induce a somewhat lopsided emphasis on the more amiable aspects of existence. It became rare for socialists to concern themselves systematically with disagreeable topics such as foreign affairs or military problems.

'Social Darwinism' represented a corruption of positivism, with its more hopeful anticipations left out and replaced by a belief in cast-iron laws which, by a curious coincidence, guaranteed *both* a species of 'progress' *and* the permanence of the *status quo*. The response to this kind of fatalism necessarily stressed the element of change, hence of human responsibility. This explains why Marxism had a liberating effect on radical intellectuals in the 1890's, notwithstanding its insistence on 'laws' of social development. We touch here upon one of the key issues of the subsequent debate over the 'revision' of Marxist doctrine: how far was materialism compatible with a belief in the ability of men to alter their environment by conscious action? Depending on how they stood in regard to this question, 'revisionist', and 'orthodox' defenders of the doctrine (as formulated by Engels), took different views of the ability of bourgeois civilisation to survive. However, we shall see that the political cleavage between 'reformists' and 'radicals' did not correspond to this ideological line-up. Marxist orthodoxy was quite capable of inducing a marked passivity in political matters, while some of the more prominent 'revisionists' were far from being peaceful 'reformists'. This situation had its reverse side: in England, where Marxism was without influence before 1918 and indeed had scarcely any competent spokesmen, philosophical idealism in some cases underpinned a radical critique of existing institutions. Neo-Hegelian emphasis upon the state and the collectivity became fashionable, via the universities, among members of the governing elite who prided themselves upon their emancipation from old-fashioned *laissez-faire* liberalism: both the 'Liberal Imperialist' Haldane and the Tory proconsul of Empire, Milner, had links with the Fabians. The latter in turn, at any rate in the persons of their intellectual leaders, the Webbs, shared the new imperial creed. The common denominator was contempt for *laissez-faire*, and an altogether novel readiness to employ political coercion—the state—for the purpose of remoulding society.

It is evident that at this point we touch upon one of the key issues in modern intellectual history: the relativity of political ideals and the closely related question of ethical value-judgments: not as a dry epistemological problem but as a question of vital significance for the culture of that particular age, which broadly speaking was the declining age of European liberalism.[1] If it can generally be said that 'philosophy rediscovers in the world that very scheme of representation which had, by a necessary process, been projected into the world from the structure and institutions of society in its earlier stages of development',[2] one need not be unduly surprised to find that the intellectual debates of the period revolved around some of the chief constituents of the liberal-humanist creed: freedom, rationality, democracy. For all these were now under attack, and the counter-movement arose not from external factors, but from the disintegration of the liberal tradition itself. Socialists—especially if they were Marxists—at that time still considered themselves immune from this mounting challenge. Only later, during the Fascist era, did they learn to their cost that no section of the humanist army was exempt from the threat. Still, for the period under review the statement holds good that the crisis affected primarily the established liberal viewpoint, which was also the traditional ideology of the European bourgeoisie. That class was now about to undergo a prolonged ideological bombardment before being exposed to the traumatic shock of the first world war. Some of the factors making for the disintegration of its accustomed way of life have been briefly indicated. None is sufficient by itself to account for the severity of the crisis that first manifested itself in 1914–18, but taken together the evidence points to a gradual loss of certitudes—political, intellectual, moral—of the sort that typically precedes a major cultural reorientation.

There is not much purpose in going into the cause-and-effect

[1] Hughes, pp. 278 ff; Schumpeter, op. cit., pp. 804 ff.
[2] F. M. Cornford, *From Religion to Philosophy*, New York, 1957, p. 126.

problem, for beyond a certain stage a movement of this kind becomes cumulative and feeds upon its own logic. The intent of these preliminary remarks will have been served if it is made clear that the rise of Marxian socialism between 1871 and 1918 is here viewed in the perspective of a transformation which affected European society as a whole. There were of course other symptoms of the same process—e.g., the surprising revival of political Catholicism in Western Europe. However, we are obliged to limit our field to one set of circumstances alone; and even here it is necessary to bear in mind that what we are dealing with are not strictly speaking 'facts' in the conventional sense, but 'situations' in which both ideas and events were inextricably involved. The crisis of liberal civilisation—or bourgeois society, if the term is preferred—concerned not merely social arrangements, but also the values incorporated in the fabric of personal and communal existence. This truth became evident enough when the collapse of the liberal integration in Continental Europe consequent upon the 1914–18 war let loose destructive and irrational forces undreamed of in the comfortable philosophy of the bourgeois age; but in a more theoretical way it ought to have been perceived before. After all, thought is not concerned with brute circumstance, but with a representation of reality to which the mind contributes its quota. Materialist philosophies are not exempt from this rule, though their adherents tend to credit themselves with a unique capacity for getting round it. If the history of Marxism during the period under review holds any lesson, it is that a simple faith in the omnicompetence of 'positive science' can itself become a philosophical illusion.

2

MARXISM, ANARCHISM, SYNDICALISM

WHAT HAS BEEN SAID so far relates to the disintegration of liberalism, principally in England and Germany, and to the growth of socialist tendencies to the 'right' of Social-Democratic Marxism. But Social-Democracy also had rivals on its other flank, notably in France, Italy, and Spain, where Anarchism had profoundly marked what was left of the labour movement after the catastrophe of the Paris Commune. It is not too much to say that Marxism as constituted around 1890 was primarily a Central European affair, while in Western Europe its progress was slowed by the Proudhonist heritage of non-political trade-unionism, and in the South it encountered Anarchism in its classic form, complete with principled rejection of state and society. Marx and Engels had taught their followers to regard such tendencies as an expression of backwardness and immaturity, and to count on their disappearance consequent upon the emergence of a modern industrial proletariat. This expectation was shaken when Syndicalism appeared in the succession of Anarchism, not merely in Spain and France but elsewhere in Western Europe and even in North America. For the Syndicalists repudiated the Social-Democratic pattern while adapting Marxism to their own purpose. Syndicalism represented a revival within the Socialist fold of tendencies inherent in the 'libertarian' doctrine of Proudhon and his French and Belgian followers, including those who had rejected his anti-political teachings; and its growth on the eve of the first world war signalised a malaise for which the official Socialist leadership had no remedy. There was even a substantial Syndicalist movement in pre-1914 England, where Social-Democratic Marxism had virtually failed to penetrate![1]

To grasp the significance of this tripartite division of forces it is necessary to recall what Anarchism had originally meant in the 1870's and 1880's: a radical protest movement of impoverished artisans (in Belgium, Austria, and Switzerland), or downtrodden rural labourers (in Spain and Southern Italy), against society and the state; while 'Marxist Socialism' during the same period had in practice come to stand for reformism in the spirit of the 1864 *Inaugural Address*: the birth certificate, as it were, of modern Social-Democracy. This division was not altogether to the taste of Marx, but as time went on he and Engels adapted themselves to the trend, and eventually Engels became so wholehearted an exponent of the new Social-Democratic creed as to cause his followers almost to forget that at one time they—or their predecessors—had shared a platform with Bakunin. Yet within a few years of Engels's own departure from the scene (1895), the ancient 'anti-authoritarian' heresy raised its head again, this time within the official Socialist fold and under the direction of men and women who repudiated every connection with Bakuninism. The new movement was not a despairing rebellion against industrial capitalism, but rather an attempt to supersede it. Its leaders rejected 'state socialism', but not the state as such. They were not even radically hostile to parliamentary politics, merely indifferent to it. Perhaps their attitude can best be summed up by saying that they were groping towards what later came to be called 'workers' control in industry'. This made them tolerant of political nostrums which ignored the fact that society was not composed exclusively of factory owners and industrial workers; and after 1917 it caused many of them to succumb for a while to the lure of the 'Soviet experiment'. But Syndicalism was essentially a radical-democratic creed, and when the authoritarian character of the Soviet regime became manifest, most of the Syndicalists who in 1917–21

[1] Cole, *History*, vol. II, *Marxism and Anarchism*, pp. 315 ff; vol. III, part I, *The Second International*, pp.. 323 ff; Ed. Dolléans, *Histoire du Mouvement Ouvrier*, vol. II, pp. 13 ff; E. Halévy, *Histoire du socialisme européen*, pp. 163 ff; R. Bothereau, *Histoire du syndicalisme francais*, Paris, 1945; Paul Louis, *Histoire du socialisme en France*, Paris, 1950.

had mistaken Leninism for a modernised version of their own doctrine turned away from it—though not towards parliamentary politics.

In a history of the Socialist movement these cross-currents would necessarily occupy an important place. They cannot do so here, since we are primarily concerned with Marxism. Yet the division is not clear-cut. After the collapse of the original Anarchist movement some time in the later 1880's, every other school of 'anti-authoritarian Socialism' was obliged to come to terms with Marx, and did so to a greater or lesser extent even when its theorists prided themselves upon their doctrinal independence. The relevant point here is not that these groups held dissenting views, but that they formulated them with reference to the dominant Marxist credo. This was a state of affairs very different from that of the 1860's when Marx was simply regarded as a rival of the more widely known Proudhon; or the 1870's when there was thought to be a choice between an 'authoritarian' and a 'libertarian' corpus of Socialist doctrine. From about 1890 onward the legitimacy of such a distinction was no longer admitted by the parties and movements which had come together in 1889 to form the Second International; and in 1896 this attitude was formalised by the refusal of the International's third congress in London to seat Anarchist delegates.[1] This did not mean that the 'anti-authoritarian' current had disappeared, though to remain orthodox its adherents now had to cut their connection with the remnant of Bakunin's old following. What it meant was that henceforth anyone who aspired to the Socialist label was obliged to conform, more or less, to the established Social-Democratic pattern and the quasi-Marxist terminology that went with it. The upshot was Syndicalism with which we cannot deal here since its spokesmen—whatever their national or regional importance—made no significant contribution to Marxist theory.[2]

[1] Cole, op. cit., vol. III, pp. 18 ff. This did not necessarily imply, as the Anarchists maintained, that the International was committed to 'reform' as against 'revolution', but in practice it did amount to a tacit recognition of the fact that the labour movement had to pursue its aims by legal means. In this sense the Second International can be said to have been 'reformist' from the start. It may be noteworthy that most of the delegates from Holland at the 1896 congress, and about half the French, were opposed to the resolution barring Anarchist participants.

[2] An exception appears to be represented by the American Socialist movement associated with Daniel de Leon (1852–1914). But though de Leon regarded himself as a Marxist—indeed as the only orthodox Marxist—it is difficult to see in what respect he developed Marxist doctrine beyond insisting that

But if doctrinal development is our yardstick, it is likewise unnecessary to consider such minor offshoots from the Central European stem as the Marxist group which came together in London in the 1880's. It is a matter of considerable historical interest that British Socialism was at the critical moment captured by the Fabians, while the rival Marxist movement never got off the ground and eventually dwindled into an unimportant sect. The revival of Marxism in England had to await the Russian Revolution, and in an important sense Marxist thinking may be said to have gained a foothold in the British labour movement only with the prolonged economic and political deadlock of the 1930's. For our purpose the period under review represents almost a complete blank so far as England is concerned. There were important political currents outside the official labour movement, but so far as theoretical thinking goes Fabianism had a near-monopoly until Syndicalism came on the scene, shortly before the outbreak of the 1914 war, in the characteristically English guise of the Guild Socialist movement; and even this took the form—at the doctrinal level anyhow—of a breakaway movement from the Fabians.[1]

We are therefore left with the Continental European countries, and here the division between the German-speaking group and the rest is fairly clear-cut. There were in the 1880's a handful of Anarchist groups in Germany, and a rather larger number in Austria, where the Socialist movement proper did not get under way until the end of the decade. But there never was a significant Anarchist *movement* in Central Europe, or for that matter anything like the Syndicalist wave which rolled across Western Europe after 1900. Nor was there a counterpart to the Populist agrarian Socialism which then grew up in Russia and the Balkans. Germany and Austria were the twin citadels of Marxian Social-Democracy, the intransigence of whose orthodoxy was rivalled only by the bureaucratic discipline imposed upon its followers. It became the special mark of this orthodoxy to refuse even to engage in theoretical discussions with adherents of the heretical 'libertarian' creed. By contrast such disputations never ceased in France, Italy, Spain, and the minor West European countries

Socialism was not synonymous with reformism. In the minds of some of his later followers de Leon benefited from the fact that Lenin expressed a high opinion of him, but even this doubtful compliment cannot secure him a niche in a history of Marxism that pays some attention to the theoretical side.

[1] Cole, op. cit., vol. III, pp. 104 ff; S. and B. Webb, *What Syndicalism Means*, London, 1913; Ch. Tsuzuki, *H. M. Hyndman and British Socialism*, Oxford, 1961; Beer, *History*, II, pp. 354 ff.

—Switzerland and Holland above all—where (non-violent) 'libertarian Socialism' had early secured a foothold; just as Socialists and Syndicalists in Western Europe never ceased to argue over the relative status of political parties and trade unions. Indeed the Syndicalist controversy turned almost entirely on this issue.

It is not possible therefore to run a straight line from the differences which split the First International to the tension between Socialists and Syndicalists in, say, France between 1890 and 1905. The issues had changed, and so had the terminology. And yet the old dividing-line between Central and Western Europe persisted. In the case of France the proximate cause of the dispute clearly lay in the insistence of the Socialist leaders—at any rate those who, like Jules Guesde, were Marxists—that the trade unions should come under the control of the political wing.[1] But when one enquires why this demand was conceded in Germany (though in the end the unions there turned the tables on the party), while it was successfully resisted in France, one comes up against imponderables: the memory of the Paris Commune, and behind it the old and deeply rooted tradition of *ouvriérisme*, i.e., distrust of middle-class intellectuals, irrespective of whether or not they were Socialists. Proudhon, himself of working-class stock, had benefited from this ingrained hostility towards Socialist theorists of bourgeois origin: it was one of the sources of his antagonism to Marx.[2] When Syndicalism revived in France from the 1890's onward, its leaders—though by now in some cases themselves of middle-class origin—instinctively groped towards a slightly modified form of the traditional *ouvriérisme*: individuals from other classes might join the labour movement, but not entire groups. Moreover, the union movement, though not 'opposed' to parliamentary activity—that would have been Anarchism, i.e., heresy—must remain strictly autonomous and independent of the middle-class lawyers who got elected to the Chamber on the Socialist ticket. The whole issue hardly existed in Germany; in France it overshadowed all others.[3]

[1] Cole, op. cit., vol. II, p. 326; Dolléans, op. cit., vol. II, pp. 23 ff.

[2] Dolléans, op. cit., vol. I, pp. 277 ff. At the Geneva Congress of the First International in 1866, the French delegates, Proudhonists to a man, opposed the admission of 'bourgeois' intellectuals into a workers' movement, and their spokesman, Tolain, expressly included 'Citizen Marx' in this category: much to the embarrassment of the British trade unionists present; cf. Dolléans, loc. cit., pp. 290–1.

[3] Dolléans, vol. II, pp. 35 ff. There is an apparent contradiction in the fact that the principal exponent of Syndicalism during this period, Fernand Pelloutier, was himself an intellectual of middle-class origin. Evidently this did not

One does well to centre attention on France, for it was here that in the period under review the dispute between Marxism and Anarcho-Syndicalism was fought out, both politically and doctrinally. Elsewhere no such head-on clash occurred, for the good reason that it takes two to produce a conflict, and one of the contestants was commonly absent. A partial exception might be made for Spain, but for the fact that the two rival movements there had tacitly agreed upon a territorial division which enabled them to practise a form of armed co-existence. There were in Spain followers of Bakunin who gradually drifted from pure Anarchism towards Anarcho-Syndicalism; and there were adherents of Marx who called themselves Socialists and looked to their French comrades—not so much to the Germans—for guidance. But there was no real communication between these rival camps; whereas in France the labour movement was sufficiently united for various shades of Socialism and Syndicalism to exist more or less peacefully under one roof, even before the adoption in 1906 of the *Charte d'Amiens* which formalised the relationship of the trade unions towards the unified Socialist party established the year before.[1] In principle the same applies to Italy where Anarchism likewise died out in the 1890's, following its expulsion from the official Socialist fold. But Italian Socialism did not as yet have much of an independent orientation.[2]

But if France is the 'classic' case, then the most one can say about the outcome of the contest is that until 1914 'Marxist' Socialism more or less managed to hold its own. It did not yield ground in its two-front struggle against 'reformist' opportunism on the 'right', and 'revolutionary' Syndicalism on the 'left', but neither did it gain much new territory. The unified Socialist party established in 1905 was a coalition within whose ranks the Marxist wing under Guesde and Lafargue barely counter-balanced the eclectic doctrines, and the somewhat opportunist tactics, of Jaurès (upon whom the party was wholly dependent for parliamentary leadership); while the trade unions, under their Syndicalist leaders, deliberately remained aloof.

matter; what mattered was that he gave expression to the prevailing sentiment of the movement.

[1] Cf. Halévy, op. cit., pp. 190 ff; Dolléans, op. cit., vol. II, pp. 117 ff.

[2] Some light has recently been thrown on this subject by the publication of letters exchanged by Engels and Turati in the 1890's; cf. *Friedrich Engels-Filippo Turati Correspondence, 1891–95*, ed. Luigi Cortese, published in the *Annali Istituto Giangiacomo Feltrinelli*, Milan, 1958, pp. 220 ff; cf. also Franco della Peruta, 'Il socialismo italiano dal 1875 al 1882', loc. cit., pp. 15 ff.

To describe this outcome as a victory for Marxism is evidently nonsense. On balance the French situation differed from the German chiefly in that the official leadership was largely 'revisionist' and made no pretence of defending every letter of the Marxist canon. This did not prevent the French Socialist movement from being on the whole rather more combative than the German; but then orthodoxy and radicalism had little to do with each other.[1]

Yet France remained important to Marxism, not merely for the obvious reason, but because of its strategic position—at any rate down to the 1890's—in the propagation of Marxist doctrine. Contrary to a widespread notion it was the first major country where a significant section of the labour movement adopted a Marxist platform. This event took place in 1880, eleven years before the German Social-Democrats followed suit.[2] The platform was a 'reformist' one, in that it tacitly repudiated both the Anarchist preachment of armed violence and the indigenous Blanquist tradition of Parisian *coups d'état*. Instead emphasis was laid on the need for the working class to build up its organisations as the only basis of the coming collectivist order. This was a return to the classic document of the First International, the *Inaugural Address*; and it marked the abandonment by Marx (who helped Guesde to draft the French party programme) of his temporary infatuation with the utopianism of the Paris Commune. It was precisely in this sense that 'Marxism' was then understood both by its adherents and by Bakunin's followers all over Europe. If Lafargue and Guesde—the latter himself an erstwhile Bakuninist —nonetheless found themselves at odds with an 'opportunist' group on their right flank, this was because the 'opportunists' had no desire to be completely cut off from the Radicals with whom they co-operated from time to time in defence of the Republic. This adherence to 'Republican solidarity' later became the principal issue between Guesde and the ex-Radical Jaurès; and the fact that Jaurès eventually

---

[1] This of course was not the view of Marx's French followers; for them it was an article of faith that political purity could be guaranteed only by doctrinal orthodoxy; cf. the correspondence between Engels and the Lafargues in *Friedrich Engels–Paul et Laura Lafargue, Correspondance, 1868–95*, ed. Bottigelli, 3 vols., Paris, 1956–9, passim. This exchange of letters, it is true, terminates a decade before the two wings of the French Socialist movement had come together, but by then the Guesdist version of Marxism had been fully developed; it was to retain its significant features even after the Communist split of 1920 had created a wholly new alignment.

[2] Halévy, op. cit., p. 191; cf. also Engels–Lafargue correspondence, vol. I, introduction, pp. xxxi ff.

imposed his outlook on the party had much to do with the evolution of French Socialism from a workers' sect into a mass movement. Yet in the 1880's, when the reawakened labour movement took its first halting steps in the political field, it was the Marxist emphasis upon complete independence from all 'bourgeois' parties, including the Radical Republicans, that enabled it to rally the surviving veterans of the Commune to its banner. Any other attitude would have left the field open to the followers of Bakunin, or alternatively enabled Clemenceau to enrol the entire working class under the Radical flag: an endeavour in which he very nearly succeeded.[1]

Thus Marxism, besides being 'collectivist' and 'authoritarian', additionally came to stand for 'reform', though not as yet for reliance upon parliamentary politics. It was the spectre of such a further development that caused the Syndicalist leaders to maintain an attitude of reserve towards the Socialist party. In so doing they unconsciously anticipated the central issue of the post-1918 situation: what was to be the role of the labour movement when confronted with a Socialist government—or worse still, a Socialist dictatorship? Before 1914 this question hardly arose in a practical form, but one can perhaps say that the Syndicalists tried to think it through; to a large extent they drew their strength from the belief that the workers' movement must at all cost preserve its autonomy even under a 'collectivist' form of society. For the rest, Syndicalism had its own 'myth' in the idea of the General Strike which would bring the social order tumbling down. This was not just a fanciful expectation of some far-off event: it conditioned the outlook, and even the tactics, of the active minority who led and organised the movement.[2]

That minority drew its fundamental inspiration partly from Marx, in considerable degree from Proudhon, and most of all from the traditions of the Paris Commune. Hostility to every form of centralised authority was not indeed something the Syndicalists needed to learn from either Proudhon or Marx, but both men had sanctioned it by their authority, though in the case of Marx with reservations

[1] Engels–Lafargue correspondence, passim; for Engels's critical attitude towards Lafargue's policy at the time of the Boulangist crisis in 1887-9—when the 'Marxists' all but washed their hands of the Republic, while their rivals joined the Radicals in a common democratic front—ibid., vol. II, pp. 139 ff.

[2] Dolléans, op. cit., vol. II, pp. 46 ff. Contrary to a popular misconception, the 'myth' of the general strike was not the invention of the romantic littérateur Georges Sorel; the latter, like other literary men, remained on the fringe of the movement and had no hand in shaping its policies. He did, however, have some influence on Mussolini; cf. his *Réflexions sur la violence*, Paris, 1908.

which enabled his followers to straddle the issue. Such traditional attitudes were hallowed by the memory of the Commune and its martyrs. There was not a Socialist in France, from the 'orthodox' Guesde to the 'opportunist' Brousse, for whom the Commune was not the ultimate test of loyalty. It was this which made it so difficult to bring French and English Socialists together in one International— an event finally consummated in 1889. With the Germans there were fewer obstacles. Praise of the Paris Commune was of course *verboten* in Germany, but since most leading Social-Democrats were in exile until 1890, owing to Bismarck's anti-Socialist legislation of 1878, they could profess revolutionary sentiments abroad. In consequence the founding of the Second International in 1889—appropriately in Paris, to mark the centenary of the French Revolution—was largely a Franco-German affair.[1]

It goes without saying that in 1889 few Socialists dreamed of repeating the tactics which had led to the great disaster of 1871. Indeed the repudiation of armed insurrection, side by side with cere-monial acknowledgment of the Commune's spiritual heritage, was the very essence of the new faith. The surviving Anarchists saw this very clearly and never ceased to marvel at the inconsequence of their opponents, who went on talking about revolution when in fact they had no intention of overstepping the bounds of legality. But this seeming incoherence had its own logic: wherever democracy had not been established—i.e., where the people did not have the vote—the Social-Democratic credo implicitly sanctioned violence, though it did not openly advocate it. This ambiguity made it possible for Social-Democracy to square its political faith with its revolutionary vocabu-lary. Nor was this simply a matter of tactics. By the 1890's it had become the conviction at any rate of Engels—Marx was no longer there—that political power resided in the vote, and that a duly elected legislature with a Socialist majority was both an attainable goal and the surest guarantee of victory.[2]

---

[1] Cole, op. cit., vol. III/1, pp. 1–36; Engels–Lafargue correspondence, vol. II, pp. 200 ff.

[2] Cf. Engels, Preface to the 1895 edition of Marx's *Class Struggles in France*, MESW I, pp. 118 ff. The Preface was somewhat toned down by the editors of the German Social-Democratic journals which originally published it, cer-tain passages dealing with the tactics of popular insurrection being omitted from fear of legal consequences. But the subsequent Leninist assertion that the sense of Engels's text was thereby radically altered does not hold water. There is nothing in the unabridged version to modify the conclusion that by 1895— the year of his death—Engels had fully accepted the democratic standpoint.

How far the movement had travelled in the quarter century since the heyday of the First International is evident when one contrasts these massive certainties with the doctrinaire debates characteristic of the congresses of the late 1860's. But something else becomes apparent too: the decreasing importance of personal and doctrinal differences. In 1872–4 the conflict between Marx and Bakunin was largely instrumental in wrecking the First International. After 1889 no two theorists, however eminent, possessed the power to disrupt what had become a mass movement. Neither the 'revisionist' controversy in Germany, nor 'Millerandism' (i.e., participation in a non-Socialist government) in France, posed a serious danger of large-scale secession. It took the 1914–18 war to bring the structure to the ground.

The interplay of theory and practice can perhaps be decisive only in the formative stage of a new movement. Not that there was ever something like a trial of strength between Marx and Bakunin at the theoretical level—if only because Bakunin was no theorist.[1] Had such an encounter taken place it would not have been difficult for Marx's opponents to embarrass him by quoting his youthful utterances; though the most recklessly utopian and libertarian of his early writings—the *Economic-Philosophical Manuscripts*—lay safely concealed in a drawer, to be brought to light only in the turbulent 1930's, when 'existentialism' was rampant in Europe and radical intellectuals yearned for mental sustenance more rewarding to the spirit than the dry dust of historical necessity. Few Socialists would have cared to give prominence to such aspirations in the sober 1890's, when official Marxism drew part of its prestige from the positivist tone of its utterances. Marx himself, in drawing up his *Critique of the Gotha Programme* in 1875, took care to lay emphasis upon the 'unscientific' character of Lassalle's rival doctrine. What was left of his original libertarianism appeared only in the form of some brief anticipations of the future—hints so guarded in tone and so ambiguous in meaning that they did not seriously incommode his followers

[1] 'A Mahomet without a Koran' was Marx's contemptuous description of the antagonist who caused him so much trouble. (Cf. Marx to Paul Lafargue, April 19, 1870, in 'Lettres et documents de Karl Marx', ed. Bottigelli, *Annali Istituto Giangiacomo Feltrinelli*, 1958, pp. 172 ff.) Bakunin's programme, he observed on the same occasion, rested 'on a superannuated idealism which considers the actual jurisprudence as the basis of our economical state, instead of seeing that our economical state is the basis and source of our jurisprudence.' (Ibid., p. 174.) Thus Bakunin was dismissed as pre-scientific, and in the eyes of Marx's followers it was this, rather than his personal and political failings, which damned him.

in opting for the present as the best of (almost) all possible worlds.[1]

In general it can be said that if libertarianism remained an effective strain within the Socialist movement in this period, it was thanks to the hold which Syndicalism had gained in Latin Europe.[2] German Socialism—notwithstanding Marx's criticism of Lassallean state-worship—remained emphatically authoritarian and bureaucratic, though perhaps no more so than the Fabianism of the Webbs. At the opposite pole, though still within the official Socialist fold, Syndicalism represented a groping attempt to work out the theory of a de-centralised form of collective ownership under which the central authority was to share responsibility with autonomous, producer-controlled, bodies. This fell short of total hostility to the state, à la Bakunin, but pointed towards its gradual supersession. At the centre of these opposing currents Marx can be watched cautiously steering his way between the Blanquist Scylla and the Anarchist Charybdis; notably in his *Critique of the Gotha Programme* where the vision of a future stateless society—a sequel to the Paris Commune and the subsequent Anarchist assault on his own position—is qualified by the reluctant admission that this goal cannot be reached until bourgeois society has been transcended.[3] In 1875 this kind of talk was bound to have an academic ring. In Germany at any rate bourgeois society, so far from being ripe for the transition to collectivism, had not even come fully into its own. But although Marx was aware of this fact, he evidently felt a need to define his attitude on an issue which was of no great importance to his German followers.

Not surprisingly the *Critique of the Gotha Programme* remained unpublished until Engels brought it to light in 1891, by which time German Social-Democracy had struck its characteristic balance between practical politics and long-term aspirations. The area where the hints thrown out in the *Critique* were to acquire practical significance was Eastern Europe, notably Russia on the eve of 1905 and 1917. Marx's impartial hostility towards Blanquism and Anarchism, his unceasing concern with the lessons of the French Revolution, his

[1] Cf. Maximilien Rubel, *Karl Marx—Essai de biographie intellectuelle*, Paris, 1957, pp. 81 ff; 103 ff. For a different view of the subject cf. Lucien Goldmann, *Recherches dialectiques*, Paris, 1959, pp. 280 ff.

[2] Including Belgium, where the anti-authoritarian tradition went back to de Paepe's efforts, in the late 1860's, to find a middle ground between Marxism and Anarchism; cf. Cole, op. cit., II, pp. 202 ff.

[3] MESW II, p. 30; an admission capped by the—purely Blanquist—concept of the 'revolutionary dictatorship of the proletariat' during the interim period.

passionate involvement with the heritage of the Commune, were barely comprehensible to his followers in Germany, where a phrase such as 'dictatorship of the proletariat' had a distinctly outlandish ring. A revolutionary break with the past was an experience lacking in the history of Germany. Moreover, the Jacobin-Blanquist phraseology of French Socialism sounded strange in German ears. There was little to connect it with the realities of German politics in the later nineteenth century. Conversely, there was much in the Eastern European setting that corresponded to the experiences which France had earlier undergone. If the Socialist movement in Eastern Europe was to take the lead in the coming upheaval, it could not fail to encounter those issues which had helped to shape French political thinking: chief among them the question whether 'the revolution' could be carried through without establishing a temporary dictatorship. In the Central European setting this was very nearly a meaningless question, since 'the revolution' here signified the democratisation of the traditional state and society. Social-Democratic Marxism after 1890 thus concealed a profound ambiguity: depending on whether it was given a 'German' or a 'French' meaning it connoted either the peaceful conquest of power through democracy, or the imposition of a Socialist dictatorship by a revolutionary minority. This unresolved tension remained latent during the period under review, but was due to explode when Eastern Europe had become ripe for revolution.

For the time being both tendencies managed to co-exist within the intellectual framework of orthodox Marxism as formulated by Engels and Kautsky in the 1890's. In many ways this is the 'classical moment' in the history of Marxist Socialism considered as a body of doctrine: the moment when the inherent disharmonies of the system were held in balance and brought to rest. It can scarcely be thought an accident that this unique constellation coincided with the rise of Germany to European eminence, or that the region of orthodox Marxism's principal influence was located in Central Europe. We are confronted with the phenomenon of German Social-Democracy in the era of its unchallenged hegemony within the international Socialist movement. Many different factors went into this constellation, but in terms of intellectual history what stands out is the temporary pre-eminence of German theorising. For a start we do well to turn our attention to Engels.

3

ENGELS[1]

THERE IS a certain ambiguity about the customary interpretation of Engels's share in the development of Marxism. For the orthodox he is simply Marx's life-long ally and helper in shaping the theory and practice of the movement—a figure of (almost) comparable size, though admittedly not quite his equal as a thinker. In the ideology of Marxism-Leninism even this distinction tends to be blurred, Engels's philosophical writings rather than those of Marx being the source of the distinctive world-view known as 'dialectical materialism' since the late nineteenth century. Some contemporary neo-Marxists by contrast tend to question the significance of his contribution, almost to the point of excluding him from the Marxist canon. Neither party to this controversy can well dispute the *historical* fact that Engels was chiefly instrumental, after the death of Marx, in giving shape to what became known as 'orthodox Marxism'. For

[1] For the following, in addition to Engels's writings cited hereafter, cf. Gustav Mayer, *Engels*, vol. II, pp. 263 ff; Kurt Brandis, *Die deutsche Sozialdemokratie bis zum Fall des Sozialistengesetzes*, Leipzig, 1931, passim; Karl Korsch, *Marxismus und Philosophie*, Leipzig, 1931, passim; Hermann Bollnow, 'Engels' Auffassung von Revolution und Entwicklung, etc.', in *Marxismusstudien*, vol. I, pp. 77 ff; Iring Fetscher, 'Von der Philosophie des Proletariats zur proletarischen Weltanschauung,' in *Marxismusstudien*, vol. II, pp. 26 ff. For a critical analysis of Engels's philosophical writings cf. Sidney Hook, *Reason, Social Myths, and Democracy*, New York, 1950, pp. 183 ff.

our immediate purpose this is all that matters. We therefore start from the well-nigh unchallengeable proposition that as a coherent system 'Marxism' came into being during the dozen years which separate the death of Marx (1883) from that of Engels (1895); to which may be added the somewhat more debatable statement that in its fully developed form the new synthesis was the work of four men: Engels, Bernstein (who later abandoned it), Kautsky, and Plekhanov; with some valuable assistance from two learned historians: Mehring and Ryazanov; and with the indirect but indispensable support of the political leaders in the strategically decisive areas: principally W. Liebknecht, Bebel, Guesde, and Victor Adler. This is all that needs to be said at this stage about the interrelation of orthodox Marxism and Social-Democracy. Later it will be shown that these terms describe two aspects of the same socio-political reality, and that both the doctrine and the movement disintegrated after the 1917–18 upheaval. But this is to anticipate. For the moment we are concerned with Engels as the founder of Marxist Social-Democracy, or Social-Democratic Marxism; for there were, and are, other interpretations of Marx. Yet it was Engels who established the central tradition. His version did not go unchallenged, but the critics placed themselves outside orthodoxy. This was made plain when the 'revisionist' controversy erupted around 1900, but the decisive step was taken in the early 'nineties, when Engels's authority was employed to fasten the new 'scientific' doctrine on a movement that at heart was still Lassallean or else simply democratic. The classic formulation of Social-Democratic Marxism in this period, the German Socialist 'Erfurt Programme' of 1891, was the joint work of its ostensible author, Kautsky, and of Engels; and its subsequent critics on the left and on the right had to reckon with the fact that fidelity to the programme was regarded as the touchstone of faith in 'scientific socialism'.

With this evocative term we have crossed the border-line from history to theory and simultaneously touched upon the vital centre of the new world-view: socialism, as understood by Engels and those who followed his lead, was above all scientific. What was the meaning of this affirmation? Plainly its significance was not exhausted by the familiar stress upon the union of theory and practice. Such a union had been envisaged by Marx as early as 1844, when he conceived the revolution in Hegelian terms, as the synthesis of philosophy and proletarian revolt. The *Theses on Feuerbach* (1845), with their proclamation of the need for thought to become 'practical' and 'change the world', represent a pragmatic doctrine of revolutionary action which cannot by any stretch of language be called 'scientific'. Attempts to justify such a use of the term, on the grounds that the *Theses* expressly repudiate philosophical thinking, turn upon an equation of philosophy with contemplation. What the *Theses* reject is the contemplative attitude in general, and German Idealism in particular; what they proclaim is a conception of the world which is no less philosophical for being couched in language hostile to traditional philosophy. In modern parlance the Marx of 1844–5 was an 'existentialist' in revolt against Hegel's all-embracing pan-logism; he was not a positivist. The notion that 'objective' thinking might furnish a guide to practical conclusions would have struck him as even more preposterous than the Kantian invocation of disembodied ideals supposedly located in the moral consciousness. Viewed from the original Marxian standpoint, scientism and moralism are two sides of the same coin. The 'union of theory and practice' is *not* science; it is a fusion of philosophy and action mediated by the vision of a unique constellation of circumstances: the approach of a social revolution which will inaugurate the reign of freedom.

In contrast to all this, the thinking of the mature Marx plainly discloses a growing emphasis upon the scientific study of processes independent of human volition, and a corresponding stress upon the concept of 'historical necessity'. The tension between this determinist mode of thought and the original vision was discharged on the plane of action, through practical-revolutionary manipulation of those very 'historical forces' which appeared on the theoretical level as blind instruments of an impersonal destiny. Marx never relinquished his hold on the two horns of his peculiar dilemma. His solution consisted in treating the socialist labour movement (whose guide and *spiritus rector* he had become in his closing years) as the prime agent of history. Because socialism was in tune with determined necessity, it could not in the long run be balked; because its victory meant the end of external determination and the establishment of the 'true realm of freedom', the attainment of its aims was synonymous with the realisation of the radical humanist programme. Faith in the impersonal necessity underlying the striving of the working class for emancipation from bondage partly replaced the Promethean urge to hurl the reigning deities from their pedestals; but the change of emphasis concealed an underlying continuity. For Marx the historical process moves towards a goal which can only be described in quasi-metaphysical terms. Its internal logic culminates in making man sovereign over his circumstances. The social revolution, determinedly propelled by causal circumstances which can be understood and guided, is the—partly conscious—agent of this transformation. The factor of consciousness is represented by the theorist who has perceived the meaning of events, and at a second remove by the socialist movement itself; hence theory and practice can be unified, on condition that the former is permitted to guide the latter. Despite an increasing tendency to emphasise the element of determination, Marx never quite abandoned his youthful vision of a breakthrough in which theory and practice interact to bring about a total transformation of the human condition. In his eyes every other goal was not merely unworthy of serious effort, but also unrealistic: if mankind aimed at less it would merely perpetuate its enslavement to circumstances not of its own conscious making.

To say that Engels—and following him Kautsky and the orthodox school in general—abandoned this perspective would be altogether misleading. What they did was to transform it from the vision of a unique historical breakthrough into the doctrine of a causally determined process analogous to the scheme of Darwinian evolution.[1] The first steps in this fateful interpretation were taken by Engels (in his *Anti-Dühring*) at a time when Marx was still alive, and indeed with his express, though possibly reluctant, sanction. In 1876–8, when Engels (with some assistance from Marx) composed his bulky rejoinder to Dühring's version of the then fashionable positivist-socialist credo, there were doubtless good reasons for Marx to acquiesce in an interpretation of his doctrine which commended it to the German public as even more rigidly 'scientific' than Dühring's own eclectic system.[2] It is apparent that he was by then more or

---

[1] Cf. Engels, 'Speech at the graveside of Karl Marx', March 17, 1883, in MESW II, pp. 153–4: 'Just as Darwin discovered the law of development of organic nature, so Marx discovered the law of development of human history.' This was to become the keynote of countless pronouncements on the meaning of 'scientific socialism'. When immediately afterwards Engels refers to Marx as 'before all else a revolutionary', he raises the curtain upon a debate which has not yet quieted down.

[2] Cf. *Herrn Eugen Dührings Umwaelzung der Wissenschaft*, last reprinted in an English translation as *Herr Eugen Dühring's Revolution in Science*, Moscow, 1954; for Marx's share in it cf. the preface to the second and third editions; also Engels Introduction to the English edition of *Socialism: Utopian and Scientific*, MESW II, p. 87.

less reconciled to such an interpretation: he had, after all, not spent half a lifetime in Victorian England for nothing. Yet the subsequent drift towards positivism and scientism—accelerated after his death and formalised by Kautsky after Engels in his turn had left the scene (1895)—went far beyond anything he can have envisaged. In the place of the original dialectical conception, in which critical thought was validated by revolutionary action, there now appeared a cast-iron system of 'laws' from which the inevitability of socialism could be deduced with almost mathematical certainty. Theory and practice virtually fell apart, the former serving principally to demonstrate the causally inevitable decomposition of bourgeois society, from which socialism was expected to arise in more or less the same manner in which capitalism had (supposedly) grown from the disintegration of feudalism. At the same time the 'goal' was transferred from the here-and-now of conscious activity to a horizon so distant as to be almost invisible. Every other attitude was denounced as 'utopian' and 'unscientific'.[1]

So drastic a 'transvaluation of values' was bound to leave its mark on every aspect of Marxian thought. In the long run its most important consequence lay in the effect it had on the central ener-gising source of the new doctrine: its theoretical and ethical value-system.

The heart of Marxism (as of rationalism generally) is the belief that insight into the nature of reality is all that is required to release the forces making for the eventual triumph of liberty and rationality. Once men come to understand that the circumstances of their lives are opposed to the fullest development of human freedom, they will spontaneously strive to throw off these external constraints. To this optimistic assurance Hegel had added the notion that what is 'truly rational' (and hence truly real) comes to empirical existence through a logical process. In contrast, Marx (following Feuerbach) had placed the emphasis on what is 'truly human', but without abandoning Hegel's certitude concerning the ultimate identity of the real (now identified with history) and the rational. Since reality is rational at its core, its unfolding through the manifold contradictions of empirical

[1] For the above cf. in particular Korsch, op. cit., pp. 5 ff; Fetscher, op. cit., passim. That this picture of Social-Democratic Marxism is not a caricature can be shown by appropriate quotation from the representative theorists of the school, notably Kautsky; but it is really quite sufficient to cite Engels in evidence. His later writings, especially *Socialism: Utopian and Scientific*, are a veritable compendium of the new positivist world-view.

existence is the ultimate guarantee of those aims which in the philo-sophy of a pre-Hegelian thinker like Kant appeared as 'ideals' counterposed to brute facts. For Marx as for Hegel, the idealist em-phasis upon the discrepancy between things as they are and things as they ought to be, is the mark of a shallow and trivial incomprehension of the ultimate identity of mind-matter. There are no 'ideals' that cannot be realised, for the emergence of new aims is itself an index to the presence of forces which make for their realisation. 'Therefore mankind always sets itself only such tasks as it can solve; since, looking at the matter more closely, it will always be found that the task itself arises only when the material conditions for its solution already exist, or are at least in the process of formation.'[1]

Now it is evident that this view implies a criterion of moral conduct, though Marx and Engels would have balked at the term. The criterion is inherent in the nature of things, being nothing else but the principle of rationality which is the essence of all that is 'truly human'. To be rational is to be in control of one's faculties; such control is freedom, and its eventual triumph is the undisclosed aim of the historical process. But men must control their self-made circumstances if they are to have mastery over nature, including their own nature; hence socialism is the goal of history and the precondition of liberty. To call this an 'ideal' is to overlook that it represents the unfolding of the human essence, which is the striving for free self-determination. This was the implication of Hegel's teaching; consequently Engels was able to assert in 1888 that socialism—as understood by Marx and himself—embodied the heritage of classical German philosophy.[2]

Yet it was Engels who took the first decisive step away from the classical conception. Marx had held fast to the identity of the real and the rational, and it was this underlying certainty which enabled him to dispense with traditional philosophy, while embodying its moral values in his own thinking. If the rationalist assumption was abandoned, the conclusions built upon it turned into a mere amalgam of factual and value judgments which lay open to attack from Kantian moralists and positivist sceptics alike. Marx's untroubled dogmatism concerning the inner principle of history (=unfolding of human nature) saved him from the difficulties which must beset every thinker

[1] Marx, Preface to *A Contribution to the Critique of Political Economy* (1859), MESW I, p. 363.
[2] Cf. *Ludwig Feuerbach and the End of Classical German Philosophy*, MESW II, pp. 326 ff; especially pp. 363–4.

not blessed with similar certainties. For if the unity of the real and the rational was dropped, there arose the familiar problem of relating normative principles ('value judgments') to 'objective', 'factual', 'scientific' statements: a problem which Marx (following Hegel) had dismissed as shallow stuff unworthy of a critical philosophy that had at last penetrated to the secret of the discrepancy between the 'truly real' and its irrational encumbrances. Once the crucial vision of a 'critical theory', which would transform the world by exposing its inner contradictions, had been exchanged for the far less exciting notion of a science of causal evolution, the ancient cleavage between what is and what ought to be—and with it the clash between factual understanding and normative judgment—was back in full force. If socialism was essentially 'scientific', it clearly stood in need of an ethical system which pointed to the connection between 'is' and 'ought'; alternatively, its motive force had to be found in the nature of science itself: a hopeless undertaking.

In 1843–8 Marx and Engels were not aware of this problem; indeed from their post-Hegelian, but still essentially philosophical, standpoint it did not exist. Their 'critical theory' which was practical and revolutionary by its very nature—because its nature was to lay bare the contradictions which spelled the imminent end of the old world—carried its own ethical implications. If the existing order was both senseless and doomed, there was no need to invoke the Kantian, or any other, moral imperative. Conversely the vision of a transformation in which the 'critical theory' would guide the 'revolutionary proletariat' could not long survive the discovery that the theory was inadequate, while the proletariat was anything but revolutionary. From about 1850 Marx and Engels were thus faced with a dilemma which became acute when the new labour movement turned to them in the 1870's. The original conception—at bottom a variant of the grandiose metaphysical construct known as German Idealism—could not be transmitted to a generation which had lost all faith in the metaphysics of revolution, the less so since its own authors had meanwhile grown sceptical of it. Yet without it the Marxian system was rendered immobile. If the 'union of theory and practice' did not signify a concrete whole of critical theorising and revolutionary action, the system's mainspring was broken. Yet every attempt to treat its pretensions seriously was bound to lay bare its non-scientific character.

The history of 'orthodox' Social-Democratic theorising from about 1875 onward—i.e., from the time when Engels was reluctantly obliged to enter the lists against rival doctrines in the name of what now came to be known as Marxism—is the story of an unceasing effort to overcome this tension between the 'idealist' core of the Marxian vision, and the 'materialist' science draped around it. What resulted from these labours was no longer a 'critical theory' in the old sense, but rather a comprehensive world-view which in due course became the ideology of the new Socialist movement: taking the term 'ideology' to signify what it did for Marx and Engels, namely a system of beliefs which partly reveals and partly conceals the nature of the reality reflected in it. From about 1880, Socialists in Germany and elsewhere had at their disposal such an ideology, now labelled 'scientific socialism'. Its classic formulation is Engels's tract against Dühring—by far the most influential Marxist composition of the period, and the source of almost all the theoretical thinking then available to the fast-growing membership of the Social-Democratic movement. To this were added such companion-pieces as *Socialism: Utopian and Scientific* (originally an extract from the *Anti-Dühring*); the essay on Feuerbach (1888) which presented German socialism as the inheritor of German philosophy; and last not least the *Origin of the Family, Private Property and the State* (1884), which may be said to have done for the labour movement what the popular writings of Darwinians such as Haeckel were simultaneously doing for the liberal middle class in dispelling the remnants of the theological world-picture. With the exception of Engels's *Dialectics of Nature*, which had to await posthumous publication until 1925, all these writings achieved canonical status in the labour movement at the very peak of Social-Democratic influence, i.e., during the period from 1890 to 1914. It was from them, rather than from *Capital* (not to mention Marx's early writings, which were still largely unknown), that most Socialists drew their mental picture of the world.

For readers who found Engels difficult to follow there was a more popular exposition of the materialist doctrine in the writings of Joseph Dietzgen, notably his *Nature of Human Brainwork*[1] to which Engels himself drew attention in his essay on Feuerbach. Dietzgen

---

[1] *Das Wesen der menschlichen Kopfarbeit, dargestellt von einem Handarbeiter. Eine abermalige Kritik der reinen und praktischen Vernunft*, Hamburg, 1869; cf. also *Josef Dietzgens Saemtliche Schriften*, Wiesbaden, 1911; *Philosophical Essays*, Chicago, 1906; *The Positive Outcome of Philosophy*, Chicago, 1906. There is a considerable literature on and around Dietzgen; for a recent account of his work cf. Lloyd D. Easton, 'Empiricism and Ethics in Dietzgen', *Journal of the History of Ideas*, New York, January 1958, vol. XIX, no. 1, pp. 77 ff.

cannot be ignored, for he is one of the sources—albeit a minor one
—of Lenin's outlook and consequently of Soviet Marxism. But he
does not compare in importance with either Engels or Kautsky as a
purveyor of the new materialist creed. At best he represents a link
between the Marxist school and the Social-Democratic movement, of
which in a sense he was more representative than its other major
theorists, being not merely an active pioneer of socialism but a
genuine working-class autodidact: a sort of German Proudhon.
Dietzgen did not lack originality; indeed, it is tempting to say that
originality was all he had. A disciple of Feuerbach and, like his
master, a radical empiricist who rejected speculative thinking, he
came on the scene at a time when Marx and Engels had already substantially pre-empted the world-view he was about to develop; but
his somewhat rough-and-ready exposition of the materialist-monist
standpoint served its purpose in helping to wean the nascent Social-
Democratic movement away from Kantian idealism. He is mentioned
here only for this reason. There is little in Dietzgen that cannot be
found in Engels, Kautsky or Plekhanov, all of whom treated him with
respect. Morally, his 'evolutionary ethics' derive through Feuerbach
from Spinoza, their ultimate sanction being a species of pantheism.
This too was not altogether novel, and has its parallel in Engels's
writings; but Dietzgen expressly rejected atheism, insisted that 'God,
truth, nature are names for the same thing', and saw a substitute for
revealed religion in 'the communion and intimate connection of all
men and things'. On the whole he probably came closest to expressing
what the average Socialist of the period thought and felt about the
world, but his thinking was too unsystematic to yield the kind of
coherent doctrine that could be opposed to the official teaching in
the universities. Something more authoritative was required, and it
was supplied by Engels.

That this something was no longer the 'critical theory' of 1843-8,
i.e., the 'revolution in thought', but rather a general 'science' of
nature (!) and history, concerns us here for reasons other than the
purely intellectual interest which anyone may take in the development
of doctrine. Marx and Engels never ceased to regard theoretical
thinking as an element of the social transformation they aimed to
bring about. It was no part of their intention to theorise about things
in general apart from their historical significance. Their growing interest in natural science from the 1850's onward reflected a tendency—
which they shared with most of their contemporaries—to see history

in evolutionary terms: a viewpoint at variance with their original conception—though, as we have seen, Engels had always been inclined to treat 'evolution' and 'revolution' as complementary.[1] The question was how this new mode of thought could be related to the old dialectical scheme of the 'critical theory', in which 'revolution' signified something radically different from mere 'change' or 'progress'. This was not an academic problem: it concerned the world-view of the Socialist movement and, in the long run, its political orientation. For better or worse, Socialist practice over the greater part of Europe came to reflect an attitude of mind which derived final confirmation from the materialist doctrine expounded by Engels in his writings of the late 1870's and 1880's. This was particularly true of Germany, then and for many years the dominant power in Central Europe and beyond. In the gradual movement of ideas from the French Revolution to the German Counter-Revolution, the transformation of Marxism into a 'scientific' doctrine emptied of genuine philosophic content—and hence powerless to stem the inrush of romantic irrationalism which began in the 1890's and reached a disastrous climax in the 1930's—was destined to be a factor of crucial importance, though negatively: it helped to bring about that cleavage between the democratic labour movement and the traditional idealist outlook of the middle-class intelligentsia which Fascism was later to exploit with such fatal results. In narrowing its perspective and adapting its level to the rather modest intellectual requirements of the labour movement, orthodox Social-Democratic Marxism obtained a political foothold at the cost of shedding those aspects of Marx's thought which bore on the human situation as such. In the long run this meant that Socialism was confirmed in its role as a sectional trend within society, and that the labour movement became a vehicle for the transmission of a somewhat old-fashioned version of the positivist faith which the middle class and the workers held in common. It is arguable that no other outcome was possible; however that may be, the failure to salvage the philosophic heritage played its part in leaving the Socialist movement defenceless against the destructive tendencies which the disintegration of liberalism after 1914 brought in its train.

[1] Cf. Bollnow, loc. cit., pp. 96 ff. It is evident from his writings and correspondence that Marx gradually came to adopt a standpoint which in some respects resembled the scientism of the age, but he never quite yielded to the temptation to recast his doctrine altogether in evolutionary-materialist terms; Engels had no such inhibition.

4

DIALECTICAL MATERIALISM

GIVEN THE CIRCUMSTANCES surrounding the emergence of the new materialist world-view, it was inevitable that the theoretical system outlined by Engels in his writings of the 'seventies and 'eighties should bear a marked resemblance to the doctrines propagated by Darwinians like Haeckel—not to mention Dühring, against whom his first and most influential tract was directed. 'From Hegel to Haeckel' might serve as a summary of the evolution of Marxist thinking between the 1840's and the 1880's, though to be sure Engels was aware that positivism left a vacuum which attracted rival philosophies.[1] As he saw it, the task consisted in showing that the scientific world-view was not incompatible with a general theory of nature and history. In the

---

[1] Cf. the original preface to his *Anti-Dühring*, subsequently assigned to the manuscript of the *Dialectics of Nature*, and eventually reprinted as an appendix to the former work (op. cit., pp. 455 ff.). 'But a nation that wants to climb the pinnacles of science cannot possibly manage without theoretical thought. Not only Hegelianism, but dialectics too was thrown overboard—and that just at the moment when the dialectical character of natural processes (sic) forced itself upon the mind, when therefore only dialectics could be of assistance to natural science in negotiating the mountain of theory—and so there was a helpless relapse into the old metaphysics.' (loc. cit., p. 460.) Engels's interest in the philosophy of science is closely related to his patriotic concern over the decay of German philosophy. For biographical data on his increasing absorption in this subject cf. Mayer, op. cit., vol. II, pp. 296 ff.

original Marxian scheme of 1843–5 the notion of such an intellectual synthesis was tied to the concept of a transformation which would b at once the 'realisation of philosophy' and the overcoming of the ancient dichotomy between idealism and materialism. In the revised version proposed by Engels in 1878 (with the tacit acquiescence, it is true, of Marx), this theme is set out as follows:

The philosophy of antiquity was primitive, natural materialism. As such it was incapable of clearing up the relation between mind and matter. But the need to get clarity on this question led to the doctrine of a soul separable from the body, then to the assertion of the immortality of this soul, and finally to monotheism. The old materialism was therefore negated by idealism. But in the course of the further development of philosophy, idealism too became untenable (sic) and was negated by modern material-ism. This modern materialism, the negation of the negation, is not the re-establishment of the old, but adds to the permanent foundations of this old materialism the whole thought-content of two thousand years of philosophy and natural science . . . *It is no longer a philosophy at all, but simply a world-outlook* (our italics) which has to establish its validity and be applied not in a science of sciences standing apart, but in the positive sciences. Philosophy is therefore 'sublated' here, that is, 'both overcome and preserved'; overcome as regards its form, and preserved as regards its real content.[1]

Instead of the 'realisation' of philosophy through *action* which transforms a world that has philosophy for its necessary comple-ment, we have here a differentiation of philosophy into 'the positive sciences'; or rather its partial differentiation, for Engels holds fast to the dialectic as 'the science of inter-connections, in contrast to metaphysics'.[2] The resulting medley of philosophy and science con-stitutes what has come to be known as 'dialectical materialism': a concept not present in the original Marxian version, and indeed essentially foreign to it, since for the early Marx the only nature relevant to the understanding of history is human nature. For the later Engels, on the contrary, historical evolution is an aspect of general (natural) evolution, and basically subject to the same 'laws'. The contrast could hardly be more glaring. That Marx put up with this travesty of his original standpoint is a factual circumstance which need not concern us, though it may be of interest to his bio-graphers. The relevant point is that Marxism came to mean what Engels, in his writings between 1875 and 1895, said it meant, namely,

[1] *Anti-Dühring*, Moscow, 1954, pp. 191–2.
[2] *Dialectics of Nature*, Moscow, 1954, p. 83.

a materialist evolutionism in which 'the dialectic' figured as a link between the old philosophy and the new science.[1]

Such a change in outlook was bound to have far-reaching consequences; it was not a matter of 'mere theory'. Few things are more pathetic than the 'practical' philistinism which fails to see the connection between the thinking that animates a movement and the practice allied to, and largely dependent upon, this thinking. Engels set the tone for a generation of Socialists, and his interpretation of Marxism acquired canonical status. In due course his philosophy—notably as set out in the *Dialectics of Nature*—became the cornerstone of the Soviet Marxist edifice. There is no mistaking the line of descent which runs from Engels, via Plekhanov and Kautsky, to Lenin and Bukharin. They all, whatever their differences, share the common faith in 'dialectical materialism' as a universal 'science' of the 'laws' of *nature* and history, as supposedly adumbrated in a confused fashion by Hegel and finally given adequate expression by Engels. To treat this as no more than a formal commitment to ideology on the part of 'practical' men is to mistake the whole temper and outlook of the Marxist movement. The 'union of theory and practice' having fallen apart, the new 'scientific' doctrine arose to take its place, determinism in thought making for dogmatism in action. The cast-iron certainty which Engels imported into Marxist thinking found its counterpart at the political level in an unshakeable conviction that the stars in their courses were promoting the victory of the Socialist cause. This faith was to survive even the Russian Revolution and its aftermath.

In terms of intellectual history, Engels's attempt to fashion a systematic body of thought patterned on traditional philosophy may be described as a revival of a certain archaic cast of mind already present in Hegel—notably the ageing Hegel who had likewise tried to comprehend nature and history in a unified system. This is the justification for treating dialectical materialism as, despite everything, a philosophy, or at least as an attempt to amalgamate philosophy with science. Not surprisingly, when one considers the derivation of this aim from the older speculative idealism, Engels felt able to look down from his eminence upon a shallow positivist like

[1] Fetscher, loc. cit., pp. 45 ff. For the logical inconsistencies of Engels's interpretation of scientific method cf. Hook, op. cit., pp. 194 ff. It is not proposed here to go at length into the question how far Engels was successful in applying his conceptual model; the important point is that the model itself represents a complete break with the pre-1848 'critical theory'.

Dühring, or a mere empiricist like Haeckel, for whom speculative philosophy had ceased to be relevant.[1] Yet his brisk polemics again~t the former, and his condescending treatment of the latter, cannot conceal the fact that in substance the materialist evolutionism of the *Anti-Dühring* and the *Dialectics of Nature* is closer to the 'mechanical materialism' of his opponents than to the old romantic philosophy of nature whose heritage he was trying to salvage. There is a fatal flaw in his attempted synthesis of speculative philosophy and positive science: if nature is conceived in materialist terms it does not lend itself to the dialectical method, and if the dialectic is read back into nature, materialism goes by the board. Because he knew this, or sensed it, Marx wisely left nature (other than human nature) alone. Engels ventured where Marx had feared to tread, and the outcome was dialectical materialism: an incubus which has not ceased to weigh heavily upon his followers, though in fairness to Engels it should be said that he cannot be held responsible for the subsequent transformation of his speculative essays into a state religion imposed upon captive audiences by doctrinaire schoolmasters scarcely more literate than their pupils.[2]

'Dialectical materialism', then, is the general theory of an evolution embracing both nature and history. As formulated by Engels, its abstract outline presents itself somewhat as follows:

There is a process in the real world of which the dialectic of concepts is the reflection, whereas Hegel had mistakenly supposed that reality is an inferior copy of logic. 'According to Hegel, dialectics is the self-development of the concept. . . . therefore, the dialectical development apparent in nature and history . . . is only a miserable copy of the self-movement of th~ concept going on from eternity. . . . This ideological perversion had to be done away with. We comprehended the concepts in our heads once more materialistically—as images (*Abbilder*) of real things. . . . Thus dialectics reduced itself to the science of the general laws of motion, both of the external world and of human thought—two sets of laws which are identical in

---

[1] *Dialectics of Nature*, pp. 300 ff.

[2] Nor should these remarks be read as a defence of the, frequently very shallow, positivist doctrines which Engels was criticising. He was quite right to despise the 'vulgar materialism' of Büchner, and the no less trivial outpourings of Dühring: the latter a fairly typical specimen of those German university men whom with the wisdom of hindsight we are now able to see as minor precursors of National Socialism. The trouble was not that he dissociated himself from such writers but that, despite his contempt for their outlook, he was himself not altogether free of their characteristic failings.

substance, but differ in their expression insofar as the human mind can apply them consciously, while in nature, and also up to now for the most part in human history (sic), these laws assert themselves unconsciously, in the form of external necessity, in the midst of an endless series of seeming accidents.'[1] In this manner the Hegelian dialectic was stood on its head 'or rather . . . on its feet', and this 'materialist dialectic' became an instrument for studying the real world.[2] However, the 'materialist' inversion of Hegel's dialectic (or to be exact of Engels's somewhat simplified version of it) does not signify that Hegel's philosophy was abandoned altogether. On the contrary, the 'great basic thought that the world is not to be comprehended as a complex of ready-made *things*, but as a complex of *processes*'[3] was retained. Rather surprisingly, Engels adds that this 'basic thought . . . has . . . so thoroughly permeated ordinary consciousness that in this generality it is now scarcely ever contradicted'.[4] However, to acknowledge the principle is one thing, to apply it in practice another. What matters now is to take seriously the notion that 'the things apparently stable, no less than their mind images in our heads, the concepts, go through an uninterrupted change of coming into being and passing away, in which, in spite of all seeming accidentality and of all temporary retrogression, a progressive development asserts itself in the end'. And with a final flourish it is stated that 'if investigation always proceeds from this standpoint, the demand for final solutions and eternal truths ceases once for all'.[5] How in the absence of normative standards ('eternal truths') it is possible to qualify the long-term development as 'progressive', Engels does not trouble to explain.

This then was the general conceptual framework into which the empirical investigation of nature and history was to be pressed. At bottom it hardly differed from the fashionable materialist evolutionism of the epoch. 'Progress', in the ambiguous sense of a development that is both inevitable and beneficial, had long become the watchword of bourgeois society, and more particularly of bourgeois radicalism. Nor was there anything novel about the moral relativism lengthily developed by Engels in such writings as the *Anti-Dühring* and the *Origin of the Family*.[6] His method consists rather in showing that

---

[1] *Ludwig Feuerbach*, MESW II, pp. 349-50.   [2] Ibid.
[3] Ibid., p. 351.   [4] Ibid.   [5] Ibid.
[6] Cf. *Anti-Dühring*, pp. 134 ff. 'The idea of equality, both in its bourgeois and in its proletarian form, is therefore itself a historical product. . . . It is therefore anything but an eternal truth.' (Ibid., p. 149.) This is a fair specimen of Engels's

if the typical assumptions of contemporary civilisation are taken seriously, the conclusions are such as to support the critics of the established order. This was to become the favourite conversational gambit of Socialists in the next generation. However effective as a debating technique it inevitably led away from the notion that the thought-forms, no less than the institutions, of society stood in need of being transcended by a critique that was genuinely radical. By the 1880's this possibility had dropped out of sight.

It is wholly characteristic of Engels's outlook that in an essay ostensibly devoted to the subject of post-classical German philosophy he introduced as a major theme such recent innovations in natural science as 'the discovery of the cell', 'the transformation of energy', and 'the proof, which Darwin first developed in connected form, that the stock of organic products of nature environing us today, including mankind, is the result of a long process of evolution from a few originally unicellular germs. . . .'[1] 'Thanks to these three great discoveries and the other immense advances in natural science', it had now (in 1888) become possible to 'present in an approximately systematic form a comprehensive view of the interconnection in nature by means of the facts provided by empirical natural science itself'.[2] Moreover, 'what is true of nature, which is hereby recognised also as a historical process of development, is likewise true of the history of society in all its branches, and of the totality of sciences which occupy themselves with things human (and divine)'.[3] What then is the difference between nature and history? It consists in this: in nature 'there are only blind, unconscious agencies acting upon one another, out of whose interplay the general law comes into operation. . . . In the history of society, on the contrary, the actors are all endowed with consciousness, are men acting with deliberation or passion, working towards definite goals; nothing happens without a conscious purpose, without an intended aim. But this distinction, important as it is for historical investigation, particularly of single epochs and events, cannot alter the fact that the course of history is governed by inner general laws. . . . That which is willed happens but rarely; in the majority of instances the numerous desired ends cross and conflict with one another. . . . Thus the conflicts of innumerable

habitual mode of reasoning, in which 'absolute' and 'relative' truths are counterposed as though Hegel had never existed.

[1] *Ludwig Feuerbach*, MESW II, p. 352.
[2] Ibid., pp. 352–3.　　　　　　　　　　　　　　　　　[3] Ibid., p. 353.

individual wills and individual actions in the domain of history produce a state of affairs entirely analogous to that prevailing in the realm
of unconscious nature. . . . Historical events thus appear on the
whole to be likewise governed by chance. But where on the surface
accident holds sway, there actually it is always governed by inner,
hidden laws and it is only a matter of discovering these laws.' The
general law asserts itself by working through a multitude of conflicting individuals. 'Men make their own history, whatever its outcome may be, in that each person follows his own consciously desired
end, and it is precisely the resultant of these many wills, operating in
different directions, and of their manifold effects upon the outer
world that constitutes history. . . . On the other hand, the further
question arises: what driving forces in turn stand behind these
motives? What are the historical causes which transform themselves
into these motives in the brains of the actors? The old materialism
never put this question to itself. . . .'[1]

What Engels puts forward in these well-known passages is an
amalgam of Hegelian and Darwinian concepts which does not add
up to a totality comparable to the Marxian critique of 1843–5 with its
stress upon historical turning-points. His evolutionary scheme is
basically Darwinian, while his appeal to 'inner, hidden laws' recalls
Hegel's 'Cunning of Reason': the providential design working
through the agency of individuals subordinated to its purpose. What
is missing from this picture is just what constituted the originality of
the young Marx: the 'coincidence of the changing of circumstances
and of human activity',[2] whereby history is 'brought to itself' and
the disjunction between general laws and particular wills is 'sublated'. By a stroke of unconscious irony Engels appended the text of
the Marxian *Theses* to his own essay on Feuerbach, which for all its
dutiful emphasis upon the novelty of Marx's conception in fact sub-
stitutes for it a thoroughly Old Hegelian appeal to what is really the
'Cunning of Reason' under a new guise. Where the youthful Marx had
envisaged a unique historical occurrence which enables mankind to
comprehend history as its own creative act, Engels presents an evolutionary pattern which in the nature of things can never come to an
end, and thus cannot yield up any definite meaning. History as a
comprehended totality can 'come to itself' by coming to a climax.
Nature is immortal almost by definition, and its study—as Engels

---

[1] Ibid., pp. 354–5.
[2] *Theses on Feuerbach*, MESW II, p. 366.

never tires of stressing—discloses no finality, but at best an endless approximation to a constantly receding limit. To assimilate the historical process to that of nature consequently means doing away with the idea of a decisive historical act that reveals the *meaning* of history. In this respect Engels, for all his polemics against the Hegelian 'system', is closer to the late Hegel than to the early Marx.

How Marx originally envisaged the relation of nature to history appears plainly enough from his early writings, where the dialectic of human, sensuous, activity and objectified 'nature' is described as a process in which man's labour *produces* the external (social) world confronting him. While 'the formation of the five senses is a labour of the entire history of the world down to the present', the world apprehended by the senses is the counterpart of the human being which grows to maturity through developing his innate faculties.[1] *There is no nature apart from man.* 'Thus the objectification of the human essence, both in its theoretical and practical aspects, is required to make man's sense *human*, as well as to create the *human sense* corresponding to the entire wealth of human and natural substance.' At the historical level, '*industry* and the established *objective* existence of industry are the open book of man's essential powers (*Wesenskraefte*), the exposure to the senses of human *psychology*. Hitherto this was not conceived in its inseparable connection with man's *essential being*. . . . *Industry* is the real historical relation of nature, and thus of the natural sciences, to man. Hence if industry is conceived as the *exoteric* revelation of man's *essential faculties*, one also understands the *human* essence of nature or the *natural* essence of man. . . . Nature, as it unfolds in human history, in the genesis of human society, is man's *real* nature; hence nature, as it develops through industry, albeit in an alienated form, is truly *anthropological* nature.' In short, for the early Marx—and in a measure for the mature Marx too—nature and man are complex realities whose interaction is studied in society. This is precisely the reverse of Engels's habit of deducing historical 'laws' from the operation of a nature conceived as an independent reality external to man.

Another consequence of his progressive abandonment of the 'critical theory' of 1843–8 is Engels's inability to appreciate the greatness of Kant, and the consequent failure of his disciples—notably the Russian Marxists of all political denominations—to make

---

[1] For this argument cf. EPM, MEGA I/3, pp. 120 ff. (Eng. tr. Moscow, 1959, pp. 108 ff.)

sense of the idealist tradition in philosophy. For this melancholy result Marx cannot be held responsible. The *Theses on Feuerbach* are there to show that he was straining after a genuine synthesis of materialism and idealism which would take account of Kant's critique. No one who had genuinely experienced the formative influence of post-Kantian philosophy could ever again rest content with the naïve naturalism of the French Enlightenment. Profoundly rooted though he was in the intellectual tradition exemplified by Holbach, Helvetius and Condillac, Marx was aware that the 'materialist' doctrine was untenable in the form in which they had left it. For one thing, their determinism was at odds with their humanism, since on their showing Man was the passive object of corrupting influences which could scarcely prepare him for the task of reshaping the institutions that had moulded him. Secondly, their naïve sensationalism—an echo of the equally naïve empiricism of Locke, from whom they were descended—was no longer acceptable after Kant (and following him Hegel) had pointed to the creative role of the mind in shaping the world of experience present to the individual consciousness. Mind was no more a passive receptacle of sense-impressions than Man was simply the product of social circumstances. The very first *Thesis on Feuerbach* expressly acknowledges the embarrassing truth that, owing to this 'defect of all hitherto existing materialism', a situation had arisen where 'the *active* side . . . was developed by idealism'. Though Kant is not expressly mentioned, the significance is unmistakable. One may say that the originality of Marx's standpoint consisted precisely in this: while the French materialists had entangled themselves in an insoluble problem by postulating a human nature passively dependent on the environment, and then superimposed upon this depressing picture an optimistic doctrine of progress, Marx pointed out that the key to the desired transformation lay in man's ability to rearrange the world of which he formed part. There was an end to the conundrum of who would educate the educator: the subject of the historical process educated himself in the course of his activity *which was nothing but the progressive unfolding of his own being*.

Of this complex dialectic Engels retained only the outer shell. Not that he formally abandoned a single element of the Marxian canon. He merely upset its equilibrium by making it appear that the purpose of the whole operation was to bring the old materialism up to date. The heart of the doctrine—the constitutive role of conscious activity

252

—was replaced by a faith in *science* as the correct description of determinate processes; matter was invested with a capacity for giving birth to mind; and Kant was rebuked for having dared to suggest that the world is partly our creation. In exchange for this retreat from the position already occupied by classical German philosophy before Marx reaffirmed its basic insights, Engels presents the reader with a static ontology wherein nature is discovered to go through all, or most, of the permutations described in Hegel's *Logic*. Marx had been attracted to Hegel's philosophy because its emphasis on the constitutive activity of mind presented him with the key to his own concept of material activity (*praxis*), wherein consciousness reappears as the specifically human form of natural existence. For Engels the stress lies on Hegel's conceptual machinery whereby material motion is invested with logical certainty. What really fascinates him is Hegel's determinism: his ability to make it appear that nature (and history) follow a pre-ordained course.

If Engels is to be believed, the 'materialist inversion' of Hegel's philosophy has for its aim not the termination of speculative system-building, but the construction of a 'materialist' ontology as systematic and encompassing as Hegel's own. He seems not to have realised that this was an abandonment of the standpoint occupied by Marx and himself in the 1840's when, under the influence of Feuerbach, they had rid themselves of Hegel's system. Whether the Absolute is called 'spirit' or 'matter' makes little difference. Engels's repeated insistence on the dialectical nature of Hegel's method, as against the static character of his system, would carry more conviction if his own exposition of the 'new materialism' were not infused with a quite evident determination to fill the vacuum left by the dissolution of Hegel's idealist ontology. The psychological roots of this urge towards systematisation are obvious; so is the *partiinost* character—to employ a term belonging to a later epoch—of the resultant 'materialist dialectic', in which the emphasis plainly rests on the materialist component. Apart from its anti-religious connotation, which was indeed important to nineteenth-century radicals, and crucially relevant to the Russian intelligentsia around the turn of the century, 'materialism' (in Engels's sense of the term) is the corollary of a certain type of radicalism which comes to the fore in every popular emancipation movement. It is an old story that authoritarianism and idealism go together; so do paternalism and moral rigorism. By contrast, the exaltation of matter—and of the *materia mater*—

makes an emotional appeal to that side of the popular consciousness which is activated by movements for human and social liberation: not least feminine emancipation, which not accidentally became a vital element in the Socialist current. These were powerful motive forces in determining the course which popular materialism and 'vulgar Marxism' actually took from the late nineteenth century onwards, but they cannot be invoked in support of an intellectual construction that purports to achieve the aim of replacing the traditional idealist ontology by a materialist one.

Does this inverted Hegelianism at least encourage an interchange of philosophy and natural science such as to warrant the assertion that dialectical materialism can promote a synthesis of these two modes of thought? Hardly, for despite occasional claims to the contrary there have been no scientific advances that could be convincingly ascribed to the application of the dialectical method. Nor is this surprising. When the dialectic is properly understood it is seen to presuppose situations in which conscious activity realises a possibility grounded in the nature of things—in other words, historical situations. In such cases human action may be said to synthesise the antithetical elements by 'negating' a definite obstacle to a chosen goal. To extend this possibility to the realm of inanimate matter is to read an element of purposive striving into the structure of reality: in other words, to revert to romanticism. Alternatively, the concept of dialectical change has to be stretched to the point of tautology, so that any happening whatever is held to equal a 'development' involving a qualitative change from one state to another. In practice the application of the dialectic to the realm of nature reduces itself to a choice between these unattractive alternatives. If this was not apparent to Engels, the reason is that for his immediate purpose it was sufficient to interpret in quasi-philosophical terms the discoveries of various interconnections in nature which were actually being made by the science of his age. This was not too difficult, once it was assumed that 'dialectics' meant the study of such connections. Given Engels's very considerable erudition and his command of philosophic metaphor, a plausible simulacrum of a universal logic of scientific enquiry could be sketched in outline—and then left hanging in the air. To this day the programme has remained unfulfilled. What was accomplished was something quite different and much less exciting, though socially of the first importance: the construction of a materialist world-view which conserved *both* the positivist outlook of the late nineteenth century *and* the language of romantic 'natural philosophy'. A good instance of this curious synthesis is Engels's assertion—against the rather more consistent materialism of the bourgeois empiricist Haeckel—that it is the *nature* of matter to give rise to human beings and hence to thought. Though hardly a 'scientific' observation, this certainly was an ingenious manner of bringing Hegel and Haeckel into some sort of balance.[1]

The formal principles employed by Engels are the transformation of quantity into quality, the identity of opposites, and the negation of the negation. His application of these Hegelian categories preserves an outward resemblance to Hegel's procedure, but necessarily lacks the consistency which permits Hegel to dispense with the customary distinction between logical and physical concepts. Because he assumes that thought and its object have their common ground in the pre-existing *logos* which underlies being and thinking, Hegel sees no inconsistency in talking of (logical) 'contradictions' in reality, or of quantity turning into quality: an impossible notion unless the identity of logical and physical structures is taken for granted. Engels, who can make no such metaphysical assumption, asserts that these dialectical concepts are abstracted from reality. His procedure then consists in trying to illustrate their validity by confronting them with the empirically obtained discoveries of scientific enquiry. This confrontation results in a set of formal analogies superimposed upon conclusions already reached by quite different methods. It does not yield a new approach, merely a useless duplication of the conceptual apparatus employed by science. This procedure is initiated in the *Anti-Dühring* and carried to an extreme in the unpublished notes for the *Dialectics of Nature*, from which Eduard Bernstein (acting on the advice of Einstein) shied away when he had occasion to edit Engels's literary remains, but which later became one of the canonical texts of Soviet Marxism and the principal source of what is now officially described as the world-view of Marxism-Leninism.[2]

The extension of 'dialectical materialism' to the realm of social history gives rise to 'historical materialism'; or rather, it does so for Engels. Marx, as we have seen, had set out his view of history in

---

[1] *Dialectics of Nature*, p. 278: '. . . the truth is that it is the nature of matter to advance to the evolution of thinking beings, hence this always necessarily occurs wherever the conditions for it . . . are present.' For a critical analysis of Engels's handling of logical concepts cf. Hook, op. cit., pp. 202 ff.

[2] *Fundamentals of Marxism-Leninism*, Moscow, 1960, pp. 29 ff; cf. H. Marcuse, *Soviet Marxism*, New York and London, 1958, pp. 136 ff.

connection with his theory of society. Here it is not even necessary to revert to his pre-1848 writings: the doctrine of historical materialism is concisely stated in the well-known preface to the *Critique of Political Economy* (1859), and expounded at great length in the posthumously published *Grundrisse* of 1857–8. Nowhere in these writings is it made to depend on a general theory of evolution, let alone a universal logic of enquiry. This notion first rears its head in the *Anti-Dühring*, and is carried further in the studies published by Engels after the death of Marx. In these writings the logic of history appears as a special case of a more general logic embracing the entire universe. At the same time Engels is at pains to deny that Marx employed a particular mode of reasoning different from that of the empirical sciences. As usual he tries to have it both ways:

The process is a historical one, and if it is at the same time a dialectical process, this is not Marx's fault, however annoying it may be to Herr Dühring. . . . Thus, by characterizing the process as the negation of the negation, Marx does not intend to prove that the process was historically necessary. On the contrary: only after he has proved from history that in fact the process has partially already occurred, and partially must (sic) occur in the future, he in addition characterizes it as a process which develops in accordance with a definite dialectical law.[1]

This is a fair description of Engels's own habitual mode of procedure, but hardly does justice to Marx.

Compared with this radical inversion of the Marxian approach, the other innovations introduced by Engels are of distinctly minor importance. That also goes for his singularly unsuccessful attempt to come to grips with the Kantian theory of knowledge, which is dismissed in a very cavalier fashion on the grounds that its assumptions have been invalidated by positive science.[2] His excursion into epistemology is nonetheless of importance: not for anything it contributed

---

[1] *Anti-Dühring*, pp. 185–6.

[2] *Ludwig Feuerbach*, MESW II, p. 336: 'The most telling refutation of this as of all other philosophical crotchets is practice, namely, experiment and industry. If we are able to prove the correctness of our conception of a natural process by making it ourselves, bringing it into being out of its conditions and making it serve our own purposes into the bargain, then there is an end to the Kantian ungraspable "thing-in-itself." ' This naive display of positivism was too much for some orthodox Marxists of the following generation, though Engels's line of argument was to find a somewhat embarrassed defender in Plekhanov. The surprising thing is that Engels did not content himself with reproducing Hegel's arguments against Kant, which unlike his own do have a bearing upon the substance of the Kantian position, but instead tried to introduce a line of reasoning quite irrelevant to the subject.

to the clarification of this well-worn topic, but because it set the tone for the idealist-materialist controversy which erupted in Germany around 1900 in connection with the 'revisionist' debate, and was later magnified into a major ideological issue by the Russian Marxists and their Soviet successors.

Engels starts from the proposition that the 'great basic question of all philosophy, especially of more recent philosophy, is that concerning the relation of thinking and being'.[1] The manner in which he develops this theme suggests that he sees no essential difference between the ancient metaphysical speculation about body and soul—which on his reading of the facts gave rise to religion, with its notions of God, immortality, and so forth—and the specifically modern debate over cognition, as inaugurated by Descartes. Both are treated under the same heading, as sources of the conflict between 'idealism' and 'materialism', as though 'the question of the relation of thinking to being, the relation of spirit to nature'[2] led straight to what he himself describes as 'yet another side' of the problem, namely, 'in what relation do our thoughts about the world surrounding us stand to this world itself? Is our thinking capable of the cognition of the real world?'[3] By running these two quite distinct themes together, Engels arrives at a confrontation between 'two great camps' in philosophy which are supposed to have confronted each other since classical Antiquity. Hegel's philosophy, which assumes the identity of thought and its object, is consigned to the 'idealist' camp, though almost in the same breath Engels invokes Hegel's support against Kant and Hume, with their scepticism as to the possibility of exhaustive knowledge of reality.[4] These confusions are then capped by the assertion that Hegel was after all on the right track, though he did not know it: his system 'represents merely a materialism idealistically turned upside down (sic) in method and content'.[5]

What emerges from this thoroughly muddled presentation of a subject with which Engels was certainly familiar, and about which he and Marx had expressed themselves quite unambiguously in the

[1] *Ludwig Feuerbach*, loc. cit., p. 334.
[2] Ibid.
[3] Ibid., pp. 335–6.
[4] Ibid. 'What is decisive in the refutation of this view has already been said by Hegel, insofar as this was possible from an idealist standpoint. The materialistic additions made by Feuerbach are more ingenious than profound.' But if Hegel rather than the materialist Feuerbach was right against Kant, what becomes of the distinction between the 'two great camps'?
[5] Ibid., p. 336.

1840's, is yet another aspect of that materialist-monist outlook which is Engels's peculiar contribution to Marxism. 'Vulgar materialism', i.e., ordinary scientific materialism, is rejected, as is Feuerbach's naive naturalism. What is required is a synthesis of Hegel's encyclopaedic turn of mind with the scientific temper. Such a synthesis must be global and embrace history as well as nature. 'For we live not only in nature but also in human society, and this also no less than nature (sic) has its history of development and its science. It was therefore a question of bringing the science of society, that is, the sum total of the so-called historical and philosophical sciences, into harmony with the materialist foundation and of reconstructing it thereupon. But it did not fall to Feuerbach's lot to do this.'[1] That task, in Engels's view, was satisfactorily accomplished by Darwin in respect of nature, and by Marx (with some assistance from himself) in regard to history; since when the 'science of society', no less than that of nature, had at last been placed upon a solid foundation.[2]

This then is 'dialectical materialism' as Engels conceived it. To point out that his exposition is flawed by the most serious logical inadequacies is merely to state the obvious. What matters in our context is not so much the theoretical shortcomings of the system as its historic function in helping to shape the outlook of the Socialist movement. As a result of Engels's decisive intervention at the critical stage, that movement now possessed a coherent world-view which simultaneously linked it to, and separated it from, the dominant ideology of 'bourgeois' radicalism and positivism. Social-Democracy as a historical phenomenon represents the unity of this world-view with a practice in large measure determined by it. The fortunes of the movement were to reflect not merely the evolution of bourgeois society's 'material base', but equally the manner in which that society reacted to the crisis which opened in 1914.

[1] Ibid., p. 340.
[2] Plekhanov subsequently improved upon this picture by claiming that 'modern dialectical materialism' had 'exploited to the full' Hegel's great discovery that 'we are free only insofar as we know the laws of nature and sociohistorical development and insofar as we, *submitting to them*, rely upon them'. Cf. his article 'Zu Hegels sechzigstem Todestag', *Neue Zeit*, Nos. 7–8–9, November 1891; reprinted in G. Plekhanov, *Selected Philosophical Works*, Moscow, 1961, vol. I, pp. 455ff, especially pp. 477 ff.

5

KAUTSKY

1883, THE YEAR OF Marx's death, is a date of importance in Socialist history. It witnessed the first successful attempt to create a Marxist school around the theoretical journal of a growing workers' movement—that of Bismarckian Germany. Hitherto 'Marxism' had been virtually synonymous with the persons of Marx and Engels. From 1883 onward it obtained a foothold in the strongest Socialist movement then in existence. The new organ of German Social-Democracy, the *Neue Zeit*, which was established in that year under Karl Kautsky's editorship, had rivals among other party publications and at the start could not purport to represent more than one current of opinion among several. This did not matter; Marxism now at last possessed what it had never had before: a regular public platform. In time, Kautsky's *Neue Zeit*, which from the start counted Engels among its contributors, imposed itself upon the Second International as the authoritative voice of what was then the fastest growing Socialist movement in Europe. When in 1890 its editor was commissioned to draft the official party programme, the fusion was complete: German Social-Democracy—already a major political party in the Reich— had officially become 'Marxist'. What did this conversion mean, and how is one to assess Kautsky's role in it?[1]

[1] For biographical data cf. *Ein Leben fuer den Sozialismus. Erinnerungen an Karl Kautsky*, Hannover, 1954; *Aus der Fruehzeit des Marxismus: Engels's*

It is easier to state what the event did *not* signify. It did not imply that German Social-Democracy had consciously adopted the role of a revolutionary popular movement dedicated to the overthrow of the Bismarckian Empire and the completion of Germany's aborted democratic revolution. If the older party leaders—principally W. Liebknecht and Bebel—ever cherished such aims, they had quietly abandoned them by 1890, when the party they led became 'Marxist'. German Socialism had been genuinely 'subversive'—at any rate from Bismarck's standpoint—in the 1870's, when it was still a fledgling growth. By 1890, with the expiry of Bismarck's anti-Socialist legislation and the steady expansion of its electoral following, it had transformed itself into a radical-democratic opposition movement within the Reich, neither more nor less dangerous to the governing caste than the Catholic 'Centre' party, and considerably less influential. Yet it was precisely at this moment that the party officially proclaimed its undying antagonism to bourgeois society as well as to the Wilhelminian regime. The 'Erfurt Programme' adopted in 1891 was mainly the work of Kautsky, and it embodied as much of Marx's analysis of capitalism as the mental comprehension of its readers seemed likely to permit. If the bulk of the platform was unimpeachably democratic and 'reformist', its preamble at least laid sufficient stress on the class struggle to satisfy Engels, with whom Kautsky was in constant correspondence.[1]

The seeming paradox of an essentially pacific and gradualist movement equipped with a revolutionary doctrine loses much of its bewildering aspect when viewed against the background of Bismarckian and Wilhelminian Germany. All German party programmes of the period were excessively ideological and tended to deduce practical demands from theoretical propositions which satisfied intellectual and emotional cravings at the expense of immediate relevance. This was unimportant, since the government of the Reich, though in form constitutional, was in fact autocratic and irremovable. Its

---

Briefwechsel mit Kautsky, Prague, 1935; *Victor Adler, Briefwechsel mit August Bebel und Karl Kautsky*, ed. Friedrich Adler, Vienna, 1954. For a critical assessment of Kautsky's role in the Socialist movement cf. Erich Matthias, 'Kautsky und der Kautskyanismus', in *Marxismusstudien*, vol. II, Tuebingen, 1957, pp. 151 ff.

[1] Cf. Kautsky, *Das Erfurter Programm*, Stuttgart, 1892, for a lengthy analysis of the document by its chief author. This 'popular commentary' of 260 pages became a Socialist classic and did much to establish Kautsky as the official party theorist. It also furnished an ample target for 'revisionist' broadsides in the following decade.

vaunted independence of the political parties had its reverse side in the irresponsibility of the latter. Since the Reichstag was virtually powerless, and the parties were condemned to the role of pressing sectional claims on the ruling bureaucracy, they were all the less ready to compromise on matters of principle. Their platforms showed the effect of this doctrinal intransigence, and the Social-Democrats did not in this respect differ as much from their Liberal or Conservative opponents as either side was wont to suppose. Germany was a doctrinaire country because all existing doctrines were held in suspense. There was no reason why the Social-Democrats should not preface a statement of aims with an exposition of their basic philosophy. What requires to be explained is rather why this philosophy took the shape it did, at the very moment when Social-Democracy had, for practical purposes, settled down to tacit acceptance of the *status quo*.[1]

German Social-Democracy was the residuary legatee of democratic tendencies which had found no outlet in Bismarck's Empire. It was also the organisation of the newly formed industrial proletariat. The party's development into a mass movement, following its virtual collapse and voluntary self-liquidation at the outset of the legal repression directed against it in 1878, coincided with the prolonged economic slump of the 1880's. Among Socialists this was widely regarded as proof that capitalism had lost its capacity for expansion. A fatalistic belief in the imminent collapse of the hated system— which was not clearly distinguished from the prevailing socio-political 'class-rule' in Bismarckian Germany—took hold of considerable strata of the movement, facilitating the subsequent adoption of a Marxist, or quasi-Marxist, platform. Among the party leaders, Bebel and W. Liebknecht were particularly prone to such attitudes, and their support enabled Kautsky to impose his peculiar brand of economic determinism upon the movement. The reverse side of this coin was the stubbornly held conviction of many leading Social-Democrats that the protectionist and militarist policies pursued by the Reich government were unfavourable to the rapid development

---

[1] Brandis, op. cit., passim; Matthias, loc. cit., pp. 159 ff; cf. also Arthur Rosenberg, *Die Entstehung der deutschen Republik*, Berlin, 1928, pp. 47 ff. The complexities of German politics after 1890 are analysed with masterly clarity in this work; in particular the author brings out the insoluble dilemma in which Social-Democracy was placed by its status as a minority movement in a country where the government could always rely on an elected majority to block progress towards full democracy.

of a more liberal and progressive form of capitalism. This assessment and the—essentially liberal—economic policies advocated by the Social-Democrats in the Reichstag and elsewhere, later became the principal political content of 'revisionism'.[1]

This background helps to account for what is certainly the oddest aspect of the 'Erfurt Programme': the yawning gap between its theoretical analysis and its practical demands. The latter were basically 'reformist', and clearly related to the backward, undemocratic, character of Wilhelminian Germany; whereas the preceding theoretical section dwelt upon the self-destructive nature of capitalism and looked forward to the socialisation of the means of production. Kautsky's perfunctory attempt to deduce the practical conclusions from the theoretical postulates was altogether unconvincing and characteristically came at the very end of his lengthy exposition of the subject.[2] His real interest lay in demonstrating the economic necessity of socialism as a consequence of the automatism of capitalist production. The political demands—e.g., for social legislation and a more democratic franchise—tacked on to the lengthy statement of Socialist principles did not greatly concern him; he seems to have regarded their inclusion as a concession to the weakness of the flesh: an attitude in which he was confirmed by his theoretical Mentor.[3]

That Engels should have taken such an attitude becomes explicable in the light of his frequently expressed conviction that the growth of Social-Democratic influence, notably in the backward East Elbian provinces which furnished most of the recruits for the Prussian army, would in due course precipitate a political upheaval on the pattern of 1848.[4] In the end he was proved right, though the collapse of 1918

[1] Cf. Brandis, op. cit., pp. 5 ff. for a destructive analysis of the official party legend concerning Socialist theory and practice during this period. Mehring's glowing account of the subject, in vol. II of his *Geschichte der deutschen Sozialdemokratie*, pp. 408 ff, testifies more to his literary ability than to his concern for strict accuracy—always his weak point.

[2] Op. cit., pp. 258 ff.

[3] Cf. Engels to Kautsky, in *Aus der Fruehzeit*, p. 300: 'At any rate the theoretical part of the programme can hold its own; the chief thing is that it should contain nothing objectionable from the theoretical viewpoint, and that has in the main been secured.'

[4] Engels to Bebel, December 11, 1884, in MESC, p. 457: 'As things are at present, an impulse from outside can scarcely come from anywhere but Russia. If it does not do so, if the impulse is given inside Germany, then the revolution can only start from the army.' Cf. also Engels to Kautsky, October 14, 1891, MESC, p. 514: 'Even in Germany conditions may arise under which the parties of the left, despite their miserableness, may be *forced* to sweep away part of the colossal anti-bourgeois, bureaucratic and feudal rubbish that is still lying

hardly lived up to Socialist advance billing of what a democratic revolution should look like. Meantime his *arrière-pensées*—freely communicated to Kautsky and the German party leaders—had the effect of confirming them in their chosen attitude of passive expectancy with regard to the coming trial of forces. The immediate task, as they saw it, was to organise the working class, and to this end it was essential to hammer home the party's relentless opposition to capitalism, as well as to 'class rule': the latter term signifying not the domination of the bourgeoisie (of which indeed in Germany there was little sign), but rather, as with Lassalle, the absence of democracy. This equivocation runs through the whole of German Socialist literature from the 1870's, and explains in large measure how a movement which had never really broken with the Lassallean heritage could regard itself as 'Marxist'. The clue to the mystery lies in the political backwardness of Germany, compared with Western Europe. Under German conditions—and the same was true of Austria-Hungary, the other citadel of 'orthodox Marxism'—democracy was still a revolutionary slogan. Indeed it was easier for the governments of the day to compromise with quasi-socialist demands which did not touch the political structure, than to yield to the growing pressure for popular rule. It was the latter, not the former, that constituted the really revolutionary aspect of the Social-Democratic movement.

If the party failed in the 1890's to work out a clear-cut strategy adapted to the situation, this was partly owing to the enforced remoteness and isolation of the only major figure it possessed. Engels does not compare with Marx as a thinker, but as a political strategist he had no equal in the Germany of his day; or if he had, his only equal was Bismarck. A full-scale confrontation between these two would have been a spectacle worth watching. Had Germany been a normal country, Engels would have stood out as the leader of all the democratic forces arrayed against the governing caste. As it was, he had to content himself with the role of grand old man and theoretical adviser to a movement whose actual leaders lacked both his comprehensive understanding of European politics and his combative temper. The drift which set in after his death was already foreshadowed in the fatalistic spirit of the 'Erfurt Programme' and in the growing sectarianism of his radical disciples. By the turn of the

there.' The reference here is to the Liberals; Engels never abandoned the hope that a political crisis of this kind would usher in a democratic revolution—as indeed was to be the case in 1918.

century the average Social-Democrat had come to abandon the idea of an imminent political struggle and settled down to the long-range task of championing labour's sectional claims; though the party did not on this account renounce the radical terminology Marx and Engels had bequeathed to the Socialism of the 1890's. In the political field, the appropriate combination of doctrinal intransigence and tactical caution was brought to perfection by August Bebel, the vastly popular and respected party leader. The corresponding theoretical synthesis was primarily the work of Kautsky.[1]

Karl Kautsky (1854–1938) is the key figure in the synthesis of orthodox Marxism and democratic Socialism which became current in Central Europe—and indirectly throughout Europe and North America—during the quarter century (1889–1914) of the Second International's rise and fall. The qualifying adjective 'democratic' needs to be stressed in view of the subsequent association of Marxism with the Russian Revolution and Leninism. For all its revolutionary overtones and the disruptive effect it actually had on the political structures of the Hohenzollern, Habsburg and Romanov empires, Marxist Socialism as conceived and formulated by Kautsky was completely integrated with democratic theory and practice. This integration was spontaneous and unforced; neither Kautsky nor Eduard Bernstein, with whom from 1880 to 1895 he was closely allied, ever thought seriously of dissociating Socialism from democracy. Nor did the subsequent dispute between these former disciples of the ageing Engels touch upon the essentials of the democratic faith they held in common. If anything, Kautsky was more intransigently committed to radical democracy than the more pliable Bernstein, who showed a hankering for mere parliamentary constitutionalism on the British model—complete with a reformed monarchy. Anything short of full republican democracy was anathema to Kautsky, just as on the other hand he resisted with inflexible stubbornness any deviation in the direction of minority dictatorship. It was this rigid commitment to a central position which so enraged his opponents on the right and left, and caused so many misunderstandings in the course of the acrid polemics in which a large part of his political life was consumed.

---

[1] Rosenberg, op. cit., passim; Brandis, op. cit., pp. 97 ff; Matthias, op. cit., pp. 163 ff; Carl E. Schorske, *German Social Democracy 1905–1917*, Harvard, 1955, passim; Gerschenkron (*Bread and Democracy in Germany*, pp. 28 ff) rightly stresses the central importance of worker-peasant relations in determining Social-Democratic strategy.

For the most fateful of these misunderstandings—the supposed identity of the new Marxism with the complete and unabridged doctrine of Marx and Engels—it would be a mistake to hold Kautsky wholly responsible. As has been shown, Engels had already reformulated the original revolutionary credo of 1843–8 in a manner conducive to interpretations which brought it much closer to positivism and its political corollary, democratic reformism. When Bernstein and Kautsky from about 1880 onward began to popularise the new world-view, they could regard themselves with reason as authentic interpreters of what was then coming to be known as Marxism; indeed Kautsky never ceased to do so. Even in his last major work, a massive treatise on the materialist conception of history completed at the age of seventy-three, he still expressly claimed to be expounding the doctrine he had adopted almost half a century earlier: albeit with critical reservations and emendations which around 1900 he would probably have qualified as 'revisionist'.[1]

The man who thus for half a century embodied the theory and practice of German Social-Democracy, and who likewise shared with G. V. Plekhanov the position of spiritual godfather to the Russian Marxists, was by temperament and upbringing uniquely qualified to act as a link between German-speaking Central Europe and the Slav world. Born in Prague, the son of a Czech father and a German mother; educated in his native city and in Vienna before emigrating abroad; brought up by his parents to look with indifference and contempt upon the decaying Habsburg monarchy; a democrat almost before he knew the meaning of the term; a Socialist sympathiser from the moment he heard of the Paris Commune; an enthusiastic student of Darwin years before he had begun to familiarise himself with Marx—Kautsky appears in his memoirs and in the recollections of his friends as one of those fortunate people who never encounter a serious doubt or feel uncertain about the direction of their interests.

[1] Karl Kautsky, *Die materialistische Geschichtsauffassung*, two vols., Berlin, 1927; cf. Karl Korsch's critical treatment of this work in the bulky essay entitled *Die materialistische Geschichtsauffassung. Eine Auseinandersetzung mit Karl Kautsky*, Leipzig, 1929. Kautsky's standing as a theorist must not be judged by this production of his declining years, which exposed him not merely to hostile criticism but even to ridicule from younger and more alert scholars, not all of them inspired by mere factional animosity. If by 1927 he was out of touch with the main intellectual currents of the time and gave the impression of being a sort of Rip Van Winkle, this was not the case with his earlier writings; though it is fair to say that few of them rose markedly above the ordinary level of competence to be expected from a professional scholar.

The beliefs and values he acquired in his youth and adolescence were also those of his maturity and old age. His commitment to them was, so to speak, organic; it took the form of an entirely unforced and unwavering certainty. There was no crisis, no conversion. This most erudite of Marxist scholars was also the most conservative of men, if conservatism signifies a profound concordance with the ideas and values of one's environment. His memoirs indicate that the thought of being anything but a Social-Democrat never occurred to him. Socialism was in the air he breathed, just as his indifference towards religion or nationalism—once he had got over the naive Czech patriotism of his boyhood—was part of the intellectual climate in which he grew up. Rarely can the theorist of a revolutionary movement have had such an untroubled attachment to his primary loyalties.[1]

This sense of unshakable commitment to ideas and values which he seems to have absorbed by a kind of osmosis gives to Kautsky's writings an air of detachment in marked contrast to the lively polemical style of Engels, to say nothing of the molten lava of Marx's prose. In reading Kautsky one is confronted with the kind of certainty that goes with the definitive formulation of a new way of thought after its first revolutionary impact has been exhausted. The immense mass of his writings—in addition to editing the *Neue Zeit* for thirty-four years and publishing some of Marx's most important economic manuscripts, he was a prolific controversialist and the author of weighty historical and economic studies—is throughout informed by a pedagogic interest inseparable from his position as the authoritative exponent of a system which he appeared to have grasped in all its ramifications; though there were others—notably Plekhanov—who excelled him in their treatment of philosophic matters. Coupled with a certain rigidity of mind, this somewhat pedantic attitude conveyed the image of a professor expounding elementary verities to a large and unruly class of pupils. As time went on this image became fixed in the minds of a growing army of critics on the right and left, and by the end of his long and astonishingly active life he had clearly lost most of the authority he once possessed. It became fashionable to

[1] These remarks are in part based on Kautsky's brief autobiographical sketch *Mein Lebenswerk*, reproduced in *Ein Leben fuer den Sozialismus*: a symposium (ed Benedikt Kautsky, Hannover, 1954) including essays on his life and work by some of his former collaborators. The massive autobiography posthumously published by his son (*Erinnerungen und Eroerterungen*, ed. Benedikt Kautsky, Gravenhage, 1960) breaks off in 1883 and is of interest chiefly for the light it throws on his early development.

see in him no more than the doctrinaire exponent of a hopelessly outmoded political and theoretical position, which in their different ways
the 'revisionists' and the Leninists had shown to be untenable. There
is just enough warrant for this assessment of Kautsky to make it seem
plausible to people whose political memory begins and ends with the
Russian Revolution; especially when such judgments are brought in
as part of an indictment of the helpless passivity which the Socialist
movement in Europe displayed in the face of the Fascist-Communist
challenge during the 1930's. Nonetheless it will not do to dismiss
Kautsky as a doctrinaire exponent of pseudo-Marxist scholasticism:
an attitude currently fashionable among the disillusioned heirs of
German Social-Democracy.[1] The man who helped to turn Marxism
from an esoteric system into the doctrine of a gigantic political movement was neither a mediocrity nor a mere populariser of other men's
ideas. For all his limitations, Kautsky is a more interesting figure than
his latter-day critics have been willing to concede.

What makes him interesting—at least to anyone whose historical
imagination is not bounded by the events of the last few decades—
is just what rendered him ineffective after 1918. In Kautsky one
encounters the heritage of nineteenth-century rationalism as—in a
more imposing form—one sees it in Freud. Indeed the two men
have more in common than is apparent at first sight. Born within
two years of each other and brought up in the Vienna of the declining
Austro-Hungarian empire, they share to a surprising degree a cast
of thought—even (at least in their correspondence) a style of writing
—which is distinctively Austrian and strikingly different from anything associated with contemporary Germany or Russia. A detached,
pragmatic, sceptical turn of mind, combined with a somewhat doc-
trainaire interpretation of scientific materialism, is characteristic of
both, as is the unquestioning acceptance of an old-fashioned—and
of course profoundly 'bourgeois'—personal morality and an equally
Victorian belief in 'progress'. To say this is after all to say no
more than that they lived and worked in a bourgeois environment;
but the resemblance goes further: for all the obvious disparity in
intellectual force and sheer originality, Kautsky's dry clinical detachment has something in common with the spirit of Freud. The long
Indian summer of Viennese intellectual life in the last decades of the

---

[1] Cf. Matthias, op. cit., passim; for a more positive, though not uncritical,
interpretation of Kautsky's work, cf. J. Marschak, 'Kautsky und die junge
Generation', in *Ein Leben fuer den Sozialismus*, pp. 69 ff.

Habsburg monarchy left its mark both on the founder of modern depth psychology and on the chief exponent of the new socio-political world-view.[1]

Kautsky's version of Marxian socialism is neither the Marxism of the *Communist Manifesto* nor its subsequent Leninist reformulation —the world-revolutionary doctrine of 1917. This is what makes it so difficult at the present time to appreciate the importance he possessed for the fast-growing Socialist movement around 1900, when the most urgent requirement was some degree of theoretical clarification. We have grown used to identifying Marxism with Communism, an equation which Kautsky, then and later, regarded as absurd. In his eyes the *Manifesto* was no more than a brilliant sketch of the fully developed system elaborated in *Capital* and in the mature writings of Engels. Its significance was that of an historical document. Unlike Bernstein and the other 'revisionists' he saw no need to repudiate it, but neither did he regard it as a *vade-mecum* for Socialists of his own generation. As he saw it, the Socialist movement had in the meantime shed its Blanquist tendencies and become democratic, without for that reason ceasing to be revolutionary. Its rise to power necessarily implied a complete alteration in the class structure, and this to Kautsky was what 'the revolution' meant, though for Germany and Austria (as well as Russia) he also envisaged the probability of a purely political upheaval which would make an end of the existing autocratic, pre-bourgeois regimes. This accomplished, democracy could be relied upon to do the rest. In Western Europe and in the United States, where democratic forms of political life had become fully established, the problem was to that degree further simplified. Here the task consisted in turning the working-class movement from a passive adjunct of bourgeois society into an instrument of labour's emancipation. The eventual certainty of such a development was guaranteed—here was the sharpest point of difference with Bernstein

---

[1] From a biographical viewpoint Kautsky's exchange of letters with Victor Adler, now included in the latter's published *Briefwechsel* (see above), is a more important source of information than his correspondence with Engels which terminates in 1895, before he had acquired his full mental stature. The letters to Adler around 1900, when the 'revisionist' debate was at its height, show him not only intellectually superior to his opponents, but equipped with a first-rate political mind and a capacity for dealing effectively with complex tactical problems—qualities which were not in evidence while he was still the disciple of Engels. Nor does his terse and incisive style of writing during those years foreshadow the pedantic caution he was to display later on, to say nothing of the pathetic weakness and garrulity of his old age.

—by the automatism of the class struggle, which in turn reflected the mechanism of capitalist economics as described by Marx. Meanwhile, however, the short-range political problem nearer home, in Central Europe, was of a different order. Here the issue was how to achieve the degree of democratic freedom already secured elsewhere. On this point Kautsky—in common with the majority of German and Austrian Social-Democrats—rejected Bernstein's optimistic appraisal as even more hopelessly utopian and wishful than his long-term economic prognosis: political tensions would inevitably increase *pari passu* with the growth of the labour movement, and in the eventual showdown Social-Democracy would obtain the support of the popular majority, though not of the propertied bourgeoisie, which had long ago turned its back on democracy. Hence the virtual certainty of (political) revolution. But mark: the revolution's function was to introduce full democracy, not 'the dictatorship of the proletariat'. The latter might indeed, in a certain sense, be regarded as synonymous with democracy, inasmuch as the working-class (taking the term in its broad meaning and giving it a generous interpretation) already constituted the majority; but no sort of Jacobin-Blanquist dictatorship was intended, or indeed—according to Kautsky— conceivable under conditions of a highly organised industrial society.[1]

This, then, in the briefest possible outline, was Kautsky's view of the situation confronting the Socialist movement. Inevitably he was drawn into controversy with critics on both wings. The 'revisionists' flatly challenged his entire interpretation of economic reality and in particular his reliance on the sharpening of the class conflict; they were especially outraged by his insistence (which he subsequently modified) that small-scale peasant farming was doomed and that the smallholders could not become reliable allies of organised labour until they had resigned themselves to this outlook. Meanwhile on the left wing a growing army of malcontents, generalled by Rosa Luxemburg and her associates, protested that Kautsky's fatalistic doctrines tended to confirm the party leadership in its traditional

---

[1] For the above cf. in particular *Bernstein und das sozialdemokratische Programm*, Berlin, 1899; *Die soziale Revolution*, Berlin, 1902; *Der Weg zur Macht*, Berlin, 1909; Kautsky's major scholarly contributions during this period— notably *Die Agrarfrage*, Stuttgart, 1899, a comprehensive study of the farm problem—were only indirectly connected with his political views, but they served to buttress them by challenging the 'revisionist' suggestion that small-scale property in industry and agriculture was holding its own.

do-nothing policy. These criticisms had already swelled into a mounting chorus on the eve of the 1914–18 war and were reinforced thereafter, when Kautsky once more entrenched himself in a central position of no-support-for-the-war and no revolutionary defeatism à la Liebknecht either. From 1917, with the victory of Bolshevism, the radical assault grew steadily in violence. Kautsky (who had meanwhile made peace with his old opponent Eduard Bernstein) was now held up as an enemy of the proletarian revolution, a renegade, an exponent of bourgeois democracy, a senile pedant, and a Darwinian in socialist clothing who had never really understood Marx.[1] These attacks soon extended from his policies to his person. Lenin poured vulgar abuse on him; Trotsky poked insipid fun at his style; younger Marxists—not all of them Communists—complained that Kautsky was hopelessly out of date. Meanwhile the heirs of 'revisionism' saw in all this pother additional proof of their old contention that democratic Socialism required an altogether different theoretical foundation. Whatever merits the Kautskyan synthesis might have possessed around 1900, it plainly no longer conveyed much to the post-war generation.

Since we are here not concerned with the post-1918 debate, these points can be set aside. The relevant period is that of the two decades between the death of Engels and the outbreak of the first world war, when Kautsky's authority was both unique and unchallenged; and the only question of importance is how far his involvement in the great controversy over the revision of Marxist theory and practice helped to clarify the issues. Was he, as his critics maintained, the doctrinaire defender of an outworn position, or did he, rather than Bernstein and the others, bring about that adaptation of theory to practice whose urgency was proclaimed on all sides? And if he did, why was the synthesis he represented so catastrophically inadequate after 1918?

At the political level the answer stares one in the face: Kautsky was the theorist of the democratic revolution that occurred in Central Europe at the end of the war. If the German and Austro-Hungarian upheavals of October–November 1918 were not his work, they were in complete accord with everything he had taught, and even more so with everything he had said in private: Germany and Austria, no less than Tsarist Russia, had to pass through revolution before Social-

---

[1] Cf. Korsch, op. cit., passim; for a more balanced though critical view cf. Matthias, loc. cit.

Democracy could come to power.[1] That this initial task devolved upon the working class was due to the exhaustion of bourgeois radicalism. In principle, regimes such as Tsarist Russia or the Habsburg empire simply had no right to exist in the twentieth century. On this issue Kautsky's doctrinaire intransigence turned out in the end to be simple common-sense. It took a certain detachment to pronounce as early as 1901 that there was no hope of further political development until these ancient structures had been cleared away, but then detachment was just what was required in a theorist. The passage in which he set out this opinion is so characteristic of the man that it is worth quoting:

> Most of our people suffer from the delusion that one can find a solution to every problem, if only one is clever enough. But there are insoluble problems, and the establishment of a viable Austria is one of them. National autonomy would not be a remedy either. It is essential for us in our propaganda and organisation, but under the given conditions, and with the present relation of forces, it is not conducive to a solution.
>
> In Austria of all places, a gradual approach to some solution or other is unthinkable. The only cure lies in complete collapse. That Austria still exists is to me not proof of its viability, nor yet evidence that we now have the political basis for a slow and peaceful development; all it proves is that bourgeois society is no longer capable of doing away with even the most rotten structures: the Sultan, Tsarism, Austria. True, one does not as yet see when we for our part shall find the strength to demolish these ruins. No doubt we shall need a great deal of patience, we are still far from our aim; but let us have no talk about our needing only an organic step-by-step development and not having to pull anything down by force in order to make headway.[2]

A passage such as this—and there are others in Kautsky's correspondence which display similar incisiveness, though in his public utterances he tended to blunt the sharp edges—discloses both his strength and his weakness as the theorist of a mass movement. At his best he could size up an entire historical situation with a ruthless clarity almost recalling that of Marx; what he lacked was the ability

---

[1] Cf. his correspondence with Victor Adler, especially Kautsky's letters of June 5, 1901, November 21, 1901, May 23, 1902, April 4, 1903, October 18, 1904, and June 20, 1907 (*Briefwechsel*, pp. 354 ff, 380 ff, 399 ff, 414 ff, 431 ff, and 478 ff).

[2] Letter to Victor Adler, June 5, 1901, op. cit., p. 354. The entire document is of great importance for an understanding of Kautsky's 'centrist' position in the controversies of his day. Among others it contains a surprisingly 'modern' assessment of the revisionist movement as an outcrop of the intelligentsia's arrival on the political scene.

to clothe the doctrinal skeleton with flesh and blood. The public role he assumed was that of a doctrinaire professor of Marxism who taught the Socialist movement to rely on the relentless march of history. This was hardly the best preparation for the crises into which the movement drifted from 1914 onward. A skilful tactician like Victor Adler, who held his party together for thirty years by pleasing all factions, had a clearer notion of what was needed to instil confidence into his followers. Yet in the long run Adler's party followed Kautsky's prescription—to the bitter end.

He was less successful in Germany. For reasons which he never quite managed to fathom, German Social-Democracy in the crisis of its fate eluded his direction. This was partly due to the accident of Bebel's death in 1913, which deprived Kautsky of his strongest support, just when the outbreak of war in 1914 threw an unparalleled strain upon German Socialism. But there were deeper currents against which he struggled in vain. The revisionist controversy at the turn of the century had already taken him by surprise. That Bernstein —'theoretically a cypher', 'no one who has understood Marxism can talk such nonsense as Bernstein is now giving out'[1]—should have been able to provoke such an upheaval struck him as incomprehensible. In the end he fell back upon a purely sociological explanation: revisionism represented a new political current to which Bernstein was giving expression without knowing what he was doing. It was part of an international trend of which Fabianism in England, and reformist Socialism in France, were parallel manifestations. The reason was that there were people who were dissatisfied with the existing state of affairs, but who did not want to go very far in the direction of Marxist Social-Democracy.[2] As the revisionist controversy was to show, this was too simple an explanation. In the

[1] *Briefwechsel*, p. 355.

[2] *Briefwechsel*, pp. 355–6: 'I think we have to expect a renaissance of bourgeois democracy. The yearning for it exists among its surviving remnants; the increasingly numerous and important oppositional intelligentsia (notably the Jews) cannot become conservative, cannot join the conservative transformation of the lower middle class; they are looking for an alliance with labour. On the other hand, the evident bankruptcy of democracy drives numerous elements into our ranks who feel ill at ease because in fact they don't belong among us; who come to us only because today we are the only democratic force, and who would be glad to link up with the residual bourgeois democracy, on condition that some concessions are made to the workers. . . . In England the Fabians have tried something of the sort. The first attempt was a failure because Liberalism was still too powerful. Its bankruptcy is likely to give rise to . . . a national Progressive party parallel to the . . . Jaurèsists.'

meantime Kautsky spent a good deal of effort trying to shore up the system he was defending. The heaviest attack had fallen upon the economics of Marxism, and his defence of this part of the fortress consequently absorbed most of his energy. By way of anticipation it may be observed that those critics of orthodoxy who more or less dimly perceived the vulnerable side of Marxian economics were not well served in the person of their leading spokesman. If Kautsky was not really a theorist of the first rank, Bernstein was no theorist at all, but rather an erudite publicist with a talent for simplifying complex matters—sometimes to a dangerous extent. This made it comparatively easy for Kautsky to demolish him, without thereby ending a debate which was nourished by a succession of political and economic issues peculiar to Germany. The story is complicated and will be considered in greater detail in the following chapter. Here it is intended only to outline Kautsky's share in it.

Revisionism began not in 1899 with the publication of Bernstein's critique of Marxism, but five years earlier with a controversy over those sections of the Erfurt Programme which dealt with farm policy and more generally with the prospects of peasant farming.[1] For reasons which cannot be extensively developed in this space, the agrarian problem was the key issue in German politics between 1890 and 1914, i.e., during the period that saw the growth of Social-Democracy to a mass movement which attracted the support of one-third of the electorate. In the 1890's this trend was already sufficiently marked for the question to be raised whether Social-Democracy should continue to represent the sectional interests of labour and the urban consumer, plus such landless farm workers as it might be able to attract; or whether the party would not do better to water down its principles and reach for the support of the millions of peasant smallholders who traditionally supported either the Catholic 'Centre' or the Liberal parties (the Conservatives had not as yet broken into this stratum, though some movements on the extreme right were making headway among the peasants). The argument had very little to do with differences over Marxism, but Kautsky's successful resistance to various attempts in 1894 and 1895 to modify the programme was in part determined by his somewhat pedantic insistence (which he

---

[1] Cf. Kautsky, 'Mein Lebenswerk', in *Ein Leben etc.*, pp. 21 ff; Schorske, op. cit., pp. 7 ff; Gerschenkron, op. cit., pp. 28 ff. For Kautsky's original view of the agrarian question cf. *Das Erfurter Programm*, especially pp. 150–3, where it is flatly asserted that peasant farming is doomed.

shared with Engels) that peasant farming was a lost cause.[1] By 1899, when the second round of the revisionist controversy was opened by Bernstein on a much wider front, Kautsky (in his major work, *Die Agrarfrage*) had already modified his original position, though not sufficiently to suit either the tactical needs of the leading South German advocates of rapprochement with the peasants or the doctrines of their chief spokesman.[2] Meanwhile the party leadership, which in 1894-5 had been disposed to make concessions to the 'agrarian' viewpoint for purely practical reasons,[3] having now taken fright at revisionist heresies, had veered round and lined up behind Kautsky. The resulting confusion is amusingly illustrated by the fact that in the meantime Kautsky for his part had come to the conclusion that he had after all been wrong about the inevitable disappearance of the peasantry! But he still refused to follow David and the other revisionists in their insistence that the family farm provided the optimal conditions for agricultural progress.[4]

Amidst this welter of fluctuating theoretical and political quarrels the first round of the revisionist controversy fizzled out, Kautsky having demonstrated that at all events Socialist theory was still in accordance both with Marx and with the facts. In this he was considerably helped by Marx's own ambiguities on the subject. Since the discussion of agriculture occurs in the unfinished third volume of *Capital*, different interpretations were possible, practically the only certainty being that Marx regarded capitalist farming (i.e., production for the market) as 'historically progressive' in the short run,

[1] Cf. Engels, 'The Peasant Question in France and Germany', MESW II, pp. 381 ff (originally published as 'Die Bauernfrage in Frankreich und Deutschland', in *Neue Zeit*, 1894-5). Apart from condemning the attempt then being made by the French Socialists to gain peasant support by committing Socialism to the defence of small landed property, Engels in this important essay set out a political strategy for German Social-Democracy which became the foundation of the radical credo: the party's task was to win over 'the rural proletariat east of the Elbe' rather than 'the small peasants of Western Germany, or yet the middle peasants of Southern Germany'. It was the fall of the East Elbian bastions of Junkerdom which would strike the death blow at the Prussian monarchy.

[2] Eduard David, *Sozialismus und Landwirtschaft*, Berlin, 1903. For David's views cf. also his speech at the 1899 party congress, in *Protokoll ueber die Verhandlungen des Parteitags der Sozialdemokratischen Partei Deutschlands*, Berlin, 1899, pp. 143 ff.

[3] Cf. Bebel to Adler, October 20, 1895, *Briefwechsel*, pp. 193 ff: 'The adoption of his (Kautsky's) resolution has blocked our progress in the countryside for years to come.'

[4] *Ein Leben etc.*, p. 22. For a full account of the controversy cf. Gerschenkron, op. cit., pp. 29 ff.

though ruinous in the longer perspective. He had even had a kind word for the smallholder, though the future was destined to belong to 'associated producers'. From this no clear tactical prescriptions could be deduced, but in general the orthodox school drew the conclusion that it was hopeless to resist the process of capitalist concentration in agriculture, though its social consequences might be deplored.

The political strategy suggested by Kautsky's analysis of the farm problem was essentially a long-range one. If the peasantry was gradually being squeezed out, or at least reduced in importance by the spread of larger and more highly capitalised units with which it could not effectively compete, its impoverishment might render it more amenable to Socialist propaganda already current among land-less agricultural labourers; but in the short run Social-Democracy, though it might try to aid the small farmer where this could be done without prejudice to its free-trade platform, could not and should not compete with the agrarian parties in sponsoring quack programmes for preserving the family farm. This had been substantially the standpoint of Engels, and in maintaining the orthodox tradition Kautsky was able to quote statistics in support of his thesis, though his opponents did the same. The importance of the agrarian issue in German politics before 1914 was such that a controversy on this subject necessarily implied a series of political choices. But from a theoretical viewpoint there is little to be gained in analysing the motives which induced the 'radical', or 'Marxist', majority within the party at the end of the 1890's to adhere to free-trade policies. If Social-Democracy wished to represent the interests of the urban consumer, it could not well adopt any other line. Marx had favoured free trade because it revolutionised society and sharpened class antagonisms. At bottom this was also the standpoint of Kautsky, but it was no longer politic to say such things. Instead, tactical considerations were invoked to support resistance to the industrial and agrarian tariff policies sponsored by the Imperial government.[1]

Kautsky's subsequent involvement in the revisionist controversy

[1] Gerschenkron, op. cit., pp. 33 ff. The tariff issue impinged directly upon the balance of political forces because it linked the East Elbian landowners and the Ruhr industrialists in a conservative 'solidarity bloc' which became the real power behind the scenes from the 1880's onward. When in 1902 the Catholic 'Centre' joined the bloc it became unbeatable, and the Social-Democrats found themselves in a permanent minority, together with their uncertain allies, the liberal Progressives. The link between them was of course free trade.

had for its chief target Bernstein's attempt to offer a new interpretation of Marxist theory, and his polemical writings thus ranged over a fairly wide field. Special mention must be made, however, of his entry into the debate on economic crises. Aside from his edition of Marx's *Theorien ueber den Mehrwert* (1905–10), his observations on the trade cycle represent his chief contribution to theoretical economics. They are of interest also because they can be viewed as an early attempt to formulate a Marxist view of the age of imperialism.

Kautsky's intervention took the form of a review-article entitled *Krisentheorien* in the theoretical organ of which he was editor, the *Neue Zeit* (1901–2, vol. II, pp. 133 ff), the immediate occasion being Tugan-Baranovsky's recently published *Studies on the Theory and History of Commercial Crises in England*. This was a product of the revisionist school, and in criticising its relatively optimistic conclusions, Kautsky went beyond exegesis and committed himself to a definite view of the future. In substance he asserted that the Marxian theory of crises was not merely adequate, but was about to come more fully into its own. Cyclical depressions, so far from becoming milder (as Bernstein and Tugan had asserted), were tending to grow sharper and more prolonged. Moreover, there was ground for supposing that capitalism was not far from a stage of chronic stagnation which would intensify the class conflict. In Kautsky's opinion such a state of affairs was already foreshadowed by the growing rivalry between the leading industrial nations, as each tried to secure a larger slice of a stagnant world market by means of protective tariffs, colonial expansion, and in the final analysis, war. *Krisen, Kriege, Katastrophen* (crises, wars, catastrophes)—this, in Kautsky's view, was the perspective of the near future, unless the working class conquered power. 'Just as so many other dreams have evaporated during the past few years . . . so the events of the coming years will dispel the dream which at present bemuses us (the fantasy) that wars and catastrophes are things of the past, while there lies before us the level road of peaceful progress.'[1] Though written under the impact of the South African War and evidently influenced by contemporary radical criticism of imperialist policies,[2] this analysis can claim a certain originality. As a contribution to what was later to become known as

[1] *Krisentheorien*, loc. cit., p. 143.
[2] J. A. Hobson's classic study *Imperialism* appeared later in 1902, but the British discussion was already in full swing, a majority of the Fabians having made their bow to imperialism by ostentatiously supporting the South African War as a 'necessary' enterprise.

the 'breakdown controversy' it does not perhaps rank very high, but the attempt to sketch a connection between structural changes in the economy and the growing bellicosity of the great powers was something new. At the very least it gives Kautsky a claim to be regarded as the first Marxist theorist to have identified one of the problems of the post-liberal era. From here it was not a long way to Hilferding's analysis of finance-capitalism, and ultimately to the political conclusions drawn by Lenin.

If Kautsky was able on the whole to ward off revisionist attacks on what to him was the core of the Marxist position—economics and the class struggle—he was markedly less successful in the field of general theory. His historical studies, including a rather laboured attempt to account in materialist terms for the origins of Christianity (*Der Ursprung des Christentums*, 1908) are respectable but prosaic essays in applied sociology. Of greater relevance to the revisionist debate was his weakness in handling philosophical concepts. *Ethik und materialistische Geschichtsauffassung* (1906), his most ambitious work in this field prior to the attempted *Summa* of 1927, displays all the characteristic failings of positivism. There is significance in the date. The book's publication came as the sequel to a lengthy polemic between Kautsky and the editors of the official party daily, whose expulsion from their editorial chairs in 1905—the year of the first Russian Revolution and of a hitherto unprecedented wave of militancy among the Social-Democratic rank and file—was not unconnected with their advocacy of political and philosophical heresies. This was almost the last occasion on which the official party leadership, traditional Marxist orthodoxy as represented by Kautsky, and the emerging left wing around Rosa Luxemburg, presented a common front. Had Kautsky been able to clinch this tactical and organisational victory by an equally crushing blow in the theoretical field, his complacent belief that revisionism was finished would have been better founded ; the facts spoke a different language. But before confronting this theme it is advisable to broaden our range so as to take in the revisionist controversy as a whole. The issues it raised were of the most general nature, and insofar as the debate turned upon the critique of Marxist theory its significance is not yet exhausted.

6

THE REVISIONISTS

TO UNDERSTAND what was involved in the great debate over Marxism which shook the European Socialist movement around 1900, it must be borne in mind that the challenge came from inside the fold. The chief protagonist had been a close collaborator of Engels, and those who shared his views were all in different degrees influenced by Marx; many of them indeed continued to think of themselves as 'critical Marxists'. Intermingled with this group, and sometimes difficult to distinguish from it, there were Socialists stemming so to speak from an earlier geological stratum; of whom it would be true to say that they were less concerned with revising Marx than with adhering to their pre-Marxian view of things, which had suddenly become more respectable owing to the outbreak of dissension within the Marxist school. In the strict sense, 'revisionism' was confined to areas where Marxism had become the official doctrine of the Social-Democratic movement: principally Germany, Austria and Russia. One cannot seriously speak of Marxism being dominant around 1900 beyond this region, though there were influential Marxists in the West European, British and American Socialist parties and sects of the period; and in consequence it is not really very helpful to contrast for example the 'Marxist' Guesde with the 'revisionist' Jaurès. The latter—aside from being the dominant figure in the Socialist movement of his country—was quite plainly the protagonist of an indigenous French Socialism largely untouched by Germanic importations (and if influenced by them, almost as deeply indebted to Kant as to Marx). To class him among the revisionists is in a sense unfair to both. As a public figure he towered above them, while as a theorist he could not well compare with the more learned and ingenious representatives of the school. On the whole his contribution to the theoretical side of the debate was limited to the subject of Socialist ethics, and here the Germans—having studied both Kant and Marx at the source —possessed an advantage which foreigners could not hope to match.[1]

If the greatest representative of French Socialism was, from the theoretical viewpoint, on the fringe of the discussion, the majority of West European Socialists hardly figured in it at all. Never having been Marxists in the full sense, there was no particular reason why they should adopt the revised version of the doctrine. For all his rigidity in doctrinal matters Kautsky saw this quite clearly, as witness his comment on the Belgian Socialist leaders who in 1902 had incurred his displeasure by mismanaging a general strike movement to obtain universal suffrage:

I maintain an entirely unprejudiced attitude towards them; the talk about their revisionism leaves me cold. They have nothing to revise, for they have no theory. The eclectic vulgar socialism to which the revisionists would like to reduce Marxism is something beyond which they (sc. the Belgians) have not even begun to advance. Proudhon, Schäffle, Marx— it is all one to them; it was always like that, they have not retrogressed in theory, and I have nothing to reproach them with.[2]

A similar degree of tolerance was not, however, extended to the Fabians. Here was an influential group of Socialists who represented a rival approach—for the most part derived from Ricardo, Mill and Henry George, plus the new 'subjectivist' school of economics—and whose activities had already stirred the disapproval of Engels, years

---

[1] For Jaurès' philosophical views cf. Karl Vorländer, *Kant und Marx*, Tuebingen, 1926, pp. 104 ff. This is the authoritative study of the revisionist movement on its philosophical side, with special reference to the derivation of its doctrines from Kantian ethics.

[2] Kautsky to Victor Adler, May 23, 1902, *Briefwechsel*, pp. 400–1. For Kautsky's critical view of the political strategy pursued by the Belgian Socialists, cf. also his letter of May 19, 1902. The May 23 letter is noteworthy among others for his insistence that universal suffrage in Belgium would mean 'the beginning of the end not only for the clerical regime, but also for the monarchy, and even the bourgeois regime'.

before Bernstein gave signs of being influenced by their views.[1] In later years it even became possible for the historian of the Society to claim, with some degree of satisfaction, that revisionism was cradled in Britain.[2] This is true in the biographical sense, at least insofar as Bernstein is concerned, for there can be no doubt that his outlook was deeply influenced by his prolonged residence in Britain.[3] But as we have seen, revisionism in theory was already latent before Bernstein had come upon the stage; in a sense it had been in the air since the appearance in 1894 of the third and concluding volume of *Capital*, with its forced and unconvincing solution of the price-value problem. To anyone concerned with Marxist theory this was a serious matter, but it was not a matter in which the Fabians took much interest; nor indeed were they competent to do so. The attack on Marxian economics was led by Böhm-Bawerk, and continued by Pareto, with some assistance from Benedetto Croce; in other words, it was centred on Austria, Switzerland, and Italy. There were excellent geographical reasons for this, just as there were good reasons for the Central European provenance of the leading Marxists of the period, but in practice it meant that the debate was confined to one particular area. No controversy worth mentioning took place either in Britain or in France. In the former country Marxism was as yet unrepresented in the theoretical field, and in France its defenders were more interested in the philosophy of history than in the dull subject of economics. Lastly, it took time for the whole of *Capital* to be translated, and in the interval all the really important debates had already taken place.[4]

[1] Engels to Kautsky, September 4, 1892; cf. *Aus der Fruehzeit*, pp. 338 ff; MESC, pp. 529–31. For Kautsky's belief that Bernstein's development was leading him 'away from German Social-Democracy, if not from Socialism', and his advice to him to become 'a representative of English Socialism', cf. his letter to Bernstein of October 23, 1898, reproduced in Victor Adler, *Briefwechsel*, pp. 272 ff.

[2] E. R. Pease, *The History of the Fabian Society*, p. 239.

[3] The best account of this subject is to be found in Peter Gay, *The Dilemma of Democratic Socialism*, New York, 1952, pp. 54 ff, 93 ff.

[4] For a brief account of the post-1894 discussion cf. Meek, op. cit., pp. 201 ff; Sweezy, op. cit., pp. 190 ff. Wicksteed's critique of Marx, which played some part in the genesis of Fabianism, belongs to an earlier phase. There was no revisionist debate in France, for the excellent reason that there were no Marxist economists in that country. Those Socialists who took an interest in Marxist theory—their number was not large before 1918—relied upon what information they obtained from the librarian at the *Ecole Normale Supérieure*, Lucien Herr, who was not only a clandestine Socialist, but possessed the then almost unique distinction, for a Frenchman, of being able to read German. His article on Hegel in the *Encyclopédie* remained for many years the only reference to that philosopher in France.

Italy, however, requires special mention in this context. Not only did it produce in the person of Antonio Labriola (1842–1904) a Marxist theoretician of some eminence who was also a full-fledged professor of philosophy.[1] It also brought forth two critics of Marxism who raised the debate to a new level: Vilfredo Pareto and Benedetto Croce; the last-named a pupil of Labriola and for some years at least a quasi-Marxist. If one cares one may attribute this surprisingly strong Italian contingent to the circumstance that Italy was more fully exposed than either France or England to German-Austrian influences. A more accurate statement probably would be to say that Italy was a borderland exposed to both Central European and Western European intellectual currents, the former including Marxism as well as neo-Hegelianism. At any rate it is a fact that Italian thinking figured prominently in the debate over Marxian theory which raged from about 1895 to 1905, just as it was an Italian, Enrico Barone, who in 1908 made the crucial contribution to the theory of socialist economic planning.[2] This, incidentally, underlines the complexity of the situation, for Barone, so far from being a Marxist, was a follower of Pareto, whose criticism of Marx (cf. *Les Systèmes Socialistes*, Paris, 1902–3) set the tone for much of the French and Italian literature of the period. Yet it was Barone who for the first time developed a coherent blueprint of a planned economy—and he did so on the basis of modern, post-classical equilibrium economics as taught at Lausanne by Walras and Pareto. Here was further proof, if the revisionists required it, that socialist theory was not dependent on Marx. To conclude this brief note on the Italian contribution, Croce during the same period produced a critique of Marxian economics which laid due stress on the weaknesses of its value theory;[3] while his countryman Alfredo Poggi, another pupil of Labriola, intervened with some effect in the debate on Kantian and Marxian ethics.[4]

With this last-mentioned theme we have crossed the threshold into the central area of discussion, both geographically and ideologically.

[1] And who should not be confused with his namesake Arturo Labriola, the founder of Italian Syndicalism, who is important in Socialist history for other reasons.

[2] In a paper entitled 'Il ministerio della produzione nello stato collettivista', now available in an English translation in *Collectivist Economic Planning*, ed. Hayek, London, 1935, pp. 245 ff.

[3] *Historical Materialism and the Economics of Karl Marx*, London, 1914. (The title of the original is *Materialismo storico ed economia marxistica*, 1899)

[4] A. Poggi, *Kant e il Socialismo*, Palermo, 1904. For an account of his views cf. Vorländer, op. cit., pp. 225 ff.

For obvious reasons the controversy over Marxism as an all-inclusive system was bound to pivot on Germany; though Austria-Hungary and Russia made important contributions. This does not mean that the level of debate was uniformly higher in Germany than in the neighbouring areas: such was not the case. But Germany was the principal battlefield, both because it was the most important country in Europe, and because of the commanding position held by German Socialism within the Second International. If this massive labour movement were to be disrupted or to shift its ground, the long-term consequences would be far-reaching. From our present vantage-point this is evident enough. In 1900 the full implications of a split were still obscure, but the cleavage was already sharp and angry. There was an even more violent conflict in the emerging Russian Social-Democratic movement, but it turned on different issues and must be considered separately. There were likewise interesting theoretical developments in Austria, but they did not quite fit the German pattern. The difference between Germany and Austria in this respect has its significance, and must be mentioned briefly before we take the plunge into our theme.

In the strict sense there was no revisionist debate in Austria. This is the more remarkable since Vienna was one of the three great centres of the 'new economics'—Lausanne and Cambridge being the other two—and consequently an ideal arena for ideological tournaments. The Austrian school of economics, as represented by Böhm-Bawerk, had in fact taken the field as early as 1896 with an assault on the third volume of *Capital*.[1] This became the starting-point of a theoretical controversy which gave the fledgling Marxist school in Vienna a chance to display its talents in a series of lively encounters with the academic economists, who in addition to Böhm-Bawerk's other pupils included the youthful Joseph Schumpeter; but it did not give rise to a revisionist movement. In Vienna one was either a Marxist or an anti-Marxist, and in the latter case an adherent of liberal economics. Some of the Austro-Marxists diluted their general philosophy a little, so as to allow for all kinds of personal ingredients, from Kantian ethics to Freudian psychology; but they never relinquished their claim to be in the central tradition, and they never

---

[1] Eugen von Böhm-Bawerk, *Zum Abschluss des Marxschen Systems*, translated as *Karl Marx and the Close of his System*, London and New York, 1898; reprinted (ed. Sweezy) New York, 1949, together with Hilferding's rejoinder and an appendix containing L. von Bortkiewicz's important paper, first published in 1907, on Marx's solution of the price-value transformation problem.

joined the German revisionists in their attempt to substitute an altogether different theoretical brew. It may be said that they merely wore their revisionism with a difference, but the difference was an important one. Vienna became a centre of Marxian Socialism and remained one even after 1918, when the majority of Central European Marxists went over to the Leninist faith.

A somewhat different situation prevailed in Russia, or to be exact, in Petersburg and among the Russian emigrants in Western Europe. Here there were theorists of some eminence who joined the critics after going through a Marxist phase. Tugan-Baranovsky has already been mentioned; Peter Struve, S. N. Bulgakov, and Nicolai Berdyaev cannot be ignored. But their example also shows how different the Russian situation was from the German. Of the four only Tugan-Baranovsky was a genuine revisionist in the sense of trying to bring Marxist theory up to date.[1] For the others the critique of Marxism was merely a stage towards a fundamentally conservative position. Marxism to them was simply the extreme form of Western radicalism-cum-materialism, and their break with it signified a return to traditional, i.e., in the last resort Russian-Orthodox, values. In consequence they contributed little to the revisionist controversy, whatever their significance in the history of Russian political thought.[2] Revisionism presupposed agreement on the fundamentals of the Socialist faith as understood in the West, and this faith was radically humanist; whether it was also necessarily 'materialist', in the sense given to the term by Engels and Kautsky, was a different question, and indeed one of the principal topics over which the disputants fell out.

After these preliminaries it is time to indicate more plainly what the great debate was about. Briefly, it concerned the adaptation of Marxism to the modern world of industrialism and democracy, as it presented itself in Western Europe and North America around 1900. This alone should serve to make it clear why Russia was on the fringe of the discussion, and why nearly all Russian Socialists remained true to Marxist orthodoxy, however much they might differ over tactics. It also supplies a pointer to the phenomenon of Austro-Marxism which will be examined later in more detail. The modern world was certainly a tangible influence in pre-1914 Austria, but its impact was

---

[1] Cf. his *Theoretical Foundations of Marxism* (1905) and his short history of Socialism, in *Der moderne Sozialismus in seiner geschichtlichen Entwicklung*, Leipzig, 1908; cf. also Kautsky's lengthy review of the latter work in *Neue Zeit*, 1907–8, II, pp. 540–51, 607–12.

[2] Cf. Vorländer, op. cit., pp. 190 ff.

not such as to encourage the notion that a peaceful transition to modernity could be made which would leave the Habsburg Empire intact. In Germany, by contrast, the break with the past promised to be less violent—or at least so it seemed to the more hopeful spirits in the Socialist movement before the first world war. This situation formed the background of revisionism. It does not 'explain' it. The explanation, if there is one, lies in the tension which Marxism set up in the minds of people who had to adjust to a new situation, but did not wish to let go of certain fundamentals they had come to accept. None of the revisionists renounced Socialism as an aim, though some came to adopt Bernstein's sceptical position, summed up in his rather unfortunate phrase 'the movement is everything, the goal nothing'. This curious formulation hardly reflected its author's real attitude, since he remained active in promoting the 'goal' to the day of his death; but it made a useful slogan and in particular gave satisfaction to all those—notably in the growing trade union movement—who did not seriously expect to see Socialism realised 'in our time', but had all the more need for some assurance that their day-to-day activities were meaningful and important.[1]

The name of the protagonist has now been invoked so often that it is necessary to fix some attention upon his views. This is not altogether easy, for Eduard Bernstein (1850–1932) was almost as prolific a writer as Kautsky, and the issues he stirred up were sufficiently numerous and complex to keep a generation of controversialists almost ceaselessly employed. Moreover, the debate gradually broadened to include such recondite subjects as the relation of Marxism to Darwinism, the possibility of constructing a Socialist ethic on the basis of Kantian idealism, the relevance of Hegel's logic to the Marxian system, and similar topics. Although Bernstein became involved in all these issues, his contributions to the more strictly philosophical disputations were not rated very highly even by his friends,

---

[1] On this subject and the whole question of Bernstein's role in the German Social-Democratic movement cf. Gay, op. cit., passim. Bernstein's main contribution to the debate, originally published under the rather long-winded title *Die Voraussetzungen des Sozialismus und die Aufgaben der Sozialdemokratie* (hereafter cited as *Voraussetzungen*) appeared in an English translation as *Evolutionary Socialism* in 1909, published by the Independent Labour Party. For a contemporary critique of Bernstein's position from the orthodox standpoint cf. Louis Boudin, *The Theoretical System of Karl Marx in the Light of Recent Criticism*, Chicago, 1907. The literature is endless, most of it in German; readers interested in a modern Marxist-Leninist comment can find one in P. Sweezy, op. cit., pp. 192 ff.

and in the end he withdrew from this part of the arena to concentrate on more immediate matters.[1] It is probably no injustice to the memory of this remarkable man to say that his autodidactic training showed up more disadvantageously in his philosophical excursions than in his political and economic writings. As a political thinker he was at least the equal of his opponents, though his cast of mind was not really attuned to the German situation; while his economic and historical writings maintained a creditable standard.[2] He can also claim the merit of having maintained an unimpeachable stand in 1914–18, when he broke with the majority of his adherents to rejoin his old enemy Kautsky in a principled opposition to his party's collaboration with the Imperial government. Nonetheless in the long run his reputation must rest upon his attempted revision of Marxism, and here a considered judgment is much more difficult to formulate.

In part this is due to the extreme complexity of the issues involved in the revisionist debate. The topics Bernstein tried to tackle in his *Voraussetzungen* (1899), as well as in his later writings, ranged from the most abstract and recondite to the simplest and most pressing, besides which his adherents raised a large number of side issues, not all of them theoretical. As time went on, the controversy over Marxist theory turned into a pragmatic dispute over tactics, and eventually it merged with a factional struggle for power. By 1910, when the theoretical debate was as good as over, Bernstein and his friends had gained the support of men—notably among the trade union leaders and senior party officials—who neither knew nor cared what the original disagreement had been about, but were quite clear that the quasi-Marxist orthodoxy of the party leadership was a brake on their instinctive reformism. Subsequent developments were to show that Bernstein was badly mistaken about the outlook of these supporters; most of them were distinctly to the right of him, a circumstance which affected both their and his orientation during the war years. Some went so far as to subscribe to the entire programme of German imperialism in 1914–18, thus offering a parallel to the Fabians, though in the German setting such tendencies necessarily had a more aggressively nationalist ring. The liberal-minded theorist who had originally started the revisionist movement was made to feel distinctly uncomfortable in this environment.[3]

---

[1] Vorländer, op. cit., pp. 176 ff; Gay, op. cit., pp. 131 ff.

[2] His historical study on radical trends in the English Revolution of 1640–60 was pioneer work and won him recognition in British academic quarters; cf. Gay, op. cit., pp. 51 ff.   [3] Gay, op. cit., pp. 251 ff.

These confusions ultimately stemmed from a single circumstance of which Bernstein's critics never failed to remind him: that Germany differed from England. Although he frequently protested his awareness of this fact,[1] Bernstein did give the impression of believing that a 'British' form of development was not merely desirable, but possible—indeed quite probable—so far as Germany was concerned, and that the Social-Democrats could do much to promote it. His criteria of judgment in any case were derived from the West European situation, compared with which Imperial Germany was indisputably lagging.[2] Prior to 1918 the question was whether this gap could be bridged without revolution; since today we know the answer it is unnecessary to remark that on the political issue Bernstein proved mistaken. As against this it is arguable that in the long perspective the type of democratic socialism he envisaged has stood the test, not merely in Western Europe but also in those parts of Germany which after 1945 were more or less willingly incorporated in Western Europe. This, however, is not exactly what the revisionists of 1900, or the reformists of 1910, had in mind when they looked forward to a Germany modelled on the Western pattern. At best their victory has been a partial and belated one.

Two further points connected with the political side of the controversy must be got out of the way before we can turn to Bernstein's strictly theoretical contribution: protectionism and militarism.

As has already been noted, the tariff was the central issue in the politics of Imperial Germany before 1914. On this matter the 'agrarian' majority stood together under the leadership of its politically and economically strongest section: the East Elbian landowners, who were also the effective rulers of the Prussian state and the Prussian army. If the Social-Democratic programme had consisted of nothing but a drastic free-trade platform, it would already have spelled revolution so far as Prussia was concerned; and the Reich as a whole pivoted on Prussia. The fact that heavy industry had entered the protectionist 'solidarity bloc' made it an ideal target for Social-

[1] Cf. Bernstein to Bebel, October 20, 1898, in Victor Adler *Briefwechsel*, pp. 260–1.

[2] Ibid., p. 263: 'Look across the German frontiers to the politically advanced countries: Belgium, Holland, Denmark, Switzerland, Norway, even France. . . . In Germany, owing to the peculiar state of affairs, the party has obtained a political power which is out of tune with the general political development. It has thereby been placed in a difficult position This situation is not alleviated by the constant banging of the revolutionary drum. . . .'

Democratic assaults, and this propaganda had no need to be socialist in order to be regarded as truly radical. Inasmuch as it menaced the economic foundations of the bloc of great landowners and great industrialists who ruled Germany, it was subversive by its very nature. When around 1900 the protectionist bloc turned imperialist as well, the conflict assumed an even sharper form, for Social-Democratic resistance to the Reich government's policy of naval expansion and hostility to Britain now merged with its attack on the political foundations of Bismarck's Empire.

All this had very little to do with socialism, but a great deal with democracy. What is important for our theme is that the revisionist debate cut across this issue, since Bernstein's faith in liberalism was not shared by all his supporters. Many came in the end to make their peace with protectionism and imperialism, until the catastrophe of 1918 sobered them. However, for the period immediately under review it is true to say that democratic reformism—as Bernstein and his immediate supporters understood it—implied a policy of free trade, European peace, and above all good relations with England. On this issue there was no conflict between the party leadership and the revisionists, save insofar as some of the latter were a little wobbly in their attachment to free trade. The real trouble was that a programme of peace, democracy, and economic liberalism had no chance of being adopted by a majority of the Reichstag. This made it impossible for German Social-Democracy to develop along the lines of the British Labour Party. It was not Marx (let alone Hegel), but the tariff, which stood in the way of revisionism.[1]

Closely linked with this issue was that of militarism—to employ the cant term in use before 1914 to describe the internal situation in Prussia-Germany. For practical purposes the Reich was governed by an uncontrollable bureaucracy centred on the Emperor and the general staff. In this respect the situation was similar to that in pre-1945 Japan; indeed the Japanese constitution had been modelled on

---

[1] Cf. Gerschenkron, op. cit., p. 67: 'In both countries free trade policies were oriented toward the interest of consumers. In England as in Germany, the labour struggle against protectionism was a struggle against imperialist policies, with the important difference that Joseph Chamberlain lost and Bülow won. But while in England the free trade policy was related to the problem of democracy only in the sense that the absence of protectionism spared the English democracy a profound internal conflict, protectionism in Germany perpetuated the economic and political existence of a class whose economic interests and general philosophy were bitterly opposed to all democracy stood and stands for.'

the German. Here again Social-Democratic policy was dictated by circumstances, and here too it required a considerable act of faith to suppose that Germany would evolve without a catastrophe in the direction Britain and Western Europe had already taken. In promoting such beliefs the revisionists certainly did not display superior insight. This became evident when on the eve of 1914 some of them began to despair of peaceful progress and to toy with the idea of a general strike to bring about constitutional reform.[1] It was becoming plain that, in Prussia anyhow, Bernstein's prescriptions would not work, and that stronger measures were needed to dislodge the autocracy. This realisation in turn promoted the fortunes of the radical wing, which aimed beyond democracy at a full-blown proletarian revolution, while Bernstein exhausted his ingenuity in elaborate paper schemes for obtaining the support of dissident Liberals in the Prussian pseudo-parliament.[2] These tactics were doomed to failure: there was in fact no way of solving the constitutional problem peacefully, and consequently no genuine choice of tactics. It is humanly understandable that this realisation was unpalatable to men who saw that war was coming and were driven frantic by the thought that in the race between militarism and democracy they were losing ground. But from our present vantage-point it is plain enough that Bernstein and his friends were conducting a fight against hopeless odds. The ruling caste was determined not to permit a significant extension of democracy in Prussia and the Reich; indeed the mere threat of such a development was enough to help precipitate the crisis of 1914 which otherwise might have been postponed for another few years. Germany, in the eyes of the governing caste, depended for its safety on Prussia, and Prussia must stand and fall with its undemocratic constitution which guaranteed the hegemony of the military aristocracy. Before Germany's rulers perforce relinquished this position to the rising democratic tide, they would hasten the inevitable European war while they still held control. All this was becoming plain even before 1914; so was the fact that what Germany needed was not a

---

[1] Schorske, op. cit., pp. 274 ff.

[2] Gay, op. cit., pp. 231 ff; Schorske, op. cit., pp. 171 ff. On the general subject of German imperialism in the Wilhelminian period cf. Eckart Kehr, *Schlachtflottenbau und Parteipolitik, 1894–1901*, Berlin, 1930; G. W. F. Hallgarten, *Imperialismus vor 1914*, Munich, 1951, passim. What those Liberals who, with some misgivings, backed the imperialist course, thought of the matter may be inferred from Max Weber's writings collected in *Gesammelte Politische Schriften* Tuebingen, 1959 ,pp. 109 ff.

socialist but a democratic revolution. It was Bernstein's achievement to have perceived this before anyone else did, but to carry his party along with him, he and his friends would have had to operate in a different environment.

After this lengthy digression it is time to consider the substance of Bernstein's theoretical position. Briefly, it amounted to a repudiation of the analysis enshrined in the Erfurt Programme. Where Kautsky in 1891 had envisaged a bleak future of mounting class tensions, increasing centralisation of wealth, and 'for the proletariat and the submerging middle strata', the certainty of 'growing insecurity, misery, oppression, enslavement, debasement, exploitation',[1] Bernstein in 1899 saw evidence of increasing order, security, tranquillity, prosperity, and more equitable distribution of wealth.[2] Where the Programme held that Marx's pessimistic analysis of social development had been fully borne out by the facts, Bernstein found statistical evidence—warmly contested by his critics—that the middle classes were holding their own, while wage-earners' incomes were rising. Capitalist concentration, in his view, was proceeding rather slowly, and small-scale enterprise continued to flourish alongside the industrial giants. Meanwhile business cycles were tending to flatten out; social tensions were lessening; and ownership of property was becoming more widespread. Since it was impossible to suppose that the actual situation had changed fundamentally between 1891 and 1899, it was apparent that Bernstein and his opponents were looking at the same set of facts through differently coloured glasses. As in the dispute between Kautsky and David over the stability of small-scale peasant farming, neither side managed to persuade the other that its reading of the situation was mistaken, though it is significant that after 1918 they moved much closer together.[3]

Had Bernstein contented himself with disputing the more unrealistic assertions of the Erfurt Programme—notably its tendency to dwell on the 'increasing misery' of the proletariat in a manner more reminiscent of the *Communist Manifesto* than of Marx's and Engels's mature writings—it is probable that his proposed revisions would

[1] *Das Erfurter Programm*, p. 2.

[2] *Voraussetzungen*, pp. 82 ff.

[3] Gay, op. cit., pp. 157–65. In some respects the debate came perilously close to hairsplitting, e.g., over Bernstein's inclusion of minor shareholders among the class of property-owners. To the orthodox, for whom control rather than ownership was the decisive criterion, this of course was simply further proof of Bernstein's tendency to backslide into liberalism.

have been largely accepted. Unfortunately for the cause he was trying to promote, he linked these criticisms to a wholesale onslaught upon every aspect of the Marxian system, from its philosophy of history to its economic doctrine. Here he was clearly out of his depth and no match for the arguments of his opponents. Not that these counter-attacks were uniformly successful; but they proceeded from a firmly held belief in the importance of theoretical coherence, while Bernstein gave the impression of being content with a good deal less. Thus in criticising Marx's value theory—whose shortcomings were indeed obvious—he made the artless suggestion that the truth might lie somewhere midway between the labour-cost approach and the 'marginalist' stress on utility.[1] This kind of eclecticism had other effects besides driving Kautsky to despair: it showed that Bernstein did not really have much of a head for theory, or at any rate that he did not greatly care for theoretical consistency. There were other blunders of the same kind, e.g., his unfortunate attempt to correct the 'one-sidedness' of the materialist conception of history, or his well-meant but singularly naive remarks on the nefarious influence of Hegel. In all these respects he was aiming at something important —a doctrine more inclusive and less rigid than the system constructed by Engels and Kautsky—but the inadequacy of his thinking was painfully evident, not least to the abler among his supporters. These included men professionally versed in philosophy who were understandably alarmed by Bernstein's amateurish incursions into their field. A brief account of these 'revisionists in philosophy' may help to set the subject in perspective.

The first thing to be noted is that almost all the writers in question were Germans, and that most of them had been influenced by the neo-Kantian revival which got under way in the 1870's.[2] This was partly a reaction to the 'vulgar' materialism of the natural scientists; in part it represented an attempt to restore unity and cohesion to the liberal world-view, as originally formulated before the great eruption

[1] Gay, op. cit., pp. 171 ff; Meek, op. cit., pp. 211 ff. For a more recent study of the revisionist debate cf. Christian Gneuss, 'Um den Einklang von Theorie und Praxis. Eduard Bernstein und der Revisionismus', in *Marxismusstudien*, II, pp. 198 ff.

[2] The definitive account of this subject is to be found in Vorländer, op. cit., pp. 112 ff. One needs to remember, though, that the author was himself a distinguished representative of the neo-Kantian school, as well as being a prominent figure in the revisionist movement. For an Hegelian-Marxist (but not Leninist) treatment of the subject, cf. Korsch, *Marxismus und Philosophie*, passim.

of positivism and scientism in the 1850's and 1860's. Being a German movement, neo-Kantianism was naturally dominated by university professors, and at its peak it more or less monopolised the official teaching of philosophy in Germany. Its leading figures (Friedrich Albert Lange, Hermann Cohen, Paul Natorp, Ernst Cassirer), and those who followed in their wake (K. Lasswitz, R. Stammler, F. Staudinger, K. Vorländer, and others), had in common a belief that the urgently necessary integration of philosophy and science could be effected by reviving those elements of 'critical' (i.e., Kantian) thinking which were independent of Kant's purely personal—and thus historically outmoded—notions on metaphysical and ethical subjects: e.g., his half-hearted concessions to the theological world-picture, his modified authoritarianism in politics, and so on. The school, in short, was neo-liberal as well as neo-Kantian and, insofar as it was neo-liberal, critical of the existing state of affairs. It was in particular hostile to every form of authoritarianism in politics or morals. Politically, its influence found expression after 1900 in the increasingly violent attacks which Max Weber—an influential adherent, though not strictly speaking a member of the school—directed against the institutions and the government of Imperial Germany. Mention of Weber, however, also indicates the limits beyond which this privileged and as it were licensed opposition could not be expected to pass (save for those who broke with 'society' and became Social-Democrats). For Weber—though critical of the regime—was unrepentantly National-Liberal and 'imperialist'. Insofar as it had political implications, the school ranged from moderate liberalism to moderate socialism. The 'extremes' were excluded.

At first sight there seems to be no obvious reason why an academic revival of Kant's philosophy—or rather of his methodology, for the neo-Kantians (like the neo-Marxians) rated method above system—should have stirred political echoes. The key to the riddle lies in Germany's incomplete and indeed precarious evolution as a national organism. The Reich had been put together by Bismarck in a manner which left a good many important problems unsolved. In particular, the Conservative-Liberal compromise of 1866–78 had failed to settle the question whether Germany was to evolve along Western lines or retain its famous 'uniqueness': the source of so much nationalist fervour. Corresponding to this political uncertainty there was a spiritual vacuum which attracted socialist criticism on the left and Nietzschean tendencies on the right, while liberalism was increasingly

291

reduced to the status of an academic creed. Although this situation had parallels elsewhere in Europe, there were in Germany's case special aggravating features which were to become more marked in 1914, and disastrously evident in 1933–9. In the perspective of history the neo-Kantian movement can be seen as an unavailing attempt to stiffen the backbone of German liberalism by making it less dependent on the uncertain market values of 'science', 'modernity', 'progress', and other fashionable deities. Not that the neo-Kantians were indifferent to empiricism and the natural sciences; they merely felt that something tougher and more coherent was needed to hold the cultural fabric together. It was this conviction, together with growing scepticism as to the permanence of liberal economics, which caused some of them as early as the 1860's to take a sympathetic interest in socialism.[1]

By the 1890's the process was sufficiently advanced to make it possible for leading neo-Kantians—who were also full-fledged university professors—to draw radical conclusions from Kant's ethics, and even to suggest a thorough-going synthesis of socialism and philosophical idealism.[2] This was about as far as any holder of a university chair in Imperial Germany could venture, Marxism being officially taboo and anyhow incompatible with Kantian idealism, to judge from Engels's pronouncements on the subject. The final and decisive step was taken when a fusion of Kantian ethics and Marxian politics was proposed by writers who were active Social-Democrats and thus outside the official fold. With the appearance of this group—principally L. Woltmann, F. Staudinger, K. Vorländer, C. Schmidt and K. Eisner—the issue ceased to be academic and became political. The question now was not whether a university teacher might profess socialist ideas in his off-hours, but whether active Social-Democrats could adhere simultaneously to Marx and to Kant. Needless to say, Kautsky and Bernstein held different views on this subject. But the matter was

[1] Cf. Vorländer's remarks on F. A. Lange, op. cit., pp. 115 ff. Since Lange was in a sense the founder of the whole movement, it is not without significance that he also counts among the pioneers of social reform. From the Marxian viewpoint he was of course no more than a democrat with vaguely socialist leanings; but in the Germany of his time this was a good deal.

[2] Vorländer, op. cit., pp. 117 ff. The dominant figure of the school, Hermann Cohen (1842–1918) went furthest in this direction, and his pupils came to figure prominently among the revisionist wing of Social-Democracy. But even so outstanding a radical as Karl Liebknecht—later to become the proto-martyr of German Communism—was philosophically an adherent of the neo-Kantian school: a circumstance deplored by his political friends.

not simple, for neo-Kantian tendencies cropped up in the most un-expected places. So prominent a representative of Marxism as the veteran leader of Austrian Social-Democracy, Victor Adler, had sug-gested as early as 1895—in an obituary article on Engels, of all places —that Kant's philosophy was compatible with Marx's sociology and might even be substituted for the materialist world-view without doing damage to the substance of Marxism![1]

Against this murky backcloth the debate at first unrolled in a manner suggestive of a fair degree of tolerance on both sides. There was also much genuine uncertainty. Not all the neo-Kantians were supporters of Bernstein, and vice versa. Some prominent revisionists managed to remain both Kantians and Marxians. Others, such as C. Schmidt, repudiated Kant's ethics while subscribing to his general philosophy.[2] Still others, notably Woltmann, were orthodox fol-lowers of Kant as well as active adherents of Bernstein's political views. Bernstein himself contributed a stream of essays and reviews, starting in the late 'nineties and culminating in 1901, in which he gradually shed his reservations and explicitly affirmed a Kantian standpoint, though his critics (who included the revisionist Socialist and orthodox Kantian K. Eisner) threw doubt on his understanding of Kant's method. The opposing camp likewise was at first far from united. Its principal representatives—Kautsky, F. Mehring, H. Cunow—shared an invincible distaste for philosophical idealism in general, and Kantian moralism in particular, but beyond that they had little in common. How confused the situation was can be seen from the fact that at one stage Kautsky deputed the well-known neo-Kantian F. Staudinger (writing under a pseudonym) to refute Bernstein's philosophical heresies.[3]

Notwithstanding these initial uncertainties, the debate did in the end give rise to something like a philosophical line-up corresponding more or less to the political cleavage. At any rate down to 1914 (when the war produced a major upheaval and even turned old enemies into friends) orthodox Marxism tended to go hand in hand with political

[1] A suggestion energetically disputed by the 'father of Russian Marxism', G. V. Plekhanov; cf. his *Grundprobleme des Marxismus*, Stuttgart, 1910, p. 137. (The German translation of a work originally published in 1908 under the title *Osnovnye problemy marksisma*; English edn., *Fundamental Problems of Marx-ism*, London, 1929.)

[2] Cf. Vorländer, op. cit., pp. 155–85, for a detailed account of the discussion; Bernstein's share in it has more recently been critically analysed by Gneuss, loc. cit., pp. 214 ff.

[3] Vorländer, op. cit., pp. 213 ff.

intransigence, or 'radicalism' as the term was then understood; while the reformist wing, by and large, came to shelter those who toyed with idealism in philosophy. Individual exceptions apart, most of those who tried to 'revise' Marxist philosophy were also revisionists in politics, which in the circumstances of the day meant some degree of accommodation to the *status quo*; while 'materialism' came to be regarded as synonymous with radicalism. This was particularly true of the left wing which emerged after 1905—the date of the first Russian Revolution—as a separate trend; but it also applied to the 'Marxist centre', as represented by Kautsky and his closest adherents. To Kautsky—as to Plekhanov in Russia, Labriola in Italy, and (so far as they understood the issue) Guesde and Lafargue in France—Marxism meant what it had signified to Engels: a 'materialist' world-view which by its nature negated every species of philosophical idealism, including the Kantian variant. Insofar as it required buttressing by the conclusions of science, the proper support was to be found in Darwinism. Kautsky indeed went so far as to put forward what he himself regarded as a satisfactory synthesis of the Darwinian and the Marxian standpoint.[1]

If one takes a severely practical view of historical developments it is tempting to dismiss these longwinded philosophical disputations as mere by-products of the 'real' political and factional struggle within German Social-Democracy. This would be a misconception. The 'real' struggle, as time went on, became divorced from the clash of ideas, but the ideological cleavage helped to cement the political alignments. The famous five-day debate on Bernstein's book at the 1899 party congress had indeed no precise sequel in later years—partly because it became clear that revisionism could not be stoned to death with cream-puffs.[2] Either there must be a split—which in fact came in 1914-18, though not on the issues raised by Bernstein—

[1] Cf. his *Ethik und materialistische Geschichtsauffassung*, Stuttgart, 1906. Notwithstanding a certain banality, this was a more influential work than the bulky treatise of 1927 which disclosed a painful falling-off in mental powers, as well as a marked failure to keep up with the changing situation in philosophy after the first world war.

[2] Cf. *Protokoll ueber die Verhandlungen des Parteitags der Sozialdemokratischen Partei Deutschlands*, Berlin, 1899, pp. 94 ff. No one could say that the annual congress of Germany's greatest party did not take the matter seriously. Bebel's speech attacking the revisionists lasted over three hours, and David replied at similar length, with Woltmann bringing up the rear and Rosa Luxemburg appearing for the extreme left. The result was a massive condemnation of Bernstein's views, which however had no practical consequences.

or the existence of two different schools had to be accepted. Once the latter course had been adopted, it became impossible to dissociate political from ideological considerations. Thus the expulsion of K. Eisner and his colleagues from the editorship of the party's principal daily paper in 1905 was as much connected with Eisner's attachment to Kantian ethics as with his lack of enthusiasm for the idea of political strikes on the Russian model.[1] Of course if one happens to believe that 'practical' politics should be strictly separated from mere ideas, all this must seem very odd, not to say absurd. But then German Social-Democracy around the turn of the century was more than a political movement. Or perhaps one ought to say that its political faith involved ethics as well as economics. At any rate the question whether or not socialism implied a new approach to morals did not seem to the participants to be wholly divorced from more practical and urgent matters.

With these facts in mind we may turn to a brief and necessarily inadequate resumé of the philosophical issue, as it presented itself to most German, Austrian and Russian Socialists down to 1914; Germany being the principal arena, if only because revisionism had its chief strength there.

The first point to be noted is that Bernstein's 'revision', and Kautsky's seemingly orthodox 'interpretation', of Marxism had at least one thing in common: both were equally far removed from the Hegelian origins of Marx's own thought, with the difference that Kautsky was nonetheless at pains to acknowledge the importance of Hegel's philosophy, while Bernstein frankly avowed his distaste for it.[2] Like the great majority of contemporary democrats, both men held an evolutionary view of historical progress. Again, in common with the dominant outlook of the age, their understanding of historical method was coloured by their somewhat uncritical acceptance of the theoretical model employed by the natural sciences. But whereas Kautsky—in conformity with Engels, and under the impulsion of his own life-long preoccupation with Darwin—conceived history as subject to immutable laws, and socialism as the determined goal of this process, Bernstein increasingly shifted the emphasis from causal determination to freedom. Historical necessity, in his view, was gradually giving way to conscious control: men were even now increasingly able to determine their circumstances in accordance with

---

[1] Schorske, op. cit., pp. 70 ff; Vorländer, op. cit., pp. 210 ff.
[2] Bernstein, *Voraussetzungen*, p. 71.

their desires. Indeed the existence of socialist strivings was proof of this. Paradoxically, Bernstein maintained that the goal was desirable just because it was *not* inevitable. Socialism represented 'something that ought to be, or a movement towards something that ought to be'. In this sense it could even be described as 'utopian'. And since it was the realisation of an ideal, its aims could not be deduced from either science or history. They were autonomous and carried their own justification.[1]

This attempted solution satisfied no one. The orthodox were frankly outraged or contemptuous; as they saw it, Bernstein had simply reverted to the pre-Marxian standpoint. Nor were his supporters altogether pleased with his intervention. In particular, his alarmingly vague definition of 'science' caused the stricter neo-Kantians to regard him as a well-intentioned amateur. Nonetheless there was no denying that he had made a breach in the orthodox position. For the first time a prominent Social-Democrat had renounced the entire corpus of doctrine bequeathed by Marx and Engels. If socialism was not the essential precondition of conscious control; if freedom was already operative, in the sense that men were called upon to determine *now* what sort of social organisation they wanted, then the Marxian distinction between 'human pre-history' and 'genuinely human history' went by the board. Bernstein's critique of Marx amounted to saying that the freedom available to men under present-day conditions was already sufficient to enable them to decide their future. If he was right, the gradual establishment of socialism signified no more than a broadening of the area of freedom already attained under liberal democracy. This of course was precisely what Mill had believed to be true; and it was precisely what Marx had regarded as nonsense. On this issue no compromise was possible.

The obverse of this coin was the revisionist assault on what the radicals called 'historical necessity'. To Engels—as to Kautsky, Plekhanov, Labriola, Mehring, Luxemburg, and the orthodox school in general—historical materialism was both the guarantor of the eventual 'leap from necessity to freedom', and the foundation of the view that bourgeois society was altogether subject to the rule of necessity. The 'iron laws' of development were laws precisely because society had no real control over the economic mechanism. If their

[1] Bernstein, *Wie ist wissenschaftlicher Sozialismus moeglich?* Berlin, 1901, passim. Cf. also Vorländer's comment, op. cit., pp. 180 ff; Gay, op. cit., pp. 146 ff.

operation did not literally spell 'increasing misery'—on this point Kautsky at least was prepared to make concessions—it certainly excluded the notion of introducing fresh determinants of the kind envisaged by Bernstein and his friends. Hence it was unrealistic to advocate a piecemeal substitution of socialist for capitalist dynamics. Irrespective of political circumstances—obviously different in Germany from the situation in other countries—it was false in principle to assert that the transition to socialism involved no more than an extension of reformist trends already in evidence: e.g., labour legislation, trade unionism, co-operation, collective bargaining, governmental regulation of the economy, etc. Such tendencies towards a more highly regulated form of society did not alter the basic laws of development described by Marx; they might have the effect of easing the transition, but the break would nonetheless be drastic and fundamental. 'Gradual change' was a fantasy. Socialism, whether or not introduced peacefully by legislation, represented both a new class interest—an aspect neglected by the revisionists—and an altogether new mode of social organisation. It was not, as Bernstein had suggested, the continuation of liberalism's incomplete work of human emancipation, but rather a new stage in history, and consequently—among other things—the precondition of a new ethic and a new manner of viewing the world.

These conclusions were tentatively set out by Kautsky in his polemic against revisionism (*Bernstein und das sozialdemokratische Programm*, 1899) in which he also defended himself with some success against the reproach of advocating 'astronomical' fatalism and elaborated on the quasi-philosophical disputes which grew out of the original quarrel. In the precise sense of the term, Kautsky's position was not really determinist, though its unintended effects operated in that direction. If Bernstein or Eisner saw no incompatibility between socialism and ethical idealism, the orthodox school placed all the greater emphasis upon the class character of the movement as the source of those moral energies whose importance the Marxists too were not disposed to deny.[1] At bottom the quarrel turned on the question whether the class struggle should be viewed as the exclusive motor of progress, political and moral. If socialist morality was essentially the expression of proletarian class interest, it was evidently impossible to subordinate its aims to an allegedly

[1] Kautsky, op. cit., passim; cf. also his article 'Klasseninteresse-Sonderinteresse-Gemeininteresse', in *Neue Zeit*, XXI, 2, pp. 265 ff.

supra-historical ethic binding upon the whole of mankind. Such an ethic could be expected to evolve—if at all—only after the existing society had been left behind. For the revisionists to seek spiritual nourishment in the writings of Kant or some other idealist philosopher, simply showed that they had not really emancipated themselves from utopian socialism, or worse still, liberalism. Yet the Marxists did not deny that moral impulses were present in the attempt to transform society. Was the source of these impulses then to be found only in the circumstances of the political struggle? The revisionists did not think so. As they saw it, socialism was making an appeal to what was fundamental in human nature, as it existed here and now. Moreover, those among them who had grasped the Kantian distinction between empirical and normative thought were well aware of the flaw in the orthodox position: 'science', in the positivist meaning of the term, might show socialism to be inevitable, but could not make it seem morally superior, or explain why anyone should trouble to hasten the process. If Marxism was 'scientific' in this descriptive sense, then it fairly cried out for a normative philosophy to complement its analysis of 'the facts'.

In trying to meet these objections the orthodox school was handicapped by what it regarded as its trump card: the determinist conception of history. For if Marxism was taken to imply that the logic of history was that of a causal process, there was no room for the notion that history might be propelled by human volition directed to the attainment of some final goal. It made little difference whether finality was denied altogether (Plekhanov) or given a biological foundation (Kautsky). In either case 'objective' science could provide no grounds for moral imperatives. Kautsky as good as admitted this when he drew a watertight distinction between 'the moral ideal, the ethical indignation against exploitation and class domination' inherent in the Socialist movement, and 'the scientific study of the laws of development of the social organism' characteristic of Marxism.[1] 'It is true', he added rather helplessly, 'that in the case of a Socialist the thinker is also a fighter, and no one can be artificially cut in two halves having nothing to do with each other; hence there appears occasionally even in Marx's scientific work the impact of a moral ideal. But he always and rightly attempted to eliminate it so far as possible. For in science the moral ideal becomes a source of error if it presumes to prescribe the goal.' With this neat dissection of

[1] *Ethik und materialistische Geschichtsauffassung*, p. 141.

Marxism into a 'scientific' and a 'moral' half, Kautsky had practically demolished his own case and surrendered the disputed ground to Vorländer and the neo-Kantians. For if Marxist theory was the study of objective 'facts'—including such alleged facts as the grounding of history in biological evolution, which Kautsky (in common with Engels) regarded as proved—then it clearly required a normative philosophy of 'values' to complement it: which was precisely what the neo-Kantians were trying to explain to their bewildered and slightly resentful opponents. The intellectual superiority of the revisionist school in this controversy was indeed so marked as to drive the opposing side back upon a somewhat philistine hostility to philosophy as such. So typical a representative of orthodoxy as F. Mehring characteristically mentioned indifference to 'philosophical brain-weaving' among the preconditions of Marx's and Engels's 'immortal achievements'.[1]

It is thus apparent that the revisionist controversy cannot be understood without reference to philosophical issues of the most general kind. For a debate which had originally begun with a pragmatic dispute over political tactics this may seem a queer ending, attributable in part perhaps to the intellectual climate of pre-1914 Germany. There is something in this explanation, but not much. It would be truer to say that the nature of the confrontation was inherent in the character of Social-Democracy as a movement which—in however diluted a fashion—represented the Marxian 'union of theory and practice'. The political attitude of the leading revisionists had general implications because Marxism implied a new world-view. As such it necessarily collided not merely with official religion and the established churches, but with liberalism as well. At the same time its ideology was itself in part derived from the classical philosophy which was also the basic inspiration of the liberal creed. When the revisionists cast around for a new theoretical foundation, they were in fact promoting that political alliance of organised labour with liberalism which the Fabians actually helped to achieve in contemporary England, and which Germany was destined to miss. Material circumstances proved decisive, but the ideological conflict was not meaningless; so far from being a mere epiphenomenon of the 'real' struggle, it was a vital part of it. The consequent failure of German Social-Democracy to win over a sizeable part of the educated middle class, in particular its inability to conquer the universities,

[1] Korsch, *Marxismus und Philosophie*, p. 51.

was to prove fatal to the Weimar Republic. These issues were already involved in the controversy of 1895–1905, though the participants could hardly be expected to realise it.

At the theoretical level, the long-drawn dispute between orthodoxy and revisionism resulted in a stalemate. This situation was especially marked in the philosophical field, where the contestants in the end came to identify their respective positions with the materialist evolutionism expounded by Kautsky, as an alternative to the neo-Kantian ethical idealism of the revisionist school. Here the deadlock was complete. After what has been said in an earlier chapter it is scarcely necessary to remark that this cleavage had its intellectual source in the interpretation given to Marxism by Engels. In this sense the revisionist controversy was part of a larger movement of ideas which, starting in the 1870's, brought about a confrontation of 'scientific materialism' and 'philosophical idealism' all over the Western world. That the split ran right through European Socialism is a tribute to the profound involvement of that movement with the basic issues of its time. Orthodox Marxism, as interpreted by Kautsky or Plekhanov, was in tune with the scientific determinism of the age. Even the philosophical helplessness of the school was after all no greater than that displayed by the founder of psychoanalysis. Its critics had indeed almost a monopoly of genuine philosophical insight. Their concern with normative values reflected the fundamental situation in philosophy; in a wider sense they were giving expression to the main problem confronting the liberal culture of their time. It was of course just this involvement with the problems of liberalism which rendered their efforts unsympathetic and suspect to the Marxists. The latter had meanwhile travelled sufficiently far away from the Hegelian origins of their creed to hold the altogether unwarranted belief that philosophy had been left behind for good. This turned out to be an illusion. The era of war and revolution was to bring about, among other consequences, a revival of Hegelianism at the heart of the Marxian system. Meanwhile the revisionist challenge was giving rise to new groupings and fresh theoretical efforts on the left wing with which we must now concern ourselves.[1]

[1] For a detailed critical account of the subject in the light of subsequent developments cf. I. Fetscher, 'Das Verhaeltnis des Marxismus zu Hegel', in *Marxismusstudien* III, pp. 66–169; the transformation of Marxist philosophy, down to the situation in the Soviet orbit after the Second World War, is here traced to the Hegelian heritage itself; cf. Korsch, op. cit., passim; Georg Lukács, *Geschichte und Klassenbewusstsein*, Berlin-Vienna, 1923, pp. 13 ff.

7

THE RADICALS

IN PROCEEDING FROM the revisionist critics of Marxian orthodoxy to
its radical defenders and heirs, we turn away from the issues predominant in the controversy of 1895–1905. The change of emphasis becomes more marked as time goes on (and as the focus shifts from
Central Europe to Russia), but already in 1905, and even in Vienna,
the intellectual atmosphere differed considerably from that of the
period described in the preceding chapter. This was partly owing to
the change in locale: Vienna, Berlin, Warsaw, and Petersburg
breathed an air quite different from that of Western Europe and
those parts of Germany most subject to Western influence. To some
degree the new mood arose from the Russian upheaval of 1905; and
in part it was due quite simply to the march of time. The post-1905
generation had begun to sense the tremors that presaged the great
upheaval of 1914–18. The problems that concerned it were the likelihood of revolution, as recently demonstrated in Russia; and the
danger of a European war. The latter was seen to arise in part from
traditional national conflicts, but principally from the new imperialist rivalries among the major powers. Revolution and imperialism
were the twin issues around which the neo-Marxist movement grouped
itself; Eastern Germany, Austria, and Russia were the areas of its

greatest strength; and the war of 1914–18 was the test of its doctrines. Beyond Central and Eastern Europe the new school at first could count on scattered support only from the more radical Syndicalists, who for different reasons were becoming critical of 'reformist' Socialism. On the eve of 1914 Marxist radicalism was still for the most part an East European phenomenon. In Germany its adherents were confined to Berlin and a few other centres; and most of its theorists belonged to the Jewish intelligentsia. This alone was enough to cut them off from the masses, though it did not diminish their influence among the minority of active militants who propagated the new doctrine.

The radicals were Marxists who had gone through the revisionist controversy and come out at the other end not merely unshaken in their faith, but more determined than ever to salvage the revolutionary core of Marxism from the temporary accretions of political reformism. Most of them were born between 1870 and 1880, and they thus represented a new generation as well as a new viewpoint. This is important because it helps to account for the difference in outlook noticeable as between the old guard of Marxian orthodoxy—Kautsky, Mehring, Victor Adler, Axelrod, Plekhanov—and the neo-Marxists. What distinguished Rudolf Hilferding (1876–1944), Otto Bauer (1881–1938), Rosa Luxemburg (1870–1919), Martov (1873–1923), Lenin (1870–1924), Trotsky (1879–1940), and Radek (1885–1941), from the older generation was first of all the fact that they had to cope with a new set of problems. That they eventually fell out among themselves, and thus gave rise to rival and violently opposed political currents, is another matter. Prior to 1914–18 they had much in common, and their bitter disputes over tactics and doctrine occurred against the background of certain assumptions foreign to most West European Socialists, including some who regarded themselves as Marxists. The most important of these assumptions was the belief that Eastern Europe—if not Europe as a whole—stood on the eve of an earthquake which would shortly make an end of all talk about peaceful progress.

For purposes of historical comparison, four different and contrasting elements composing the 'generation of 1905' can be distinguished: (1) the Austro-Marxists, with Vienna as their natural centre; (2) the German-Polish group around K. Liebknecht, R. Luxemburg, L. Jogiches, A. L. Parvus, and K. Radek; (3) the Menshevik group, of which Trotsky was *de facto* a member; and (4) the

Bolsheviks around Lenin. All four were involved, though in varying degrees, in the upheaval of 1905–6 which heralded the greater cataclysm of 1917–18; and the effect was to give them a common orientation, at least to the extent of making them aware that the political fortunes of Germany, Austria-Hungary, and Russia, were linked together. This was something Bernstein and his friends never grasped until it was too late, whereas among the older generation Kautsky and Victor Adler had seen it quite clearly. Though politically more moderate than the rival Russian and German-Polish factions, Kautsky's Austrian pupils inherited his conviction that Eastern Europe was about to enter a revolutionary era; and Vienna thus became a centre of political radicalism as well as theoretical Marxism. In this respect it differed from Berlin where left-wing Socialism was a fringe phenomenon confined to intellectuals and a minority of radicalised workers. This state of affairs reflected an important distinction between Germany—now about to make its first bid for European hegemony—and Austria-Hungary, which was visibly falling to pieces already before 1914. In the capital of Imperial Germany, then at the height of its power, even Socialists might think that a revolutionary cataclysm could be avoided; in Vienna such illusions were more difficult to sustain. Here even the most moderate and gradualist of Austrian Social-Democrats could not help noticing that the Habsburg structure had become shaky. Since the neo-Marxist group in Vienna was the oldest of the four, and the one furthest to the right in politics, it is convenient to begin with its leaders.

Karl Renner, Rudolf Hilferding, Otto Bauer, Friedrich Adler, and Max Adler, are commonly regarded as the principal representatives of the Austro-Marxist school. Of the five, Renner (1870–1950) was the senior in years and experience, and the most sympathetic to gradualism. In 1914–18 he adopted the standard patriotic attitude while his more radical associates went into opposition. Yet he continued to regard himself as a Marxist, therein resembling Bernstein with whom indeed he had a good deal in common. Had the Habsburg monarchy as a whole been modelled on German Austria, where the political and cultural ambience resembled that of Southern Germany, his version of democratic Socialism might very early have become the official doctrine of Austrian Social-Democracy. But Vienna before 1918 was the capital of an empire very different in structure from the peaceful Austrian Republic over whose fortunes Renner was to preside after 1945; and Austro-Marxism had to concern itself with national, imperial, and European issues which pointed straight to the cataclysm of 1914–18. Insofar as he became involved in these controversies, Renner sided not merely with the revisionists, but with those Social-Democrats (including the former radical Parvus) who in 1914–18 worked for a German victory and a German-controlled *Mitteleuropa*. This made him anathema to the extreme Left, but it did not mean that he had become uncritical of imperialism. It also did not diminish his standing in the Austrian Socialist movement, of which indeed in some respects he was more representative than the radical theorists who formed the core of Austro-Marxism. Considering the violence provoked by these cleavages elsewhere, it is a remarkable tribute to the maturity of the Viennese group—possibly also a manifestation of the peculiar *genius loci*—that a degree of mutual respect and tolerance was somehow preserved.

If Renner was an untypical adherent of the school, in that he was a Marxist without being a radical, the other members of the group stood close to Kautsky and shared his political outlook. Unlike him they combined firm attachment to doctrine with considerable elasticity in practice. Being younger and more up to date, they managed to straddle some of the issues first raised during the revisionist controversy, without thereby ceasing to be orthodox—at least in their own estimation. Their interests ranged from general ideas to specifically Austrian problems, and the philosopher of the group, Max Adler, was not thought to be less of a Marxist for being a Kantian in his general outlook;[1] any more than Friedrich Adler (another prominent member and subsequently something like a left-wing rebel) incurred suspicions of heresy because he was attracted to the philosophy of Ernst Mach. The very first pronouncement of the group in 1901 was directed against Bernstein, and more generally against the various current attempts to 'revise' Marxism out of existence.[2] Again, when Max Adler and Hilferding came forward in 1904 with a massive symposium of theoretical studies, the editors, for all their proclaimed readiness to 'develop' the inherited corpus of

---

[1] Cf. M. Adler, *Kausalitaet und Teleologie im Streit um die Wissenschaft*, in *Marx-Studien*, I, *Blaetter zur Theorie und Politik des wissenschaftlichen Sozialismus*, ed. Dr. Max Adler and Dr. Rudolf Hilferding, Vienna, 1904, pp. 193–433. For Renner's contribution to this first systematic publication of the Austro-Marxist school, cf. J. Karner (Karl Renner), *Die Soziale Funktion der Rechtsinstitute*, loc. cit., pp. 65–192.

[2] Vorländer, op. cit., pp. 235–6. Hilferding's defence of Marxian economics against Böhm-Bawerk has already been mentioned.

doctrines, expressly laid claim to the title of 'orthodox Marxists':
not without some polemical side-glances at people whose demand for
greater intellectual latitude only served to conceal their lack of a
firm standpoint.[1]

For all these affirmations of doctrinal consistency, the Viennese
neo-Marxists were separated from their elders by the change in the
general intellectual climate which had occurred since the 1880's,
when Engels laid down the principles of orthodox Marxism. The
intervening period had witnessed a revulsion against scientific
materialism and a revival of interest in philosophy; it was this which
had driven the revisionists back to Kant, and correspondingly caused
the defenders of orthodoxy to emphasise their dislike of metaphysics.
The greater sophistication of the Viennese school was immediately
made evident by their ingenious attempt to reconcile the Marxian
analysis of society with a qualified adherence to neo-Kantianism in
philosophy. Marx was discovered to have been primarily a sociologist
—indeed the founder of modern scientific sociology. Epistemological
scruples could be laid at rest by recalling that Kant had preceded
Marx in treating experience as a logical construct.[2] That Marx had
been seemingly unaware of this fact was readily explained in terms
of his intellectual upbringing: in the 1830's and 1840's Kant had been
temporarily eclipsed by Hegel, whose metaphysical system nonetheless rested upon Kantian foundations, inasmuch as it was Kant who
introduced the 'critical' method into philosophy. In short, Marxian
sociology was fully compatible with Kantian philosophy. More than
that: Marx's analysis of social reality in *Capital* (a work not accidentally sub-titled *Critique of Political Economy*) had been essentially
Kantian in spirit, seeing that his method consisted in isolating the

[1] Preface to *Marx-Studien*, pp. v–vii. Not surprisingly the new venture was
welcomed by a reviewer in Kautsky's *Neue Zeit*, vol. XXIII, pp. 196 ff,
242 ff.

[2] M. Adler, loc. cit., passim; cf. also his lecture on the centenary of Kant's
death, February 9, 1904, reprinted in M. Adler, *Kant und der Marxismus*,
Vienna, 1925. Of Adler's numerous writings, his two anniversary essays, *Marx
als Denker* (Berlin, 1908), and *Engels als Denker* (Berlin, 1920), may be mentioned for their somewhat simplified exposition of his really quite complex
approach. The latter is lengthily expounded in *Das Soziologische in Kants
Erkenntniskritik*, Vienna, 1924. For Adler's critique of Kautsky's naïve positivism, cf. Vorländer, pp. 244–5. The whole discussion is still of interest to
historians of modern philosophy, its intellectual level being at least equal to
that of the contemporary debate among the neo-Kantians—Rickert, Simmel,
Stammler, and Windelband—on the methodology of the natural and historical
sciences.

logic of the economic process by abstracting from the surface phenomena present to mere uncritical reflection, and thus penetrating to
the reality concealed behind them.[1] For Marx as for Kant, the world
of experience was not simply 'given', but mediated by the human
mind. His theory was a 'critique' in the Kantian sense, specifically
a critique of *society*. The latter was to be understood as a living
totality of material forces and ideal (psychological) strivings, the
social organism being subject to historical 'laws' (processes) which
in the last resort yield a rational harmony of individual and social
interests. Human activity (practice) realises the aims of philosophy,
the latter being nothing but the ideal norms of human nature cor-
rectly understood, i.e., nature actuated by reason. Scientific and
normative thinking have their common denominator in the critical
understanding of what it is that constitutes man's social being. There
is no unbridgeable gulf between science and ethics, causal laws and
ideal aims, materialism and philosophy. One can be a scientific
sociologist and at the same time subscribe to the aims of Socialism,
since the latter are grounded in a critical perception of the social
whole as it affects each individual. A rational order would be a
Socialist one, hence rationality tells us how we ought to act. Thus
Adler, whose ingenious synthesis of neo-Marxism and neo-Kantianism gained the support of the Viennese school, though Kautsky
remained sceptical and publicly regretted the young generation's
tenderness for idealist moral philosophy.[2]

Though the historian of ideas turns with some reluctance from
these philosophical disputations to the rather less fascinating subject
of economics, it must be confessed that the real achievement of
Austro-Marxism did not lie in the field of general philosophy. However highly one rates M. Adler's intellectual *tour de force*, it did not
signify a theoretical break-through. On the other hand, Otto Bauer's
work on the national question, and Rudolf Hilferding's study of
finance capitalism, represented something new and important. The
two works are best considered jointly, for despite their dissimilar
starting-points they terminate in an analysis of imperialism which

---

[1] M. Adler, *Kausalitaet und Teleologie*, loc. cit., pp. 316 ff; cf. also *Marx als
Denker*, passim; *Engels als Denker*, pp. 45 ff. In the last-mentioned essay, the
point is made that Marx's so-called 'materialism' was simply 'the positivism
of modern science', not an application of philosophical materialism in the
traditional meaning of the term (p. 50).

[2] Cf. his lengthy debate with Otto Bauer in *Neue Zeit*, 1905-6, II, pp. 485-99,
516-29; for a critical review of the discussion cf. Vorländer, pp. 250 ff.

was to become the special characteristic of the neo-Marxist school.[1] Both men owed more to Kautsky than is generally recognised. In other respects their writings hardly bear comparison. Bauer's erudite volume of almost 600 pages appeared when its author was all of twenty-six years old, and though a brilliant achievement for so youthful a writer, it rather lacked finish. The book's lengthy theorising about the sources of national culture, the origins of European history, and the nature of the Jewish problem, makes quaint reading today, and even in 1907 some readers must have had difficulty struggling through a mountain of information on the Austrian nationality problem before arriving at Bauer's theory of imperialism. It was this which established him as a new magnitude in the field of Marxist scholarship, though within three years his brilliant sketch was to be superseded by Hilferding's massive treatise. In passing it may be remarked that for all its weaknesses and its occasional touches of naïvete, Bauer's analysis of the national question in Eastern and Central Europe was so far superior to the subsequent productions of the Leninist school that only the massive ignorance of an age fed on popular pseudo-histories can account for its present relative neglect.

What Bauer has to say about imperialism is of importance, although in the light of later developments his essay today reads like an anticipation of Hilferding's more systematic theorising on the subject. His starting-point is the growth of global rivalries and the consequent relative shrinkage of interest in purely European affairs.[2] The question he raises is why the great powers increasingly tend to place their foreign and military policies in the service of expansion to the less developed regions of the globe, and the explanation he suggests is that the periodic cyclical depressions characteristic of capitalism accentuate the urge of capital to secure guaranteed spheres of influence in pre-industrial countries, where investment opportunities are better and profit rates higher. Put thus baldly the argument sounds both trite and doctrinaire, but Bauer backed it with a detailed analysis of protectionist policies under conditions of industrial cartelism. He thus helped to popularise a thesis which has now become familiar, but was far from being widely accepted in the first decade

---

[1] O. Bauer, *Die Nationalitaetenfrage und die Sozialdemokratie*, in *Marx-Studien*, II, Vienna, 1907; R. Hilferding, *Das Finanzkapital*, Vienna, 1910. For Renner's view of imperialism (which for the most part derived from Bauer and Hilferding, though his political attitude differed from theirs) cf. his *Marxismus, Krieg und Internationale*, Vienna, 1917.

[2] *Die Nationalitaetenfrage etc.*, pp. 461 ff.

of the century.[1] Moreover, he did not content himself with stating the obvious, namely that protectionism makes it possible for cartelised industries to dump their products abroad; he also stressed that free-trading England was the chief victim of the protectionist policies adopted by other nations, notably Germany and the United States.[2] At the same time he closed the circle of his own argument, which had started from a description of the nation-forming process, by suggesting that imperialism was making an end of nationalism in the older liberal-cosmopolitan sense of the term.[3]

Some of Bauer's theses were not strictly related to his views on protection, but rather derived, in a somewhat doctrinaire fashion, from the Marxian value concept. From this he deduced that in any exchange between industrialised and backward areas, even under complete free trade and in the absence of political control, surplus value is pumped out of the latter into the former, because the 'higher organic composition' of capital under advanced technological conditions means that surplus profit accrues in a proportion favouring the capitalists of the more industrial region, at the expense of those with whom they trade.[4] This argument had the interesting, though possibly unintended, consequence of suggesting that imperialism was primarily a relationship between industrial and agricultural countries, the former supplementing their normal trade profits by subjugating the latter. It would seem that Bauer adopted this notion from Kautsky, who first formulated it in 1901 and then elaborated it in 1914—much to the indignation of Lenin, to whom it was proof of Kautsky's unwillingness to regard imperialism as a necessary outcrop of monopolistic capitalism.[5] If one takes Bauer's somewhat confused presenta-

---

[1] Cf. Schumpeter, *Imperialism and Social Classes*, pp. 104 ff. It is noteworthy that Schumpeter in this essay, written during the first world war and originally published in 1919 ('Zur Soziologie der Imperialismen', *Archiv fuer Sozialwissenschaft und Sozialpolitik*, vol. 46) takes a more favourable view of the Bauer-Hilferding analysis of imperialism than in his later writings.

[2] Bauer, op. cit., p. 468.   [3] Ibid., pp. 473 ff.

[4] Bauer, op. cit., pp. 246 ff; for a different view cf. Sweezy, *The Theory of Capitalist Development*, pp. 290–1. As Sweezy notes, Bauer's position was later taken by H. Grossman, in *Das Akkumulations- und Zusammenbruchsgesetz des kapitalistischen Systems*, pp. 431 ff; cf. also M. Dobb, *Political Economy and Capitalism*, pp. 223 ff.

[5] Cf. Lenin, *Imperialism, the Highest Stage of Capitalism*, in V. I. Lenin, *Selected Works*, London, 1947, vol. I, pp. 710 ff; for Kautsky's views cf. *Neue Zeit*, vol. XXXII, part II, Sept. 11, 1914, p. 909; vol. XXXIV, part II, pp. 107 ff. The first formulation of Kautsky's thesis occurs in his *Handelspolitik und Sozialdemokratie* (1901), a work which had a considerable influence on Bauer and Hilferding.

tion of the subject as a whole, the stress of his argument would seem to lie on the idea that capitalist expansion leads to imperialist annexation because under modern conditions the strongest concentrations of capital—the cartelised industries and their allies, the banks—require guaranteed markets and politically controlled fields of investment from which foreign competitors are excluded. His attitude towards this development was somewhat ambiguous and even left room for the suggestion that the whole process is economically progressive, in that it equalises profit rates and helps to establish a global economy. 'What was effected by the establishment of an ordered system of courts and administration within the European countries, is now being accomplished everywhere by modern militarism and marinism. The navies of the European powers are so to speak the world police, which everywhere establishes the requisite legal conditions for the investment of European capital.'[1] He even conceded that the workers might profit from protectionism and expansionism, at any rate in their capacity as producers, though on balance the adverse effects of cartels and tariffs were harmful to their interests as consumers.[2] From this it followed for Bauer that the working class would tend to adopt an attitude of sober financial accounting in judging the promised fruits of imperial expansion. 'It desires to establish in each case whether the favourable results of imperialism are worth the sacrifice.'[3] It is only when the political consequences of imperialism—mounting armaments, weakening of parliamentary control, spread of authoritarian attitudes at home—come into play that this systematic distrust changes into open hostility on the part of the class-conscious workers. Hence, Social-Democracy and imperialism are incompatible, the more so since imperialism clearly heightens the danger of war, while at the same time it undermines democracy at home. It will be seen that Bauer takes some time to arrive at this conclusion, which in the end rests upon non-economic considerations: chiefly motivated in his case by the conviction that Social-Democracy safeguarded the long-term aspirations of labour by

[1] Bauer, op. cit., p. 470.

[2] Ibid., pp. 476 ff. For a critique of the belief that export dumping and protection offer economic benefits to the workers, cf. Schumpeter, op. cit., pp. 111 ff. His argument in this passage is explicitly directed against 'neo-Marxist doctrine' which concedes the possibility of such temporary benefits: an instance of Liberal anti-imperialism showing greater theoretical (and political) consistency than the rival Socialist school.

[3] Bauer, op. cit., p. 487.

transcending its narrower short-term economic interests. Though impeccable in logic, such a conclusion could hardly have been stated in these terms without giving rise to some rather awkward questions. For if labour's long-term and short-term interests were not identical, but required to be harmonised by a party which yet regarded itself as the 'expression' of proletarian class interest, it was at least conceivable that a situation might arise in which people would prefer to follow a rival movement which promised them more immediate satisfactions: at the expense of conquered races and in the name of 'National Socialism'. It was to be Bauer's misfortune that in the 1930's such a situation did in fact arise, and that his party proved helpless to meet it.[1]

For all its ingeniousness, Bauer's cursory sketch of the subject (casually included within the context of a massive study of Central and Eastern European national and political problems on the eve of 1914) was hardly more than a harbinger of later systematic studies. The task of underpinning the embryonic theory of imperialism suggested in the writings of Kautsky fell to another member of the Viennese group who had the advantage of being a trained economist. In 1910 Rudolf Hilferding came forward with a massive treatise whose very title, *Das Finanzkapital*, proclaimed its author's belief that the time had come to bring Marx up to date. Sub-titled 'A study on the most recent development of capitalism', Hilferding's work at once established its author as the leading authority in the field of neo-Marxian economics, and for good measure enabled every contemporary Socialist (including Lenin) to relate the theory of imperialism to the analysis of monopoly and protection. This was something the academic economists had failed to see, economic sociology not being their strong point. It was left to the neo-Marxians to describe the

---

[1] Cf. Bauer, *Zwischen zwei Weltkriegen*, Bratislava, 1936. Written after the rise of Fascism in Central Europe and the temporary eclipse of the labour movement, this final production of the Austro-Marxist school may be regarded as its author's political testament. Though conceived under circumstances very different from the hopeful anticipations of 1906, it displays the same unshakeable confidence in the ultimate triumph of democratic socialism. There was a remarkable consistency in Bauer's outlook: he had no illusions about the 'revolutionary proletariat'—in fact he said bluntly that it could exist only where capitalism and democracy were not yet fully developed (op. cit., pp. 243 ff)—but he relied on the internal dynamic of class conflict under capitalism to bring about the socialist transformation. As he saw it, capitalism and democracy were becoming incompatible, and it was just this which would compel the labour movement to abandon its reformist illusions and undertake the conquest of political power.

'functional change in protectionism' which enabled cartelised or trustified industries to turn tariffs to their advantage, while at the same time engaging in a policy of price dumping and intensified capital export abroad.[1]

Hilferding's argument—in this part of his work, for he also goes at great length into other subjects, e.g., monetary management and the theory of banking—may be summarised as follows: the growing concentration of corporate ownership in all major industrial countries has the effect of narrowing the range of competition, while at the same time it creates a homogeneous class of decision-makers in charge of the leading banks and industrial monopolies. It thus makes possible a degree of conscious control over the economy, but 'in antagonistic forms', i.e., without eliminating the conflicting class interests characteristic of capitalism. The contradiction between the rational management of particular branches of production, and the basic irrationality of the system as a whole, finds expression in attempts to 'plan' those sections of the economy which have fallen under corporate control: either in the form of cartels (i.e., producers' associations to keep prices high and stable), or unified combines (trusts) controlled by the largest investment banks. The counterpart of this increasing trend towards monopoly is the growth of tariff protection, which in turn favours the formation of further cartels and trusts, until the entire economy of the country in question is controlled by them—a monopolistic price policy requiring an adequate tariff wall in order to become effective. Nationally, this trend leads to the gradual disappearance of competition and the subordination of the smaller entrepreneurs to the large corporations, which for technical reasons are strongest in heavy industry. Internationally, it eliminates free trade and thereby intensifies political antagonisms. For whereas under free trade 'foreign' markets and raw material sources are in principle as accessible to all as 'domestic' ones, protection—when allied to cartelisation and monopoly—leads to a state of affairs where rival groups in different countries seek to monopolise markets and raw material sources. The home market needs to be protected by tariffs so that the cartelised industries may be able to raise

---

[1] Schumpeter, op. cit., pp. 104 ff. Once the point had been grasped, Liberal and Socialist critics of protectionism and imperialism had a common platform: witness Schumpeter's account of the subject, which is simply a summary of the Austro-Marxist argument in terms of Austro-Liberalism, i.e., minus Hilferding's assertion that free trade was dead and protectionist monopoly had come to stay.

prices, while abroad they pursue a policy of dumping to get rid of products unsaleable at home at the higher price. Thus whereas in the formative stage of capitalist industrialisation tariffs needed only to be high enough to equalise the chances of domestic producers (the 'infant industry' argument), their purpose now is to exclude all foreign imports which might compete with the monopolies. Since the competing groups of 'national' monopolies, and their respective states, pursue the same incompatible aim of protection at home and intensified dumping abroad, the result is economic warfare which threatens to turn into political and military warfare. Colonial imperialism, i.e., armed expansion into undeveloped regions, is a by-product of this process, for in conjunction with tariff protection it enlarges the area controlled by the national monopolies. The end result of this contest is war, or at least warlike tendencies on the part of the nations concerned. Thus in the last analysis the centralisation of capital leads to international anarchy, mounting national antagonisms, and finally armed conflict.[1]

Two further points are noteworthy: first, the entire argument is derived from Marx's analysis of capitalist concentration, notably in *Capital*, vol. III, though the growth of protectionism and monopoly described by the neo-Marxians was a more recent phenomenon, of which Engels had barely glimpsed the first signs when he came to edit Marx's manuscripts. Secondly, the thesis does not depend on the Marxian theorem—freely employed by Hilferding—concerning the falling rate of profit. Though he abandoned the perspective of automatic breakdown, Hilferding was sufficiently orthodox to maintain that the average rate of profit tends to decline with the growing 'organic composition' of capital, and that this trend reinforces the drive to equalise profit rates by eliminating competition.[2] But his argument is not logically dependent on this assumption, and the process of cartelisation, growing tariff protection, and intensified national

[1] Hilferding, op. cit., pp. 234 ff, 265 ff, 400 ff, 416 ff. The above is of course a very schematic outline; for details cf. Sweezy, op. cit., pp. 254 ff. Schumpeter's very similar analysis, loc. cit., pp. 104 ff, includes a summary of Hilferding's thesis which is rather more concise and less doctrinaire than Sweezy's elaborate attempt to rephrase the Austro-Marxist theory in Leninist language.

[2] *Das Finanzkapital*, pp. 242-5. The argument turns upon the fact that it is the capital-intense industries which stand to gain from the elimination of competition, because their superior equipment enables them to appropriate part of the profit which under genuine competition would accrue to the less advanced branches of industry; they are thus enabled to offset the fall in the average rate of profit. (All references are to the 1920 edn.).

competition, can be plausibly traced to the functioning of the economic mechanism without attempting to decide whether there is in fact a long-range tendency for the average rate of profit to decline. This naturally extends to the political consequences as well: other Socialists did not have to share all his assumptions in order to realise that what he called 'the economic policy of finance-capital'[1] must necessarily turn economic rivalries into political conflicts. In fact the same conclusion could be drawn by writers who started from the conventional free-trade premises.

If the whole argument has come to sound familiar and even somewhat trite, one reason is that for the past forty years it has been popularised in Leninist literature, when it was not quietly taken over and adapted by Liberal critics of imperialism. The reader of Lenin's well-known study on imperialism—written in 1916, but against the background of a discussion already in progress since 1902—is hard put to discover anything not already said by either Hilferding or Hobson. This, however, only applies to its rather slender theoretical content. The *political* bias of Lenin's pamphlet differs strikingly from the productions of the Austro-Marxist school. In particular, there is not a great deal in the earlier literature to prepare the reader for Lenin's highly charged picture of imperialism as a system 'for oppressing a thousand million people (in the colonies and semi-colonies), that is, more than half the population of the globe', in the interest of an increasingly parasitic group of 'civilised' Western countries. Some such conclusion could indeed be drawn from the theoretical premises worked out by Bauer and Hilferding, but Lenin's simplified version ignored what was essential to the neo-Marxian thesis: the notion that, insofar as the whole process served to equalise profit rates and promote capital exports to backward countries by 'policing' the latter, it was still rational, even though its peculiar rationality was increasingly undermined by the danger of war. As was usual with him, Lenin disregarded these subtleties and contented himself with the part of the argument that could be put to immediate political use.[2]

[1] Op. cit., pp. 400 ff; the implication being that the banks are the ultimate controllers of the whole process. This was questionable even when he wrote, and is certainly not true today, but the argument does not depend on it.

[2] Cf. Lenin, *Imperialism*, loc. cit., pp. 646, 688, 699 ff, 717 ff. Anyone curious to trace the sources of the anti-Western bias prominent in Soviet thinking is well advised to ponder these instructive passages. By previous Marxist standards Lenin's pamphlet was a rather poor performance, but it has been immensely influential for reasons having little to do with its meagre intellectual content.

In 1914–18 a situation favouring the spread of some such simplified theoretical model had clearly arisen, but it needed the Bolshevik conquest of power in 1917 to replace the hitherto accepted Marxist critique of imperialism by the much cruder Leninist doctrine. On its own merits Lenin's war-time pamphlet would have failed to impress even contemporary Russian Marxists, let alone those of other countries. After 1917 intellectual considerations increasingly gave place to political and propagandist criteria. Even so, the prolonged discussion among Marxist economists in the 1920's and 1930's on the innate tendencies of capitalist accumulation owed nothing to Lenin, and those Soviet theoreticians who took part in it tacitly followed the example of their Western colleagues in treating the Leninist concept as a *political* doctrine.[1]

More will have to be said on this subject. For the moment let us turn to the other important group of Marxist theorists active on the eve of 1914: the German-Polish radicals around Rosa Luxemburg, and their few but influential Russian adherents, notably Trotsky. Here again a brief introductory note on the political background imposes itself before considering their long-range ideas. Since the leading figures of the group were full-fledged theoreticians, the distinction is somewhat artificial, but it cannot be avoided. The closer one approaches the great cataclysm of 1914–18, the more difficult it becomes to separate the politics of Marxist radicalism from its doctrinal pronouncements; yet somewhere there is a dividing-line. Rosa Luxemburg's controversial theory of imperialism, for example, was not logically related to her political activities in the East European Socialist movement, though it clearly had some bearing on her anti-war stand in 1914–18. Few Russian or Polish Socialists of the time were greatly concerned to know whether she was right or wrong to take a critical view of Marx's theory of accumulation. What mattered to them was her hostile attitude towards the Polish national movement, and her consistent support of the Menshevik group in the struggle within Russian Social-Democracy. Conversely, her German

---

[1] Cf. N. Bukharin, *Der Imperialismus und die Akkumulation des Kapitals*, Vienna-Berlin, 1926, passim. Being then the chief exponent of Soviet Marxism, Bukharin naturally paid tribute to Lenin's views on the subject of imperialism (loc. cit., pp. 123–6), but he was too good an economist to pretend that Lenin had much to say on the theoretical side of the matter. Such notions had to await a more propitious intellectual climate. For Bukharin's earlier, and rather academic, disputation with the Austrian marginalists cf. his *Economic Theory of the Leisure Class* (1919).

friends, who greatly valued her theoretical acumen, were largely in-different to her involvement in what appeared to them an obscure factional wrangle among Russian and Polish Socialists. And indeed the two sets of circumstances were quite distinct, though they came together in the thinking of East European Marxists—chiefly Luxemburg, to a lesser extent Trotsky and Radek—who happened to be concerned both with the approaching East European upheaval *and* with the debate on the causes of international rivalry. The latter problem concerned Germany principally in its capacity as a European country in competition with England; while the complex issue of 'proletarian revolution' was primarily relevant in Russia, where indeed a dress rehearsal had already occurred in 1905. Still, Central Europe—Germany and Austria-Hungary—extended sufficiently far east for the more alert minds to be aware of both sets of problems, while Russian emigrants in Vienna or Berlin might do likewise.[1] This was the background to such intellectual productions as Rosa Luxemburg's doctrine of revolutionary radicalism, or the 'permanent revolution' concept elaborated by her associate Parvus in 1904 (with some assistance from the youthful Trotsky). Unless it is kept in mind that the questions prominent in all this theorising stemmed from two different sets of circumstances, it is easy to underrate the intellectual ingenuity required to bring them together. On the other hand, it ought to be remembered that the protagonists occupied a kind of political no-man's-land between Germany and Russia, peopled for the most part by national minorities—including the numerous and important Jewish minority—and not really quite in tune with the dominant strivings in either of these two great centres of power (not to mention the Western world, whose peculiarities even Germans found it a little difficult to grasp).[2]

[1] For a non-Marxist study of the Russian political situation by a contemporary thinker who was alive to the coming world-political upheaval, cf. Max Weber, 'Zur Lage der buergerlichen Demokratie in Russland', and 'Russlands Uebergang zum Scheinkonstitutionalismus' (1906), both in Max Weber, *Gesammelte politische Schriften*, Tuebingen, 1959, pp. 30–65 and 66–108.

[2] For R. Luxemburg's theory of imperialism, cf. *Die Akkumulation des Kapitals*, first edn. 1913, new edn. in *Gesammelte Werke*, Berlin, 1923, vol. VI (including her reply to critics); English edn. (minus the anti-critique, but with a preface by Joan Robinson), London, 1951. This is by far her most important work; her political writings, originally published in the *Gesammelte Werke* of 1923–31, have become largely unavailable, save for a characteristically inadequate and tendentious two-volume selection published after the war in East Germany: *Ausgewaehlte Reden und Schriften*, Berlin, 1951.

Bearing in mind then that our two points of reference are, on the one hand, the Russian upheaval of 1905, and on the other, the growing international tension which finally exploded in 1914; and that the theorising to which these events gave rise at first possessed no common denominator—we are in a better position to answer the question what exactly it was that radical Marxism stood for during this period. To some extent the answer is implicit in the question. For if the coming Russian cataclysm was only externally connected with the approaching world war—in the sense that Tsarism was likely to collapse under the strain of conflict, and thus open the road to revolution—any theorist who tried to relate these two sets of issues was really confronted with a quite desperate task. It speaks for the ingenuity of the leading Marxist radicals that in the end they did manage to evolve a doctrine which appeared to make sense of the situation. This notable *tour de force* was primarily the achievement of four writers—Luxemburg, Parvus, Radek, and Trotsky—two of whom were subsequently to play a key role in the Communist International. This in itself suggests one reason for the ultimate failure of that organisation to make a more lasting impact on the Socialist movement in Western Europe: the circumstances of its birth predisposed even its most learned and ingenious theorists towards plausible but erroneous syntheses, on the pattern of the rather more successful thinking they had developed down to 1914. The most celebrated example—Trotsky's 'permanent revolution' concept—is somewhat outside the subject of this study, the more so since Trotsky went on refining his thesis throughout the 1920's and 1930's; but since the idea goes back to the pre-1914 discussion, it must be briefly considered before we move on to Rosa Luxemburg's rather more consequential theory of imperialism.[1]

The basic notion—which seems to have occurred first to A. L. Parvus (then a close associate of Rosa Luxemburg) in 1904—was that modern capitalism had outgrown the existing political system. In particular the European nation-state had become too small for the coming age of global contests, and was doomed to disappear in a series of frightful convulsions which would leave only the strongest and best-equipped empires standing amidst universal wreckage. This

[1] For an account of the Parvus-Trotsky partnership cf. I. Deutscher, *The Prophet Armed*, London-New York, 1954, pp. 98 ff; Trotsky's ideas on the subject are scattered throughout his voluminous writings, starting with a pamphlet he wrote in 1906 and climaxing in his *History of the Russian Revolution* (1930–2).

was not indeed an altogether novel thought; many leading political figures of the time held that there was a tendency for larger supranational agglomerations to be formed. The imperialist movement in the Britain of Joseph Chamberlain, and in the America of Theodore Roosevelt, drew a good deal of stimulus from this prospect. So did some of the leading Fabians and revisionists in England and Germany. But Parvus gave a startling emphasis to the idea by linking it to the notion of capitalism as an economic system propelled forward by crises in which the weaker went to the wall. He also took a more pessimistic view than other contemporaries of the European nation-state, which on his reading was unlikely to survive the coming collision between the imperial giants; and lastly, he connected this analysis with the approaching revolution in Russia. For in this new perspective Russia was the weak link in the global chain, owing to its political and social backwardness, for which the Tsarist regime had no cure. As Parvus saw it, the coming revolution would do more than modernise the country and render it fit to participate in the power struggle for global domination. Already in 1905 the alignment of forces within the revolutionary movement was such that a proletarian upheaval was probable, which in turn could not fail to react upon the political climate of the more advanced countries. 'The Russian revolution will shake the bourgeois world . . . and the Russian proletariat may well play the part of vanguard of the social revolution.'[1] At the time this seemed an improbable forecast, but the youthful Trotsky was impressed and employed it henceforth in support of his own belief that the coming upheaval in Russia would lead straight to a socialist dictatorship. This in turn—since such a regime could not long maintain itself in backward Russia—must seek to establish links with revolutionary movements in more advanced countries. The further perspective evidently rested on the assumption that the industrial countries—specifically the European nations, now faced with a transformation which threatened their independence—would be compelled to relinquish both their traditional political structure and their socio-economic system: the two being linked, since European capitalism had grown up together with the nation-state and could not well survive the disappearance of its political carapace. Hence the coming revolution would be both international and socialist. Whatever may be thought of the rather sweeping fashion in which this synthesis was put together by its authors, one cannot fail to admire the intellectual

[1] *Iskra*, no. 82, January 1905 (quoted by Deutscher, loc. cit., p. 104).

boldness and ingenuity that went into it. Events did not in the end shape themselves quite in accordance with the forecast, but after two world wars the picture has certainly come a good deal closer to the revolutionary prospectus of 1905 than to the rather more common-place expectations of the moderate school.[1]

So far we have looked at the 'permanent revolution' concept in terms of what it implied for the world as a whole, and more particularly for Europe. But the phrase already had a precise significance in Marxist thinking, going back to Marx's writings during the 1848–52 period, where 'permanent revolution' signified a *national* upheaval patterned on the French model of 1789–94. The roots of this conception—as was shown earlier—were essentially Jacobin-Blanquist, and this portion of the Marxian inheritance could with the greatest ease be related to the strategy of the coming Russian revolution—as indeed was being done by all factions of Russian Marxism.[2] What then was the connection between this familiar and as it were traditional employment of the term 'permanent revolution' (meaning a democratic revolution climaxing in 'proletarian dictatorship'), and the Parvus-Trotsky forecast of a coming world-wide upheaval? The answer is that the link was chiefly verbal; or, if one prefers it, the connection existed in Trotsky's mind before it was established in reality. Not that it was difficult to draw a plausible picture wherein the Russian Revolution—both before and after its actual occurrence —figured as a key element in a global transformation. But though almost every Marxist before 1914 toyed with this notion, Trotsky was unique in going through with it and building an entire political

---

[1] With two qualifications: the reader who remembers Kautsky's sombre prognosis of 1902 (cf. supra) will realise that the left-wing radicals were not really quite as original as all that; and secondly, some of the revisionists were equally apocalyptic in their vision of the shape of things to come. It is also worth noting that in 1914 Parvus himself went over to the extreme right-wing group within German Social-Democracy, which preached support for a Pan-German *Mitteleuropa* (and war to the bitter end against 'plutocratic' England) in the name of—socialism! But all this does not lessen interest in the genesis of an intellectual construction which was in part inherited by the Leninists and thus became an integral element of the Soviet Communist world-view.

[2] For a summary of the discussion cf. L. H. Haimson, *The Russian Marxists and the Origins of Bolshevism*, Harvard, 1955, passim. It is evidently impossible to list even a fraction of the literature on this subject, since to do so would be to take in the entire controversy over Lenin's tactics in 1905 and 1917, as well as the subsequent dispute over Trotsky's role. Here it is merely intended to indicate the link between this well-worn topic and the pre-1914 debate among European Socialists.

world-view on it. He alone among East European Marxists maintained from the start that the imperialist era, the crisis of the European nation-state, the revolution in Russia, and the imminent collapse of capitalism as a global system, were *organically* linked, so that the 'world revolution' could not even be conceived, let alone directed, in terms of a series of unconnected happenings. Least of all was he prepared to accept the 'reformist' view—which eventually became that of his former Menshevik associates—that only advanced industrial countries were ripe for (gradual and piecemeal) socialisation. On this issue he stood ready in 1917 to throw in his lot with Lenin, however much he might differ from him in other matters. Hence when all is said and done, Trotsky must be allowed his claim to have anticipated the Leninist standpoint of 1917, when Bolshevism became what it had not been before: a world-revolutionary doctrine.[1]

After this lengthy digression—made necessary by the remarkable consistency of Trotsky's thinking, which on this pivotal question never really altered in essentials between 1905 and his death in 1940 —we are obliged to retrace our steps so as to consider the other notable intellectual production of the school: Rosa Luxemburg's theory of capitalist development. Here the ground is more familiar and less encumbered by political land-mines, for in her theoretical work R. Luxemburg was quite simply a—slightly unorthodox—follower of Marx. Her politics are another matter. They were in part animated by a species of Syndicalist romanticism, and for the rest they related to three different, though concentric, circles: German Social-Democracy; the Polish Socialist movement (within which she championed the unpopular anti-nationalist position); and the Russian revolutionary movement, where she generally supported the Mensheviks, or at any rate the Menshevik group led by Martov (and occasionally by Trotsky) which was reliably internationalist. All this is of importance to the history of Socialism, but we cannot deal with it here and must content ourselves with considering her contribution to Marxist theory.

This took the form of a critical investigation into certain aspects of

[1] This topic has been debated at such length in the writings of Trotskyist and Stalinist partisans that an enumeration of the relevant passages would be both impracticable and pointless. It must be sufficient to say that Trotsky's writings (as well as the biographical studies devoted to him by his followers and others) have consistently stressed this theme. The best summary of his position is still to be found in his pamphlet *Die Permanente Revolution*, Berlin, 1930, where his principal literary target turns out to be—his old associate Radek!

Marx's theory of the capitalist process, coupled with an attempt to suggest an economic explanation of the manner in which industrial capital expands into backward areas. So far as subject-matter is concerned we are thus back with the theme of the Austro-Marxist school, but Luxemburg's concern with the question of how capitalism manages to avert automatic breakdown pointed forward to the discussions of the 1930's.[1] That is why her work, for all its analytical faults, strikes today's reader as relevant. The twin points of her analysis—capital accumulation in a 'closed' system, and capital expansion into pre-industrial areas—are of obvious importance to any theory, liberal or socialist, which seeks to explain the mechanism of economic growth. But the immediate political relevance of her thesis, as formulated in 1913, lay in a different context: by appearing to have demonstrated that capital accumulation was impossible in a closed system, and that capitalism could maintain its rhythm—and avert automatic breakdown—only by constant expansion into backward areas, she seemed not merely to have accounted for the contemporary phenomenon of imperialism, but to have indicated a definite *historical* limit to the process. For the non-capitalist sector of the world economy was steadily shrinking, and thus the moment was approaching when the process of accumulation would falter. Capitalist expansion was undermining its own foundations, and the system's breakdown had become a *historical* certainty.[2]

The analytical faults of this construction did not escape her critics, among whom the Austro-Marxists took the lead immediately upon the book's appearance in 1913.[3] The relevant point here is that these critics fastened upon her assertion that capital accumulation was impossible in a closed system, and then proceeded to demonstrate—on the basis of Marx's own theoretical model, in *Capital*, vol. II—that she was mistaken. In this they were joined by the Dutch Marxist A. Pannekoek, a left-wing radical whose political views might have predisposed him in favour of her thesis. The debate was thus genuinely scientific, not factional. Nonetheless the theoretical dispute did

---

[1] Cf. Joan Robinson's introduction to the English translation of *The Accumulation of Capital*, pp. 13 ff; quotations are from this edition.

[2] For a critique of Luxemburg's thesis from the orthodox Marxist standpoint cf. Bukharin, *Der Imperialismus etc.*, passim; some of her earlier critics were answered in the (untranslated) second part of the German edition of 1923.

[3] For Luxemburg's rather irritable reply to her Austrian critics—principally O. Bauer and G. Eckstein—as well as her comments on Hilferding's work, cf. *Die Akkumulation etc.*, part ii, *Anti-Kritik*, pp. 401 ff.

imply an important difference of emphasis which had political over-tones.[1] If Bauer and Hilferding were right in holding that capitalist accumulation could in principle continue without limit, and that Marx's analysis did not presage anything in the nature of automatic breakdown, it was not altogether clear on what grounds Socialists were confident of victory. Bauer's assertion that the working class would make an end of capitalism, even though it continued to func-tion satisfactorily, did sound a little unconvincing. At any rate it failed to explain why a viable capitalism should breed a class-con-scious proletariat ready and able to establish a socialist system. But then the same might be said of Luxemburg's notion that economic breakdown would have such results.

The remarkable thing about Rosa Luxemburg's performance is that, although her central thesis was mistaken, she managed to draw attention to the peculiar mechanism of economic growth underlying the world-wide expansion of capitalism during the past two cen-turies.[2] The analytical fallacies which invalidate her argument have often been emphasised; they were indeed evident to her critics from the beginning. What was less evident—and presumably accounted for her angry refusal to relinquish her vision of the total picture—was that she had stumbled on something important: for although it is not true to say that capitalism keeps going only by expanding into non-capitalist regions, it is a fact that such a process of expansion had become characteristic of the system as it operated in the era of Western hegemony. If one abstracts from her rather mechanical breakdown theory, her analysis of economic imperialism is valid enough; so is her trenchant critique of the disruption worked by European colonialism upon primitive Asian and African peasant societies.[3] Lastly, she saw that the intensified militarism and navalism of the pre-1914 era had an economic function (though she exaggerated its importance). On all these counts she anticipated later theoretical developments. But for her doctrinaire assertion that it was 'necessary for capital progressively to dispose ever more fully of the whole

---

[1] *Anti-Kritik*, loc. cit., pp. 476–81. Part of this work was written during the 1914–18 war, and its angry tone reflects the factional animosities of the period. Even so she did not impute to her critics the desire to prove that capitalism might last for ever, though she lamented their obtuseness. For a note on the debate which seems to suggest that these critics were animated by fear of revolution cf. Sweezy, op. cit., pp. 202 ff.

[2] Robinson, loc. cit., pp. 25 ff.

[3] *The Accumulation of Capital*, pp. 368 ff.

globe', and that in respect of the supposed problem of 'realising' additional surplus-value 'the solution . . . lies in the dialectical conflict that capitalism needs non-capitalist social organisations as the setting for its development',[1] her critics would have found little to question in the descriptive parts of her work. Unfortunately it was essential to her thesis that the necessity of economic breakdown should be *logically* demonstrable on the basis of Marx's assumptions. When it was suggested to her by Bauer and others that capitalist accumulation might under certain circumstances be self-perpetuating, she seems to have felt that such a notion was fatal to socialism, as well as being theoretically wrong.[2] It was in fact fatal to her rather apocalyptic vision of economic breakdown giving rise to political catastrophes. Clearly it was this vision which connected her thinking with that of Parvus and Trotsky, though her reasoning was a good deal more abstract. That the 'breakdown' thesis was not really essential to 'catastrophism' became apparent a few years later, when most of her former adherents—as well as such unattached radicals as Karl Radek—went over to Lenin; for Lenin's doctrine did not operate with any kind of mechanical causality so far as economics was concerned. In his empirical fashion, Lenin was ready to make use of any material that came to hand, while steering clear of controversies that had no bearing upon his immediate political aims. Nor was Trotsky inclined to make his prognosis dependent upon one particular theory of imperialism rather than another. It was enough for his purpose that imperialism should be understood as a global tendency rooted in the conflict between the world-wide development of society's productive forces and the oppressive straitjacket of the obsolescent national state. Once Lenin had accepted these notions —or as much of them as was necessary to buttress his standpoint— the Communist theory of imperialism could be said to have taken the place of the older, pre-1914, Socialist model.[3]

---

[1] Ibid., pp. 358, 366; cf. also p. 446: 'Imperialism is the political expression of the accumulation of capital in its competitive struggle for what remains still open of the non-capitalist environment.'

[2] *Anti-Kritik*, loc. cit., pp. 410–11. Yet Lenin, who rejected her theoretical analysis, saw no need for a long-term perspective founded on the belief that depressions would grow worse and that the working class would eventually revolt against the system. For his own purpose, the Hobson-Hilferding analysis of capital export leading to imperialist conflicts was quite sufficient.

[3] Bukharin, op. cit., pp. 113 ff. For Bukharin's theoretical work in general cf. Peter Knirsch, *Die oekonomischen Anschauungen N. I. Bucharins*, Berlin, 1959. Trotsky's post-1917 appreciation is set out at length in his *Critique of the*

To put the matter in this form is equivalent to saying that the emergence of an entirely new doctrine concerning the future of capitalism as a world system depended on the revolution in Russia; or to be exact, on the conquest of political power by the faction of the Social-Democratic movement led by Lenin. The paradox inherent in this statement is not lessened by the reflection that Bolshevism down to 1917 was a distinctly 'Russian' doctrine with a certain parochial flavour. There was little in Lenin's pre-war writings to presage his later role as the key figure in a revolution with world-wide pretensions. It was not even certain that he and his group aimed at the displacement of capitalism in Russia, though their tactics at least permitted the inference that such a development was considered desirable. Down to 1917 most Social-Democrats—including the majority of Lenin's followers—would have regarded a democratic but non-socialist revolution in Russia as the most probable outcome. Even Parvus had merely suggested that such an event might become the starting-point of a socialist transformation in the West. That Russia would not merely give the signal, but actually try to promote and direct the world revolution on the basis of her own experience, was a possibility not even conceived by Trotsky, who on the contrary always maintained that the real decision would fall in Europe, specifically in Germany. All this is relevant in our context, as well as for the general history of the period, for it meant that when the new doctrine came to be fashioned, it was an East European one; hence the 1917–18 upheaval implied a further eastward shift compared with the pre-1914 situation, when the gravitational centre of the radical Marxist group lay somewhere between Vienna and Berlin; though Petersburg and Warsaw certainly figured in the movement. Neither the German-Polish nor the Austro-Hungarian Marxists in those days had any notion of viewing the imminent political upheaval in Russia as more than a sign that the Europeanisation of that country was at long last beginning in real earnest. Since the political fortunes of Germany, Austria-Hungary, and Russia were closely connected, such a prospect was naturally welcomed; beyond this it would be difficult to point to any evidence that European Socialists expected Russia to break new ground. At any rate it can be said that down to

Draft Programme of the Comintern (1928) written to demolish Stalin's and Bukharin's joint theses submitted to the Sixth Congress of the Communist International in that year. (Cf. *Die Internationale Revolution und die Kommunistische Internationale*, Berlin, 1929.)

1914 the intellectual hegemony of Germany and Austria within the Socialist movement had not been seriously challenged. Marxism was still essentially a Central European doctrine, and the Russian Marxists —including Lenin—looked to Germany for theoretical and political leadership. The notion of reversing this traditional state of affairs had not yet occurred to anyone.

All this of course is merely to say that even those who stood closest to the scene were unaware of the cataclysm that was preparing. Today we can see that the Russian Revolution did give an altogether new direction to Marxist theorising, as well as to European history. Among others it lent an East European imprint to what had hitherto been a Western, or at most a German, doctrine; though paradoxically it also revived some elements of the Jacobin heritage which had been lost from view while Marxism was identified with German Socialism. Though in terms of geography the secular trend had been from west to east, the arrival on the scene of a Russian revolutionary movement inevitably rekindled those long dormant elements of the original Marxian synthesis which went back all the way to French utopian Socialism, and further to the French Revolution itself. This is the justification for concluding the historical part of our study with some reflections on the antecedents of Bolshevism.

8

LENIN

PRIOR TO 1917 the prospect of a revolution in Russia figured in Socialist thinking primarily as an event that would make Europe safe for democracy by removing that traditional bulwark of reaction, the Tsarist regime. This attitude had become standard since 1848-9, when indeed it was common to democrats of all shades of opinion, and around 1900 it would have been difficult to discover any group or faction within either the Russian or the international Socialist movement which held a different view. The fact is merely recalled here in order to stress the extraordinary change which was to supervene after the event had actually occurred. Since we are not concerned with the pre-history of the 1917 upheaval, but with its place in the development leading from the French Revolution, via 1848 and the Marxist synthesis, to the Leninist seizure of power in 1917, we need not enquire into the national origins of Bolshevism—or for that matter of Populism (*Narodnichestvo*)—beyond the point where Marxist influence can be traced. Likewise there is no need to go into the question what Marx and Engels at varying stages of their career thought of Russia and the Russians.[1] But two points need to be borne in mind:

[1] The interested reader can discover this for himself by consulting the standard Russian source, *Perepiska K. Marksa i F. Engelsa s russkimi deyatelyami*, Moscow, 1947; there is an entertaining criticism of Marx's somewhat Victorian views on the subject of early Russian history, by the greatest of Russian Marxist

first, neither Marx nor Engels doubted after about 1870 that the Tsarist regime would soon collapse; and secondly, they regarded this event, whatever its importance from the *democratic* standpoint, as marginal in terms of *Socialist* developments in the West. This distinction may seem artificial; and it *was* artificial insofar as the Social-Democratic movement in the era of the Second International (1889–1914) rested upon a confluence of democratic and Socialist tendencies which—notably in Germany and Eastern Europe—were often difficult to tell apart. But the distinction was nonetheless important to anyone who tried to think seriously about the long-range significance of a revolution that did away with the Tsardom. For the disappearance of the autocracy would presumably lead to the installation of a social order modelled on Western institutions; in which case the choice lay between constitutional monarchy patterned on Bismarckian Germany, or a democratic Republic inspired by the French example. In general, Western democratic thinking—while obviously favouring the second alternative—was quite prepared to treat the first as at all events a considerable step forward. Specifically, German Social-Democracy—for very good reasons of its own—was ready to welcome any political change in Russia which seemed likely to promote a more democratic orientation within Germany, and a lessening of military tensions in Europe. It must be remembered that the age of the Second International was also the era of the Franco-Russian military alliance against Germany, and that already in the 1890's German Socialism—as represented above all by Engels—had to face the awkward prospect of a future war in which Germany's national existence might be at stake. In this perspective the Tsarist regime appeared as the principal obstacle to the triumph of Social-Democracy, as well as being—in Engels's opinion anyhow—the sworn enemy of European peace and progress.[1]

scholars, D. Ryazanov, in *Neue Zeit, Ergaenzungsheft*, No. 5 (1908/9), March 5, 1909. The selection of writings by Marx and Engels published under the title *The Russian Menace to Europe* (ed. Blackstock and Hoselitz, London, 1953) does not quite live up to its aim, but can serve as an introduction to the subject.

[1] For Engels's unremitting hostility to Tsarism (and to the Franco-Russian alliance) cf. Engels-Lafargue correspondence, vol. III, passim, and his correspondence with Bebel (Berlin, 1958). That Engels believed there was a race between revolution in Russia and war in Europe is evident from his important essay 'The Foreign Policy of Russian Tsarism', originally published in the Russian emigré *Sotsialdemokrat* (Geneva, No. 2, 1890) and in the *Neue Zeit*, vol. VIII (1890), pp. 145–54 and 193–203, as well as in French and English translations. For an analysis cf. Blackstock and Hoselitz, loc. cit., pp. 242 ff (text pp. 25 ff).

Marx's own approach had been somewhat different. During his lifetime the Franco-Russian alliance had not yet begun to weigh upon the minds of German Social-Democrats, while the traditional Anglo-Russian antagonism over Turkey did not engage his theoretical interest, though he never ceased to champion the Anglo-Turkish standpoint.[1] This accounts in part for the philosophic detachment with which he followed the disputes among Russian Populist Socialists in the 1870's and early 1880's. His own work during this period involved an intensive study of Tsarist economic conditions and frequent correspondence with Russian economists of the Populist school, as well as contact with the growing Russian emigré milieu in Western Europe. An incidental outcome of these exchanges were some lengthy unpublished drafts for a brief letter to Vera Zasulich—then no longer a Narodnik though not yet a Social-Democrat—in 1881, in which he carefully refrained from taking sides in the growing controversy over the prospects of capitalist development in Russia.[2] Today his notes on the subject make truly fascinating reading. Had these drafts been published in the 1890's, when the controversy between the Russian Marxists and their Populist rivals was at its height, both parties to the debate might have found support in them for their respective views concerning the extent to which the Russian peasant economy had been able to resist capitalist encroachments. As it was, they had to content themselves with the tantalisingly brief statement made by Marx and Engels in their joint preface to the second Russian edition of the *Communist Manifesto* early in 1882, to the effect that 'if the Russian Revolution becomes the signal for a proletarian revolution in the West, so that both complement each other, the present Russian common ownership of land may serve as

[1] And consequently the Tory interpretation of British interests as against the Liberal readiness to make concessions to Russia at the expense of the Ottoman Empire; this was one of the sources of his persistent distrust of Gladstone, whom he suspected (as he had earlier suspected Palmerston) of being willing to condone Russian expansion in the Balkans and the Near East.

[2] Published first in Russian translation in *Arkhiv K. Marksa i F. Engelsa*, vol. I, Moscow, 1924, pp. 270–86; and two years later in the French originals, in *Marx-Engels Archiv*, vol. I, Frankfurt-am-Main, 1926, pp. 309–42, with a preface by D. Ryazanov; the latter draws attention to the curious fact that the Zasulich-Marx correspondence of February–March 1881 did not come to the attention of the Russian Socialist group in Geneva, and seems later to have been forgotten even by Zasulich—possibly because Marx's rather unorthodox reply to her enquiry did not quite fit her own prepossessions. Cf. also B. Nikolaevsky, 'Marx und das russische Problem', in *Die Gesellschaft*, Berlin, 1924, vol. I, no. 4, pp. 359–66; Blackstock and Hoselitz, loc. cit., pp. 275 ff.

the starting-point for a communist development.'[1] Like Marx's earlier reply to Zasulich's enquiry, this non-committal formula was deliberately phrased so as to preserve neutrality in the dispute among the Russian factions, of whom the one headed by G. V. Plekhanov, P. B. Axelrod and V. Zasulich in the following year (1883) duly constituted itself on a Social-Democratic (i.e., 'Marxist' and non-Populist) programmatic basis. Marx's personal sympathies seem to have been fairly evenly divided between the rival groups. After his death, Engels gradually became more severe with the Narodniks, who by the 1890's had come to reject the entire Marxian analysis as inapplicable to Russia (as well as unsympathetic to their general outlook, which broadly speaking was Comteist and Anglo-French rather than Marxist and German).

The relevance of these seemingly arid disputes became evident in the second half of the 1890's, when the growing Social-Democratic movement laid successful siege to the Populist strongholds in the universities. It is perhaps unnecessary to emphasise that the entire dispute was confined to the intelligentsia: not merely in the obvious sense that nearly all those who took part in the literary and theoretical wrangles were intellectuals—in this respect the situation did not differ from that in Western Europe—but in the more important sense that the intelligentsia as a group provided the social milieu within which the politico-ideological conflict was fought out; at any rate down to the revolution of 1905, when something like normal political life came into being and the competing groups and sects were able to open their ranks to non-intellectuals. When one speaks of the conflict between Populists and Marxists in the 1890's, one is referring to a factional struggle within the radical intelligentsia, including the numerous and important proletarianised semi-intelligentsia which later became the chief support of Bolshevism. The conflict was waged principally over the question whether Russia was already engaged in the 'normal' process of capitalist development, or whether she could still hope to escape from it. Since Marx's only existing direct reply (his unpublished letter to Zasulich) had been non-committal, the disputants were compelled to seek enlightenment through diligent

[1] MESW I, p. 24. For the history of this document cf. Blackstock and Hoselitz, loc. cit., pp. 281 ff. For Engels's views on the subject cf. his article 'Soziales aus Russland' (1875) in the essay collection *Internationales aus dem Volksstaat* (Berlin, 1894), with the reply to P. Tkachev's *Open Letter*. (Partly reprinted in Blackstock and Hoselitz, loc. cit., pp. 229 ff; also in **MESW II, pp. 46 ff.**)

study of his major theoretical works. In this respect the posthumous publication in 1894 of the concluding volume of *Capital* had an effect similar to that produced in Germany and Austria, but for different reasons: in Western Europe readers of the work fastened on the price-value problem, the falling rate of profit, and anything else that contributed to the analysis of mature industrial capitalism; in Russia it was read chiefly for confirmation of what Populists and Marxists had come to believe with regard to the impact of capitalism on the peasant economy: the Narodniks asserting that the village community was holding its own, and the Marxists denying it.[1] Hence the curious phenomenon of 'legal Marxism' after 1894, i.e., legally published Marxist literature designed to show that capitalism was making progress in Russia despite the country's general backwardness. It was only with the subsequent quarrel among the Marxists themselves—one group holding out for positive encouragement of capitalism along liberal lines, another (the 'Economists') combining this perspective with emphasis on trade unionism, and the third (and largest) insisting on Social-Democracy's *political* task in overthrowing the autocracy—that the dispute ceased to be academic; and thereafter it still needed the further decisive split of the Marxist Social-Democrats into Bolshevik and Menshevik factions in 1903–5 to produce something like a clear-cut political alignment.[2] Even then the analogy with German and West European conditions is misleading. In particular, there is very little to support the notion— energetically propagated by Lenin himself, and subsequently elevated to the rank of dogma by his followers—that the split corresponded to the revisionist controversy in the West. Russian intellectuals who broke away from Marxism for the most part opted for liberalism in politics, following the example of Peter Struve, the first of the 'legal Marxists' to transform himself from a theoretical Socialist (and co-author of the 1898 Social-Democratic 'Minsk Manifesto') into a practising Liberal. The only Russian 'revisionist' really to deserve this title was Tugan-Baranovsky. Few of Lenin's Menshevik opponents after 1903 were revisionists in any meaningful definition of the term. Plekhanov, the 'father of Russian Marxism', was at least as

[1] Cf. Lenin, *The Development of Capitalism in Russia*, Moscow, 1900 (new English edn., Moscow, 1957, pp. 11 ff); cf. also Lenin, 'Who are the "Friends of the People" etc.' in *Collected Works*, Moscow, 1960, vol. I, pp. 133 ff.

[2] Cf. Haimson, *The Russian Marxists*, pp. 75 ff; E. H. Carr, *The Bolshevik Revolution*, London, 1950, vol. I, pp. 7 ff; L. Schapiro, *The Communist Party of the Soviet Union*, London–New York, 1960, pp. 19 ff.

orthodox as Kautsky, and neither Martov nor Axelrod, nor any of the other principal figures of Menshevism—not to mention Trotsky— had the smallest sympathy for reformist Socialism in the West European sense. Their opposite numbers in Germany were the left-wing radicals: Parvus, Rosa Luxemburg, and their circle. Indeed, as we have seen, Parvus and Trotsky eventually came to form a faction of their own.

These considerations do not, of course, dispose of the argument that Lenin's intervention marked a fundamental cleavage. They are merely intended as a comment on the popular notion that in the ensuing struggle Bolshevism represented the 'orthodox' Marxist viewpoint. Nothing could be further from the case; if anyone introduced a profound 'revision' of Marxist doctrine, it was none other than Lenin himself. This was immediately perceived by his opponents, who at the time included almost every Marxist of note, from Plekhanov and Kautsky to Luxemburg and Trotsky.[1] The difficulty lay in defining just what the new element represented. In 1903–4 the controversy raged mainly over organisation, and specifically over Lenin's insistence upon dictatorial control within a 'narrow' party of 'professional revolutionaries'; later the debate switched to the seemingly quite distinct subject of political strategy during the Russian upheaval of 1905–6; and later still it involved the question of whether there should be a conspiratorial organisation of Social-Democrats side by side with the 'open' democratic labour movement that was growing up in Russia before 1914. Finally in 1917 there came the biggest shock of all: Lenin's conversion to the Parvus–Trotsky doctrine of 'permanent revolution', and his insistence—to the utter bewilderment and dismay of his own lieutenants—that the Bolshevik party should usurp power in the name of a proletarian revolution with Socialist aims: in other words, that it should do what for fifteen years he had declared to be impossible. In the face of so many seemingly disconnected issues, all turning upon one man's apparent readiness to subordinate all else to the single aim of seizing

---

[1] Haimson, op. cit., pp. 182 ff; Carr, op. cit., pp. 26 ff; Deutscher, op. cit., pp. 88 ff; Schapiro, op. cit., pp. 54 ff; 71 ff. Trotsky's pamphlet, *Our Political Tasks* (Geneva, August, 1904), is usually mentioned in this context for its strangely prophetic statement that Lenin's conception of political organisation was Jacobinical and must lead straight to dictatorship; but he was simply giving polemical formulation to a generally held view. Rosa Luxemburg, as might have been expected, agreed wholeheartedly with the Mensheviks in condemning Lenin's organisational model.

power, it is not surprising that even his followers frequently failed to grasp the purpose underlying his baffling changes of front. Indeed one has the impression that there were moments when he had himself run out of formulas which satisfied his theoretical conscience, and had to fall back upon improvisation. Still, taking Lenin's theory and practice as a whole—notably in the light of what it was that he actually achieved—the essential coherence is more striking than the frequently bewildering changes of tactic and vocabulary. However little the reality of Soviet society may have corresponded to his expectations, the actual seizure of power in 1917—the 'October Revolution'—was very much the kind of thing he had anticipated and worked for. And if this is granted—as it must be on any dispassionate study of the evidence—one must also grant that his theorising and his actions complemented each other; though the official doctrine of 'Leninism', as it was shaped after his death, does little to clarify the circumstances.

In trying to understand the political novelty that Bolshevism represented, it is important to abstract from merely doctrinal squabbles over side-issues, such as the not very fascinating dispute over materialist philosophy which absorbed some of Lenin's energy in 1908, and to which quite disproportionate attention was given after Leninism had become the official ideology of Soviet society. Whatever the significance of his philosophical writings for the mental climate of the USSR, their purely intellectual standing—whether in terms of traditional Marxist thinking or simply of philosophy in general—is not such as to invite prolonged consideration; perhaps the only thing which needs to be said is that Lenin's naively realistic theory of knowledge is incompatible with the dialectic.[1] Again, it is not really very relevant in our context to enquire into the purely national origins of his general outlook. Broadly speaking, his manner of looking at the world did not differ from that of his fellow-Marxists, or for that matter from the political philosophy of the average radical of his time. When one bears in mind that all factions of the revolutionary

[1] Cf. Lenin, *Materialism and Empirio-Criticism* (Russian text in *Sochinenya*, vol. 14; English edn., Moscow, 1952). Lenin's *Philosophical Notebooks*, a collection of notes on Hegel's *Logic* dating back to 1914–16 and posthumously issued (*Filosofskiye tetradi*, Moscow, 1947; cf. *Collected Works*, vol. 38), are of greater interest, though hardly important enough to warrant the humourless solemnity with which they are treated in Soviet literature; cf. Wetter, *Dialectical Materialism*, pp. 118 ff. For an extract from the 'Notebooks' cf. Raya Dunayevskaya, *Marxism and Freedom*, New York, 1958, pp. 326 ff; for a critical dissection of Leninist philosophy, cf. Marcuse, *Soviet Marxism*, pp. 136 ff.

movement shared the assumptions of the nineteenth century Russian radicals, this is hardly surprising. Anyone who takes the trouble to read Herzen or Chernyshevsky can easily discover what these assumptions were; just as anyone who bothers to read Plekhanov's painstaking exposition of materialist fundamentalism[1] can find out for himself where Lenin—who thought very highly of the older man's work—acquired his more technical philosophic notions. All this belongs to the history of Russian Marxism as it gradually arose from its Populist chrysalis. But while it is important to realise that the Russian Marxists stemmed from the Populist movement of the 1860's and 1870's, and that in general they preserved its fundamental values even when they repudiated its politics, this still does not explain the phenomenon of Leninism. In a way it even renders it more bewildering; for if Leninism is simply Populism with a Marxist infusion (as one is sometimes tempted to feel), the question arises why the true Populists—the Narodniks of the 1890's, and the vastly more numerous and better organised Socialist-Revolutionaries of 1903–1917—were unable to hold their own against the diminutive Bolshevik assailant. With so many giant creatures floundering about in the political jungle, why did victory go to the Bolsheviks?

The question may be unanswerable in this form. Accidents played their part, Lenin's control over a centralised organisation enabling him to exploit what was perhaps only a fleeting opportunity in 1917. Certainly the disastrous failure of the democratic parties to take Russia out of the war, and satisfy the peasantry's demand for land, was not written in the stars, or anchored in the class structure. It was part of a situation which Lenin turned to advantage, as no one else could have done; but it was no more than an opportunity. To treat the Bolshevik seizure of power in October 1917 as an event of the same order as the fall of the Monarchy eight months earlier, i.e., as the *necessary* consequence of Russia's internal development, is not only nonsense, but the reverse of 'historical materialism'. To do him justice, Lenin himself did not pretend that the 'October Revolution' was 'necessary' in the sense of being inevitable; on the contrary, he insisted all through the critical months that if the chance were missed, it might never return. This was quite true; and it is the

[1] Principally in his lengthy polemical tract entitled *The Development of the Monist View of History* (1895; the English edition of 1947 bears the less cumbersome title *In Defence of Materialism*). Cf. also his 'Notes to Engels's book L. Feuerbach' in *Selected Philosophical Works*, vol. I, pp. 486 ff, for Plekhanov's theory of cognition.

best possible comment on the obstinate attempt of his disciples to have the event inscribed in the Marxist canon as a manifestation of historical inevitability. What it really showed was that in a fluid situation it was possible to bring off a successful *coup d'état* of the sort Blanqui had planned, but for which mid-nineteenth-century France was already too highly organised—and too conservative! For of course the urban rising needed an agrarian revolution to complement it, just as the Jacobin seizure of power in 1793–4 had done. Once the peasantry had ceased to be a revolutionary force, the age of successful proletarian insurrections was over. In this respect the experience of 1848–71 had been conclusive—which was just why European Socialism after that date had turned 'reformist'.

This is the negative side of the matter. But an analysis of Leninism which stops at this point is in danger of underrating the originality of Lenin's achievement. After all, there were other Socialists—even other Marxists—in the Russia of 1905–17 who perceived all this with a fair degree of clarity. The uniqueness of Lenin—and of the Bolshevik organisation which he founded and held together—lay in the decision to make the agrarian upheaval do the work of the proletarian revolution to which all Social-Democrats were in principle committed. Here again it is necessary to distinguish between doctrine and performance. The bare notion that the democratic and the socialist revolution might be merged, or telescoped, was not peculiar to Bolshevism. On the contrary, Lenin tended to fight shy of it—until the decisive moment in April 1917, when he suddenly committed his party to it and thus touched off the cataclysm. Even then his rationalisations lacked the logical coherence of Trotsky's formula.[1] But Trotsky had been able to develop the pure logic of his argument precisely because—being in a minority of one even among the

---

[1] Cf. L. Trotsky, *Die Permanente Revolution*, pp. 21 ff; 88 ff (published simultaneously with the Russian original, *Permanentnaya Revolyutsiya,* Berlin, 1930). Attention is drawn in this work to Trotsky's earliest formulation of his thesis, in his essay *Itogi i Perspektivy* (*Results and Prospects*) which first appeared in a collection of writings under the title *Nasha Revolyutsiya*, Petersburg 1906. Its substance was reproduced in Trotsky's subsequent account of the 1905–6 events, *Russland in der Revolution* (Dresden, 1908), which is partly a translation of the earlier work. (Cf. in particular pp. 32 ff.) At the end of 1917 the original essay was published by itself under the title *Perspektivy Russkoi Revolyutsii*. The abridged English translation of the 1906 volume, which appeared in New York in 1918 under the title *Our Revolution*, includes the greater part of the 1906 essay. The more mature formulations which appear in the 1930 work—already overshadowed by the controversy over 'socialism in one country'—do not diverge basically from the original thesis.

333

Mensheviks—he was reduced to theorising about the probable course of events. (To say nothing of the fact that, not being rooted in Russian life to the same extent as Lenin, he could afford to make light of circumstances ever present to the older man.)

Chief among these circumstances was the central importance to Russia of the agrarian problem, and the key role which the peasantry was certain to occupy in any thoroughgoing democratic revolution. No study of Lenin's writings from the 1890's onward, when he first formulated his criticism of Narodnik policy and ideology, can overlook the fact that concern with this subject was basic to his thinking. This did not make him less of a Marxist, but it gave an emphasis to his theorising which, to say the least, was unusual among Social-Democrats. The reader who comes to Leninism from the Populists, by way of the 'legal Marxist', 'Economist', and Menshevik diatribes against the simple-minded Narodniks who denied the reality of capitalism, experiences a feeling of having returned to the starting-point after a lengthy digression through unfriendly territory. In this connection it is immaterial that Lenin was himself almost certainly a Populist for a brief period in the late 1880's before becoming a Marxist, for this kind of evolution was quite common. What mattered was that he retained his sense of the village and the peasantry after he had broken with the Populists and become a convinced— even a doctrinaire—Marxist Social-Democrat. Throughout his career —down to the moment in November 1917 when he quite simply appropriated the Populist platform on landownership, and left the rival Socialist-Revolutionary party (still far more numerous than his own, but already split into hostile factions) to shiver in the wind without its clothes—he conveys a sense of determination to put a radical solution of the agrarian problem foremost among the tasks of the revolution. This was more than ordinary tactical realism; it reflected an order of priorities—ultimately a hierarchy of values— different from that of the average city-bred radical.

But of course there was more to the Bolshevik union of theory and practice than the bare strategy of a radical-democratic movement which in the end overstepped its own limits. There was the conception of the party as a tightly centralised organisation of 'professional revolutionaries', and the perspective of revolution under the control of a party of this type: ultimately, of 'revolution from above'. This has become a familiar theme, so much so that the essence of Leninism has come to be seen in its organisational model. But here caution is indicated: the record shows that with Lenin the vision of 'total' revolution preceded the 'totalitarian' party structure. As early as 1898—four years before he outlined the 'vanguard' concept—he was already urging the strategy of such a revolution upon the nascent Social-Democrat movement. Moreover, he employed arguments which implied, if they did not actually state, that the coming revolution would be carried through by the proletariat.[1] 'In the struggle against the autocracy', he wrote, 'the working class must single itself out from the rest, for it *alone* is the truly consistent and unreserved enemy of absolutism, it is *only* between the working class and absolutism that compromise is impossible, *only* in the working class has democracy a champion without reservations, who does not waver, who does not look back.' And yet more emphatically, '. . . the proletariat alone is capable of bringing about the *complete* democratization of the political and social system, because such democratization would place the system in the hands of the workers.'[2] To say that these statements breathe the spirit of the *Communist Manifesto* and the *Address of the Central Committee to the Communist League* is another way of saying that the Russia of 1898 was fifty years behind Western Europe. But this circumstance was recognised by all Socialists of the period, and the conclusion which Lenin drew in 1898 was accepted by the exiled Social-Democrats of the 'Liberation of Labour' group in Geneva, headed by his future Menshevik opponents: Plekhanov, Axelrod and Zasulich; else his pamphlet would not have been published by them, with a laudatory preface by Axelrod who described it as a 'commentary' on the official Party manifesto drawn up in the same year.[3]

Nonetheless there was an important difference between the Marxian model of 1848–50 and Lenin's tentative formulation. In 1898 Lenin did not as yet venture beyond the suggestion that 'the proletariat, led in its class struggle by Social-Democracy, is the vanguard of Russian democracy.'[4] The revolution to which he looked forward was a democratic one which would do away with the Tsarist regime and clear the ground for the subsequent class struggle between bourgeoisie and proletariat. The notion of merging or telescoping both phases did not occur to anyone before 1905, and by that date Lenin had developed his own theory. This was set out successively in

[1] 'The Tasks of the Russian Social-Democrats', in *Selected Works*, vol. I, pp. 131 ff.
[2] Ibid., pp. 137–8.   [3] Carr, op. cit., p. 14.   [4] Lenin, loc. cit., p. 139.

two important pieces of writing to which somewhat disproportionate attention has been given in recent years: the essay on party organisation, *What Is To Be Done?*[1] and the analysis of Bolshevik strategy in the 1905 upheaval, *Two Tactics of Social-Democracy in the Democratic Revolution*.[2] Between the dates of appearance of these two programmatic statements of Leninist organisation and policy—respectively 1902 and 1905—there lay the split of 1903 into Bolshevik and Menshevik factions, in consequence of which even those who in 1902 had raised no objection to the thesis of *What Is To Be Done?* discovered after the event that they had really disapproved of Lenin's 'Jacobin' ideas all along. By a familiar process this retrospective view was then projected forward into the debate over the proper attitude to be taken by Socialists in the 'bourgeois-democratic' upheaval of 1905–6. Instead of going into the details of this controversy, which has been analysed often enough by historians of the period, let us try to isolate the essential elements of the Leninist concept.[3]

In *What Is To Be Done?* (written before the Bolshevik-Menshevik split, and in the main directed against the 'Economist' group of Russian Marxists who regarded political activity as a by-product of the class conflict between employers and workers) Lenin developed at greater length the basic idea of his 1898 pamphlet, namely that Social-Democracy could not confine itself to the proletarian class struggle, but must take the lead in the coming democratic uprising against the Tsarist regime. From this unimpeachably orthodox—from the Marxist standpoint—thesis he proceeded to what at first glance seems a quite irrelevant dissertation on the 'socialist consciousness' of the workers which—in contrast to his opponents—he insisted on treating as an extraneous element, not rooted in the 'spontaneous' life process of the working class, but injected into it by the radical intellectuals who were the carriers of the socialist world-view.[4] Though decked out with appropriate quotations from

---

[1] *Selected Works*, I, pp. 149 ff.   [2] Ibid., pp. 351 ff.

[3] For the actual course of events and the intra-party discussions of the period cf. Carr, op. cit., pp. 26 ff; Haimson, op. cit., pp. 142 ff; Schapiro, op. cit., pp. 36 ff; Alfred G. Meyer, *Leninism*, Harvard, 1957, pp. 107 ff.

[4] Lenin, op. cit., *Selected Works*, I, pp. 175 ff. Among non-Russian Marxists, Rosa Luxemburg went furthest in repudiating Lenin's organisational model and urging faith in the revolutionary initiative of the masses, as against the inevitable rigidity of the party bureaucracy. This showed a curious misunderstanding of Lenin's real aim. It also raises an interesting psychological problem: Lenin's diatribes in *What Is To Be Done?* were largely directed against E. D. Kuskova's *Credo*, a document which in his view preached a type of 'spontaneous labour

Kautsky, this notion was at best of dubious orthodoxy. But what really caused the subsequent rift between Lenin's followers and all other groups in the Social-Democratic movement—including the left-wing radicals around Luxemburg—was his evident tendency to identify the 'conscious' element with the 'professional revolutionaries' whom he wished to place in undisputed control of the 'spontaneous' mass movement—*in other words, of the real workers' movement!* Since the 'professionals' were either intellectuals of bourgeois origin, or former workers who had shed their proletarian character and assumed a 'classless' identity in the conspiratorial underground movement—the forerunner of the victorious party organisation which was to dominate the state after the revolution—the Leninist model in fact amounted to the political expropriation of the proletariat and its subjection to a dictatorial machine operated by the Bolshevik leadership: a leadership which was essentially self-constituted and irremovable, though in theory democratically controlled. This consequence of Lenin's organisational model was promptly perceived by his Menshevik opponents—at any rate after the split of 1903–4 had opened their eyes to his 'Jacobin' temper—and systematically denounced by them from that time onward. As Trotsky in particular never tired of pointing out, it represented a throwback not merely to the immature proto-Marxism of 1848–50, but to pre-Marxist forms of organisation. In fact, the only reason for not describing it as 'Blanquist' was that Blanqui had never envisaged anything quite so thorough-going.[1]

This is one side of the matter; the other side, to which less attention has been given in Western literature, is Lenin's approach to the problem of revolutionary strategy in 1905. Unless the link between

movement' certain to promote 'the ideological enslavement of the workers to the bourgeoisie' (loc. cit., p. 177). Now Kuskova was certainly a 'reformist', and perhaps genuinely indifferent to the political side of things, whereas R. Luxemburg staked everything on the hope of a revolutionary mass movement. This suggests that their shared reliance on 'spontaneity' against 'consciousness' may have had psychological roots. At any rate there is the fact that both were women, and that Luxemburg throughout her career gave the impression of regarding conscious control as a threat to spontaneity—a typically feminine notion.

[1] The other possible argument against this identification—namely that Lenin himself was frequently at pains to disclaim any partiality for Blanqui's conspiratorial ideas and tactics—is not a very good one, since for all his protestations Lenin in 1917 did in fact organise a seizure of power modelled on Blanqui's Parisian *coups*: of course with the important difference that he succeeded where Blanqui had failed.

these two aspects of his attitude is grasped, the secret of his eventual success remains obscure. So does the place of Leninism in Marxist history, and the progression from the French to the Russian Revolution, of which Marxism was the theoretical instrument. For of course the bare statement that Marx in 1848–50 had toyed briefly and experimentally with some notions which Lenin put into practice seven decades later, tells us little. The question is what enabled him to square his conception of the party with his doctrine of revolution. It is not enough to say that he remodelled his doctrine until it fitted the unique circumstances of 1917, for the fact is that in 1905 he had already worked out the strategy—though not yet the complete theoretical formula—of a revolution which, though democratic, was not 'bourgeois'. This peculiar achievement requires some consideration. The difficulty lies in disentangling what was said from what was implied, and still more in discriminating concepts that were genuinely operational from notions which achieved prominence *post factum*. Thus after the Bolshevik triumph in 1917, Communist writers took to quoting Marx's observation (in a letter to Engels of April 16, 1856) that the outcome of the expected 'second round' in Germany (which never materialised) would depend 'on the possibility of backing the proletarian revolution by some second edition of the Peasant War.'[1] Although this notion was in reality no longer applicable to Germany when Marx wrote, it could be regarded as having forecast in a very general way what took place in Russia in 1905, and more particularly in 1917. But apart from Trotsky, who was quite isolated on this issue, no Social-Democrat in 1905 ventured to draw such conclusions, and even in 1917 Lenin had the greatest difficulty in getting his party to adopt the strategy of 'permanent revolution', i.e., proletarian-socialist revolution 'backed by' an agrarian upheaval. The orthodox view that in a backward country only a 'bourgeois-democratic' revolution was possible, still predominated when Lenin arrived in Petrograd in April 1917. This doctrine, moreover, had in 1905 been Lenin's own.[2] Indeed for years thereafter he still

---

[1] MEGA III/2, pp. 131–2; MESC, p. 111. For Trotsky's comment on this subject cf. *Die Permanente Revolution*, pp. 26 ff, pp. 129 ff. The first edition of the Marx-Engels correspondence including this remark appeared in 1913, but similar observations could be culled from Marx's published writings before this date. Only—this is the point—they did not lend much support to Lenin's tactics in 1905 (nor to those of his Menshevik opponents).

[2] Cf. *Two Tactics*, loc. cit., p. 378: 'We cannot jump out of the bourgeois-democratic confines of the Russian revolution, but we can vastly extend its boundaries, and within those boundaries we can and must fight for the interests

maintained that the correct strategy was to aim not at a socialist dictatorship—for which the preconditions did not exist in backward Russia—but at a 'democratic dictatorship of the proletariat and the peasantry.'[1]

Before trying to extract the meaning of this curious formula, it is worth pondering what Lenin in 1905 had to say about the prospects of social development after the expected fall of the Tsardom:

Marxists are absolutely convinced of the bourgeois character of the Russian revolution. What does this mean? It means that the democratic changes in the political system, and the social and economic changes which have become indispensable for Russia, do not in themselves imply the undermining of capitalism, the undermining of bourgeois domination; on the contrary, they will for the first time really clear the ground for a widespread and rapid European, and not Asiatic, development of capitalism; they will, for the first time, make it possible for the bourgeoisie to rule as a class. The Socialist-Revolutionaries[2] cannot grasp this idea, for they are ignorant of the rudiments of the laws of development of commodity and capitalist production; they fail to see that even the complete success of a peasant uprising, even the redistribution of the whole of the land for the benefit of the peasants and in accordance with their desires ('Black Redistribution' or something of that kind), will not destroy capitalism at all, but will, on the contrary, give an impetus to its development and hasten the breaking up of the peasantry into classes. The failure to grasp this truth makes the Socialist-Revolutionaries unconscious ideologists of the petty bourgeoisie. Insistence on this truth is extremely important for Social-Democrats, not only theoretically, but from the standpoint of practical politics, for from it follows the necessity for the complete class independence of the party of the proletariat in the present 'general democratic' movement. But it does not at all follow from this that a *democratic* revolution (bourgeois in its social and economic substance) is not of enormous interest for the proletariat. It does not at all follow from this that the democratic revolution cannot take place in a form advantageous mainly to the big capitalist, the financial magnate, and the 'enlightened' landowner, as well as in a form advantageous to the peasant and to the worker.[3]

This seems straightforward enough; but as one reads what Lenin has to say about the character of the coming 'bourgeois revolution',

of the proletariat, for its immediate needs, and for the conditions that will make it possible to prepare its forces for the complete victory that is to come.'

[1] *Two Tactics*, loc. cit., p. 381. In the subsequent factional disputes this formulation became the principal Leninist shibboleth, at any rate down to 1914.

[2] The party name then taken by those Populists who adhered to the Narodnik tradition of agrarian socialism, radical republicanism, and terrorist methods of combat.

[3] *Two Tactics*, op. cit., p. 375.

there gradually appears an ambiguity in his thinking which he seems to have been reluctant to face. On the one hand, the fall of the Monarchy was to clear the ground for a democratic Republic, bourgeois rule, and the most rapid development of modern capitalism. On the other hand, the revolution itself was to be carried through by the working masses in town and country, against the probable resistance not only of the old regime, but of the liberal bourgeoisie, whose major aim—a constitutional regime under a reformed Monarchy—necessarily precluded radical democracy. The 'bourgeois revolution' would thus have to be pushed through against the will of those elements whom ultimately it was certain to benefit, republican democracy being no part of the bourgeois programme. This paradox was capped by another: although the revolution was not to be a proletarian one in the Marxist sense—i.e., it was not to aim at socialism—it would nonetheless bring the proletariat and the peasant masses to the forefront, seeing that the propertied classes could not be expected to wage a resolute fight against the autocracy:

We know that owing to their class position they are incapable of waging a decisive struggle against tsarism; they are too greatly handicapped by the shackles of private property, capital and land, to enter into a decisive struggle. They need tsarism, with its bureaucratic, police and military forces against the proletariat and the peasantry far too much for them to be able to strive for its destruction. No, the only force capable of gaining 'a decisive victory over tsarism' is *the people*, i.e., the proletariat and the peasantry, if we take the main . . . forces and distribute the rural and urban petty bourgeoisie (also part of 'the people') between the two. 'A decisive victory of the revolution over tsarism' is the *revolutionary-democratic dictatorship of the proletariat and the peasantry*.[1]

This was to become the pivotal element of Bolshevism for the entire period from 1905 to 1917, when Lenin adopted the 'permanent revolution' strategy of a *socialist* dictatorship. In retrospect it is evident that the 1905 formula was an.biguous, in that it left open the possibility that the 'revolutionary-democratic dictatorship' might take matters into its hands and decide to transcend the limits of the 'bourgeois revolution'. It is likewise apparent that, whatever the tactical advantages of such an elastic formula, its real—though probably unconscious—function was to conceal from others the inherent ambiguity of Lenin's standpoint.[2] Two further considerations

[1] *Two Tactics*, loc. cit., p. 381.
[2] For Trotsky's critical analysis of the 'democratic dictatorship' concept cf. *Die Permanente Revolution*, pp. 60 ff.

are likewise relevant in our context: first, Lenin's terminology— notably his employment of the term 'the people', for all the subsequent qualifying clauses—quite obviously stems from the Populist tradition; and secondly, his conception of a 'revolutionary-democratic dictatorship' which would carry through the *bourgeois* revolution in radical fashion against the resistance of the bourgeoisie, was clearly Jacobin. To be exact, it was modelled on the Marxist interpretation of Jacobinism as a radical-democratic movement which employed dictatorial means to clear the ground of pre-bourgeois encumbrances. As Lenin remarked complacently on the same occasion, 'If the revolution gains a decisive victory—then we shall settle accounts with tsarism in the Jacobin, or if you like, in the plebeian way.'[1]

It is a matter of history that in 1917 Lenin abandoned this perspective and in substance adopted the 'permanent revolution' strategy, although down to 1916 he had continued to polemicise against its exponents, who at that date included Bukharin and Radek as well as Trotsky.[2] The proximate cause of this change of mind appears to have been the war: specifically, the radicalisation of his thinking after 1914, which led him to propose the new party name 'Communist' in 1917, in place of the traditional 'Social-Democrat.' It can hardly be thought accidental that while thus reverting to the outlook of the *Communist Manifesto* he also adopted the strategy adumbrated in that document. Marx after all had been the first man in Europe to spell out the implications of 'proletarian dictatorship' and the *Manifesto* had given the first clear hint of how a 'bourgeois revolution' might be transformed into a proletarian one. The distance travelled by Lenin in this respect between 1905 and 1917 can be measured by two quotations:

The Jacobins of contemporary Social-Democracy—the Bolsheviks . . . or whatever we may call them—wish by their slogans to inspire the revolutionary and republican petty bourgeoisie, and especially the peasantry, to rise to the level of the consistent democratism of the proletariat. . . . They want the people, i.e., the proletariat and the peasantry, to settle accounts with the monarchy and the aristocracy in a 'plebeian manner', ruthlessly destroying the enemies of liberty, crushing their resistance by force, making

[1] *Two Tactics*, loc. cit., p. 383. Biographers have not been slow to note that Lenin's unyielding hatred of the Tsarist autocracy was much his strongest political emotion—certainly in his early writings he displayed no particular animosity against the bourgeoisie; but he was rarely as explicit as on this occasion.

[2] Cf. Trotsky, op. cit., p. 82.

341

no concessions whatever to the accursed heritage of serfdom, of Asiatic barbarism, and of all that is an insult to mankind.[1]

By 1917 the aim had shifted to full-blooded Communism in the sense of the 1848 *Manifesto* and Marx's pamphlet on the Paris Commune:

We ourselves, the workers, will organize large-scale production on the basis of what capitalism has already created, relying on our own experience as workers, establishing strict, iron discipline supported by the state power of the armed workers. . . . This is *our* proletarian task, this is what we can and must start with in carrying out the proletarian revolution.[2]

In the place of the 'widespread and rapid European, and not Asiatic, development of capitalism' which Lenin had envisaged in 1905 as the goal of radical-democratic revolution, there now appeared —in a perspective drastically foreshortened by the war and the anticipated socialist upheaval in Europe—the messianic vision of a Russia liberated from the curse of capitalism and free to 'build socialism' in its own fashion. From his own rather more sophisticated standpoint, Trotsky was able to welcome this as a belated conversion to his long-held view that a thoroughgoing democratic revolution would automatically result in a socialist dictatorship. Where he continued to differ from most Bolsheviks after 1917—as he had differed from Lenin, on other grounds, before that date—was in refusing to believe that socialism could in fact be constructed in a backward country: Russia could only give the signal; it was for Europe to accomplish the main task.

But if a proletarian revolution in Russia did not spell socialism, what exactly was its import? From 1905 onward Trotsky had insisted that the course of events in Russia would inevitably bring 'the workers' to power, since no one else could give direction to the inchoate strivings of the peasantry. In 1928–30—having meantime been obliged to refurbish his thesis in opposition to the new doctrine of 'socialism in one country'—he achieved a rather more general formulation which incidentally cast a good deal of retrospective light upon his own and Lenin's role in 1917. The concept of 'permanent revolution', he wrote,

demonstrated that the democratic tasks of backward bourgeois nations in our epoch lead to the dictatorship of the proletariat, and that the dictator-

[1] *Two Tactics*, loc. cit., p. 384.
[2] *State and Revolution*, in *Selected Works*, II, p. 174; cf. also 'The tasks of the proletariat in the present revolution', ibid., pp. 17 ff.

ship of the proletariat places socialist tasks upon the agenda. That was the central idea of the theory. If the traditional view held that the road to proletarian dictatorship ran through a lengthy democratic period, the doctrine of permanent revolution asserted that for the backward countries the road to democracy leads through the dictatorship of the proletariat.[1]

The advanced industrial countries had no place in this scheme, which is hardly surprising; but then neither did they play a very convincing part in the revised post-1917 Leninist-Stalinist model. Russian Communist theorising from 1918 onward has tried in vain to formulate a global doctrine applicable both to nations industrialised under capitalism, and to countries whose condition resembles Russia's arrested development under the Tsarist regime. Any such doctrine, to be realistic, would have had to concede that a 'proletarian revolution' is possible only in a retarded country; whence it follows that Communist dictatorship is a concomitant of backwardness; and this is just what no Leninist can admit and remain true to himself. Even Trotsky refused to draw this conclusion, though he more than once came close to stating the fact. His favourite escape from the dilemma lay in asserting that the revolution in Russia was part of a global upheaval which was undermining capitalism in the advanced industrial countries as well, though for different reasons: in the West, capitalism had become 'overripe', while in the East—specifically in India and China—its very absence or weakness facilitated the tasks of the revolution. This was an ingenious way out of the embarrassment of having to admit that the 'October Revolution' had sprung from a unique constellation of circumstances; but it was hardly more than a verbal escape-hatch. The logic of his argument really entailed the recognition that the Russian Revolution had done for Eastern Europe and parts of Asia what the French Revolution in its time accomplished for Western Europe and Latin America. But where the prospect of 'world revolution' was concerned, logic had to give way. Nor was orthodox Communist doctrine after 1918 willing to concede that Western Europe and North America might represent a reality against which revolutionary movements inspired by Russian example would beat in vain.

It remains to consider the link between Lenin's strategy of revolution and his doctrine of the party; for of course this is really the core

[1] Trotsky, op. cit., pp. 27–8. A large section of this pamphlet is devoted to an analysis of the abortive Chinese revolution of 1925–7; this accounts in part for the significant stress laid on social backwardness as a precondition of 'proletarian dictatorship', i.e., Communist dictatorship.

of the matter. Anyone might have decreed a 'revolutionary-democratic dictatorship' in 1905, or a proletarian one in 1917, but only
Lenin was in a position to translate these notions into reality. It was
a case of theory and practice coming together. Such situations are
rare, and when they occur it is not always clear whether the theory
was shaped by the pressure of events, or vice versa. To a large extent
Lenin in 1917 undoubtedly followed the drift of events. Thus he
adapted himself to the spontaneous emergence of the Soviets, and the
'dual power' relationship in which they stood to the Provisional
Government; and having decided to use them as the springboard of
revolution, he proceeded to rationalise his tactics by establishing a
historical connection between the Soviets and the Paris Commune.[1]
He had been just as ready to experiment with political forms in 1905
and in the years following. Nonetheless it is impossible to study the
record without seeing that there was an underlying consistency, and
that all the tactical turns and twists had a single aim in view and were
sustained by a remarkably coherent vision of what was possible in
Russia. The Lenin of 1918 is already present in the youthful author of
the modest 1898 pamphlet which so delighted the exiles in Geneva;
he is clearly discernible in the 'Jacobin' doctrinaire of *What Is To
Be Done?* (1902) and *Two Tactics* (1905). But where is the link between these writings and the strategy of the 'October Revolution'?

Notwithstanding a great deal of fascinating literary and historical
detective work in recent years, the best answer to this question is still
that provided by Trotsky. Lenin (he wrote after the event), staked
everything on a radical solution of the peasant problem—to the
extent of virtually identifying the 'bourgeois revolution' with the
agrarian revolution.[2] This implied the overthrow of the Monarchy
and—since the liberal bourgeoisie was sure to resist such a drastic
measure—an upheaval in which the urban proletariat and the
peasantry would march together. Their joint victory would be secured
by the 'democratic dictatorship'—a bewilderingly vague formula

---

[1] *State and Revolution*, S.W. II, pp. 141 ff. This is one of his worst pieces
of writing and also one of the least significant, in that it contains not a single
genuinely operational concept, but rather a profusion of sophistries designed
to justify a radical break with Marxist orthodoxy. (Cf. in particular pp. 188
and 197, where the distinction between democracy and dictatorship is con-
jured away by what can only be called a sleight-of-hand.) The reader who
judges Lenin by this pamphlet does him a serious injustice. When he dealt
dispassionately with a subject he had closely studied—e.g., the agrarian question, or the economics of Russian development under Tsarism—he reached a
much higher level. [2] *Die Permanente Revolution*, pp. 22–3.

whose intentional obscurity allowed Lenin to envisage at different
times such mutually exclusive goals as a democratically elected legislature with a peasant party majority,[1] and a 'proletarian' dictatorship based on urban and village councils dominated by his own
party.[2] The consistent line of thought running through all his
argumentations from 1898 onward was directed against the assumption—which the Mensheviks inherited from the 'legal Marxists' of
the 1890's—that a 'bourgeois revolution' could only bring the
Liberals to power. Even in 1905, when he still protested against the
'absurd semi-anarchist ideas about putting the maximum programme
into effect immediately, about the conquest of power for a socialist
revolution',[3] he envisaged a 'provisional revolutionary government' which would be both dictatorial and 'democratic', in the
sense that it would push the democratic revolution as far as circumstances permitted: in other words, a 'Jacobin' government. This
was quite in accordance with the tradition of *Narodnichestvo* (minus
the Narodnik fantasies about agrarian socialism founded on cottage
industry). It was in fact a highly original fusion of the Populist and
the Marxist vision; and just because it combined elements of both, it
proved politically superior to either. In the crisis of 1917 Lenin was
able to organise a seizure of power which no democrat could pardon,
but which in terms of his own definition of 'democracy' was quite
legitimate: its purpose after all was to promote the 'democratic'
dictatorship of the 'toiling masses' in town and country over their
exploiters (among whom he now included the capitalist class in
general).[4] The fact that this was actually feasible in Russia because
the country was still relatively backward—in other words, because its
economy was still to a large extent bureaucratically controlled—lifted
the programme out of the realm of utopia into that of practical politics. Even so, 1917 was probably the last date for the premature
socialisation of a semi-developed Russia. A few more years of
industrial development (and avoidance of war!) would have undermined the entire basis of Bolshevik strategy.

[1] *Two Tactics*, Sel. Works, I, p. 414.
[2] *The Tasks of the Revolution*, loc. cit., II, p. 127.
[3] *Two Tactics*, loc. cit., p. 360.
[4] *The Impending Catastrophe And How To Combat It*, Sel. Works, II, pp. 86 ff.
In this pamphlet, written in September 1917, i.e., shortly before the seizure
of power, state control of industry and the banks—though not full-blown
socialism—is declared to be feasible and listed foremost among the tasks of a
genuinely revolutionary 'provisional government'.

What Lenin does not seem to have realised—but then neither did his opponents—was that a political party which put itself at the head of such a movement would inevitably become the instrument of state-controlled industrialisation as soon as the emergency was over. But this subject belongs to the post-Lenin era with which we are not concerned. The question here is what enabled the Bolshevik party to play the role Lenin had imposed upon it.

Part of the explanation clearly has to do with the centralised character of its organisation, and more particularly with the Leninist conception of revolutionary politics which made the party an instrument of the changing purposes of its self-appointed leadership. This is an aspect of Leninism to which considerable attention has been given in recent years, generally under the heading of totalitarian politics in the modern age. There is no particular reason why the subject should not be approached from this angle, so long as one remembers that we are dealing with a revolution which was intended to be a democratic one, and which in fact arose from the normal conflict between an archaic regime and an evolving society. Russian Social-Democracy after all was the beneficiary of a long-standing radical-democratic tradition which already had its heroes and martyrs, as well as its prophets and doctrinaires. Even the Bolshevik variant at first did not appear to mark a fundamental break with this tradition. The totalitarian element lay concealed in the 'vanguard' concept which Lenin—like Tkachev and Lavrov before him—had inherited from the French Revolution: to be exact, from the Populist misinterpretation of the Jacobin heritage, for in actual fact the brief Jacobin dictatorship was no more than an emergency operation, and was so regarded by all concerned. Though there was a genuinely totalitarian element in French radical (Babouvist) thinking after the failure of that experiment, it had already been considerably weakened by the time French Socialism got under way in the 1840's, and thereafter Marx and Engels diluted it further. The *Communist Manifesto* is dictatorial enough in all conscience, but the authoritarian rule it envisages is to be short-term, and the subsequent evolution of Marxism pushed even this notion into the background. In any case the peculiar character of Leninism cannot be wholly deduced from the filiation of ideas. There must have been a structural element in the Russian situation which responded to the revival of concepts and attitudes dating back to the pre-1848 era.

It has become a commonplace that this element was furnished by the radical intelligentsia; but though not wrong, this explanation still leaves unanswered the question why the Bolshevik party functioned as it did in a situation where *all* revolutionary groups appealed to this social stratum for support—in some cases with greater initial success than Lenin's party. What was it that facilitated the triumph of the only potentially totalitarian one among them? Or to put it differently: given the fact that Lenin's aims were totalitarian—though until 1917 neither he nor anyone else realised the full implications of his attitude—what was it that enabled him to map out both a political strategy and an organisational model which prefigured the fully developed system of the Stalin era? To say that the latent totalitarianism of the intelligentsia had already become institutionalised in the pre-revolutionary Bolshevik party is only half the answer. The other half is supplied by that Leninist key concept, the 'democratic dictatorship'. Taken together they go a long way towards clarifying the problem.

Lenin's political strategy from the start envisaged a victorious popular uprising and the seizure of power by the radical wing of the revolutionary movement. While the social content of the new regime was left undefined, its political character would correspond to the aims of the radical intelligentsia, notably its more plebeian strata who eventually became the real shock-troops of Bolshevism. This is the justification for treating Lenin's conception as part of the Jacobin heritage which he shared with the radical Populists of the 1870's[1]—but not with the Mensheviks, who (as good left-wing Social-Democrats) maintained that in a 'bourgeois' revolution the party of the proletariat must remain in opposition and should not try to seize or share power. In Lenin's view, the seizure of power was needed to consolidate the revolution, the 'democratic dictatorship' representing both the peasants and the urban workers, just as the Jacobin dictatorship was supposed to have done. (Whether in fact it did is immaterial in this context, since we are only concerned with Lenin's view of the matter.) Since two different social classes were involved, a political force standing above or outside them was needed to hold the alliance together, if the 'democratic dictatorship' was not to come apart immediately. Lenin seems at different times to have envisaged various approaches towards this problem, including a coalition with an authentic peasant party. But in the end his cast of mind inclined him to the solution which was in fact adopted by the Bolsheviks from

[1] Franco Venturi, *Roots of Revolution*, London, 1960, pp. 389 ff.

1917–18 onward: the untrammelled dictatorship of his own party, which was thus to represent the peasantry (or at any rate the 'poor peasants') as well as the proletariat. That this could not be done by a genuine Socialist labour party of the Menshevik type—or rather of the type the Mensheviks were hoping to evolve—should have been obvious. How far it was in fact clear to Lenin is doubtful, but at any rate he always insisted that the party—*his* party—must be more than a representative of labour's class aims, however generously interpreted.[1]

What he does not seem to have grasped is that a coalition of two classes—workers and peasants—could be directed only by a third force. Or rather, he realised this clearly enough where 1789–94 was concerned, since Marx had taught him to look for the reality of bourgeois rule behind the façade of republicanism. It was common coin among Social-Democrats that the bourgeoisie had been in control of the French Revolution, whence indeed the Mensheviks derived their fatalistic certainty that the same thing would happen in Russia. Trotsky might counter this by asserting that in default of the bourgeoisie, which had lost its taste for revolution, the proletariat would 'lead' (i.e., dictate to) the peasantry. But Lenin, who obstinately refused to accept this conclusion, could only cling to the idea that somehow 'the party' would do the trick. Logically he should have concluded that the party could only succeed in this role if it represented an independent force, namely the 'classless' intelligentsia, which alone could staff the cadres of a ruling political elite. But although in *What Is To Be Done?* he came to the very brink of stating this fact, the full realisation was hidden from him, and for good reason: had he possessed it, he could no longer have acted in good faith when he asserted that the 'vanguard' represented the proletariat. The organisation of 'professional revolutionaries' which on the morrow of its victory transforms itself into the nucleus of a new ruling elite is a twentieth-century phenomenon, and Lenin's conceptual apparatus was derived from an earlier age. Like other great revolutionaries, he was rooted in the conditions of an era which his own victory was helping to bring to a close.

[1] 'The Social-Democrat who disparages the proletarian tasks in a democratic bourgeois revolution becomes transformed from a leader of the people's revolution into a leader of a free labour union.' (*Two Tactics*, loc. cit., p. 423.) Cf. also the well-known disparaging remarks about 'mere' trade-union consciousness among workers not firmly led by a vanguard of 'professional revolutionaries', in *What Is To Be Done?* loc. cit., p. 170.

That the revolution ultimately took the form it did was not of course entirely due to Lenin. The war provided him with an opportunity which, had it been postponed even for a few years, would probably not have occurred. What counts is that he was able to seize upon those elements of the Marxian synthesis which went back to the Jacobin strain in Marx's own thinking. In this perspective 1848 appears as the connecting link between 1793 and 1918, which is another way of saying that Marxism was the bridge between the French and the Russian Revolution. It was also a great many other things, e.g., a theory and practice of democratic Socialism, for which there was no adequate foundation in Russia—but Lenin naturally saw only what lay closest to his purpose. Moreover, in 1918–19 it did look for a moment as though the upheavals in Central Europe might fuse with the Russian Revolution to produce something like a Socialist triumph. The simultaneous breakdown of the three Eastern Empires had revived memories of 1848, with the difference that Russia was now in the van of the revolution. If Communism reigned in Moscow, Social-Democrats were in power in Berlin and Vienna. It did not seem altogether fanciful to suppose that all of Central Europe would be swept into the current. Had this occurred even temporarily, the nationalist aspect of Bolshevism—ultimately an inheritance from the Populist movement—would have been overlaid by the new faith in proletarian revolution on a world scale. Leninism might then have merged with a broader international current. This never happened, but for a brief period it seemed about to happen, which explains *inter alia* why so many Syndicalists, and other left-wing radicals in the West, mistook the Bolshevik victory for the triumph of their own cause, and the shadowy workers' councils for 'proletarian democracy'. It took time—and the failure of 'world revolution'—for the true nature of Leninism to disclose itself. Years passed before it began to dawn on Communists in the West that the October Revolution, so far from being the first great proletarian uprising, might be the last.[1]

[1] There were of course critical voices from the beginning, e.g., Rosa Luxemburg, whose pamphlet on the Russian Revolution (written in 1918) does not figure in Communist editions of her works. But it took the Kronstadt rising of 1921 to open the eyes of those Syndicalists who had hoped for 'workers' democracy'; and even then the true nature of the new regime remained for long a puzzle to left-wing opponents. The subject cannot be pursued here. It belongs to the history of the Communist International, with which we are not concerned The 'orthodox' misinterpretation of Leninism as the theory and practice of proletarian revolution dates back to the early 1920's, a typical example being

The core of the new Communist synthesis was the party and its 'historic role' in leading the proletariat to victory over its enemy, the imperialist bourgeoisie.[1] To this was later added the 'building of socialism' in the USSR under the direction of the same party, which thus came to occupy two quite distinct, and ultimately incompatible, functions. The resulting tensions and conflicts belong to the history of the post-revolutionary society which emerged from the chrysalis of the Bolshevik dictatorship, much as nineteenth-century French society evolved from the turmoil of the Revolution. To that extent the parallel holds true, while in other respects it has misled both critics and apologists of the Soviet regime. In particular, too much has been made of superficial analogies between Jacobin and Bolshevik rule. The Jacobins were not a party in the modern sense, but a political club which for a while succeeded in terrorising its opponents. Moreover, their ideology was not really attuned to the practice of a totalitarian reconstruction of society from the top downward, being heavily impregnated with classical liberalism. Lastly, they came upon the scene at a moment when the state in Western Europe was genuinely tending to 'wither away', at any rate so far as the direction of economic life was concerned; while the Bolshevik seizure of power coincided with an enormous expansion of state power in all the advanced countries and most of the backward ones. Few historical misconceptions are more pathetic than Lenin's vision of a classless and stateless society, as outlined in *State and Revolution*, at the moment when the revolution he led was about to give birth to the first great totalitarian system in modern history. It was of course just this world-wide trend towards centralisation and state management which made the later successes of Soviet planning possible. In this sense, i.e., if state ownership and central control were accepted as adequate criteria, the regime could even lay claim to being socialist.

For the rest, the march of events was to confirm what critical observers of the labour movement had already begun to suspect,

Zinoviev's *Geschichte der Kommunistischen Partei Russlands*, Hamburg, 1923. This is a good introduction to the subject, just because the author naively ignores all the real problems.

[1] Zinoviev, loc. cit., p. 206: 'The hegemony of the proletariat is impossible without the hegemony of the Communist party. The dictatorship of the working class finds its expression in the dictatorship of the party which it has created and which stands at its head. The history of the Russian Communist party is the history of the Russian working class.'

viz., that political 'rule' by the working class was an impossibility, whether in advanced or backward countries. A class which encouraged or tolerated the dictatorship of a body such as the Communist party was clearly not fit to exercise political power, and possibly inhibited from such a role by something more permanent than mere immaturity. Even on the orthodox Communist assumption that the party represented the working class—which in fact it never did—the only conclusion possible from the course of events after October 1917 was that this class had been obliged to split itself in two, and give its leading stratum dictatorial powers over itself. This hardly accorded with the traditional Socialist expectation of workers' democracy, but it did not fit the original Communist vision either. Conversely, if the Communist party had simply institutionalised the rule of a new directing stratum in control of the centrally planned economy, the question arose how and why 'the masses' had passively tolerated this act of political usurpation. On either assumption, Leninism turned out to be just what on Marxian principles one might all along have suspected it of being: the ideology of a revolution whose outcome was wholly at variance with its professed aims, and whose principal beneficiaries constituted a new privileged stratum. Marxian sociology might without difficulty account for this outcome—indeed treat it as confirmation of its own working hypotheses—but in that case the unity of theory and practice was broken, and Marxism was reduced to the status of an intellectual system operative after the event rather than before; the event being a revolution undertaken for the express purpose of realising the aims outlined in Marx's reflections upon the failure of the earlier attempt made in France.

At this point it seems convenient to break off and return to our previous perspective. If Communism is to be understood as the (negative) fulfilment of the radical programme derived, via German philosophy, from the French Revolution, then we can complete our study by asking what is left of the Marxian synthesis, now that its materialisation has made it possible to distinguish its utopian postulates from its scientific insights.

PART SIX

THE DISSOLUTION OF THE MARXIAN SYSTEM
1918–1948

1

WAR AND REVOLUTION

THE WAR OF 1914–18 closed the liberal epoch in which Marxism had taken shape, and inaugurated an era as different from the preceding one as the nineteenth century had been from the age which ante-dated the French Revolution. The war itself was the outcome of national rivalries rooted in Europe's past, and the attitude of the various Socialist parties was determined as much by traditional reflexes as by patriotism. The German Social-Democrats in particular displayed the deeply rooted Russophobia with which German demo-cratic opinion had become imbued since 1848. For this attitude they could claim respectable authority. Socialist participation in an osten-sibly defensive war waged by Germany against Russia and France had been a virtual certainty since the 1890's, and the terms employed by their spokesmen to justify their patriotic attitude in August 1914 were merely a paraphrase of Engels's statement in 1891 that in such a war Germany would be fighting for its national existence.[1] If left-wing

[1] Cf. Engels, 'Der Sozialismus in Deutschland', *Neue Zeit*, 1891–2, No. 19, p. 371; Engels to Bebel, September 29, 1891, in *Briefe an Bebel*, pp. 180–4; cf. also his interview with the Paris *Eclair* of April 6, 1892, reprinted in Engels–Lafargue correspondence, III, p. 421. The real break with this tradition was signalised not by Lenin's polemics, but by Rosa Luxemburg's pamphlet *Die Krise der Sozialdemokratie* (Junius-Broschuere), Berlin-Zürich, 1915–16, re-printed in *Ausgewaehlte Reden und Schriften*, pp. 258 ff. And even she held fast to the doctrine that the correct attitude was to combine national defence with 'Jacobin' opposition to the Imperial government (loc. cit., p. 372).

Marxists like Lenin and Luxemburg were now to claim that such arguments no longer fitted the case—Germany having meantime become an imperialist power—this was another way of saying that classical Marxism was not appropriate to the new situation; and so it proved. Liberals were in the same plight. None of them had previously doubted that citizenship implied the duty to defend one's country, but wars of conquest were another matter and might justifiably be opposed, especially if a suspicion arose that imperialism tended to make them permanent. Wars of conquest, however, were unlikely to be billed as such, which made it an awkward matter to stand out against one's countrymen. In 1914–18 it was still common form among the belligerents to disclaim any purpose but the time-honoured one of defending the national soil against foreign invasion. The Fascist glorification of warlike expansion for its own sake, and enslavement of 'inferior' peoples as a matter of course, was yet to come; so was 'revolutionary defeatism' on the Leninist model. The nineteenth century had not prepared either Liberals or Socialists for such apparitions. The 1914–18 war still had its traditional side; that of 1939–45 was fought in circumstances not remotely foreseen either by Marx or by the first generation of his followers.[1]

What rendered the breach fundamental was not the fact of war

[1] Lenin's polemics against those who supported the war—or opposed it mainly on pacifist grounds—are to be found in vol. 19 of the official *Collected Works* (2nd edn.); an earlier German-language selection (Lenin and Zinoviev, *Gegen den Strom*, Hamburg, 1921) is noteworthy for its emphasis upon the theme that war can and must be transformed into civil war. On the whole, the clearest formulation of the internationalist position is to be found in Radek's essay on the subject, in *Vorbote*, Zurich, 1916, pp. 28 ff; Kautsky's standpoint —essentially a qualified acceptance of national defence, coupled with the traditional democratic opposition to imperialism and military annexation—was summed up by him in *Die Internationalitaet und der Krieg*, Berlin, 1915; his analysis of imperialism (cf. *Nationalstaat, Imperialistischer Staat und Staatenbund*, Nuremberg, 1915; *Neue Zeit*, April 30, 1915; May 28, 1915) is in substantial agreement with the traditional liberal critique of militarism and protectionism, and for the rest urges the gradual abandonment of war as an instrument of national policy. On the extreme right of the German Socialist movement, Paul Lensch (*Die deutsche Sozialdemokratie und der Weltkrieg*, Berlin, 1915) anticipated some of the characteristic Fascist slogans of the subsequent period, notably the theme of Continental European 'liberation' from the reactionary yoke of plutocratic England. On the whole, the party leadership clung to an intermediate position validated by Engels's advice to Bebel in 1891: Germany's national existence being at stake, the working class must defend the country, all the more since a Russian victory would menace European democracy; this latter argument of course lost much of its weight from March 1917 onwards, when Tsarism collapsed while on the other hand the USA entered the war on the Allied side.

itself, or even the collapse of the International in 1914 and the consequent split within European Socialism, but the Bolshevik capture of the Russian Revolution. It was this constellation which turned Leninism into the theory and practice of a world movement. It would be tempting to describe this outcome as fortuitous, were it not that Lenin's doctrines so closely matched his tactics. Convinced as he was that Tsarist Russia would prove the weak link in the global chain, he laid stress on its combination of internal backwardness with an aggressive foreign policy which really demanded an altogether different 'infrastructure'. Alone among the major European countries, Russia was ripe for revolution precisely because of her backwardness. The logical corollary of this view should have been that Western Europe was correspondingly immune. Lenin did not draw this conclusion, but he did say (in 1915) that revolutionary strategy had a better chance in Russia than in the West.[1] What he failed to see— and what no Leninist has yet been able to admit—was that 'revolutionary defeatism' could be advocated with any hope of success only in a country so retrograde that the bulk of its population was altogether outside the mainstream of national life. Elsewhere such a slogan would simply have been regarded as treasonable, not merely by 'the bourgeoisie', whom Lenin credited with a monopoly of patriotism—or, in his terminology, 'chauvinism'—but by 'the masses'. Insofar as he had some residual qualms on this point he got over them by denouncing first the Tsarist government, and then after March 1917 the provisional government, as the slavish campfollowers of Western imperialism. This enabled him and his followers to square national sentiment with revolutionary doctrine: if the exploiting classes who promoted imperialism were in the pay of foreign capital, they were doubly damned. The shot went home because the strength of the Populist tradition was such that it was fatal for any regime or party to be branded as the tool of Western

---

[1] Cf. his article entitled 'On the defeat of one's own government in the imperialist war': 'The latter argument is particularly important for Russia, because Russia is the most backward country, where the Socialist revolution is not immediately possible. Precisely for this reason the Russian Social-Democrats had to come out first, in theory and practice, with the slogan of defeat. . . . The opponents of the slogan of defeat are simply afraid of themselves and refuse to see the evident connection between revolutionary agitation against the government and the promotion of defeat.' (Originally published in *Sotsialdemokrat*, Zurich, July 26, 1915; cf. also 'On the United States of Europe Slogan', ibid., August 23, 1915, English translation in *Selected Works*, London, 1947, vol. I, pp. 630 ff.)

capitalism. Without knowing it, Lenin had hit upon the *leitmotiv* of 'anti-imperialism' among the intelligentsia of backward countries in the years to follow. Since Russia bordered on Asia as well as on Europe, the 'October Revolution' assumed a twofold significance: depending on whether one looked at it from the West or from the East, it was a proletarian revolution in the most backward of the great European countries, or a national and 'anti-imperialist' revolt against the West. In its first aspect it appealed to (mainly European) workers, in its second to (mainly Asian, but latterly also African and Latin American) peasants. All this was implied in Lenin's assertion (itself a revival of the earlier Narodnik doctrine) that Russia's backwardness rendered a 'proletarian' revolution feasible. It is true that in 1915–17 this, to most of his followers, was a novel and surprising view, but once they had got over the shock, its potentialities turned out to be very great indeed.

After the event—and especially after the Communist victory in China: an historic sequel to the Bolshevik triumph, as it were, on a lower level—the whole process acquired a meaning quite different from that which it possessed for contemporaries in 1917–18, when the simultaneous fall of the Russian, German, and Austrian monarchies was universally viewed in the light of East European history. It is this which has made it increasingly difficult for Communists and Social-Democrats to find a common language, even when both sides employ Marxist terms. To anyone brought up before 1918 in the Social-Democratic tradition, Russia was an East European country which happened to extend into Asia. This had been the unquestioned assumption of Plekhanov as well as Kautsky; one may say that down to the last years of his life it was still the dominant view of Lenin, but thereafter it was no longer that of Stalin and the Stalinists.[1] In the 'Eurasian' perspective increasingly prominent after the industrialisation drive of the 'thirties and the military victory over Germany in 1945, the 'October Revolution' assumed a significance altogether different from that of the parallel upheavals in 1918–19

[1] They could of course point to Lenin's last published utterance, the article 'Better fewer, but better' (*Selected Works*, II, pp. 844 ff), with its evocation of a coming showdown between 'the counter-revolutionary imperialist West and the revolutionary and nationalist East' (loc. cit., p. 854). This perspective is already implicitly Stalinist—and incidentally helps to explain why the majority of old-guard Bolsheviks after Lenin's death preferred the Stalinist orientation to that of Trotsky and other Westernisers; cf. E. H. Carr, *Socialism In One Country*, London, 1959, vol. II, pp. 36 ff.

which brought Germany and Austria closer to Western Europe. The second world war and its aftermath deepened the division and thereby confirmed the prime lesson of 1917–18, which was that Russia and Central Europe were fated to follow divergent paths of development. No Communist of course could accept this, and the history of the Communist International from 1919 onward is largely the story of unavailing attempts to bridge this ever-widening gap. The sequel—the Russian military occupation of East-Central Europe in 1945 and the forcible imposition of Communist regimes upon countries whose spontaneous development pointed in quite a different direction—really belongs to the sphere of international relations. Whatever its political significance, it holds little theoretical interest (save possibly for historians of pan-Slavism, who may treat it as evidence that the October Revolution ultimately helped to promote the traditional aims of Russian imperialism).

It is worth stressing that after 1918 the sharpest line of division gradually came to be drawn between orthodox followers of Lenin and those left-wing Socialists in the West who pinned their faith to the revolutionary potential within the working class. The political cleavage involved Communist and Social-Democratic parties, but from a theoretical viewpoint the significant difference lay between those who with Lenin believed in the possibility of socialist revolutions in backward countries, and those who—like Luxemburg, the Austro-Marxists, or the Syndicalists—did not. (Trotsky, after a lengthy period of sharing the Bolshevik faith, in the end reverted to the orthodox Marxist standpoint.) In this matter Lenin's followers were compelled by events to go far beyond their original starting-point. Beginning around 1905 with the flat assertion that the coming Russian revolution would be 'bourgeois-democratic' and pave the way for modern, 'European' capitalism, they gradually came round to the idea that a socialist revolution was possible in Russia, and eventually they committed themselves to the construction of a socialist society in a country artificially isolated from the world market. In so doing they inevitably revived some elements of the traditional Populist faith in the possibility of a direct transition to socialism on the basis of the village community (minus the Populist thesis that capitalist development was impossible in Russia for economic reasons). Under Stalin the issue was increasingly posed in terms of the nationalist doctrine first put forward by the Narodniks half a century earlier: Russia was supposedly offered a choice between becoming a colony of the West or evolving into a socialist future on the basis of her own —fortunately still intact—pre-capitalist foundations. All this was of little interest to the labour movement in advanced industrial countries but relevant enough to intellectuals in backward pre-industrial societies who had to wrestle with similar problems. Hence the varying fortunes of the key term 'revolution'. In 1917–18 it still meant to Communists what it had signified to European radicals ever since France set the pattern: the liberation of society from outworn political and spiritual fetters. From the 1930's onward it came to stand for the reshaping of society by a dictatorial regime in control of a centralised state apparatus and an all-pervading party organisation. Both meanings could hardly continue forever to coexist without friction; hence the peculiar moral climate of Stalinism, with its secret doctrine for the elect, its contempt for 'the masses', and its elevation of the individual conscience to the role of public enemy number one.

In terms of traditional Marxist thinking, this transformation of socialism into the ideology of an industrial revolution in backward countries was both unforeseen and awkward. It could of course be fitted into the theoretical framework: Marx himself had cautiously admitted the possibility of a socialist development in Russia (the popular notion to the contrary is based on ignorance). Moreover, after the event it was easy to see that Lenin had exploited a situation which was bound to recur. Put schematically, he had shown that it was possible to steer the 'bourgeois revolution' into anti-bourgeois channels. It is now a commonplace that the impact of industrialism on backward societies sets up strains which—in conjunction with the concurrent popular revolt against autocracy, and intellectual revolt against traditional culture—make for a revolutionary situation. But a sociological formula of this kind takes no account of the historical links connecting the Russian Revolution, by way of Marxism, with its French predecessor.

The simplest way of putting the matter is to say that the situation erroneously assumed by Marx and Engels in 1848 to exist in Germany turned out, seventy years later, to be present in Russia. By then, however, Marxism had become synonymous with European Socialism and the latter had become democratic. Hence the October Revolution—though it confirmed Marx's own estimates concerning Russia—endangered the integration of Marxism with the Western labour movement, which was henceforth split between Communists and Social-Democrats, both in theory followers of Marx. This was bound to happen from the moment Germany and the rest of Europe refused to follow the Russian example. The resulting split disclosed that in any advanced industrial country the labour movement was committed to democracy: a circumstance not grasped by Communists in the utopian climate of 1918–20, and barely apprehended by their successors. There is nothing in all this that does not fit with perfect ease into the framework of Marxism as a *theory* of social development. But historically the outcome has been to identify the original Marxist programme of 1848—though not the revised version of 1864—with the forcible industrialisation of the less advanced portions of the globe: which is scarcely what Marx and Engels expected to happen when they first formulated their doctrine. To say that the centre of gravity has shifted eastwards is a considerable understatement. The fact is that Marxism as a movement fails to make sense outside the European context, or at any rate outside the context of a world centred on Europe. Its basic assumptions are too closely bound up with the Victorian perspective of European leadership to retain much of their significance when transposed to a world scene dominated by the global conflict between North America and Eurasia.

The awkwardness of this conclusion—for anyone trying to adhere to the traditional Marxist perspective—is sufficiently dramatised by the East–West split which has become the principal issue in world affairs since 1945–8. This is not so much because of the obvious dangers arising from what is popularly known as the 'cold war' but because the very nature of the conflict—whether conducted peacefully or not—implies a political choice in terms of competing power blocs. In this perspective there is no real difference between 'cold war' and 'coexistence'; they are simply two sides of the same coin. The real issue in any case concerns the social structure of countries adhering to one side or the other. Given the assumptions current in the Soviet orbit since the 1920's, it was perfectly logical for Communists to conclude from 1948 onward that the global transition to a new form of social organisation implied a shift in world leadership towards the group of countries led by the USSR. In less refined language, the coming victory of 'socialism' (as defined in the orbit) was expected to take the form of Russian—or Sino-Soviet—hegemony in world affairs. This conclusion was never stated in so many words, but it was implicit in the evolution of Stalinist doctrine after 1945; indeed in a sense it was already implied by Lenin's formula in

1923, though this still had a defensive ring. In Marxist terms such a prospect might be justified on the grounds that historically every major change in socio-economic organisation has been associated with the emergence of a new group of countries who took over from their rivals. Examples might include the industrial-capitalist break-through which enabled England to play the dominant role for a century or more. (The awkward feature of this transition: that it was conservative England, not revolutionary France, which emerged as the leading power from the Napoleonic wars, is not of course stressed in Soviet literature, since it would spoil the neatness of the argument.)

Whatever attraction such an outlook may have for Soviet patriots —or for nationalist intellectuals in backward countries recently emancipated from Western control—it is totally at variance with the traditional Marxist-Socialist conception in which Western Europe and North America figured as the pivotal areas of the coming social transformation. Marx and Engels took it for granted that, just as England and France had in the nineteenth century provided the model for the liberal age, so Western Europe and North America would take the lead in promoting the advance to a higher level of organisation. While they did not exclude the possibility of socialist transformations in backward countries, it never occurred to them that the latter might identify their belated industrial revolutions with socialism, and on this ground stake a claim to world leadership, to the point of solemnly offering to reorganise the civilised nations of the West! Such a perspective would have struck them as grotesque. Their internationalism did not imply any abandonment of the West's his-toric claim to leadership. On the contrary, they assumed that the advanced countries would be the first to transcend the limitations of the established order.[1] In 'correcting' this perspective to make

[1] Cf. Engels to Kautsky, September 12, 1882, MESC, p. 423: 'Once Europe and North America have been organised, they will represent such a colossal power and such an example that the semi-civilised countries will naturally be taken in tow; economic necessities will see to it; as to what sort of social and political stages these countries will have to go through before they too arrive at a socialist organisation, we can, I think, at present formulate no more than vague hypotheses.' (Quoted by Kautsky, in *Sozialismus und Kolonialpolitik*, Berlin, 1907.) It is noteworthy that in commenting on this passage in October 1916, Lenin still took the entire argument completely for granted. As usual, this did not prevent him from ignoring it in practice, when a year later he com-mitted his party to a socialist revolution in backward Russia. Lenin never 'revised' or repudiated a single element of the Marxian canon; he merely disregarded anything that happened to interfere with his changing political requirements.

room for their own national goals, the leaders of Russian Communism were in the end driven by the logic of their argument to underwrite the corresponding—and therefore even more patently absurd—claims of Mao Tse-tung and his colleagues: to the point where even the most blinkered Stalinist might have begun to suspect that something had gone wrong. What that something was should by now have become clear. It remains to see how the evolution here described has affected the theoretical model of Soviet Marxism.

Ever since Lenin in 1915–17 committed himself to the thesis that the first world war had ushered in a new age of imperialist conflicts and proletarian revolutions, Leninist doctrine has oscillated between utopian anticipations of imminent world-wide breakdown, and hard-headed insistence upon the chances offered to any country that managed to escape from the capitalist maelstrom. The roots of this two-fold attitude are traceable to Lenin's wartime writings and his subsequent utterances, after the conquest of power by his party, when he tended to stress, now the certainty of further global upheavals, now the opportunity for Russia to push forward with the construction of socialism. As early as August 1915 he envisaged a victorious socialist revolution as a sort of local breakthrough 'in a few countries or even in a single country', and by implication outside Europe, since part of the argument was devoted to deflating the traditional conception of Europe as the natural centre of democracy and socialism.[1] In its original form the thesis was rather sketchy, the possibility of isolated socialist revolutions being simply deduced from the 'uneven economic and political development' characteristic of capitalism. Yet behind this nebulous formula there clearly lurked a very definite political notion: the belief that backward Russia might burst the bonds of the international system in which she was entangled. Though currently one of the 'imperialist marauders' who were fighting to divide the world among themselves, she might through revolution become the focus of a new global development. After 1917 these hints were expanded into what for want of a better term must be reluctantly described as the theoretical system of Leninism-Stalinism.[2] This involved *both* the definition of Leninism

---

[1] 'On the United States of Europe slogan', *Selected Works*, I, pp. 630–2.

[2] Stalin, 'The Foundations of Leninism', in *Problems of Leninism*, Moscow, 1947, pp. 13 ff; cf. also 'The October Revolution and the Tactics of the Russian Communists', ibid., especially pp. 103 ff, for Stalin's attempt to deduce from Lenin's observations that Russia could very well build a socialist society within her frontiers.

as 'Marxism of the era of imperialism and of the proletarian revolution', *and* the ascription to Lenin of the characteristically Stalinist thesis that the establishment of 'socialism' in the USSR did not by any means depend on international developments.[1] In the twenties such an assertion might still be disputed; later such attempts became distinctly unhealthy, and the meaning of Soviet Marxism, or 'Marxism-Leninism', was identified with a set of beliefs which Marx would never have dreamed of putting forward.

A further stage was reached after 1945, when the implicit sense of the 'unequal development' thesis was, as it were, turned back upon its critics: henceforth it was the USSR's emergence as an industrial and military giant—and not as before her backwardness—which was held to demonstrate that history proceeded by leaps and bounds rather than in a straight line. Having skipped the capitalist phase of development, the Soviet orbit now confronted a Western world which, by Leninist-Stalinist standards, was politically retrograde and socially conservative. The wheel had come full circle, and Marxism, from being a critique of bourgeois society in terms of that society's own liberal aspirations, was now employed to buttress the faith of a regime which prided itself on its freedom from bourgeois traditions (always very weak in Russia, and nowhere more so than in the sphere of political liberties). After that it only needed the extension of the Communist triumph to China for Marxism to be stood entirely on its head. By Stalinist standards even a work like Lenin's *Development of Capitalism in Russia* (1900), with its stress on the validity of the traditional Marxist model, had become, if not heretical, at any rate pointless. It was no longer necessary to argue that capitalism represents progress for backward countries, the USSR having demonstrated the possibility of an alternative. Naturally, the connection between Communism and backwardness was not admitted, though it should have been evident. National pride has its own logic. Just as Lenin's brief and sketchy tract on imperialism, or his scholastic exercises in *State and Revolution*, must be affirmed to constitute a major theoretical breakthrough, so Soviet 'socialism' as a whole is conceived in the official ideology to represent a new and higher stage in the development of mankind. That such claims are not acceptable to Westerners is put down to political hostility. The obvious explanation, in terms of continued Russian backwardness in

[1] Stalin, loc. cit., pp. 119 ff; for Trotsky's viewpoint cf. *Permanentnaya Revolyutsiya*, passim.

most spheres outside technology and the natural sciences, is no more admissible than the truth that Soviet Marxism is intellectually incompetent to sustain a genuine theoretical confrontation with rival modes of thought. All such dangerous notions are simply excluded from the official consciousness.

This state of affairs makes it difficult to come to grips with the theoretical affirmations offered by Soviet Marxists, whose point of departure today is not simply Leninism but Stalinism, i.e., the theory and practice of a planned 'revolution from above' in a backward country (minus those irrational excrescences which could be, and have been, blamed upon the personality of the late dictator). In this respect a significant change has supervened since the 'twenties and early 'thirties, when genuine theoretical discussions were still possible between Leninists and Western Marxists, or for that matter between Communists and non-Marxian Socialists. However inadequate Lenin's or Bukharin's theoretical exegesis of Marx's system might appear to non-Communists, there was enough common ground to make rational controversy possible. This situation came to an end when the Stalinist codification of Lenin was superimposed upon the already disastrously narrow and schematic Leninist interpretation of Marx. Since then—roughly speaking since the middle 'thirties—Soviet Marxism has taken on the character of an official ideology whose internal coherence is preserved at the cost of increasing rigidity and growing remoteness from reality. In the circumstances a head-on confrontation is no longer possible; or rather, it is possible only in political terms, since every challenge to the theoretical structure resolves itself into an investigation of its political premises. One cannot, for example, analyse the Leninist theory of imperialism, or the Stalinist doctrine of the state, without coming upon ideological postulates—anti-Westernism in the one case, acceptance of autocracy as the only rational political system in the other—of which Soviet Communists are unaware, but which are in fact the unexamined premises of their thinking. This is as much as to say that Leninism must be understood as an ideology in the Marxian sense of the term, i.e., as a system of thought which obscures the facts it purports to describe. Since Marxism—almost by definition—is a method of sociological critique, it is not very surprising that when applied to Soviet reality it turns out to be thoroughly subversive. Yet this reality embodies at any rate *some* aspects of Marxism, so that if pushed sufficiently far the critique turns back upon itself: the Marxian method cannot halt before the Marxian system—i.e., the comprehensive world-view which Marx and Engels bequeathed to their followers and ultimately to the Socialist movement from which Leninism was to arise.

It is necessary to see both the continuity and the point where the fatal break took place. After what has been said earlier, this point can be defined without too much trouble: it was constituted by Lenin's (and subsequently Stalin's) systematic misuse of the term 'proletarian revolution' to describe the totalitarian rearrangement of society *after* the capture of power by a party which originally conceived itself to be in the 'classical' tradition. Simultaneously, the democratic revolutions of Western society since the seventeenth century were denigrated as 'bourgeois.' Behind these verbalisms there lies the reality of an experience quite different from that of the West, but quite in accordance with the traditional Russian pattern of autocratic reorganisation of society by the state—except that it took the Revolution to make the state genuinely totalitarian, i.e., capable of refashioning the social order from top to bottom. Once this goal was defined as the purpose of 'socialism', all the rest followed, and it only remained to recast the vocabulary of Marxism so as to bring it into line with the practice of the Communist party.[1]

---

[1] For the historical roots of this attitude, cf. Venturi, op. cit., passim. It is now widely recognised that the characteristic Bolshevik synthesis of revolutionary and authoritarian beliefs was prefigured within the radical wing of the nineteenth-century Populist movement. Totalitarianism and elite-worship both have their source in the conspiratorial sects of the radical intelligentsia; one may even suspect that there was a direct filiation between the most intransigent of these groups and the Bolsheviks. Lenin's Menshevik opponents had drawn attention to this issue at a fairly early stage. (Cf. J. L. H. Keep, *The Rise of Social Democracy in Russia*, Oxford, 1963, passim; Samuel H. Baron, *Plekhanov: the father of Russian Marxism*, Stanford, 1963, passim.)

2

STATE AND SOCIETY

TO EXTRACT the theoretical essence of Soviet Marxism is a simpler
matter than might appear from the enormous literature on the subject—itself no more than a fluctuating and uncertain mirror-image
of the complex reality portrayed therein. The theme appears in-
exhaustible, concerning as it does the Revolution and its impact on
Russia; thereafter—if such a distinction is possible—the theory and
practice of the Communist party, the conflicts between its various
factions, the rise and fall of the Communist International, and the
gradual transformation of Leninism from a doctrine of 'proletarian'
revolution into the ideology of a new ruling class. Merely to enumer-
ate these topics is to show why no study intent on isolating the
theoretical structure of Marxism can attempt to pay more than passing attention to them. In taking them all for granted one is not for
this reason obliged to draw an artificial frontier between history and
theory; still less between the analysis of ideas and that of political
events. Historical treatises on the revolution, and analytical studies of
the regime, come together in the attempt to lay bare the common
root of the reality we call Soviet Communism. In the process, the
party is discovered to be the link between the old and the new society,
between the pre-revolutionary and the post-revolutionary significance of the term 'Communism', and finally between the practice

of the regime and the ideology of its articulate stratum: the Soviet intelligentsia. All this belongs to the pathology of the Revolution—taking the term to stand for the whole vast transformation effected since 1917—and has no immediate bearing on our subject. There is indeed the theoretical problem of accounting for the role played by the party, which was surely unique and suggestive of a new historical determinant unknown to the liberal nineteenth century. Yet this problem is not peculiar to the Soviet regime, the Bolshevik party being evidently a variant of the characteristically modern phenomenon known as totalitarianism. No one understood this better than the theorist who after 1918 helped to bring the Italian Communist movement into being, and who from his prison cell under Mussolini went on to develop a doctrine more totalitarian than that of his gaolers:

The modern prince, the myth-prince, cannot be a real person, a concrete individual; it can only be an organism; a complex element of society in which the cementing of a collective will, recognised and partially asserted in action, has already begun. This organism is already provided by historical development, and it is the political party: the first cell containing the germs of collective will which are striving to become universal and total.[1]

From a different starting-point and in language reminiscent of nineteenth-century German romanticism—but with the same Hegelian commitment to truth as the 'comprehended totality' of history—the doctrine of the party as the incorporation of the revolution *and* the nucleus of the new society, was simultaneously worked out by the only other original thinker the Communist movement has produced since 1917: the Hungarian philosopher Georg Lukács.[2]

It may seem strange that two European writers should be cited in this context, but then Leninism is an international phenomenon, though centred on Russian Communism. Moreover, its national

[1] Antonio Gramsci, 'Notes on Machiavelli's Politics', in *The Modern Prince and other writings*, London, 1957, p. 137. Cf. also loc. cit., p. 139: 'The modern prince must and cannot but be the preacher and organiser of intellectual and moral reform, which means creating the basis for a later development of the national popular collective will towards the realisation of a higher and total form of modern civilisation'—a pretty drastic inversion, this, of the traditional Marxian scheme, but quite in accordance with Gramsci's intellectual descent from Hegel and Croce: not to mention his Catholic upbringing.

[2] Cf. Lukács, *Geschichte und Klassenbewusstsein*, Vienna-Berlin, 1923 passim. For an analysis of this seminal work, and of Lukács's role in adapting Marxian philosophy to the requirements of the totalitarian epoch, cf. Morris Watnick, 'Georg Lukács: An Intellectual Biography', *Soviet Survey*, London, Nos. 24 and 25, April–June and July–September, 1958.

roots (to which attention has been drawn elsewhere) had their counterparts in countries like Italy and Hungary which were a little outside the West European mainstream. Gramsci's concern with Jacobinism is more illuminating for our purpose than an exegesis of the dreary writings penned by the Webbs in their old age. In contrast to these and other essays in misinterpretation, the leading theorist of the Italian Communist party comes straight to the point:

The *Modern Prince* must contain a part dedicated to Jacobinism . . . as an example of how a collective will was formed and operated concretely, which in at least some of its aspects was an original creation, *ex novo*. It is necessary to define collective will and political will in general in the modern sense; will as working consciousness of historical necessity, as protagonist of a real and effective historical drama. . . .

Any formation of a national-popular collective will is impossible unless the great mass of peasant cultivators breaks *simultaneously* into political life. Machiavelli understood this by his reform of the militia, which is what the Jacobins did in the French Revolution, and in this understanding we can see the precocious Jacobinism of Machiavelli. . . .[1]

One may also see that Gramsci had intuitively grasped the nature of Leninism, as the theory and practice of a revolution in a retarded country where the masses were suddenly hurled upon the political stage under the leadership of the Bolshevik vanguard. The next stage—the transformation of the revolutionary party into a new ruling elite—was concealed from him: in part by the accident of his relatively early death in 1937 (after eleven years in prison), but even more effectively by his illusions. He would certainly not have approved of the Stalinist doctrine, expressly invented to justify the permanent rule of a party which concealed the social domination of a new privileged stratum; but by then the matter had been taken out of the hands of theorists like himself and entrusted to the practitioners of the new order. Moreover, his own approach was quite consistent with the totalitarian assumption that revolutions are made by elites, though his personal commitment was to the hope that the proletarian revolution might be self-liquidating.[2]

[1] Gramsci, loc. cit., pp. 138–9 (for the original text cf. *Note sul Machiavelli, sulla politica e sullo stato moderno*, Turin, 1949).

[2] Cf. *The Modern Prince*, p. 143: 'In the formation of leaders the premise is fundamental: does one wish there to be always rulers and ruled, or does one wish to create the conditions where the necessity for the existence of this division disappears? In other words, does one start from the premise of the perpetual division of the human race, or does one believe that this is only an historical fact, answering to certain conditions? . . . In a sense it can be said that this division is a product of the division of labour, that it is a technical fact.'

Totalitarianism raised its head in Gramsci's writings for the good reason that he was confronted with the reality of Fascism. What he had to say about it—e.g., that under modern conditions it is the party which founds the state; that the totalitarian party 'will exalt the abstract concept of "State" and will seek by various means to give the impression that the function of "impartial force" is active and effective'[1]—was intended as criticism of Mussolini's regime, but could have been applied word for word to Stalin (under whose rule Gramsci would have been unlikely to fill entire prison notebooks with philosophical reflections). We owe it to the accident of this gifted writer's incarceration under Fascism that there is such a thing as a Marxist critique of totalitarianism, 'from the inside', as it were. The various opposition groups which split off from the Russian Communist party in the 1920's and 1930's produced a great many critical reflections on the operation of the regime, but—with the doubtful exception of Trotsky's last writings—nothing like a principled rejection of the central idea of totalitarianism, which is quite simply the idea of a social order created by force: perhaps the most 'un-Marxian' notion ever excogitated by professed Marxists.[2]

Communist theorists like Lukács and Gramsci were able in the 1920's and 1930's to pose the issue with a degree of clarity not paralleled in Soviet literature, where after Lenin's death apologetics predominated. Although—or because—the Bolshevik regime had evolved in the direction of totalitarianism, there was no corresponding development on the theoretical level. The official exegesis remained helplessly suspended between Lenin's revival of the 'proletarian dictatorship' concept and his simultaneous insistence that this dictatorship could and should take the form of radical 'popular democracy', to the point where the state would begin to 'wither away'.[3] During the Stalinist era these evident contradictions were supplemented by the even more patent disharmony between the utopian slogans of 1917 and the drive for rigid control while the 'second revolution' was in progress. It is true that Lenin had led the

[1] Ibid., p. 146; cf. also Gramsci, *Lettere del carcere*, Turin, 1947 (tr. *Lettres de la prison*, Paris, 1953), passim.

[2] For Lukács's views cf. in particular his essay 'Methodisches zur Organisationsfrage', in *Geschichte und Klassenbewusstsein*, pp. 298 ff: an impressive exercise in Hegelian logic to the end of drawing out the full implications of Lenin's doctrine of the vanguard. The attempt was so successful that the entire work was promptly placed on the Communist Index. Some doctrines are easier to practise than to preach.

[3] Cf. *State and Revolution*, in *Selected Works*, II, p. 223.

way in this respect. Although *State and Revolution* is full of quasi-anarchist passages, it also contains a significant reference to the 'iron discipline' required during the transitional period, while 'we ourselves, the workers, will organise large-scale production on the basis of what capitalism has already created.'[1] After this promising start it was not too difficult for Stalin to assemble scriptural justification for his decision to invest the managers of the planned economy with practically unlimited powers over 'their' working personnel.[2]

At first sight it might seem that there is no good reason for linking this subject with the issue of totalitarianism. But it must be remembered that it was the state-party which created the party-state, and that Leninism-Stalinism is essentially the doctrinal reflex of this transformation. Speaking generally, totalitarianism is the outcome of a situation in which the state is captured by a party which has resolved upon the wholesale reorganisation of society. Whatever may be said about the participation of 'the masses' in furthering this aim, the whole process can only go forward under 'conscious direction', i.e., by unremitting pressure from above. This is especially so if the state-party is committed to socialism, which by its very nature involves both conscious control and central direction. Before hastening to conclude that socialism therefore spells monolithic rule by a caste of planners, it is well to remember that historically this danger was perceived quite early by the nascent labour movement which for precisely this reason insisted that socialism should be democratic. It was the emancipation of the Bolshevik party—ultimately of the Soviet dictatorship—from all forms of democratic control that made possible the identification of 'planning' with the untrammelled rule of a new privileged caste. And it was the centralised structure of Lenin's party that enabled it to usurp power under conditions where, for the first time in modern history, a genuinely

[1] Ibid., p. 174.

[2] Cf. *Problems of Leninism*, pp. 359 ff: 'New Conditions—New Tasks in Economic Construction' (Speech delivered at a conference of business executives, June 23, 1931). This document includes *inter alia* the following instructive passage: 'No ruling class has managed without its own intelligentsia. There are no grounds for believing that the working class of the USSR can manage without its own industrial and technical intelligentsia.' (Loc. cit., p. 369.) In this context the terms 'ruling class' and 'working class' clearly have a meaning remote from ordinary usage; it is not too much to say that in the fanciful picture drawn by Stalin, the real social relationship between the workers and the technical intelligentsia—the core of the new 'ruling class'—has been reversed. Not that Stalin was necessarily aware of this fact.

'total' attempt to refashion society had become technically feasible. It would be tempting to describe this as a coincidence, were it not for the disagreeable fact that since 1917 such trends have shown up elsewhere—and not only in backward countries. They evidently correspond *both* to the peculiar problems of retarded societies in a transitional age, *and* to the bureaucratic tendencies characteristic of highly industrialised countries. In the 1930's it even looked for a while as though Fascism and Stalinism might coalesce; and we have seen that it was an Italian Marxist under Mussolini who unwittingly described the nature of totalitarianism in terms applicable to both regimes.

In trying to cope with this complex of theoretical and practical issues, neither Socialists nor Communists could draw much comfort from the classics. On the democratic side, the practice of German and Austrian Social-Democracy after 1918 corresponded more or less to the advice Engels had given their leaders in the 1890's,[1] while the doctrine and policy of French, Italian or Spanish Socialist movements might be said to constitute a judicious gloss upon Marx's varying recipes for France. Neither Marx nor Engels had envisaged the kind of situation which arose from the consolidation of the Bolshevik regime in Russia. For the domain of socialist economics this was obvious: *Capital* contained at most the rudiments of a theoretical model applicable to the problem of planning (in vol. II). Questions of political rule had been discussed by both Marx and Engels at greater length, but for the most part with reference to social conditions which did not prevail in Russia and which after 1918 were being eroded in the West. It is hardly surprising that the founding fathers did not concern themselves overmuch with the institutions of parliamentary democracy, since they regarded them as appropriate to liberal society and thus of no particular interest to socialists—save in the obvious sense that the labour movement had to make use of them. On the other hand, their dislike of utopian blueprints prevented them from trying to envisage the political model of a socialist society. Leaving aside Marx's sketchy observations on the experiments undertaken by the Paris Commune, and his quasi-Jacobin reference to 'proletarian dictatorship' during the transition period,[2] his followers were left without guidance. It is true that Marx was not

---

[1] For a different view cf. R. Schlesinger, *Central European Democracy and its Background*, London, 1953, passim.

[2] *Critique of the Gotha Programme*, MESW II, p. 30.

nearly so utopian as he is often represented as being. It was Engels, not he, who as late as the 1870's committed himself to the assertion that the state would 'wither away'.[1] His own occasional hints were sufficiently ambiguous to leave room for the suggestion that even the higher stage of the communist society would not be completely stateless.[2] In more immediate terms, his stress on the need for a transitional dictatorship could be cited as evidence that he would have approved of the Leninist experiment. But all these exegetical labours come to a dead stop in view of the evident impossibility of squaring the Marxist doctrine with the reality of modern Communist domination. The simple fact is that totalitarianism was as little dreamed of in Marx's philosophy as in that of Mill. In this respect classical liberalism and Marxism have more in common than either side could have suspected before 1918.

Marx's attitude to the state was closely connected with his theory of class, and like the latter a product of the liberal epoch. At the risk of some simplification his standpoint can be summed up by saying that the state is an epiphenomemon of the class struggle. A clear formulation of this belief—which was not really very different from the prevailing democratic view in the West, while sharply opposed to the Hegelian state worship endemic in Germany—is to be found in a fairly early utterance of his, two years after the publication of the *Communist Manifesto*. Commenting on a French work of the period which advocated the virtual abandonment of centralised administration and the establishment of a self-regulating system of taxation, Marx observed that bourgeois society could not do without the state, though its functions could be reduced to the level then prevalent in North America:

Behind the abolition of taxes there is concealed the abolition of the state. The abolition of the state has meaning only for Communists, as the necessary result of the abolition of classes, with which the need for the organised power of one class to hold down the others disappears of itself. In bourgeois countries the abolition of the state signifies the reduction of state power to the level it has in North America. . . . In feudal countries the abolition of

[1] *Anti-Dühring* (Eng. edn.), Moscow, 1954, p. 389.
[2] MESW II, p. 30: 'The question then arises: what transformation will the state undergo in communist society? In other words, what social functions will remain in existence there that are analogous to present functions of the state? This question can only be answered scientifically. . . .' For an illuminating discussion of the whole question cf. S. F. Bloom, 'The "withering away" of the State', *Journal of the History of Ideas*, vol. VII, no. 1, New York, January, 1946.

the state means the abolition of feudalism and the establishment of the familiar bourgeois state.[1]

The state is an outcome of class rule, and class society is due to disappear with the transition to communism, defined as 'an association which will exclude classes and their antagonism', and where in consequence 'there will no longer be a political power properly so called, since political power is precisely the official resumé of the antagonism within civil society'.[2] The already common objection that the disappearance of the old society might simply give rise to a new form of class rule—and hence to a new form of political oppression—is countered by the assertion that the working class cannot emancipate itself without getting rid of class rule altogether, 'just as it was a precondition of the emancipation of the third estate, the bourgeois order, that all estates and all orders should be abolished'.[3] This ingenious argument can hardly be termed anything but an evasion of the issue: the very fact that the disappearance of the estates had not ushered in the promised reign of freedom might have suggested the conclusion that the abolition of classes would likewise fail to make society truly self-governing. Subject to this caution, however, the argument is effective enough: classes, like estates, are transitory forms of social organisation, and the oppressed class—like the oppressed medieval order before it—can attain its aims only by transforming the society of which it is part.

Before turning to the examination of Marx's concept of class in the light of latter-day reality, it is worth recalling that his hostility to the state was held in check by a decidedly authoritarian doctrine of political rule during the transition period: prior to being consigned to the dustbin of history, the state was to assume dictatorial powers. In different terms, authority would inaugurate freedom—a typically Hegelian paradox which did not worry Marx though it alarmed Proudhon and Bakunin: both Hegelians like himself, but temperamentally disposed to fear that authority would simply breed more authority. All three, it might be added, had this in common: they envisaged the coming transformation in the light of the 'bourgeois revolution', as it had taken shape since the eighteenth century,

[1] Review of *Le Socialisme et l'Impôt*, by Emile de Girardin (Paris, 1850), in *Neue Rheinische Revue*, No. 4, April 1850 (cf. Mehring, *Nachlass*, vol. III, p. 438).
[2] Marx, *Misère de la philosophie*, in MEGA I/6, p. 227; cf. *The Poverty of Philosophy*, London, 1956, p. 197.
[3] Ibid., p. 196.

notably in France; the difference being that Marx fastened on the state as the chief instrument of political change while simultaneously affirming that the revolution would cause the state to disappear. This is the point where the Leninist model later inserted itself into the framework of the Marxian conception. Paradoxically, it was Marx's contemptuous treatment of the state as a mere instrument of reconstruction which has made it possible for modern Communists to obscure its role in promoting the 'total' reorganisation of society. The state as an epiphenomenon of class rule, and the state as the prime agent of revolutionary change, exist on different planes of the complex Marxian structure. Depending on whether Marxism serves as a theory of bourgeois society, or as a doctrine of social revolution, the emphasis shifts from one aspect to the other, though the tension never quite disappears. Indeed the only way to make it disappear is to impose a general prohibition upon political thinking, and in particular upon the realistic study of political institutions. This accounts for the fact that institutional sociology is unknown in the USSR. Any attempt to introduce it would undermine the official taboo surrounding notions such as that in the Soviet Union the working class has acquired political power and 'ceased to be a proletariat in the proper . . . meaning of the term.'[1]

While the gradual development of Leninist-Stalinist doctrine on the state plainly reflects the growth of new hierarchical relationships in Soviet society which make nonsense of the egalitarian slogans proclaimed in 1917, the inadequacy of this doctrine has deeper roots. Mention has already been made of the uncertainty which from the start afflicted Marx's view of the state's function in history. To this must be added the no less paradoxical conception of political 'rule' by a class envisioned as the dialectical negation of the socially dominant bourgeoisie. This notion already raises its head in the *Communist Manifesto* where 'the first step in the revolution' is described as an act which will 'raise the proletariat to the position of the ruling class, to win the battle of democracy'.[2] Leaving aside the fact that in 1848 the proletariat was nowhere the majority, and that the only revolution then in question was precisely a 'bourgeois'

---

[1] *History of the Communist Party* (*Bolsheviks*), Moscow, 1939, English edn., pp. 314–15. Though superseded in 1959 by a revised party history, the essential theses of this well-known primer—the so-called *Short Course*—have not been abrogated; indeed it is difficult to see how they could be abandoned without a renunciation of the whole Leninist conception.

[2] MESW I, p. 53.

one, there clearly is a paradox involved in the notion of turning political control over to those who, almost by definition, are without effective power in society. Conversely, if the working class is thought of as 'leading' the people as a whole, so that its 'rule' is synonymous with democracy, we are confronted with what is probably the oldest conundrum in the history of political thought: if 'the people' are the rulers, who is there left to be ruled?[1] This question has received different answers since its first formulation in classical Antiquity, the typical modern solution being the doctrine of majority rule within a representative system; but in 1848 Marx and Engels were debarred from taking this line by their belief that the representative system camouflaged the domination of the propertied minority. Hence they were obliged to fall back upon the Jacobin idea of a temporary dictatorship to pave the way for a new order 'in which the free development of each is the condition for the free development of all'. This conception was not merely incompatible with democracy in the short run; it stood in flat opposition to the actual character of the labour movement, as it gradually came to free itself from the political model of the 'bourgeois revolution' and evolved its own characteristic ideas and modes of procedure. One could get out of the difficulty (as most Socialists did after 1871) by treating the *Manifesto* as a youthful escapade on the part of its authors, but one must not blind oneself to its crucial importance for Lenin's political strategy. The fact is that in 1917 no other rationale was possible for the Bolshevik party, once it had determined upon the conquest of power. Moreover, once the fateful decision had been taken it became a psychological necessity to affirm that the doctrine held good not merely for backward countries, but for the world in general. Hence the obstinate refusal to admit that under capitalism the state might be something other than the 'executive committee' of a diminishing number of monopolists; and the equally blind inability to perceive that the labour movement cannot possibly abandon its concern for democracy.

In actual fact the rudiments of a doctrine of the state transcending the 'executive committee' notion were already present in the writings of Marx and Engels, inasmuch as they recognised the obvious

---

[1] Cf. Richard Wollheim, 'Democracy', *Journal of the History of Ideas*, New York, April 1958, vol. XIX, no. 2, pp. 225 ff; for the growing tension between fact and myth in Soviet doctrine on this subject cf. H. Marcuse, *Soviet Marxism*, pp. 120 ff.

truth that every government, however class-bound, is obliged to represent the essential interests of society as a whole.[1] These and other hints became important to Soviet Marxists once the Stalinist era had encouraged a somewhat unorthodox emphasis upon the 'creative role' of the 'political superstructure'. By that time, however, it had become impossible to approach the problem realistically, since every serious analysis of the regime was bound to lay bare its true character. In consequence Soviet theory is distinguished by a persistent, if hopeless, attempt to demonstrate that in the USSR the state serves the general interest, without being in any way beholden to those who are actually in control of it. This naïve determination to dispense with the simplest elements of Marxist thinking where the USSR is concerned, is made easier by the actual role of the Communist party as the mediator between the privileged stratum and the masses. Since the party knows itself to be doing what in principle every ruling power must do: namely, hold the balance between the socially dominant class and the working people, it can with a fairly good conscience repudiate the charge of serving the interests of the privileged upper crust. What its ideologists fail to see is that the Soviet state is not unique in harmonising social conflicts, preserving law and order, and in general functioning as the executive organ of society as a whole. The possibility of such a condition of things existing outside the borders of the 'socialist camp' is stubbornly denied, whence the total sterility of Soviet political thinking. This thinking in effect combines the sectarian narrowness of the original Leninist approach with the disingenuousness characteristic of every autocratic regime which dare not submit its decrees to popular ratification. Even if this gap should gradually be bridged—in principle not an impossibility, as the new order comes to be more or less acceptable to the majority—the ideological character of Soviet thinking would be bound to persist as long as its presuppositions remain unquestioned.

What characterises every ideology is discordance between the actual state of affairs and the socially determined pressure to re-arrange reality in the light of certain overriding concepts which may be altogether at variance with what the individuals know to be the

[1] Cf. Engels, *Origin of the Family*, MESW II, p. 290: 'As the state arose from the need to hold class antagonisms in check . . . it is as a rule the state of the most powerful, economically dominant class. . . .' This at any rate suggests that the state on occasions harmonises social conflicts, while at the same time serving the interests of the dominant class.

case within the limits of their own experience. That is why under a totalitarian regime the private existence of people becomes a source of danger. Since individual needs cannot in fact be met—least of all the need for freedom—the claim that liberty and democracy have already been established comes up against the widespread perception that reality differs from its presentation in the official system of beliefs or quasi-beliefs. This leads to scepticism, which in turn endangers the ability of the party-state to mobilise popular energies towards further 'social engineering'. Since it is of the essence of a totalitarian regime to be dynamic, it cannot function in an atmosphere of public indifference. A conservative autocracy requires no more than passive obedience, for the good reason that its aim is to keep things as they are. A regime which aims at reshaping society is driven towards totalitarianism by the logic of its functioning, and this drive compels ideas, as well as material circumstances, to change their shape in conformity with the central purpose animating the revolutionary mechanism. In this overheated atmosphere, theoretical consistency and ordinary veracity are among the first and most lasting casualties. Hence it should cause no surprise that the relationship of state to society—the central problem of Soviet totalitarianism—is surrounded by a barrier of taboos impenetrable to mere argument. The official ideology performs the basic service of protecting the self-appointed guardians of the status quo from the danger of acquiring too clear a notion of their veritable role.

To such criticisms Soviet Marxism typically replies by impugning the credentials of the critic. Alternatively, it appeals from 'mere' fact to the 'higher', or 'deeper' truth laid up in the doctrinal heaven. The argument runs somewhat as follows: one cannot criticise Soviet reality without implicitly invoking an ideology and a purpose opposed to Marxism-Leninism; for no criticism can be formulated that does not involve a commitment to certain aims, and these aims are either socialist or non-socialist; hence the critic of Soviet reality is by definition opposed to the attainment of socialism; q.e.d. Now one must indeed be careful not to fall into the empiricist trap of appealing from ideological constructs to so-called facts which commonly turn out upon inspection to be simply rival constructs. But the circular character of the argument should nonetheless be obvious: it begins by affirming the factual truth of certain statements, e.g., the statement that Soviet totalitarianism is the political form of a democratic socialist order; when these assertions are disputed, it replies that the challenge involves a different, and inferior, theoretical approach, and that recourse must bé had to an adequate theory, i.e., its own. This kind of verbal ingenuity may be effective for debating purposes, but its hollowness becomes apparent as soon as one contrasts the traditional signification of certain political concepts—class, state, socialism, democracy—with the use made of them in Leninist-Stalinist doctrine. The custodians of this doctrine cannot afford a genuine confrontation with rival modes of thought, for the internal consistency of their approach depends upon the ability to manipulate certain key concepts in such a manner as to exclude the semblance of discord between theory and practice. One need only consider the weird argument that a multiplicity of political viewpoints corresponds to the presence of antagonistic class interests, from which it is inferred that one-party rule is the ideal form of socialist democracy! The manner in which 'the party' —i.e., in the last resort the ruling oligarchy which *inter alia* controls the central party apparatus—interprets its own role, is closely linked to its ability to function as the political elite of a society that officially denies any distinction between rulers and ruled. In this domain as in others, the effective critique of ideology consists in making plain what lies concealed at the bottom of the doctrinaire ink-well.

3

SOCIALISM AND CLASS CONFLICT

MARXISM, which views class conflict as the principal feature of historical change, cannot be said to have operated with a definite conception of what it is that constitutes a class. The paradox has often been noted that Marx's major work breaks off at the very point where its author for the first time attempted a systematic consideration of this topic. Yet the fragmentary notes assembled in this unfinished chapter are enough to show that for him, as for his predecessors among the classical economists, the field of study was defined by the existing division of European society into landowners, capital owners and property-less labourers; and the question to be answered was 'what makes wage labourers, capitalists and landowners the formers (*Bildner*) of the three great social classes?'[1] Thus the theoretical model already familiar to Ricardo was taken for granted. Even before

[1] Cf. *Capital*, vol. III, chapter 52. Among recent literature on the subject, *Class and Class Conflict in Industrial Society*, by R. Dahrendorf, London, 1959, is distinguished by its comprehensiveness; for a qualified defence of the Marxian approach cf. M. Dobb, 'The Economic Basis of Class Conflict', in *On Economic Theory and Socialism*, London, 1955, pp. 93–103; R. Schlesinger, *Marx*, pp. 212 ff; for an appreciation of Marx's doctrine in terms of intellectual history cf. S. F. Bloom, 'Man of his Century: a reconsideration of the historic significance of Karl Marx', in *Journal of Political Economy*, New York, vol. LI, no. 6, December 1943, pp. 494 ff.

the breakthrough associated with the industrial revolution, the general notion underlying it had acquired prominence in the literature of the preceding age. That 'those who hold, and those who are without property have ever formed distinct interests in society', was a circumstance well known to the authors of the American Constitution, who probably did not need Madison to inform them that moneyed, manufacturing and other interests 'grow up of necessity in civilised nations, and divide them into different classes, actuated by different sentiments and views'.[1] By the time the physiocrats, the Scottish historians, and Adam Smith himself, had formulated the eighteenth-century view of the subject, there was little for Ricardo to add, or for Marx to elaborate, so far as the general principle was concerned. Yet pre-industrial society, being relatively static, did not invest the concept of class with an operational meaning. It was commonly employed to distinguish the different 'ranks' of a social order still in many respects hierarchical and regarded as permanent even by its critics.

In its characteristic modern sense the notion of class—as distinct from that of rank or estate—may be said to have arisen in the course of the French Revolution, from an empirical awareness that the removal of legal privileges did not by itself result in social equality, but rather laid bare an enduring conflict of interest dividing the propertied minority from the bulk of the labouring poor. In its embryonic form this view is still compatible with the pre-socialist standpoint affirmed by the Jacobin left-wingers who prepared the ground for the 'utopian socialists.' By the 1830's when the radical wing of the intelligentsia had got the socialist movement under way in both France and Britain, a dynamic element had been added by the discovery that class antagonisms were being sharpened by the industrial revolution. It was the conjunction of these ideas that lent a new and pointed significance to the radical view of democracy as the self-government of the non-privileged majority. Socialism as a political movement and a set of ideas takes wing from the moment when the newly formed industrial proletariat is identified by the radical intellectuals, who function as its spokesmen, as the class destined to

---

[1] *The Federalist* (1937 edn.), p. 56. Cf. Locke, *Of Civil Government*, para. 94: 'Government has no other end but the preservation of property.' A. Smith, *Wealth of Nations* (ed. Cannan, New York, 1937), p. 674: 'Civil government, so far as it is instituted for the security of property, is in reality instituted for the defence of the rich against the poor, or of those who have some property against those who have none at all.'

inherit the earth. By 1848, with the growth of intellectual sophistication consequent upon the fusion of socialism with political economy, Marx was able in the *Communist Manifesto* to formulate the new standpoint in a manner conspicuously superior to the naive moralising protests of his socialist predecessors. One may say if one likes that between 1776—when Adam Smith and Thomas Jefferson simultaneously summed up the eighteenth-century doctrine of society—and 1848, when Marx challenged that doctrine, the 'bourgeois revolution' in the West had run its course. Yet it is worth noting that Marx continued to operate with the traditional three-class model he had inherited from Smith. Class as a socio-economic concept belongs to the bourgeois age, and it is questionable whether it can be made to work under circumstances where property in the means of production is no longer the characteristic line of division between the major groups in society.

It is, however, not much use trying to assess Marx's standpoint without reference to what he was trying to accomplish. This consideration rules out the greater part of what is commonly said on the subject by writers who happen not to be interested in *historical* problems. For the Marxian theory is exclusively concerned with historic change, and with what is assumed to be its characteristic mechanism: social conflict. It has no bearing on 'status-seeking' or other phenomena devoid of long-range significance. If this were better understood there would be fewer attempts to prove Marx wrong by invoking 'status differences' as distinct from class relations. For of course Marx was not unaware of the texture of social life: as an inhabitant of Victorian England he could hardly fail to notice the complex interplay of class and caste relationships, and in fact his writings supply ample evidence that—like any other nineteenth-century observer of the social scene—he was alive to their significance.[1] Where he differed from contemporary sociologists and historians was in the particular angle from which he observed the

---

[1] Cf. his distinction—already referred to—between the British 'governing caste' and the middle class, which latter held effective political power but did not care to exercise it. Nor did Engels, with his Manchester background, have to be told anything about the latent tension between the oligarchic 'establishment' and the provincial manufacturers; and both men were of course fully aware of the even more complicated social texture of their native Germany. Anyone active in politics would be bound to notice such things. The notion that 'status' is a modern discovery could only have occurred to people who have never been outside a university.

transformation of pre-capitalist forms of dependence into class relationships, i.e. relationships governed not by legal or social status, but by property and, in the last analysis, by ownership of the means of production. The transformation itself was an observable phenomenon; the question was what it would lead to. For reasons which have already been discussed,[1] Marx's view of class relations under industrial capitalism was unduly pessimistic, but this forecast arose from his analysis of the economic mechanism, not from his class model; the latter was simply an extrapolation from the social conflicts of the age, which pitted landowners, manufacturers, and workers against each other—though they also encouraged temporary alliances among them.

Marx's sociology of class turns upon a fusion of historical and economic elements, of which 'surplus value' is the best known, though far from being the best understood. At bottom it is a way of stating the historical fact that in every known form of society a minority has been able to live at the expense of those engaged in physical labour. Control over means of production is the strategic factor because it enables the minority to compel others to work. It is obvious that the term 'working class' is here defined in such a manner as to account at once for the fact of social subordination and for the phenomenon of unearned income. Class society, by definition, operates so as to place effective power beyond the range of those whose unpaid labour sustains the privileged minority in control of the instruments of production. The doctrine of the state follows from these assumptions. Its briefest and most pregnant formulation occurs in the passage where Marx observes that 'the specific form in which unpaid surplus labour is pumped out of the immediate producers determines the relation of domination and subjection', which relationship in turn constitutes 'the final secret, the hidden basis of the whole construction of society, including the political patterns of sovereignty and dependence, in short of a given form of government.'[2] The class that controls the means of production (including the means of intellectual production) wields effective political power. Internal conflicts within this stratum may disturb the underlying pattern, but do not normally disrupt it. Genuine social revolutions, which always signify the displacement of one ruling class

---

[1] Cf. part IV, ch. 5, passim.

[2] *Das Kapital* (1949 edn.), vol. III, pp. 841–2; cf. *Capital* (1960 Moscow edn.), vol. III, p. 772.

by another, are rare. What commonly pass for such are mere political upheavals which do not alter the fundamental class structure, though they may interact with it.

Whether or not this model is adequate in relation to the 'bourgeois revolution' and more generally to bourgeois society, need not concern us here. It is at any rate empirical and scientific. Its principal weakness would appear to lie in a failure to discriminate methodically between socially dominant classes and political ruling strata. Not that Marx was unaware of the distinction, but although it figures quite prominently in his political writings, it has no real place in his theoretical system. On his assumptions this was defensible, since if political power was a mere epiphenomenon of a particular mode of social organisation, the long-run development could be analysed in terms of the latter. In this attitude he was probably guided, quite without being aware of it, by the actual relationship between the territorial aristocracy and the industrial bourgeoisie in nineteenth-century Europe, which could in fact be discussed in such terms; though the mere existence of an entrenched ruling stratum which was no longer the dominant social class might have suggested awkward problems for the future. The fact is that Marx did not investigate the matter in any very systematic fashion. He did notice the commanding position of the state bureaucracy in Continental Europe, but did not accord it more than passing attention. His references to the bureaucracy are invariably contemptuous and make it clear that he regarded it as an artificial 'caste' lacking a dynamic of its own—apart from a tendency to swell in numbers—and incapable of playing an independent and socially significant role. If the state now and then appeared on the scene in the guise of mediator—e.g., under Bonapartism—that was a temporary anomaly which could not long survive the contest of interests and ideas between the 'true' classes of society.[1]

In the Marxian model classes are not 'income groups', nor are they coterminous with social strata arising from the division of labour. Rather they are defined by property, a concept to be understood not in terms of wealth, but dynamically, as 'ownership of means of production', themselves subject to constant technological

[1] Cf. *The Eighteenth Brumaire of Louis Bonaparte*, MESW I, pp. 332 ff. Marx's contemptuous attitude towards the bureaucracy seems to have stemmed from his Rhineland background. Like other radical thinkers of his time he was more profoundly affected than he knew by the outlook of the liberal era, which in this instance is no longer very helpful.

change.[1] Since control over means of production is the key to social, and therefore indirectly to political power, every class represents an ensemble of relationships held together by an overriding commitment. Social classes are by definition rooted in 'production relations', which in turn give rise to income relations. Their political power, if any, also arises from the 'relations of production'.[2] Latent *economic* power becomes *socially* effective through the instrumentality of *politics*. When this final stage has been reached, the class may be said to have attained its fullest development. A class that lacks political power—*a fortiori* one that lacks consciousness of its position in society—is not as yet fully constituted as a class. It is evident that the entire construction has little in common with the static models employed in academic sociology, with its stress on the functioning of a given 'structure'. Not that such models cannot be constructed with the help of Marxian concepts; but they do not amount to Marxism. For a theory of social change to be Marxist it must be embedded in a *historical* perspective.

Must it also be committed to the particular perspective which Marx and his followers deduced from his analysis of nineteenth-century capitalism? For Marx the question would have been meaningless, since his thinking about society arose as a by-product of his critique of *bourgeois* society. Modern sociologists who employ the Marxian conceptual apparatus are clearly in a different position. There is no good reason why they should rely on extrapolations from the social struggles of his day, or subscribe to his fusion of economic sociology and the theory of class conflict as exemplified in the 'bourgeois revolution'. Social historians in particular can make use of the Marxian notion of class conflict as the dynamic element in history, without thereby committing themselves to any particular orientation.[3] Indeed his general theory can be given a distinctly conservative

[1] For a detailed analysis of this theme cf. Dahrendorf, op. cit., pp. 11 ff; the problem is complicated by the casual and unsystematic nature of Marx's utterances on the subject, but his meaning can be reconstructed without much difficulty.

[2] Or non-production: the proletariat of imperial Rome was a non-producing class and *therefore* had no effective political power, though naturally it had to be kept quiet with the help of political bribes; the latter were distributed by an irremovable governing class which had effectively monopolised power.

[3] Cf. Talcott Parsons, *Essays in Sociological Theory*, Glencoe, 1954, pp. 323 ff. Nor, it may be added, are they obliged to 'choose' between Marx's modus operandi and that of the German school founded by Max Weber. As has rightly been remarked, the whole of Weber's sociology of religion fits without difficulty into the Marxian scheme.

interpretation: ruling classes, after all, act as repositories of tradition (including cultural tradition), and hence tend to stabilise a given social order, at any rate so long as the underlying relations of production are themselves fairly stable. A class which preserves the degree of social cohesion necessary to the functioning of the economic system clearly performs an essential role, and any incidental privileges it may have acquired are easily justifiable on these grounds.

In actual fact it may be doubted whether the Marxian concept of a ruling class which monopolises both political and economic power can be made to apply fully to any post-medieval situation. European feudal society—a unique creation nowhere paralleled in either ancient or modern times—did represent such a constellation, and the long reign of its dominant 'class' impressed itself deeply upon the consciousness of the rising urban bourgeoisie which gradually managed to erode its position. Even after the aristocratic monopoly of military and political power had been broken, the land-owning nobility continued to hold a privileged position, and for a long time imposed its standards upon social strata that were beginning to rival it. The case of nineteenth-century Germany is of particular relevance in this context, because Marx's outlook was shaped by the struggle to transform a rigidly stratified society which was still pre-bourgeois, and whose radical intellectuals quite naturally transferred their own thought patterns to the nascent labour movement. This is the ultimate source of his 'Jacobinism'. Conversely, the mental attitude bred in youthful middle-class rebels by a society of this kind was inevitably an aristocratic one, in that their outlook was unconsciously shaped by a classical education which had preserved the ideals of the *polis*, i.e., the historic achievement of the Greek aristocracy. Clearly the Marxian ideal of the freely developed personality is both classical and aristocratic; it is not specifically 'bourgeois', and manifestly not 'proletarian'. In this Marx was not of course unique. The classical German philosophy of his age was held together and validated by the cult of Antiquity. Its ethos rested upon a fusion of aristocratic and bourgeois elements—quite unlike the vulgar utilitarianism of Bentham and his followers which Marx thought so deplorable. Thus we have the curious fact that Marx protested against bourgeois society in the name of the aristocratic *polis* ideal, while at the same time professing to see in the bourgeoisie another ruling class similar to the nobility which had for so long held power in Western Europe. Yet the aristocratic power monopoly (as

Marx well knew) had originally rested upon a unique combination of land-ownership, territorial rule over unfree peasants, and exclusive possession of military force through the instrument of armoured cavalry. No such unparalleled concentration of military, social, and economic power was at the disposal of the European bourgeoisie, least of all the German bourgeoisie whose feebleness had originally induced Marx to transfer his hopes to the proletariat. If he nonetheless went on ascribing to it a position in society corresponding to that of the aristocracy in medieval Europe, he was plainly being inconsistent—except on the not very frequent occasions when he argued that in its 'pure' form, bourgeois society was not to be found anywhere outside the United States. One cannot say that his three-class model was wrong; but it was adapted to a state of affairs fully developed only in Western Europe, and within that area it might have suggested a somewhat different conclusion. For if Europe was unique in having given rise first to feudalism and then to bourgeois society, it was unlikely that it would also be the geographical home of the next major social transformation. The mere fact that the European bourgeoisie had largely abandoned political power to the aristocracy, or entered into a symbiosis with it, might have suggested to Marx that post-bourgeois industrial society would evolve in the main upon soil not encumbered with so many antique formations.

Failure to distinguish between the concept of historical class and that of social stratum is at the origin of most of the unsuccessful attempts made by latter-day sociologists to employ isolated fragments of the Marxian theory, while neglecting its historical bent. Recognition of this fact is increasingly common in modern literature, where it is usually coupled with an analysis of post-capitalist society in terms derived from Marxian sociology, though divorced from the political perspective which Marx imposed upon his general picture.[1] These writings necessarily lack the intellectual excitement generated by a doctrine which unifies historical and sociological categories in the Marxian manner. It may be said, however, that Marx himself failed to establish the necessary correspondence between the concept of class and that of historical epoch. As we have seen, his classes

[1] Dahrendorf, op. cit., passim; G. D. H. Cole, *Studies in Class Structure*, London, 1955; T. B. Bottomore, *Classes in Modern Society*, London, 1955; T. H. Marshall, ed., *Class Conflict and Social Stratification*, London, 1938; Theodor Geiger, *Die Klassengesellschaft im Schmelztiegel*, Cologne, 1949; Paul Sering, *Jenseits des Kapitalismus*, Nuremberg, 1947; Franz Borkenau, *Pareto*, London, 1936; James Burnham, *The Managerial Revolution*, New York, 1941.

are distinguished from ordinary social strata in that each corresponds to a definite stage in the evolution of society. The landowning class, e.g., stands for the feudal order, with its aristocratic culture and the corresponding forms of spiritual life, at the same time that it denotes a particular phase in the development of society's productive forces, a particular arrangement of economic relations, and a definite type of political sovereignty. The bourgeois epoch likewise is characterised by an ensemble of historically conditioned traits linked to the evolution of a new form of socio-economic organisation, and determining a specific mode of life and a unique culture. It is only in relation to these antecedent stages of history that socialism acquires the dignity of a principle—ultimately derived from the role of labour —capable of replacing earlier forms of organisation. Unlike Hegel's 'epochs of the spirit', which in appearance they closely resemble, Marx's 'historical stages' lend themselves to empirical study; but it is just this which has thrown the whole construction into disarray, for the close of the bourgeois epoch has not yielded the anticipated results. Post-bourgeois industrial society, whether capitalist or socialist, does not accord with the expectations current in the nineteenth century. If no new ruling class is visible which could take the place of aristocracy or bourgeoisie, there is all the more stratification of a type unwelcome to liberals and socialists alike. Moreover, the working class, so far from generating a spontaneous drive towards socialist democracy, has shown an alarming tendency to acquiesce in patterns of socio-political domination which promise to guarantee economic advance and full employment at the cost of freedom. The least one can say is that the Marxian perspective of a socialist transformation propelled by labour's collective drive towards emancipation seems rather less plausible that it did a century ago.

As was remarked above, Marx formulated neither a systematic account of the class structure under industrial capitalism, nor yet a consistent view of the relationship between state and society during the—presumably lengthy—transition period preceding the establishment of the socialist order. His hostile attitude to the bureaucracy has been noted; yet in places it is tempered by a grudging recognition that 'modern society' requires a certain degree of central control.[1]

[1] Cf. *The Eighteenth Brumaire*, MESW, I, p. 340. 'The centralisation of the state that modern society requires arises only on the ruins of the military-bureaucratic government machinery forged in the struggle against feudalism.' This uncharacteristic observation is preceded by a lengthy diatribe against the bureaucratic despotism established in France by Napoleon and continued under

The context suggests that 'modern society' here stands for industrial society, and more specifically for the socialist form it is expected to take after the irrational encumbrances still blocking its evolution have been removed. A rational organisation of modern industrial society must be socialist: thus Marx could (and on occasion did) define his standpoint; but this formulation left the role of authority undecided, save for specifying that it should be reduced to the minimum compatible with centralised control.

Marx's view of what constitutes economic rationality cannot be divorced from his analysis of the labour process. At the genesis of his thinking about social organisation there lies an unresolved conflict between alternative ways of envisaging the future pattern of industrial society. In 1846–7 he had argued, against Proudhon, that the rational organisation of work in the factory might become a model for industrial society as a whole.[1] In *Capital*, written some twenty years later, with far greater command of fact, this line of thought is crossed by another one. There is a realm of economic necessity which calls for a certain minimum of social organisation. '. . . the capitalist process of production is a historically determined form of the social process of production in general.'[2] With the shedding of the temporary historical determination it becomes possible to isolate the logic of the process, which at bottom consists in the application of scientific technology to nature. This involves, on the one hand, co-operation between the producers; on the other hand, the 'orchestration' of their separate tasks. The latter function need not be exercised by the entrepreneur, for 'the process of production, separated from capital, is simply a labour process. Hence the industrial

his successor. 'How could it be otherwise, seeing that alongside the actual classes of society he is forced to create an artificial caste for which the maintenance of his regime becomes a bread-and-butter question?' (Ibid., pp. 338–9.) This view of the bureaucracy as a parasitical stratum battening on the productive classes of society is thoroughly in accordance with the classical liberal standpoint, but it does not help us much today.

[1] 'Society as a whole has this in common with the interior of a workshop that it too has its division of labour. If one took as a model the division of labour in a modern workshop, in order to apply it to a whole society, the society best organised for the production of wealth would undoubtedly be that which had a single chief employer distributing tasks to the different members of the community according to a previously fixed rule.' *The Poverty of Philosophy*, Moscow, 1954, p. 151. Cf. Lenin, *State and Revolution*, loc. cit., p. 210: 'The whole of society will have become a single office and a single factory, with equality of labour and equality of pay.'

[2] *Capital*, III, p. 798 (1960 edn.).

capitalist, as distinct from the owner of capital, does not appear as operating capital, but rather as a functionary irrespective of capital, or as a simple agent of the labour process in general, as a labourer and indeed as a wage labourer.'[1] He can therefore be replaced by a salaried manager. Indeed, 'the capitalist mode of production has brought matters to a point where the work of supervision, entirely divorced from the ownership of capital, is always readily available. It has therefore come to be superfluous for the capitalist to perform it himself. An orchestra conductor need not own the instruments of his orchestra . . .'[2] Yet the need for a directing function does not vanish. 'The labour of supervision and management is naturally required wherever the direct process of production assumes the form of a combined social process, and not of the isolated labour of independent producers.'[3] What changes is the specific historical form of capitalist control. 'All labour in which many individuals co-operate necessarily requires a commanding will to co-ordinate and unify the process,'[4] but it need not be that of capital. The kind of supervision which 'necessarily arises in all modes of production based on the antithesis of the labourer, as the direct producer, and the owner of the means of production,' is destined to disappear. Not only are entrepreneurs increasingly being replaced by salaried managers, but 'co-operative factories furnish proof that the capitalist has become no less redundant as a functionary in production as he himself, looking down from his high perch, thinks the great landowner redundant'.[5] The kind of directing function which 'originates from the social form of the labour process, from combination and co-operation of many in pursuance of a common result' is a permanent necessity, or as Marx puts it, 'is just as independent of capital as that form itself as soon as it has burst its capitalistic shell'.[6] Can it be exercised democratically? 'In a co-operative factory the antagonistic nature of the labour of supervision disappears, because the manager is paid by the labourers instead of representing capital counterposed to them.'[7] Rather inconsequentially, the immediately following sentence adds: 'Stock companies in general—developed with the credit system—have an increasing tendency to separate this work of management as a function

---

[1] *Capital*, III, pp. 374–5.
[2] Ibid., p. 379. (The wording of this translation has been slightly modified.)
[3] Ibid., p. 376. [4] Ibid.
[5] Ibid., p. 379. [6] Ibid. [7] Ibid., p. 380

from the ownership of capital, be it self-owned or borrowed, just as the development of bourgeois society itself witnessed a separation of the functions of judges and administrators from land-ownership, whose attributes they were in feudal times.'[1] This leaves it uncertain whether the basic line of development is towards co-operation or to the replacement of entrepreneurial by managerial control. The 'transformation of the actually functioning capitalist into a mere manager, administrator of other people's capital, and of the capital owner into a mere . . . money capitalist'[2] signifies 'the abolition of the capitalist mode of production within the capitalist mode of production itself, and hence a self-dissolving contradiction which *prima facie* represents a mere phase of transition towards a new form of production'.[3] There is a cautious suggestion that the new mode of production will be co-operative and self-governing. 'The co-operative factories of the labourers themselves represent within the old form the first sprouts of the new, although they naturally reproduce, and must reproduce, everywhere in their actual organisation all the shortcomings of the prevailing system. But the antithesis of capital and labour is overcome within them, if at first only by turning the associated labourers into their own capitalists, i.e., by enabling them to use the means of production for the employment of their own labour. They show how a new mode of production naturally grows out of an old one, when the development of the material forces of production, and of the corresponding forms of social production, has reached a particular stage.'[4] Yet though capitalist control over the labourer disappears, social control does not; the need for planning and management remains, or is even enhanced.[5] 'Freedom in this field can consist only in this, that socialised man, the associated producers, organise their interchange with nature rationally, bring it under their common control, instead of being mastered by it as by some blind force; that they accomplish their task with the minimum expenditure of effort and under conditions most favourable to, and

---

[1] Ibid.   [2] Ibid., p. 427.   [3] Ibid., p. 429.

[4] Ibid., p. 431. This perspective accords well enough with the tenor of the 1864 *Inaugural Address* which Marx wrote at about the time he drafted the unfinished manuscripts later assembled by Engels in *Capital*, vols. II and III. (Cf. Engels's preface to vol. II.)

[5] Ibid., p. 830: 'After the abolition of the capitalist mode of production, but still retaining social production, the determination of value continues to prevail, in the sense that it is more essential than ever to regulate labour time, to distribute social labour among the various production groups, and lastly to keep books for this purpose.'

worthy of, their human nature. But it nonetheless still remains a realm of necessity.'[1] True freedom lies beyond the sphere of production undertaken to satisfy material wants.

Though hardly a utopian perspective, this is not finally a convincing one. Marx has not really faced all the implications of the problem of social control in a planned economy. A society in which such control is exercised by paid functionaries need not have classes in the nineteenth-century sense of the term, but its 'classlessness' does not exclude new forms of social differentiation incompatible with the ideal of industrial self-government. Nor is it apparent why the progressive replacement of capitalist by managerial control should be viewed as a mere transitional phase towards a co-operative order. Today we are better placed to notice the missing links in the chain of reasoning, but this does not altogether protect Marx against the reproach of having broken off his analysis at the point where his empirical investigations threatened to impinge upon his underlying vision of the historical process. The fragmentary nature of his theory of class cannot finally be divorced from his concern to safeguard the thesis that class society stands and falls with private ownership in the means of production. On the assumption that 'class' signified what it did in the nineteenth century, this thesis could be defended—but only as long as the second phase of the industrial revolution had not given rise to a new social hierarchy independent of the property relations with which Marx was familiar. The emergence of new forms of dependence and control, both under corporate management and state-controlled planning, has 'sublated' the historic antagonism of capital and labour, and established a new perspective from which to view the conflict of classes. Paradoxically, Marx's theory of class, insofar as he can be said to have formulated it, has been undermined by the transformation of bourgeois society to whose analysis his major work was directed.

---

[1] *Capital*, III, p. 800. For a contrasting view, though one equally derived from Natural Law doctrine, cf. Locke, *Of Civil Government*, para. 124: 'The great and chief end, therefore, of men's uniting into commonwealths, and putting themselves under government, is the preservation of their property; to which in the state of Nature there are many things wanting.'

4

BEYOND MARXISM

THE EVOLUTION OF MARXIST thinking since 1918, and in particular since 1945, has not kept pace with the growth of socialist influence in the Western world and beyond, let alone the expansion of Communism in the wake of the Russian and Chinese revolutions. While Marxism has become the official ideology of totalitarian reconstruction in the Soviet orbit, and the unofficial creed of radical intellectuals in backward countries, its internal development has stagnated since the 1930's, when it still contributed a coherent, though inadequate, explanation of the world economic crisis and the fascist challenge. In recent years it has not been more successful than liberalism in formulating either a theory of post-capitalist society, or a programme of social reconstruction adapted to the needs of the democratic labour movement. Where it has not congealed into an apologetic of Stalinist industrialisation and 'revolution from above', its theoretical model has been employed for the analysis of societies still on the threshold of the industrial revolution. At the opposite extreme of social development, in countries already far advanced and possessing a long tradition of democratic rule, it has been turned into a critique of modern society as such. The most recent advance in fact has been in the utilisation of Marx's early writings for the purpose of underpinning the intelligentsia's rejection of the world created by modern industry and scientific technology; and the principal battle-ground of this debate has been furnished by the universities. It is tempting to abstract a general rule to the effect that a new doctrine becomes academically respectable only after it has petrified. How-ever that may be, it is undeniable that interest in Marxism as a system has not in recent years been matched by success in the application of its method.

There are variations in this picture. Intellectual paralysis has been total in the USSR, and almost as complete in its satellites, with the significant exception of Poland. In the West it has been countered by the liberalising influence of conflicting ideas, and by the rediscovery of those aspects of Marx's own thought which link it to the central tradition of Western philosophy. Even so, the discussion has no-where recaptured the excitement of the 1920's, when the impact of the Russian Revolution upon Central Europe produced a ferment of ideas in an environment already affected by the first world war and the upheavals of 1918–19. In some respects the current situa-tion in France and Italy resembles that in Germany and Austria during the earlier phase; but where the Central European debate turned upon the union of (philosophical) theory and (political) prac-tice, the post-1945 discussion in Western Europe quickly became academic and fastened upon those elements of the Marxian system which were furthest removed from political action. In the 1930's and early 1940's, the rediscovery of Marxian economics in the Anglo-American world still possessed practical significance. After 1945 the breakdown of intellectual isolation in France gave rise to a literature which went back to Hegel and the early Marx as part of a belated re-orientation within the philosophical sphere. Protective walls long defended by the old guard of Cartesianism had collapsed without warning, and German philosophy, no less than Russian political practice, called for re-examination by an elite predisposed in favour of intellectual system-building. The resulting flow of critical and analytical comment, while impressive in quantity and quality, has increasingly come to bear the stamp of academicism. The absorption of Central European thought into French—and in a lesser degree Italian—intellectual life is clearly a cultural phenomenon of some im-portance; but in terms of what has been happening to Marxism since 1918 it bears all the marks of an elaborate *post mortem*.[1]

[1] For the above cf. the works listed by Calvez, op. cit., pp. 647–9; Cottier, op. cit., pp. 373–8. Fetscher, 'Der Marxismus im Spiegel der franzoesischen

It is scarcely surprising that this debate has been confined in the main to Western Europe, though some echoes have reached Britain and the United States. In the latter country Marxism continues to be thought of as a politico-economic doctrine that supplies one-half of the Marxist-Leninist synthesis: an opinion also held in the USSR. As regards Britain, the statement that Marxist thinking has stagnated since the 1940's needs to be qualified insofar as it leaves out of account the recent fertilisation of sociology, history, and anthropology, by unorthodox concepts that are clearly of Marxist origin. This development, however, represents not so much a new intellectual breakthrough as a time-lag in the assimilation of ideas which had already left their impact on Continental European thought a generation earlier. However highly one values the contribution made by scholars working with a conceptual apparatus in part derived from Marx, there is nothing in this phenomenon to alter the impression that Marxism has achieved academic status at the cost of ceasing to be the theory of a revolutionary practice.[1]

With this state of affairs in mind it may now be asked what has caused the stagnation. Clearly this is not just a conceptual matter. An analysis in terms of what has been happening to Marx's theory since it was first formulated must take account of the discrepancy between the theoretical model and the real world. If the latter departs from the model, no amount of juggling with concepts will restore the precarious balance of theory and practice which Marx and Engels established in the second half of the past century. Nor does it help to allege that the whole question has been raised to an altogether different (and of course higher) level by the emergence of the USSR and the other members of the 'socialist world'. This recourse to political language is open only to Leninists. For those who do not share their assumptions, the problem presents itself as one of growing divergence between theoretical premises inherited from the liberal era, and totalitarian practices developed to cope with crises stemming from

Philosophie', *Marxismusstudien*, I, pp. 173 ff, supplies both an analysis and a critical commentary on some of the major writings. Cf. also Jean Duvignaud, 'Neo-Marxism in France', in *Soviet Survey*, London, April–June 1960; Daniel Bell, 'In Search of Marxist Humanism', ibid. It is impossible here to go beyond the bare statement that much of the literature in question is philosophical and devoted to the search for a synthesis of traditional Cartesian thought forms with Hegelian, Marxian, and Existentialist, notions.

[1] For an account of the influence of Marxism upon recent sociological work, cf. Bottomore and Rubel, op. cit., pp. 29 ff.

the breakdown of the liberal system. What needs to be clarified is in what precise respect the Marxian analysis has ceased to provide a working model for socialists.

When Marx and Engels conjectured the probable future of bourgeois society in the Western world, they started from the commonly held assumption that state and society are clearly distinguishable spheres, and that society is the determining one. In terms of this analysis (which in essentials did not differ from the corresponding liberal doctrine) it could plausibly be held that a political 'superstructure' resting upon a society dynamically propelled by class conflict would eventually take a socialist form; the more so since the industrial working class was tending to become the majority of the population in all advanced countries. These assumptions form a whole in which it is not too difficult to recognise the 'inverted mirror-image' of the social philosophy held by Marx's bourgeois-liberal contemporaries. This applies above all to the ascription of superior reality to the socio-economic, as distinct from the political, sphere. Their interaction was thought to be of such a kind that *in the long run* the 'superstructure' must follow the movement of society; the latter in turn being propelled forward by an economic system which, moving under its own steam and following a logic as blind as that of the market itself, would steadily transform itself into its own opposite. The whole construction clearly assumes that the political realm is secondary. That the relationship between state and society might alter so as to make the state the dominant partner, was not taken into account. Hence it was not foreseen (leaving aside the hypothetical case of a revolutionary dictatorship during the transitional period) that the state might reshape society. Even less were Marx and Engels able to foresee that their own doctrine might become the ideology of a technocratic elite intent on imposing its authority upon the workers, in the name of—socialism!

Were Marxism merely a sociology attuned to the defunct age of liberal capitalism, these theoretical failings would matter only in the context of academic debate. Their practical-political relevance stems from the Marxian commitment to 'change the world'. Marx's analytical mistakes are not politically neutral, for they serve to underpin a doctrine that is the counterpart of a definite political orientation. The difficulty in trying to isolate them lies in the fact that some of his most important operational concepts are not of an empirical nature; they cannot be tested by factual investigation, and are thus immune to disproof. In this connection it does not perhaps matter much that the three-class model is not applicable to modern industrial society, since in principle it can be brought up to date. Nor is it very important that the Marxian analysis is defective or incomplete in relation to such practical problems as the business cycle under capitalist, or the planning of production under socialist, auspices. The real trouble is that Marxism tries to do duty both as a theory of society and as a philosophy of history, and that its philosophical postulates are hopelessly at variance with its scientific insights.

In the Marxian system, class conflict culminates historically in the antagonism of bourgeoisie and proletariat, the latter representing not simply one essential element of industrial society, but rather the external form of the rational principle itself. Reason asserts itself throughout history as the organising principle of society, but it does so imperfectly until the transition to a planned and collectivist order has been accomplished. That order, moreover, is conceived as harmonious as well as rational, in that it eliminates social antagonisms. Merely to state these notions is to make plain why they cannot be empirically validated; they belong to the class of philosophical postulates which Marx inherited from Hegel. But neither can they be divorced from the corpus of Marx's doctrine, for they are inherent in his vision of history as the self-emancipation of mankind through labour. The process whereby man develops his latent faculties, while at the same time 'alienating' his nature and fixing it in antagonistic social institutions, would be incomplete—indeed meaningless—were it not to culminate in a higher stage where these obstructions are transcended. This stage is the classless society, in which full freedom for every individual is established on the basis of socialised property. It is classless because on Marx's assumption classes exist and stand in antagonistic relation to each other only as long as the means of production are controlled by a ruling minority. This notion enables him to forecast the actual disappearance of class conflict on the quasi-empirical grounds that socialisation is a necessary consequence of the economic process; while defining socialism in terms of classlessness. From this it follows that the socialist order is the consummation of history (or rather pre-history, since 'genuine' history can only begin after society has at last emerged from the stage associated with class rule).

It may be argued that these notions are extraneous to what is really important about Marxism, namely its sociology; but this is to introduce an arbitrary separation between elements of the system which must be viewed as a whole. Moreover, the idea of a classless society was not simply a philosophical extravagance. Its practical significance was indeed less than Marx and Engels supposed: in Social-Democratic parlance 'the class struggle' really signified the attainment of *equal rights* by the class of industrial workers; while 'the classless society' was simply another name for democracy. But these equivocations—of which Marx was quite aware and which he never ceased to deplore—did not touch the core of the doctrine, and the latter finally became operational after 1918, when the Communist movement set out to establish the 'proletarian dictatorship' in dead earnest. So far as the utopian expectations of the first generation of Communists went, the attempt was a gigantic failure; but it was a failure which in its turn gave rise to the phenomenon of totalitarianism. In the fully developed Leninist system—of which Stalinism is simply the final consequence—the general interest of the working class is hypostasised in the party. The latter in turn legitimises its rule by claiming to embody the rationale of history. Hence the state it governs is the incarnate ratio, and its own monopoly of power the necessary sanction of mankind's march towards the stateless and classless society of the future. It would be an exaggeration to say that this entire development was already inherent in the original doctrine, seeing that Bolshevism evidently stems from the traditional messianic and universalist outlook of the Russian revolutionary intelligentsia which fastened upon Marxism as an instrument of its own will to 'change the world'. But the Marxian scheme clearly lent itself to utilisation by revolutionaries in search of a system which validated their drive towards total reconstruction; and it did so because Marx's starting-point had been the all-inclusive rationalism of Hegel, with its conception of history as the realisation of liberty. In terms of this philosophy—which in its idealist form had already gripped the Russian intelligentsia long before Marxism came on the scene—the idea of the classless society had nothing extraordinary about it.

That so abstruse and far-fetched a notion could become genuinely operational was clearly due to the exceptional circumstances attending the impact of Marxism upon Russia: a relatively backward country whose radical intellectuals had broken with religious tradition, but retained its chiliastic inheritance, and transferred their hopes to the revolutionary doctrines imported from Western Europe. The flow of secularised religious energy which had almost run dry in the

West with the growing disillusionment over the results of the French Revolution, was still sufficiently powerful in the East to revive the utopian or messianic idea at the core of the Marxian system. The outcome was Communism: not as the reality of Soviet society—which is simply another instance of modern planned and bureaucratised industrialism—but as the ideology of that society, and more particularly of its ruling elite organised in the Communist party. The fact that this elite stems directly or indirectly from the radical intelligentsia which made the Bolshevik revolution, enables the party to bridge the obvious gap between the pre-revolutionary faith and the post-revolutionary accomplishment; though this does not exclude a growing awareness of tension between belief and practice. In this respect, however, the problem facing it is not radically different from that which has confronted all revolutionary movements in modern history, from the Puritans onward; and though one may suspect that it is the official ideology rather than the state which in the end will 'wither away', this does not necessarily mean that the party cannot adapt itself to a situation where its function is simply to preserve the *status quo*. Transformations of this kind have occurred before, though admittedly never in a situation where a totalitarian regime operated something like a 'permanent revolution from above'. Yet the exhaustion of the revolutionary dynamic need not entail the disappearance of the party and the conversion of the political elite into an ordinary ruling class without an ideology. Such an outcome indeed is unlikely, at any rate in the short run. Since Soviet society is asserted to be classless by definition, social differentiations cannot become overt beyond a certain point without threatening the moral foundation of the regime. The party as the mediator between the upper and the lower levels of the 'classless' hierarchy retains its importance even after faith in the imminence of full Communism has quietly been abandoned, at any rate by those in control of the apparatus. For though the controllers may eventually cease to be doctrinaires and to take their ideology seriously, they cannot dispense with a unifying conception of their own role. In all probability the doctrine of classlessness can be transformed into one of social harmony—especially if the inconvenient concept of 'class' is dropped and replaced by a politically neutral term. Examples of such a procedure are not lacking, and in taking this course the party would anyhow merely pursue its already traditional role of reinterpreting doctrine to fit the circumstances.

Where, however, does this leave the link between the Marxian concept of revolution and the Communist vision of the classless society? The candid answer must be: nowhere. If the dynamic let loose by the proletarian revolution fails to transform society in such a way as to eliminate the distinction between rulers and ruled, then Marx's doctrine loses both its philosophic sweep and its practical import. In scientific terms this may be a gain, but it signifies the failure of the attempt to unify critical thought and political practice. This conclusion holds also in the face of those democratic-socialist versions of Marxism which are free from totalitarian tendencies and independent of the Soviet model. Socialist planning as the *sine qua non* of rational political organisation in a modern democracy is a perfectly valid conception, but no substitute for a unified world-view transcending the political sphere. A doctrine which demonstrates no more than the likelihood of a planned (and centrally controlled) society taking the place of an unplanned one, is not a 'critical theory' in the original Marxian sense of the term. The latter stands and falls with the belief that human action can bring about the end of 'pre-history'. Unless this claim is made good, the socialist revolution cannot be regarded as a radical break with the past. To the pragmatic outlook of the modern socialist movement this conclusion may come as no great surprise, but it spells the dissolution of the Marxian synthesis and the end of the eschatological hopes embodied in it.

CONCLUSION

IN HIS *Lectures on the Philosophy of History* Hegel expounded the thesis that philosophy supplies the general criteria for the understanding of the march of events through time. The meaning of history is disclosed to an intellect who has mastered the most general categories available to man in his capacity as a reflective being. In this role he transcends the accidents of age and locality, and places himself at the level of the historical process itself. Man therefore is able—provided his concepts are of sufficient generality—to take in at a glance the whole of his past and to envisage the future. Man here is 'generic man', the embodiment of mankind as a whole, and his understanding relates not to this or that aspect of history, but to the goal of the process itself. In attaining this insight, philosophy rises to a comprehension of past and present reality, now seen to incorporate the rational principle which strives to bring existence into conformity with its own essence. Hegel, however, held that this end had already been achieved and that the struggle was over. In contrast, Marx reasserted the revolutionary credo which measured progress by the fulfilment of its ultimate aims: liberty and autonomy. His 'generic man', who is also 'autonomous man', attains true status only in a 'realm of freedom' which has left Hegel's rational State behind, and brought to a close the reign of constraint and the tyranny of material necessity.

This realm is the classless society. In envisioning it, Marx, by an unconscious stroke of genius, combined the romantic longing for natural harmony with the idealised image of the classical *polis*. This image, as transmitted in European literature, belonged by tradition to the heritage of an aristocratic humanism and liberalism which had never seriously made contact with political life until the French Revolution hurled the radical leaders of the Enlightenment upon the stage. Because the revolutionaries strove, however unsuccessfully, to

401

translate the radical programme into reality, Marx—and following him all genuine Marxists—regarded their brief reign as a turning-point in history and the true opening of the modern age. They did not extend a comparable welcome to the English and American revolutions of the seventeenth and eighteenth centuries—for all that they were equally decisive in bringing the modern world into being—because they had not been accompanied by a parallel emancipation from the theological world-view. In the Marxian perspective the attainment of freedom implies the adoption of a this-worldly standpoint. Because in the later nineteenth century this problem acquired decisive importance for the Russian intelligentsia which had entered into the French revolutionary inheritance, Marxism in Russia became a creed, whereas in Germany it had to content itself with the status of a philosophy. Germany, though traditionally the home of metaphysical speculation, had made its break with medievalism in a more gradual fashion, and German Social-Democracy for this reason adopted a more tolerant attitude towards religion. In its classic, or German, phase Marxism therefore lacked the revolutionary drive and the totalitarian character it was to acquire in Russia.

In the conventional view—shared by Marxists as well as others—this development is to be viewed as an aspect of the rise of nineteenth-century capitalism. On this reading, Marxism is both a theory of the industrial revolution in its European phase, and an ideology of the socialist movement during the struggle for democracy. While plausible enough so far as it goes, this interpretation falls short of explaining what it was that made Marxism the instrument of total revolution and reconstruction on Russian (though not on German) soil. In particular it overlooks the fact that modern capitalism revolutionised European society only after it had been extensively secularised, i.e., placed on a rational foundation. Late medieval and Renaissance economic development effected nothing of the kind; while as late as the seventeenth century, the 'bourgeois revolution' in England was intermingled with a religious struggle which was certainly more than a sham. It was only in the late eighteenth century that the dissolution of the traditional religious world-view gave rise to modern secularism, and it was then that the French Revolution proclaimed a totally new conception of politics as the application of rational principles to human affairs. This breakthrough has determined the entire history of nineteenth-century Europe, and placed its stamp upon liberalism and socialism alike. These two movements, for all their antithetical views of society, are ideological twins; they arise almost simultaneously from the intellectual crisis at the opening of the century. At first liberalism, through its association with the now briefly triumphant middle class, is better able to exploit the forces unleashed by the industrial revolution; later it is overtaken by socialism which fastens upon the revolt of the proletariat. But the two strains are intermingled from the start, and nowhere more so than in Marxism, which affirms the fulfilment of the common humanist programme. It is only with the transformation of Russian Communism into the official ideology of a totalitarian regime that Marxism is really wrenched out of this context and divorced from its West European origins; and the reaction to this development within the Communist camp itself promptly gives rise to a new form of 'revisionism', which once more seeks to recapture the libertarian spirit of the original socialist message.

But though in Eastern Europe it became the instrument and the ideology of 'total' revolution, Marxism also functioned as the theory of the Socialist labour movement, whose aims were more limited and practical than the goals proclaimed in philosophy. And thirdly it provided the causal explanation—derived from classical economics—of a process which actually transformed the structure of society all over the world. As such it breathed life into sociology and fused economic theory with its own peculiar doctrine of historical stages. The fusion, however, operates at a level which takes for granted—as did contemporary liberalism—the permanence of those very arrangements which were challenged by the social revolution: Western hegemony, bourgeois civilisation, and the rule of law. Hence in the twentieth century Marxism suffers the fate of liberalism: it is found wanting as a theory of post-bourgeois society, which no longer has a single centre, and whose increasingly rigid structures resist the drive towards social equality and the unification of physical and intellectual labour. In the light of these conditions, Marx's humanism comes to appear utopian, while his political programme is travestied by totalitarian regimes in the pre-industrial hinterland of the modern world. The supposed totality of Communism reveals itself as a grotesque distortion of industrial society, as its exists everywhere of necessity under the conditions of the modern age. At the same time the reduction of democratic socialism to the modest dimensions of an essay in economic planning destroys the mystique of a movement which had identified its coming triumph with the emancipation of mankind from the reign of bondage. Hence Marxism—originally conceived as the 'union of theory and practice'—now confronts the dilemma experienced by philosophy from its beginning: it too becomes the repository of ideals and values not attained in actuality, and perhaps not capable of attainment. Socialism joins liberalism as an attempt to salvage the original humanist programme under conditions hostile to liberty and equality alike. The planned and centralised society of our time offers fewer opportunities to radicals of either species than did the bourgeois nineteenth century, though it speeds the rate of technological advance and does away with the grosser material obstacles to human progress. Freedom, so far from reigning unchallenged, is threatened in its very birthplace, while rationality is shown to be compatible with despotism. In this prolonged retreat from the certainties of the liberal era, Marxism disintegrates as a system, though it conserves its importance as a tool of analysis. Paradoxically, its sharpest edge is now turned against the illusory claims made on its behalf by regimes which purport to represent the fulfilment of its aims.

In looking back upon the century which gave rise to this movement against the established order, we are today less struck by its revolutionary character than by its profound though unconscious conformity with the established principles of the age. The great divide of two world wars, the Russian Revolution, and the rise of totalitarianism in its various forms, has cut us off from an era in which the basic certainties of liberal bourgeois culture were taken for granted even by its opponents. Marx and Mill have more in common with each other than either has with the representative thinkers of the next generation, let alone those of our own troubled age. The basic assumptions of the mid-nineteenth century reflect the self-confidence of a civilisation whose radical critics still adhered to ideas and values which have become genuinely problematic only since 1914. By present-day standards the Victorian age must be reckoned one of almost unparalleled stability, at any rate for the middle class—and the critics of that class still belonged to it, even if they were not, like Engels, actually members of the industrial bourgeoisie itself. A certain simplicity and solidity is characteristic of them all. Even their most revolutionary pronouncements take the form of an extrapolation from the unquestioned certitudes of the time: freedom, autonomy, rationality, democracy. The great upheaval of the French Revolution had been absorbed; the greater

Russian cataclysm was barely on the horizon, and was expected to re-affirm what the world had been taught by France, not to inaugurate a wholly new era. It is this combination of a fundamental certainty, even complacency, with radical ideas and strivings, that sets its seal on what may now in retrospect be called the golden age of the European bourgeoisie.

In generalising the notions elaborated by this era of material expansion and ideological ferment, historical materialism attained the paradoxical result of making the century conscious of its own achievement. Capitalism received its true, and not wholly unflattering, portrayal in the writings of its greatest critic. The grandeur and the horror of its achievement are for ever stamped upon the record because Marx broke through to a deeper level of reality than that portrayed in the official panegyrics. In so doing he rendered bourgeois society a service whose significance becomes visible only now that this society has disintegrated. But by the same token he misconstrued the immediate future. In the twentieth century, bourgeoisie and proletariat have both been 'sublated' in a higher unity which is not that of socialism as conceived in 1848. The dissolving class society of the liberal century turns out to have been too closely bound up with its geographical centre in Western Europe to serve as a model for the second, global, phase of the industrial revolution. The scale on which events have shaped themselves has dwarfed the dimensions of the Victorian era. Its small wars between great nations, its violent conflicts over limited issues, the intellectual and moral certainties of its leading figures, belong to an age that has vanished.

In nothing has this transformation expressed itself more profoundly than in the disappearance of the characteristic radical faith in the union of theory and practice. The liberal era opened with an unparalleled outburst of utopianism and—after an interval imposed by the partial defeat of the French Revolution—it witnessed a second climax in mid-nineteenth-century Germany. The advanced thinkers of the time were confident that the reign of thought was about to be succeeded by a triumph of will, a revolutionising of reality by way of action:

It is a psychological law that, once the theoretical spirit has been liberated, it turns into practical energy, emerging as *will* from Amenthes' realm of shades and rounding upon the world of external reality.[1]

In this act, philosophy realises its aims and at the same time ceases

[1] Marx, *Doktordissertation*, MEGA I/1, p. 64.

to exist, its disappearance implying the birth of a world in which the cleavage between ideal and reality has been overcome. Although the offspring of German metaphysics and youthful idealism, this was only the most extravagant formulation of a faith which runs through the entire period from the French to the Russian Revolution, linking the second upheaval to the first—and terminating in the discovery that after the most strenuous exertions the gulf between reality and ideal remains as unbridgeable as ever.

Midway between these two crucial dates the Victorian compromise offered the radicals of that age a chance of turning philosophy into science. The Marxian system is a response to this challenge and at the same time its negation. It responds to the reality of Western bourgeois society by a critical analysis of economics which, after an enormous detour, presents the conclusions already briefly formulated in the pre-1848 'critical theory'. These conclusions, suitably amended and modified, were adopted by the Socialist labour movement, and to all appearances validated by the catastrophe of 1914–18. The latter, however, while it delivered a mortal blow to European civilisation, failed to transform Europe into a Socialist commonwealth. The cataclysmic events it set in train are now seen to have resulted in the virtual destruction of the society which gave birth to the industrial revolution. Therewith Marxism disintegrates in the only manner suitable to a system that represents the union of its own theory with the practice of a revolutionary movement: its accomplishments are shown to be incompatible with its ultimate aims, which thus disclose their essentially metaphysical, i.e., transcendental and unrealisable, nature. What remains is, on the one hand, the travestied fulfilment of these aims in a reality which is their actual negation; and on the other, the *caput mortuum* of a gigantic intellectual construction whose living essence has been appropriated by the historical consciousness of the modern world; leaving the empty husk of 'dialectical materialism' to the ideologists of a new orthodoxy. In the sunset of the liberal era, of which Marxism is at once the critique and the theoretical reflection, this outcome confirms the truth of its own insights into the logic of history; while transferring to an uncertain future the ancient vision of a world set free.

INDEX

For authors cited in the footnotes, reference is made in this Index, unless for some special reason, only to that footnote in which full bibliographical particulars of their cited work are given. Footnote references to books or papers by Marx, Engels, Lenin, and others are not generally indexed.

407